⊷ THE OTHER ⊷
TRAIL OF TEARS

THE OTHER TRAIL OF TEARS

The Removal of the Ohio Indians

Mary Stockwell

WESTHOLME
Yardley

Westholme Publishing, LLC
904 Edgewood Road
Yardley, Pennsylvania 19067
Visit our Web site at www.westholmepublishing.com

First Printing March 2016
10 9 8 7 6 5 4 3 2 1
ISBN: 978-1-59416-258-9
Also available as an eBook.

Printed in the United States of America.

To my sister
Kathleen Stockwell

Contents

List of Maps

Prologue

MANY TRAILS OF TEARS

Any professor of the history of the United States in the early nineteenth-century has to say only two words to get a reaction from students. Those two words are "Andrew Jackson." The response is usually swift and visceral, running something along the lines of: "We hate him!" No amount of defending our seventh president as the hero of New Orleans, the champion of the Common Man, or the guardian of the people against the "Hydra" of the Second Bank of the United States can silence his many critics in and out of the classroom. When asked to explain this all-pervasive dislike of President Jackson, the answer is always the same —"The Trail of Tears!"

The story of the removal of the "Five Civilized Tribes" as they were designated by historians in the late nineteenth-century, most especially the Cherokee, who had a government based on a constitution, a written language with their own alphabet, and cotton plantations in northern Georgia—has seared itself into our collective imagination. So much was lost on the "trail where tears were shed," along which the Cherokee and four other tribes were driven from their homes in the southeastern United States to the Indian Territory across the Mississippi River.[1] Thousands of Cherokee, Choctaw, and Chickasaw died on the long trek to the present-day state of Oklahoma. Hundreds of American soldiers perished fighting the Creeks and Seminoles who refused to leave Alabama and Florida.

But perhaps the greatest loss came to Jackson's own reputation. Even his best contemporary biographers have not been able to repair it completely. Robert Remini, Jackson's greatest defender in the late twentieth-century, concluded that the president had decided long before the passage of the Indian Removal Act in 1830 that the "good of the nation and the tribes required their removal."[2] Not even the country's most resolute chief justice, John Marshall, could stop the process once Jackson had made up his mind that the Cherokee and the other southern tribes must be sent packing for their own good. For Jackson, there was no turning back from this basic point, and so there was never any regret. Remini described this best in *Andrew Jackson and His Indian Wars*, his final work on the life of President Jackson. "To his dying day on June 8, 1845," Remini explained, "Andrew Jackson genuinely believed that what he had accomplished rescued these people from inevitable annihilation."[3]

More recently Jon Meacham, in his Pulitzer Prize-winning work, *American Lion: Andrew Jackson in the White House* (2008), explains that Jackson was neither a "humanitarian" nor a "blind bigot" when it came to Indian removal. Instead he was "practical." He knew the Indians were increasingly being crowded out by white settlers who demanded their land. Georgia, in fact, was on the brink of taking the Cherokee's land by force. Jackson weighed the situation and sided with the average American, who wanted property of his own. After stating that there was nothing heroic, right, or brave about this decision, Meacham added, "Not all great presidents were always good, and neither individuals nor nations are without evil."[4]

Yet there is something tragic in believing that if we explain why Andrew Jackson drove the Cherokee, Choctaw, Chickasaw, Creek, and Seminole west to Oklahoma in the early nineteenth century, we have explained Indian removal. The tragedy lies in the fact that the struggle between Jackson and the southern tribes was only one part of a wider story that reaches back across time to the closing months of the War of 1812, back through many states—most notably Ohio—and back into the lives of so many other tribes, including the Delaware, Seneca, Shawnee, Ottawa, and Wyandot. They, too, departed down many trails of tears— sent west in a process that leaves a great deal of responsibility and blame to pass around among citizens of the United States and Indian nations alike—not just to Andrew Jackson.

A closer look at what the major Ohio tribes passed through in the period leading up to their official removal sheds light into how complex that process truly was. While the conflict between Jackson and the Cherokee, as well as with the other southern tribes, reads like a mythic battle between good and evil, the struggle of Ohio's historic Indians to find a place for themselves in a rapidly changing world comes closer to the tragedies of Shakespeare. There is no black-and-white scenario of perfect characters on one side to root for, nor wholly evil characters on the other side to condemn. Instead, there is only the tale of the many individuals who tried to come to terms with the fast pace of change on America's western frontier. While they often disagreed with one another on how to proceed, they all attempted to move toward the best possible future. In the end, Ohio became a microcosm of how people with conflicting views and competing interests strove to find the surest way forward, even in the face of the relentless press of time.

ONE

Turning Back the Clock at Ghent

The Flemish capital of Ghent, founded as a trading post in Roman times, and thriving in recent years as a staging point for armies heading east to fight Napoleon, seemed a world away from the ancient forests and rolling prairies of the old Ohio Country. But in the summer of 1814, its citizens were bound together in the same moment in time that brought ambassadors from Great Britain and the United States together in Flanders to end the war between their two nations. Viscount Robert Stewart, the British foreign secretary better known as Lord Castlereagh, had turned down overtures from the Russian tsar, Alexander I, to hold the negotiations in St. Petersburg, and also from the Swedes to hold them in Gothenburg. He chose Ghent, instead, because the city was on the road he would be continually taking in the coming months to the Congress of Vienna, where the fate of Europe would be decided now that Napoleon had been exiled to Elba.

Every time Castlereagh traveled through Ghent, he could pass on instructions to his three commissioners, who were negotiating peace with the Americans. He would make sure that Lord James Gambier, an admiral in the Royal Navy who had served in North America; William Adams, an expert on maritime law who would defend British rights on the high seas; and Henry Goulburn, a

Tory member of Parliament and the undersecretary of war and the colonies would implement the most important requirement of the upcoming negotiations. They were to demand as a sine qua non of any treaty that an Indian nation be created south of the Great Lakes and north of the Ohio River. Here the many tribes that had allied themselves with the British during the War of 1812 would have a permanent homeland, which the Americans could neither conquer nor purchase.[1]

Two of the five American commissioners—Albert Gallatin, the secretary of the treasury; and James Bayard, a Federalist congressman from New Jersey—were the first of their delegation to arrive in Ghent. Secretary of State James Monroe had chosen Gallatin because he was European by birth, having grown up in Switzerland, and because he now hailed from Pennsylvania, a state whose soldiers had fought bravely against the British in the American Revolution and the War of 1812. The Senate had resisted Gallatin's appointment, not wanting to lose the most knowledgeable secretary of the treasury since Alexander Hamilton— especially not in wartime—but in the end had relented. Congress had no objection to appointing Bayard since he would represent the middle states, and who was still fondly remembered for breaking the tie in the House of Representatives that made Thomas Jefferson the president over Aaron Burr in 1801.[2]

Gallatin and Bayard had traveled together across the Atlantic on the *Neptune* from New Castle on the Delaware coast to London, where they witnessed the wild celebrations over the fall of Napoleon. They saw hundreds of thousands of people crowd into Hyde Park to cheer for old King Louis XVIII on his way back to Paris, where he would reclaim the French throne for the Bourbons. Night after night, they watched fireworks light up the sky outside the window of their hotel on Albemarle Street, and each morning over breakfast they read the newspapers filled with attacks on the upstart Americans, who had dared to declare war on Great Britain in her most desperate hour.[3]

Once safely in Ghent, Bayard and Gallatin sent dispatches back to Secretary Monroe reporting every rumor circulating about what the triumphant British were planning for their former colonies. They were going to teach the United States the painful lesson that "war is not to be declared on Great Britain without impunity." Upwards of 25,000 soldiers might already be on their way to North America from Europe, where they were no longer needed.

These were crack troops led by the best commanders who had served under the Duke of Wellington. This huge and disciplined army would occupy the state of New York and split the nation in two. The Royal Navy, now freed from its duty of blockading Europe, was probably at this moment sailing west to capture every American port on the Atlantic. New York City, Baltimore, and Norfolk would be reclaimed as part of the British Empire. Patrols would come up the Potomac River and burn down the capital city of Washington. American fishermen would be banned from the Grand Banks of Newfoundland, and the nation's commercial fleet would be wiped off the high seas. Still, amid all these frightening rumors, there was no mention of a plan to establish an Indian state in the western country.[4]

Gallatin and Bayard were to serve alongside John Quincy Adams, who had been appointed lead negotiator at Ghent. Adams finally arrived from St. Petersburg, where he had served as the ambassador to Russia since 1809. There he witnessed similar celebrations for the victory over Napoleon, which had come at a terrible price for the Russian people. He spent long hours standing beside the family of Tsar Alexander I and listening to *Te Deums* sung in thanksgiving to God for delivering the Russian people from the hated dictator.[5] Anxious about the upcoming negotiations, Adams tried to calm himself by continuing his normal habit of rising before dawn and walking in the last dark moments of the night to observe the heavens. As the dawn grew brighter, he would have seen the stars disappear behind the three great towers at the center of Ghent. The blue-gray spire of the church of Saint Nicholas and the still higher tower of St. Bavo's Cathedral would have come clearly into view. But the city's belfry, rising nearly three hundred feet, would have loomed the largest in the morning light. Here, the tolling of the bells had counted time and warned of danger for centuries. John Quincy Adams took all this in and returned to his quarters, where he recorded every observation he had made about Ghent, as well as the movements of the heavens above the town, in his diary.[6]

But nothing could calm Adams's fear that his country would not long survive in a world ever more firmly in the control of Great Britain. Brilliant and lonely, he brooded that his fellow commissioners (who had all finally arrived in Ghent) were not as worried about the nation's future as he was. They wiled away their time smoking cigars and drinking bad wine. Adams was especially annoyed at Henry Clay, the former speaker of the House of Representatives from Kentucky, who had resigned his position to help negotiate the peace. Clay usually went to bed after a long night of playing cards, while Adams headed out to ponder the stars.[7]

Despite his apparent nonchalance, Clay was just as anxious about the coming negotiations as Adams. He wanted to end the war even more surely than Adams, for he knew from firsthand experience how the conflict had torn Americans apart. Clay had been the leader of the War Hawks, the young nationalists in the Twelfth Congress who had called for war against Great Britain to defend the nation's honor. They had gotten their way, only to see their fellow countrymen turn against each other once the war started. Monroe had appointed Clay to represent both the West and South, where support for the war remained high, along with Jonathan Russell, a former War Hawk from Rhode Island, who was to represent New England, where the war was so hated that people spoke openly of secession.[8]

None of the five American ambassadors had received any instructions on what to do if the British demanded an Indian nation on the western frontier. Instead, they had been told first and foremost to convince Great Britain to abandon the practice of impressing sailors on American ships. Monroe was clear about this in every set of formal notes he sent to his commissioners: This "degrading practice must cease; our flag must protect the crew," he wrote in January 1814, "or the United States cannot consider themselves an independent nation." Monroe confided that President James Madison might be willing to ban British citizens from working on American merchant ships. But the point that impressment was wrong must still be made. As Monroe explained, this was imperative, since a "vast amount of treasure" had already been expended to prove this point in the war. The commissioners were also to convince the British government to restore the wages that American sailors had lost while serving in the Royal Navy.[9]

Demanding that Great Britain abandon impressment of sailors might make sense to Monroe, standing in the momentary safety of his nation's capital. But for the American commissioners to demand this in Ghent, as a condition of any peace treaty, seemed next to impossible, given the fact that Britain had just defeated Napoleon in large measure because of its navy. The crowds that lined the streets of capital cities throughout Europe for one victory parade after another cheered for the British soldiers and sailors who had saved them. Along with their commanding generals and admirals, they were the heroes of the moment.[10]

William Crawford of Georgia, who had made a name for himself as a War Hawk alongside Henry Clay and other southerners, like John C. Calhoun of South Carolina, was now the ambassador to France. He witnessed the celebrations that gripped Paris when Arthur Wellesley, the Duke of Wellington, and his troops marched through the city. After seeing this, Crawford lost all hope that the American commissioners could win a concession from the British on impressment. "I believe they will insist upon the unqualified admission of their right to impress on board American vessels at sea," he wrote to Clay in June 1814. "This I trust will never be conceded." It would be better for the United States "to return to our colonial relations with *our mother country* than to submit to this condition." Crawford was certain the negotiations about to begin in Ghent would break down over impressment, and then all Americans would hopefully unite, realizing that peace could "only be obtained by the most vigorous prosecution of the war."[11]

But Monroe would not back down. He believed the United States must win the day on impressment as a matter of principle. The fight was part of a wider struggle to define the rights of neutral nations in wartime, especially on the high seas. This was not an abstract issue for the United States, since Britain had impressed thousands of American sailors and taken hundreds of American ships during their war against France. Was the world to be a place governed by the demands, and more importantly, the navy of the most powerful nation on earth or one governed by law based on the most humane and just principles applied to all nations? For

Monroe, the honor, future, and very existence of the United States of America depended on answering yes to this question, even in the face of a Great Britain more powerful than during the American Revolution.[12]

While he was most concerned about ending his nation's troubles along the eastern seaboard, Secretary Monroe added a few instructions on rectifying the damage done by the British in the west and south. He blamed Great Britain for the many Indian attacks on Americans, including defenseless women and children, along the frontier. British fur traders sold guns to the tribes, who then turned these weapons on settlers living on isolated farms. The gun trade only survived because the Royal Navy patrolled the Great Lakes. Monroe therefore told his commissioners to demand that Great Britain recall its traders from the west and its warships from the lakes. While he believed that real peace would only come once the British ceded Canada to the United States, he did not press his commissioners to ask for this in the negotiations. However, he did tell them to make sure Great Britain returned all slaves that had been taken during the war and sold in the West Indies.[13]

With Monroe's instructions in mind, but with deep misgivings, the American commissioners headed for the Hôtel des Pays-Bas, where they had agreed to meet their British counterparts at one o'clock on the afternoon of August 8. At first they were pleasantly surprised at the friendly demeanor of the men who sat across the table from them. James Gambier had made a name for himself during the Napoleonic Wars by refusing to send fire ships against the French navy at the Battle of Basque Roads in April 1809. He considered the practice of loading ships with explosives and launching them against an enemy fleet at anchor "a horrible and anti-Christian mode of warfare." The Americans could only hope that he would be as merciful to them as he had been to the French.

They were not disappointed at first. Gambier began the proceedings by admitting that his nation deeply regretted the war between their two countries. William, the Prince Regent, ruling on behalf of George III—who was still alive, but by all accounts quite mad—sincerely desired its termination. The admiral said he was as anxious as the prince and his government to end this terrible conflict and restore amicable relations with the United States.

Surely the blessings of Divine Providence would rain down on both countries once this had happened. Admiralty lawyer Dr. William Adams added that he felt both the American government and the American people wanted to end this war that was "so contrary to the interests of both nations." John Quincy Adams was so relieved when he heard this that he thought for a moment that he and Dr. Adams might be related.[14]

But the mood in the room changed when Henry Goulburn took the floor. Although at thirty years of age, he was the youngest commissioner, the Americans quickly realized that he was the point man for the British. As Adams explained in a letter to Monroe, young Goulburn was the plenipotentiary "most in the confidence of his Government."[15] But what Adams and the rest of the American delegation did not understand was how deeply involved Goulburn had been in the prosecution of the war. As the undersecretary of war and the colonies, he had directed Britain's political and military leaders in North America throughout the conflict. From the perspective of the Colonial Office, the cause of the war was not impressment, but the relentless drive of the United States to conquer Canada. In fact, the primary goal of the British throughout the war had been to preserve Canada. They had achieved this in large measure by recruiting Indian warriors, who had already lost much of their land to the Americans, to fight with them. At the peace negotiations, the British were determined to win a treaty that would protect both Canada and the Indians from any further American aggression long into the future.[16]

Goulburn took the matter of impressment off the table right from the start. He told the American commissioners that the question of the "forcible seizure of mariners," who as "native-born subjects" owed their allegiance to the British Crown, would not be open to debate.

Instead, he and his fellow negotiators had been instructed to forge a treaty that would "embrace Great Britain's Indian allies." More specifically, they were told to demand that a permanent boundary be set between the tribes and the United States as a "*sine qua non* to the conclusion of any treaty of amity and peace." Goulburn said his government believed this was the only way to achieve a lasting peace.

"There should be fixed a boundary for the Indians which should not be liable to be encroached upon," he explained. When Goulburn added that the border between Canada and the United States would have to be adjusted as part of the process, the implication was clear: the new Indian state, which would lie beyond the new boundary, would be part of a much larger Canada. The British, in fact, were so intent on strengthening Canada that they would no longer allow Americans to fish off the Grand Banks, nor dry their catch on the shores of Newfoundland. Even though they had agreed to this in the treaty that ended the American Revolution, they could offer no "equivalent" as an alternative at the moment.[17]

The American commissioners were caught off guard by Goulburn's demands. John Quincy Adams repeated back what he thought he had heard him say, and then asked: "Then we will be allowed to discuss the issue of impressment?" "No," Goulburn replied. The British government did not consider the matter worthy of debate. His response only added to the confusion among the Americans. They had come ready to argue that the practice of impressment was immoral and must be abandoned. Instead, they were told that an Indian nation was about to be created somewhere in the western country belonging to the United States. But where exactly? No one dared to ask this question, even if they could have even formulated it at the time. They had received no instructions from Monroe nor from anyone else in Madison's administration on what to do if the British proposed the creation of an Indian state on American soil.

The unflappable Adams looked at his fellow commissioners for help, and getting none, asked for a postponement of the negotiations until the following day. Goulburn, seeing the confusion, and realizing that the Americans had obviously received no instructions on the matter of an Indian homeland, said his government was not trying to win more territory for themselves or the tribes. This only confused the American commissioners further. How could this nation be created within the borders of the United States without taking away American territory? Unable to wrap their minds around so impossible a concept, they were at least able to agree to meet at eleven o'clock on the following morning at the lodgings of the British ambassadors in Ghent's old Carthusian monastery.[18]

While all the commissioners were deeply shocked, John Quincy Adams was particularly so. The British seemed to have hurled him back through time to more than thirty years earlier, when his father, John Adams, had negotiated an end to the American Revolution. All the same issues were now staring him in the face, including his nation's western boundary, the Indians, and even the Atlantic fisheries. He was fighting for the survival of the United States all over again. How could the British not understand that the impressment of American sailors on the high seas had caused this war? The United States had been treated like a colony with its sovereignty ignored, and now its borders and thus its very existence were threatened.[19]

Somewhere between the declaration of war in June 1812 and the start of formal peace negotiations in August 1814, Adams and the rest of the commissioners had forgotten that there was more to the conflict than stopping ships on the high seas and kidnapping sailors. The causes, as listed in President Madison's speech calling for an official declaration of war, included the impressment of American seamen and the Orders in Council, instructions from the prime minister's cabinet directing the Royal Navy to blockade Napoleon's European empire and seize any ship bound for the Continent. But Madison had also listed the unrest of the "savages" on the western frontier, fomented by the British in Canada, as the third cause of the war. That unrest could be summarized in one word: Tecumseh.

Inspired by the visions of his younger brother Lalawethika, or the "Loud Mouth," the Shawnee warrior Tecumseh had pieced together the largest Indian confederation in history. Its main purpose was to push American settlers out of the western territories of the United States and leave the country to the Indians. Between 1805 and 1810, Tecumseh, traveling on foot, by canoe, and on horseback, had spoken to most of the tribes living in the old Ohio Country, and even to a few tribes farther east. Charismatic and eloquent, he impressed everyone who heard him and swayed many people, especially younger chiefs and warriors, to join him. He told the Indians to think of themselves as one people, not as separate tribes. They must recognize that they held the land in common; therefore no chief could sell any more territory to the insatiable Americans, who would not be satisfied until they drove the Indians into the sea.

As he built his confederation in secret, his brother, now calling himself Tenkswatawa, or the "Open Door," and best known as the Prophet, preached openly to the crowds that flocked to hear him. He told them that the Great Spirit had shown him frightening visions in which two paths lay open before the tribes. One path led to perpetual happiness, but the other led to fiery damnation, where drunken Indians swallowed cups of molten lead for all eternity. The Great Spirit had assured him that if the Indians gave up the white man's ways, especially his whiskey, and returned to the customs of their forefathers, then he would protect them in this world as well as in the next. Tenkswatawa urged the tribes to follow him, first to his village at Greeneville, Ohio, and later to Prophetstown on the Tippecanoe Creek in the Indiana Territory, promising that if they did all he asked, the Great Spirit would reward them with a permanent homeland, which the Americans could never take away.[20]

How would the Shawnee brothers win the country promised by the Great Spirit? At times, Tecumseh said he would simply demand it from the Americans once he had united all the Indians under his leadership. But at other times, he spoke of a day when he would send a miraculous signal to his followers to strike the Americans one fatal blow. On that terrible day, he would stamp his foot on the ground, and all the earth would shake. His warriors would then know that now was the time to rise up and kill every American man, woman, and child living west of the Appalachians. Surely, he believed, the frightened Americans would flee back east across the mountains and give the country north of the Ohio River and west to the Mississippi back to the tribes as their own nation. If only he could stay hidden in the shadows, away from the prying eyes of territorial officials, and strike the Americans before they discovered his plans, then the dream of the Shawnee brothers for their people might be fulfilled.[21]

Maybe if William Henry Harrison, longtime governor of the Indiana Territory, had been chosen to treat for his nation at

Ghent, he could have explained all this to his fellow commissioners. Harrison had warned the Madison administration for years in weekly letters to the War Department that there was more to the Prophet than anyone suspected. He fretted constantly over the growing unrest swirling about Tenkswatawa. Harrison could not believe that a one-eyed Shawnee holy man, who wore a black patch over his sightless right eye and wrapped himself in a cloak of eagle feathers, was the true leader of the many Indians gathering at Greeneville and who now lived along the Tippecanoe Creek. When he finally learned that the Prophet's older brother was the true "Moses" of the family, Harrison demanded that Tecumseh come to his capital at Vincennes. The two men met on the lawn before the governor's mansion in two dramatic encounters; one in August 1810, and the other in the following summer.

At their first meeting, they nearly came to blows. Tecumseh declared that he had united all the tribes in a confederation and that he would soon demand a separate country for his people, always claiming his intentions toward the United States were entirely peaceful. Governor Harrison just as boldly declared that the moon would sooner fall to the earth than would the Americans give up their country to the Indians, and accused Tecumseh of listening to the British in Canada, who had undoubtedly plotted this whole scheme right from the start. Calling Harrison a liar, Tecumseh brandished a war club at him while the governor raised his sword to defend himself.

Yet Harrison came to admire the Shawnee leader, even telling the War Department after their final meeting in July 1811 that Tecumseh was "one of those uncommon geniuses" who rise up to "overturn the established order of things." If not for the United States, he might have been able to build an empire on the order of the Aztecs or the Incas. "No difficulties deter him," Harrison explained. "You see him today on the Wabash and in a short time you hear of him on the shores of Lake Erie or Michigan, or on the banks of the Mississippi and wherever he goes, he makes an impression favorable to his purposes."[22] But as much as he admired him, Harrison was determined to break up Tecumseh's confederation before the daring chief had a chance to launch a fatal attack on American settlements along the western frontier.

He got his chance in the late summer of 1811, when Tecumseh left on a trip to the South, where he hoped to win the Chickasaw, Choctaw, and Creek to his cause. Harrison took advantage of Tecumseh's absence to lead an army toward Prophetstown.[23]

Tecumseh had left specific orders with his brother to disperse their followers if Harrison approached their capital on the Tippecanoe Creek. He could not take the chance that his men might fight and be defeated, which would ruin their confidence and send them fleeing back to their own country, thus making a surprise attack on the Americans impossible. But under pressure from the many young warriors who surrounded him, the Prophet ignored his brother's instructions. He ordered an attack on Harrison and his men, who had camped on a small bluff about a mile away from Prophetstown. Tenkswatawa promised the warriors he would use his powers to make sure the bullets of the Americans would not harm them. He also remembered Harrison always rode a white horse, so he told them to kill every man riding one.

But when the Indians attacked the American camp at dawn on the morning of November 7, 1811, Harrison could not find his usual mount in the confusion. He rode a dark horse throughout the battle and so saved his own life without knowing it. The Prophet's magic did little good, either, as his young men fell to the American bullets. After several hours of fighting, the Indians fled the battlefield. Harrison headed for Prophetstown and burned it to the ground. He then marched his men back to Vincennes as quickly as he could. He was worried that Tecumseh might have returned from the South and could be waiting to ambush his army somewhere along the Wabash.[24]

Tecumseh, however, was nowhere near the Indiana Territory. Instead, he was on his way to the Osage country across the Mississippi River, having completed his tour of the southern tribes. The Chickasaw and Choctaw had flatly rejected him, but he struck a chord among the Muscogee, or Creek, Indians. Speaking at their main town of Tuckaubatchee in October 1811, and painted black from head to toe, he called for the total destruction of the Americans. "Burn their dwellings—destroy their stock—slay their wives and children, that the very breed may perish," Tecumseh proclaimed. "War now! War always! War on the living! War on the dead!"[25] Though only thirty warriors followed Tecumseh when he left for the Osage country, he had inspired many of the young men who remained behind to dream visions of their own. Prophets among the Upper Creeks, who had resisted acculturation with the whites, now taught that the Master of Life was about to remake the world. The time was ripe for war, not yet against the Americans, but instead against the Lower Creeks, who had forgotten their heritage.[26]

Tecumseh would not reach the Tippecanoe Creek until February 1812. When he saw his village deserted and all his warriors fled back to their own towns, he called himself a ruined man. He searched for his younger brother among the remains of their burned-out capital. After the terrible and unexpected loss to Harrison the previous November, the Prophet had barely escaped with his life. Winnebago warriors took him to their camp on Wildcat Creek, some twenty miles east of Prophetstown, where they beat him and left him tied to a post before returning to their villages along the northern Great Lakes. The Prophet made his way back to the Tippecanoe Creek, where Shawnee and Wyandot stragglers kept him alive. When Tecumseh finally found him, he shook him so hard he nearly killed him. He told his brother to get out of his sight, for he never wanted to see him again. But he soon relented, and together the two brothers began the difficult task of rebuilding their confederation by calling their followers back to Prophetstown.[27] Tecumseh also sent a message to Harrison, asking him to arrange a visit with President Madison; but the governor refused, telling him there was no hope of restoring peace now. Fighting had already broken out between bands of Indians and settlers all along the frontier in Indiana and Illinois. Attacks on lives and property became so frequent that many settlers abandoned their farms and moved their families into hastily built blockhouses. Others huddled for protection in nearby towns, and some even withdrew to safety across the Ohio River.[28]

No matter where they had taken refuge, Americans on the frontier agreed with Governor Harrison that the British in Canada were to be blamed for the Indian uprising. Surely they had directed Tecumseh in his dastardly plans, arming and supplying his followers who were now on the warpath. The turmoil on the frontier grew even worse in the early spring of 1812, when a comet lit up the night sky, and earthquakes centered at Cape Girardeau in the Missouri Territory shook the entire Mississippi River valley. People from the Great Lakes to the Gulf of Mexico felt the ground tremble beneath them. Many Indians said this was the sign that Tecumseh had promised long ago to launch his war against the United States. With the official declaration of war at least six months away, the War of 1812 was already under way in the western country.

With the frontier aflame in an Indian war, the War Hawks in Congress made an even stronger case that the British were holding the United States in a stranglehold. To the east, on the Atlantic, they were destroying American commerce and national pride, while to the west, they were uprooting frontier settlements. The nation had no other choice but to declare war on Great Britain, even though it barely had an army or navy to defend itself. The War Hawks argued that this was not an issue, since Great Britain was tied down in Europe fighting Napoleon, and could not afford to send troops against the Americans. In fact, the United States held the upper hand because, once war was declared, volunteer armies would rise up and conquer Canada, finally breaking the tie between Great Britain and the Indians that had led to the near tragedy of Tecumseh's confederation. The loss of Canada would likewise be a profound blow to the British since they needed the lumber, grain, and naval stores pouring out of their colony if they ever hoped to defeat Napoleon.[29]

Everything had seemed so clear in the first half of 1812. Even former president Thomas Jefferson, who had avoided war with Great Britain at all costs, preferring instead to impose a self-inflicted embargo that crippled American commerce to an open conflict on the high seas, believed that the "acquisition of Canada this year will be a mere matter of marching."[30] But just two years later, the American negotiators at Ghent seemed to have forgotten that their nation's confident boast to take Canada in retaliation for British support for Tecumseh's confederation had helped bring about the war. Maybe it was the sheer speed of the military disasters along the Canadian border in the opening months of the War of 1812 that made them forget. Instead of conquering Canada by simply marching into it, the Americans had come up against a small but powerful force of British regulars, Canadian militia, and hundreds of Indian warriors, led by Tecumseh, determined to defeat them.

As Governor Harrison had suspected, the British had made contact with Tecumseh well before the start of the War of 1812. They met often with him as part of their attempt to rebuild the "silver chain of friendship" between their nation and the Indians. The chain had remained strong during the American Revolution and throughout the next decade. Canadian officials supported the many tribes living across the Great Lakes in their fight against the advance of the Americans across the Ohio River. They supplied them with arms and ammunition from their forts on American soil at Detroit, Oswego, Niagara, and Michillimackinac which they had refused to surrender after the revolution ended. But the chain had broken, seemingly past repair, after American Major General Anthony Wayne defeated the Indians at Fallen Timbers in 1794. The warriors fled from the battlefield a mile north down the Maumee River in northwestern Ohio to Fort Miamis, the new British post built just four months earlier. Expecting to be welcomed there, they were shocked when Major William Campbell, the commander of the post, fearing that General Wayne was right behind them, closed the gates in their faces. The warriors had no choice but to flee back into the surrounding woods. Tecumseh, then a twenty-six-year-old warrior who had left his older brother Sauwaseeka dead on the battlefield, vowed never to forgive the British for their betrayal.[31]

During the next two years, the bonds between Great Britain and the tribes were strained even further. In 1795 the Indians, knowing they could no longer count on the support of the British, signed the Treaty of Greeneville with Wayne, which drew a line through the modern state of Ohio, allowing the Americans to settle south of it, while the Indians could still live to the north. With Jay's Treaty, which went into effect a year later, the British finally gave up their forts on American soil. Great Britain then concentrated on settling Upper Canada (now the province of Ontario) with American Loyalists, Iroquois from New York, and immigrants from England, Ireland, and Scotland. Officials still gave presents to the Indians, who made annual pilgrimages to the new posts at Fort Malden on the Detroit River in Amherstburg, to Fort George on the Niagara frontier, and to Fort St. Joseph's near Mackinac. However, with the war against France under way on the continent of Europe and on the oceans of the world, the amount of gifts was greatly reduced. The few officials who remained in the Indian service were ordered to keep accurate records of how much they spent on the Indians each year.[32]

But the situation changed dramatically in the summer of 1807, after the British frigate HMS *Leopard* sailed up the James River in Virginia and attacked an American ship, the frigate USS *Chesapeake*, impressing four sailors whom the *Leopard's* captain accused of being deserters, hanging one, and impressing the other three into the Royal Navy. Cries for war against Great Britain now rang out across the United States.

Sir James Craig, the new governor general of Canada, decided the time was right to restore the chain of friendship between Great Britain and the Indians. Craig was certain that if war were declared, the Americans would cross over from Detroit and easily conquer Canada. The only hope for defending their colony was to recruit Indian warriors to protect its western border. In May 1808 he called a grand council with the tribes living across the Great Lakes at Fort Malden, hoping the Indians had forgotten Fallen Timbers and so would be willing to support Great Britain in the coming war. A special invitation went out to the Prophet, who was well-known beyond the borders of the United States.[33]

Canadian officials, including the lieutenant governor, General Francis Gore; William Claus, superintendent of Indian affairs at Fort George; and Matthew Elliott, Fort Malden's Indian superintendent, were surprised when Tecumseh, the Prophet's older brother, arrived instead. They were deeply impressed with the Shawnee warrior's efforts to build an Indian confederation and win a homeland for his people. They promised to arm and supply his followers, hoping to hold them in check until the very moment that they were needed in an actual war. Tecumseh remained leery of the British, remembering the betrayal at Fallen Timbers, and hoping to defeat the Americans on his own. For their part, the British kept their promise and sent regular packtrains to Prophetstown. Even after the disaster at Tippecanoe, throughout the winter and spring of 1812, Indian agents at Fort Malden continued to supply Tecumseh and the Prophet as they struggled to rebuild their confederation. Finally, in May 1812, when all hope seemed lost for Tecumseh, who was forced to defend his actions against angry chiefs at a council in Mississenewa in northeastern Indiana, a black wampum belt arrived from Fort Malden. Tecumseh immediately understood the belt's meaning. The British were letting him know that war with the United States was immi-

Tecumseh by Benson Lossing, c. 1848, after an 1808 sketch from life by a French trader. (*National Museum of the American Indian*)

nent. He must bring his followers to Canada and help defend it against an American invasion.[34]

Tecumseh arrived in Fort Malden in June 1812, just as the United States declared war on Great Britain. There he met with Sir Isaac Brock, the governor general of Upper Canada, who had been planning the defense of his province for some time. He had already alerted Robert Dickson, the most important British trader on the Upper Mississippi, to be ready to send warriors to defend Canada's border on the Detroit River. He had alerted Captain Charles Roberts, the commander of Fort St. Joseph's, to take Michillimackinac once the war began. Tecumseh was so impressed with Brock that he said to his followers, "This is a man!" Brock was just as impressed with Tecumseh. He wrote to Henry Goulburn at the Colonial Office and the prime minister, the Earl of Liverpool, urging them to secure a separate country as a reward for the Indians in any future peace negotiations. Sir George Prevost, Canada's current governor general, agreed with Brock and also wrote to Goulburn in support of an Indian state.[35]

Now fighting openly alongside the British, Tecumseh and his supporters participated in attacks against the Americans all along the western frontier. Fort Michillimackinac fell to the British and

Indians on July 17, 1812, just one month after the United States had declared war. Tecumseh and his warriors next helped the British turn back the American invasion of Upper Canada. An army, led by the old Revolutionary War brigadier general William Hull, had crossed from Fort Detroit to Sandwich, Ontario. After facing heavy resistance on the way to Fort Malden, Hull and his three thousand men had returned to the safety of Detroit. Tecumseh and his warriors followed him there, harassing his communication and supply lines in skirmishes at Brownstown and Maguaga, south of the fort. Returning to Fort Malden, Tecumseh mapped out the region around Detroit for General Brock on a piece of elm bark and recommended an immediate attack. Although the American forces outnumbered his own, Brock knew from letters captured by Tecumseh's men that Hull's troops had little faith in their commander, and that many were unwilling to fight for him.

On the night of August 14, Tecumseh crossed the Detroit River from Canada with six hundred warriors. They took up positions to the north and west of the fort, further disrupting Hull's communications. Brock arrived on the next morning and positioned his troops south of the fort. He sent word to Hull, calling for the immediate surrender of Detroit. Playing on the commander's fear of Tecumseh and his followers, he told Hull that he would not be able to control the savagery of the Indians once fighting broke out. He also let the Americans capture a false dispatch that claimed five thousand warriors were on their way to Detroit from Michillimackinac. After bombarding the fort from Sandwich, and before either he or Tecumseh could strike the first blow, Hull surrendered Detroit without firing a shot. It was August 16, just two months since the United States had declared war.[36]

President Madison could not have forgotten this terrible time. He had been so distraught after receiving news of the fall of Detroit that he was never quite the same man again. People who knew him said that he aged overnight.[37] Secretary of State Monroe could also not have forgotten these awful days, especially since he was the first person to whom the president turned for help. After the surrender of Detroit, Madison planned to commission Monroe as a major general and send him north with a volunteer army to prosecute the "campaign against Upper Canada." Monroe accepted the phantom commission, proudly telling his friend Thomas Jefferson that he was raising an army to retake Detroit, and hopefully Canada as well.[38]

But soon more terrible news came in from the West. Pottawatomi warriors massacred Americans who were fleeing toward the Indiana Territory from Fort Dearborn (now Chicago). The attacks of Ottawa warriors on settlers fleeing from the Maumee River valley were so brutal that Matthew Elliott, the Indian agent at Fort Malden, reprimanded them for their cruelty. Even the Prophet, emboldened by his brother's victory at Detroit, joined in the fight against the Americans by directing Pottawatomi bands to attack Fort Harrison at Terre Haute on the Wabash, and later at Fort Wayne on the headwaters of the Maumee. By September Tecumseh and his followers, along with British soldiers under the command of Captain Adam Muir, were on their way from Detroit to lay siege to Fort Wayne. If the post fell, settlers throughout Indiana were convinced that Tecumseh and thousands of his warriors would attack Vincennes, probably by the next full moon. As the British and the Indians took control of much of the old Ohio Country, the mirage of the United States easily taking Canada slipped away.[39]

Having suffered one setback after another in the West, the Americans preferred to look out to the Atlantic where in the deep waters of the grey green sea they could see their fight against impressment justly reflected. The American commissioners at Ghent would have to regroup if they were to convince their counterparts of the error of Great Britain's ways. The fight might be doomed from the start, however, since the British saw nothing that troubled them when they looked out toward the wide Atlantic, neither in August 1814, nor in June 1812, or all the way back to the terrible summer of 1789, when the nightmare of the French Revolution began. For twenty-five years, Great Britain's highest purpose as a nation had been to defeat France: first as a republic bent on tearing up the old order, and then as an empire propelled across Europe and the world's oceans by Napoleon's ambition.

The British had staked their future, and in their opinion the future of the world, on the premise that France must be stopped. To accomplish this, they pieced together a continental alliance that raised armies to defeat Napoleon on the battlefield. They blockaded Europe and let nothing pass that might help the dictator succeed. To man the many ships needed for the blockade, they boarded merchant vessels on the high seas at will, and pressed into service anyone suspected of being born a subject of their king. The Royal Navy had employed this practice for more than three hundred years. Press gangs regularly raided towns along the coast of the British Isles, or stopped merchant vessels, taking all the able-bodied men they needed to keep the navy afloat. Kidnapped sailors served for twelve years and were never allowed on shore during any of that time for fear of desertion.[40]

If the outraged Americans had only waited a few more weeks in the summer of 1812, thought many of the British, then their outrage might have abated. Napoleon had started for Russia on June 18, the very day the United States declared war on Great Britain. Five days later the prime minister's cabinet repealed the Orders in Council. This was the beginning of the end for the French dictator, and so the beginning of the end for the blockade and impressment. Why could the Americans not understand that their "troubles were the troubles of the age?"

Some forty years after the War of 1812 ended, an English author, writing in Toronto, Canada, prepared a history of the conflict from the British point of view. Basing his work on eyewitness accounts and primary sources, Gilbert Auchinleck best expressed the sentiments of his nation that still remained after the passage of so much time:

> Tyrants aiming at universal dominion cannot send their whirlwinds of men and steel over the earth without causing general suffering—and the United States suffered. With the breaking of the oppressor's rod, their sufferings would have ceased. The tide of French invasion once driven back, the ancient landmarks would have reappeared; the rights of nations, the renewal of commerce; everything in short worth contending for would have followed the fall of Buonoparte, since it was by his conquest and decrees alone that the order and true happiness of the world had been

interrupted. The United States, by throwing themselves into the contest, only delayed that happy consummation.[41]

Locked in their final struggle against Napoleon, the British considered the War of 1812 a battle for the North American continent rather than a fight for freedom on the high seas. They were determined to retain Canada against every American invasion. They had spent years rebuilding their relationship with the Indians to help defend it. In the process, they had met Tecumseh, the Shawnee warrior who came to them with plans of creating an Indian nation just beyond the borders of Upper Canada. When the war finally broke out, the British made Tecumseh's cause their own. Together they would turn back the Americans and establish an Indian state, somewhere in the old Ohio Country, that would be a permanent buffer between the United States and Canada. Never again would the Americans dare to invade the territory of Great Britain or of the Indians.[42]

This is what the British commissioners were fighting for at Ghent. In their eyes, the cause they championed was far more worthy than the American quest to abolish impressment. Still, there was a problem with their own demand for an Indian nation to be created within the borders of the United States. While all had gone well for Great Britain in the opening months of the war, with Detroit, Mackinac, and Dearborn falling quickly, the tide soon turned against them. In August 1812, Tecumseh and Captain Muir failed to take Fort Wayne. Two months later Great Britain suffered an even more terrible loss when General Brock was killed at the Battle of Queenston Heights, on the Niagara frontier. His successor, Brigadier Henry Procter, hated Tecumseh, and considered his followers little more than wild animals, better suited for massacring innocent men than for fighting real soldiers in battle. He made no attempt to prevent the Indians from massacring prisoners, a practice that Tecumseh opposed. In January 1813, after the surrender of an American army along the river Raisin in present-day Monroe, Michigan, Procter allowed the Indians to slaughter the captured soldiers. Procter and Tecumseh tried to set aside their differences in order to defeat Major General William Henry Harrison, who had been given command of the Army of the Northwest. While Madison had hoped to appoint

Monroe, he chose Harrison instead, after letters poured in from the West demanding that the hero of Tippecanoe lead the Americans against the British and the Indians.[43]

As part of his nation's campaign to retake Detroit, and maybe still conquer Canada, Harrison built Fort Meigs on a bluff overlooking the Maumee River, not far from the battlefield at Fallen Timbers. The British and Indians under Procter and Tecumseh failed to dislodge Harrison's army from the post after two assaults in May and July 1813. They failed again in their attack on Fort Stephenson, some fifty miles to the east in the following month, and in September 1813, when an American flotilla under Commodore Oliver Hazard Perry defeated a British fleet under Commander Robert Barclay at Sandusky Bay in the Battle of Lake Erie, the British and Indians abandoned Detroit and fled into Upper Canada toward Niagara. With Harrison's army now in hot pursuit, Tecumseh demanded that Procter make a last stand against the Americans. Late on the afternoon of October 5, 1813, Tecumseh led his followers against Harrison's army at the Battle of the Thames River. The Americans remembered hearing him over the gunfire, shouting commands to his men. But then his voice fell silent, and no one knew for certain if he had been killed or fled with the British. Unable to find Tecumseh's body on the battlefield, and fearing that he might still be alive, Harrison retired to Detroit, leaving Upper Canada to the British, but ensuring that the United States held onto the Ohio Country. Only later did he learn that Tecumseh was dead, gunned down by a musket ball to his heart. His closest followers had taken his body from the battlefield and buried him in a secret grave.[44]

So much had already happened in the war between the British and the Indians on one side and the Americans on the other leading up to the negotiations at Ghent. So much was still at stake for both sides when the Americans arrived at the lodgings of the British ambassadors at eleven o'clock on the morning of August 9. Goulburn and his fellow negotiators, who had dominated the first session, came ready to fight for an Indian state. The Americans, who came determined to control the second session, planned to force the British to clarify the exact meaning of their government's sine qua non. Adams and Gallatin grilled Goulburn, hitting him with one question after another. Why were the British making such an issue out of the Indians on the western frontier? Surely the trouble between the Americans and the tribes would come to an end once the war was over. As Clay liked to say, the branch would fall from the tree once the trunk was toppled. A treaty had probably already been signed with Tecumseh's allies that established a border between the United States and the Indians. Goulburn answered that the British would never abandon their Indian allies, who were so much weaker than the Americans. Adams and Gallatin raised still more questions: What was the real purpose of this Indian state? Where exactly would this new state be located? Could the Indians sell this land? Goulburn answered that the Indians would be allowed to sell their land, but that no American would be allowed to buy it. He became so flustered and angry at the barrage of questions that he burst a blood vessel in his throat and was unable to speak for a week.[45]

When the commissioners met again on August 19, Goulburn, under even more intense questioning from Adams and Gallatin, as well as from Bayard and Clay, about the purpose of the new Indian state, blurted out that it was meant to be a buffer between the United States and Canada. Never again would the Americans think of invading Canada and taking it away from the British. This new state had, in fact, been a war aim of the British right from the opening days of the war, when Brock and Prevost first recommended it to the Colonial Office. Goulburn himself had promised the tribes that the "security of the Indian possessions" would never be compromised at the negotiating table.[46]

He now told the American commissioners that the southern border of the new Indian nation would be the old Greeneville treaty line, hammered out between General Wayne and the tribes a year after their defeat at Fallen Timbers. The line ran south from Lake Erie along the Cuyahoga River, crossed on a diagonal southwest to Laramie's Station and then ran northwest to Fort Recovery, and finally headed on another diagonal to the southwest toward the Ohio River. If this became the southern boundary of the Indian homeland, then the state of Ohio, along with the Indiana, Michigan, and Illinois territories, would be surrendered to the tribes. Since the Americans had invaded Canada, and not the other way around, Goulburn added that the lakes must be controlled by the British navy; and since the British needed a road between Halifax and Quebec, they would also be taking the northern half of Maine. When the Americans protested, asking what would become of the more than 100,000 people already living north of the Ohio River, Goulburn at first said that maybe the border could be adjusted, but then flatly stated that they would have to move.[47]

The arguing back and forth between the American and British commissioners went on throughout late August and early September. Each day the negotiators took turns meeting at the lodgings of the other delegation. On some days, they did not convene at all, but instead spent their time preparing written statements that messengers carried back and forth between them. The British had the advantage of sending letters to London asking for instructions on how to counter the Americans. Once, Lord Castlereagh even came in person, and admitted he too was baffled as to why the Americans refused to admit that their aggression toward the Indians and the subsequent invasion of Canada were the true causes of the War of 1812. The Americans wrote home as well, sending reports back to Washington, on the frigate USS *John Adams*. They could only wait and hope that answers would arrive from Monroe telling them that the war with the Indians had actually been settled just as they had asserted.

While only silence came back to them from across the wide Atlantic, they were at least relieved that Bayard had a printed copy of all the laws and treaties of which America had ever been a part since colonial times. He had brought it with him on the barque USS *Neptune*, which was still anchored in Antwerp. The commissioners read through them and discovered that, in 1762, the French had tried to force the British to include the Indians in treaty negotiations to end the Seven Years' War. The British had been just as furious as the Americans were now, and refused to allow it. Their own review of the treaties convinced them that the United States of America had been the only nation that ever treated the Indians with respect, not simply taking land away from them as the European powers did, but meeting with their headmen and offering to buy the land from them, not just once, but in yearly payments or annuities of money, food, blankets, and guns. Even without specific instructions from Monroe, on September 9 they wrote to Gambier, Adams, and the hated Goulburn, informing them that, based on this evidence, both a separate Indian nation and British control of the Great Lakes were "inadmissible."[48]

While John Quincy Adams might have understood the Indian question less than the other commissioners, he grasped the implications of the sine qua non better than the rest. He knew that the British saw themselves as the ultimate victors in a worldwide struggle against their rule, their commerce, and their navy that had begun not at Washington in 1812, nor in Paris in 1789, but at Lexington and Concord in 1775, and that they were now dictating the terms of the peace. In Ghent and Vienna, they were staring down at maps and redrawing the borders of the world in their favor. The cries of the wildest War Hawks—that Great Britain did not consider the United States of America a real nation and therefore could take her sailors and her ships at will while arming the Indians against her on the western frontier—suddenly came back with a terrible chill. But now those cries seemed a mere whimper against the frightening reality of a United States dismembered and handed back to, as Adams described them, the "savages." Surely, he worried it would not end with the loss of one-third of the nation to the Indians. The British would also demand Maine, the southern shores of the St. Lawrence and the Great Lakes, and maybe even the Mississippi River, the Louisiana Territory, and all of the far western country out to the Columbia River.[49]

Albert Gallatin came to share many of Adams's fears, and wrote home to Secretary Monroe that the situation at Ghent was far more dangerous than he originally guessed. He knew the British people were quite bitter toward the Americans. It was impossible not to know this since the newspapers were filled with angry editorials against the United States. While few letters were making it across the sea from America, British newspapers arrived on a regular schedule, and their attacks were increasingly vicious. They were filled with cartoons of the machinations of the sickly President Madison, who had replaced the Emperor Napoleon as the king of evil. "There is no public feeling in the country stronger than that of indignation at the Americans," said the *London Times*. "As we urged the principle, no peace with Bonaparte! so we must maintain the doctrine of, No peace with James Madison!"[50]

By the summer, the *Times* was calling not only for the protection of Canada but also for indemnities for damages incurred in the war, a review of the legality of the Louisiana Purchase, and punishment for American attacks on Florida. "Our demands may be couched in a single word—submission." Gallatin had hoped that officials in the British high command, who were obviously behind all this commotion, were only stirring up the people to stay in power. But now he feared that their goal was to acquire territory within the borders of the United States. They would not stop at taking land for their Indian allies at Ghent on paper, but were probably on their way across the Atlantic to take land away from the Americans by force. He hoped his letter explaining all this would beat the Royal Navy to America, because he thought they would not then attack the Atlantic coast, but would instead head first to the land they seemed to most desire, the Indian country in the western Great Lakes, before moving on to the real prize of New Orleans and control of the Mississippi River.[51]

By late September, the American commissioners were overcome with the sickening fear that the real purpose of the British in demanding an Indian state at Ghent was merely to use it as a delaying tactic. The American government would put all its efforts into the peace negotiations and then be caught off guard when the Royal Navy, along with the army its ships carried, arrived off America's shores. This foreboding sense of doom was accurate, for plans had been under way since the exile of Napoleon in April 1814 to shift thousands of Wellington's veterans from the Peninsula campaign to America. They had left from Bordeaux in May with at least ten thousand troops heading for Quebec and then Montreal for the invasion of New York by way of Lake Champlain.

Governor General Prevost had been told to take Detroit and restore the "Michigan Country" to the Indians, and then occupy New York and hopefully most of New England, bringing them back into the empire as the colony of New Columbia. During the first week of the negotiations at Ghent, a squadron under Sir Alexander Cochrane had arrived in Chesapeake Bay. Cochrane's ships carried a thousand soldiers under the command of Major General Robert Ross, who was ordered to take the nation's capital. Once they had finished off Washington, and hopefully Baltimore as well, the British under Cochrane and Ross were to rendezvous at Negril Bay in Jamaica and wait for another four thousand reinforcements from England before heading straight for New Orleans.[52]

Only Henry Clay thought the situation was not hopeless. At first, he had been just as angry as the other commissioners and even wanted to leave Ghent, but now he told his fellow Americans to be patient and wait. He was certain that the British would "finish by receding from the ground they have taken." Perhaps because he was an expert card player and a gambler at heart, he knew that luck rarely holds out for long. The British had been lucky for some time, and therefore things were bound to change. Clay predicted that the British would back down from their demand for an Indian country. His fellow commissioners angrily asked him, "Why would they change their minds when they had called this demand the *sine qua non* of the negotiations?" Events would go against them, he explained, for such was the nature of politics, and such was the way of the world.[53]

As proof that he was right, he shared the news that had just arrived in a mail packet from America on September 29. His supporters had written their congratulations to him upon his reelection to Congress, and had included clippings from the *National Intelligencer* (Washington), which described the peace treaty recently concluded between the United States and the Indians on the western frontier. General William Henry Harrison, along with Lewis Cass, governor of the Michigan Territory, which was supposed to be handed back to the Indians, had met with chiefs from seven major tribes in the old Ohio Country at the exact spot where Anthony Wayne had signed the Treaty of Greeneville in 1795. These were the very people that the British had been fighting for at the negotiating table at Ghent—the Delaware, Shawnee, Seneca, Ottawa, and Wyandot living in the state of Ohio along with Miami and Pottawatomi living in the Indiana and Michigan territories.

In the treaty, the tribes agreed to end all hostilities toward each other and the United States. They promised to send warriors to fight alongside the Americans if fighting with the British on the western frontier continued. In turn, the United States promised to return to the boundaries with the tribes that existed before the war began. All the tribes were now under the protection of the United States of America, "and of no other power whatever." The greatest chiefs had agreed to the treaty, including Tarhe the Crane of the Wyandot, Captain Anderson of the Delaware, and Black Hoof of the Shawnee. For all practical purposes, the war between the United States and most of the Indians in Tecumseh's confederation had been over since July 22, 1814, when the second Treaty of Greeneville was signed. Clay advised his fellow commissioners to pass this information on to the British. Surely they would then ask themselves, who would be a part of this new Indian nation that they were demanding so vociferously?[54]

Not only had the Ohio tribes made peace with the Americans, but so had Tecumseh's allies among the Creeks. Nine months after Tecumseh gave his fiery speech in Tuckaubatchee, the Red Sticks—warriors and prophets among the Upper Creeks named for the red war clubs they carried—attacked Lower Creek towns throughout Alabama. They were determined to tear up the white man's ways that had taken root there. At first they had no intention of attacking the Americans, at least not until Tecumseh had won more significant victories in the North. But after a militia company from Mississippi attacked a party of Red Sticks at Burnt Corn Creek in southwest Alabama in July 1813, the Upper Creek warriors retaliated by massacring nearly 250 Americans huddled for safety at nearby Fort Mims. The Creek War now widened to include the Americans fighting with the Lower Creeks and the Cherokee against the Red Sticks. Colonel Andrew Jackson, who commanded the militia of western Tennessee, became the hero of the day, leading his often mutinous men in one skirmish after another, culminating in his final victory over the Red Sticks at their main town of Coweta at Horseshoe Bend in March 1814.[55]

Two months later, the British arrived along the coast of the Gulf of Mexico, hoping to recruit Creek warriors to fight with them against the United States. While they easily took Pensacola from the Spanish, they were stunned to learn that the Americans under Colonel Andrew Jackson had brutally defeated the Upper Creeks at the Battle of Horseshoe Bend. The Red Stick warriors who survived fled with their families to the safety of British forts, set up first at Apalachicola, and later at Prospect Bluff, where the British trained the Indians, along with runaway slaves, to help them defend Pensacola and capture the town of Mobile. But both campaigns failed, with the British losing Pensacola for a time to Jackson. They retreated to Prospect Bluff, where they could do nothing to stop Jackson and his government from taking twenty-three million acres away from the Creeks in the Treaty of Fort Jackson, negotiated in August 1814. The treaty punished the Lower Creeks, who had been allies of the Americans, equally with the Upper Creeks. When the chiefs of the Lower Creeks protested, Jackson said they were just as responsible for the war since they should have arrested Tecumseh the day he spoke at Tuckaubatchee.[56]

Surprisingly, a major victory for Great Britain over the United States brought more bad news for Henry Goulburn and his fellow negotiators at Ghent. The first reports of the burning of Washington, DC, arrived on the Continent in early October. Major General Ross had entered the city at eight o'clock on the evening of August 24, and after a sniper shot his horse out from under him, he torched the Capitol, the president's house, the Treasury buildings, the arsenal, and the soldiers' barracks, which had just been evacuated under the watchful eye of James Monroe once he had judged the situation as hopeless. Admiral Cochrane came ashore to oversee the destruction of the *National Intelligencer* presses, which had so severely criticized the Royal Navy. While the American commissioners were heartsick at hearing the news, and now understood why no answers had come back across the Atlantic from Monroe since August, the British commissioners, however, were ecstatic. Goulburn sent clippings from several London newspapers describing the destruction of the American capital to Henry Clay, along with a note that he might find them pleasant reading.

The British high command was equally delighted with the news, and celebrated the destruction of the American capital by firing the Tower of London's guns and ringing the bells of Westminster Abbey. But voices were soon raised throughout Europe against the attack on Washington. Even many of England's major newspapers condemned the attack as a barbarous act. London's *Statesman* wrote, "The Cossacks spared Paris, but we spared not the capital of America." Suddenly the British did not seem quite so high minded and pure. They had been veritable gods who had saved Europe from Napoleon, but now they appeared as power mad as he, burning a capital city when they clearly held the upper hand over its citizens. Suddenly it was the Americans who were the heroes. The commissioners were cheered and feted everywhere they went, while the British were ridiculed or ignored. Even more remarkably, many people wondered what was really going on in Vienna. Were the British there to build a better world, or to bully the nations into doing their bidding? Would the new Europe be better than the old? Had Napoleon, still alive on Elba and still capable of escaping and building an army, really been so terrible after all?[57]

The British army and navy no longer seemed so invincible when even more bad news came across the Atlantic in early October. On September 1, Prevost, still governor general of Canada, had led fifteen thousand crack troops south across the Canadian border toward Plattsburgh, New York, on Lake Champlain. He was to take the town as the first step in setting up New Columbia, while Captain George Downie, commanding a British fleet from his flagship, HMS *Confiance*, would defeat the pitiful American navy on the lake. But when the armies and navies met on September 11, nothing went as planned. An American flotilla, hastily built, manned by prisoners and runaway slaves, and under the command of thirty-year-old Lieutenant Thomas Macdonough, smashed the British fleet, killing a quarter of the sailors, including Captain Downie, before the Royal Navy finally surrendered. On shore nearby, an American army of at most five thousand militiamen under General Alexander Macomb, many of whom were sick or inexperienced, held off Prevost at Plattsburgh, taking such a terrible toll on his army that, after watching the defeat of Downie's fleet on Lake Champlain, he retreated back to Canada as his men deserted to the Americans by the hundreds.

Two days later, Admiral Cochrane's fleet sailed from the Chesapeake after losing Ross to a sniper's bullet and failing to take Fort McHenry outside Baltimore, even after a twenty-four-hour bombardment. Like Francis Scott Key, who had watched the fight from the hold of a British ship where he had come to arrange a prisoner exchange, Cochrane and his men could see the giant American flag, sewn by the ladies of Baltimore, torn but still flying over the battered fort. How had this happened? The greatest army and navy in the world, so great that they had defeated Napoleon at last, and so bold that they had been sent to complete the job of dismembering the United States begun at Ghent, stood humiliated, a laughingstock in the eyes of Europe, and maybe even in the eyes of the still-ambitious Napoleon on Elba.[58]

Despite all the bad news, the British commissioners, taking directions straight from a defiant Lord Castlereagh, upped the ante in Ghent by demanding the Americans agree to let the western country go as an Indian nation based on the ancient Roman principle of *uti possidetis*, or "right of possession." It took the Americans, who by now were as tired of each other as they were of the fruitless negotiations, three days to write a joint response. Instead of saying the obvious, that the British could not demand land by right of possession (which they did not actually possess), they wrote that they had not been given instructions on this point, and therefore could not turn over territory without the authority to do so. Would the British play another hand? Would they bluff, or would they fold?

Only the gambler Clay seemed to remain calm, and waited for the next move, which at that moment was being played behind the scenes. The British commissioners turned to Castlereagh, who in turn sought out the advice of the Duke of Wellington, now serving as the British ambassador to France. He had refused to lead the three-pronged attack currently under way in the United States, saying instead that he must stay in Europe to hold together the latest coalition against Napoleon. The Duke now grew impatient, as more and more pressure was placed on him to sail to America and dismember the United States, perhaps not on the grand scale planned since April, but still at least on behalf of an Indian state north of the Ohio River. Wellington had all of Europe at his feet, and he was not ready to leave the wealth, honors, and women coming his way for the wilds of North America.[59]

The general bluntly told his own government what the Americans did not say: the British had won a few battles, but they had never truly been able to best the United States. In fact, they seemed incapable of winning decisively on the North American continent and had not taken any new territory, especially where they were now demanding an Indian nation. Therefore it was shameless to demand an Indian state based on the principle of *uti possidetis*. How could they so boldly demand territory on American soil that they had not won on the battlefield, especially now that Tecumseh, the mastermind of this new nation, was dead for more than a year? Even more important, Wellington could have added that many of Tecumseh's former allies had signed a treaty with his nemesis, William Henry Harrison, that recognized this same land as American territory. Since Andrew Jackson, who defeated the Red Sticks at Horseshoe Bend, had already negotiated a treaty with the Creeks to surrender their country, then for whom, exactly, were the British fighting? If they wanted to save Canada, then they needed to secure its southern border and, in the process, abandon their Indian allies. Wellington urged them to settle the American war quickly, since they might be fighting Napoleon before the year was out.[60]

All of the American commissioners, except Henry Clay, were surprised in late November when the British sent a note stating that the creation of an Indian nation, which was to be a buffer between America and Canada, would no longer be a requirement for writing the peace. They were now willing to take the Americans up on their offer to return to status quo antebellum. The offer had come by way of a deeply shaken James Monroe, who had finally sent off instructions to his commissioners on October 4. It had been a terrible six weeks leading up to this decision for the secretary of state. Monroe had escaped from Washington just as the British were marching into the city. He made it to the Rokeby Plantation across the Potomac, where the president's wife, Dolly Madison, had also escaped. Together they watched the sky turn red in the east, knowing their capital was burning in the night. By October, Monroe had convinced

Madison that the issues of impressment and neutral rights meant little, now that there was peace in Europe. Therefore the nation's commissioners—from whom he had heard not a single word since midsummer—should fight for the borders that existed before the war started. He had no idea, and would not learn for another week, that this was exactly what the American commissioners had been trying to do since August.[61]

Negotiations on the precise wording of the Treaty of Ghent now began in earnest. All territorial holdings, with the exception of several islands off the coast of Maine that were still in dispute, would be just as they were before the war: prisoners, property, artillery, slaves, and archives or records of any kind taken during the war would be returned. Both nations recognized that ships might be inadvertently taken by either side in the immediate future. Specific limits for such captures were laid out across time and space—twelve days off the American coast; thirty days in the northern Atlantic; forty days in the Baltic, North, and Mediterranean seas; sixty days in the Atlantic below the equator; ninety days south of the equator elsewhere; and a hundred twenty days "for all other parts of the world without exception." Future seizures that occurred within these limits would be forgiven as long as the ships and their crews were safely returned.

Most of the balance of the treaty, including Articles IV, V, VI, VII, and VIII, went into great detail on determining the exact border between Canada and the United States. The British were determined to secure Canada's southern boundary through these five articles. Future commissions would decide who owned the disputed islands off of Maine, how the control of each of the Great Lakes would be divided, where the northern boundaries of Maine and New York were located, and where the far western border between Canada and the United States near the Lake of the Woods actually ended. Article X described how both sides were opposed to the Atlantic slave trade, but made no provisions on how to stop it. The eleventh and final article promised that both sides would approve the treaty, as written with no changes, in four months' time or even sooner.[62]

Even though they were cutting their losses and saving Canada with a precise border stretching from the Atlantic to the northwestern corner of the Ohio Country, the British could not completely abandon their Indian allies. They could not forget Tecumseh, the daring chief who had given his life in the end—not to win a homeland for his people, but to preserve Canada. Even after his death, the British had still tried to win an Indian state north of the old Greeneville treaty line. But as the Duke of Wellington had so clearly pointed out, their many defeats on land and sea made setting the clock back to 1795 impossible. Still, they must find a way to end the bloodshed on the western frontier that had plagued the continent for centuries. If the United States and the Indians could somehow go back to the world that existed before Tippecanoe happened, then maybe the old hatreds and fears on both sides could be forgotten. The three British commissioners, on behalf of their government, packed all their nation's hopes for a better future into Article IX. It called for an end to hostilities between the United States and Great Britain on the one hand and the Indians on the other. All sides would return to the world that existed sometime during 1811. The section that applied to the United States read as follows:

> The United States of America engage to put an end immediately after the Ratification of the present Treaty to hostilities with all the Tribes or Nations of Indians with whom they may be at war at the time of such Ratification, and forthwith to restore to such Tribes or Nations respectively all the possessions, rights, and privileges which they may have enjoyed or been entitled to in one thousand eight hundred and eleven previous to such hostilities.[63]

On the afternoon of Christmas Eve 1814, the commissioners had agreed to sign the final peace treaty in the monastery where Gambier, Adams, and Goulburn had stayed since August. The three British commissioners regretted that they had failed to accomplish all they had hoped for their nation at Ghent; yet they and their government leaders took some comfort in the fact that Canada remained in the empire. It was also too late to recall the fleet carrying General Sir Edward Pakenham and eight thousand troops toward New Orleans right at this moment. Maybe there would still be a chance to redraw the map of North America once the city was taken. They greeted the five American commissioners who arrived at four o'clock in the afternoon, and after reviewing the document for nearly two hours, all were ready to sign the treaty by six that evening. The Americans were relieved that the United States of America remained intact; but how their nation's troubles with the Indians could be over by going back in time to 1811 seemed at the moment beyond any of them to comprehend. Clay had explained it best in a letter to Ambassador Crawford by saying that the British meant to take everyone back just "prior to the battle of Tippacanoe [*sic*]." Now all they could do was hope, and perhaps even send up a silent prayer on this evening filled with prayers and the sound of church bells tolling throughout the city that this was even possible.[64]

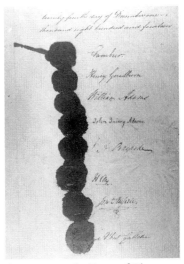

Signatures on the Treaty of Ghent, December 24, 1814. From top to bottom, British representatives [James Lord] Gambier, Henry Goulburn, and Willliam Adams; American representatives John Quincy Adams, J[ames]. A. Bayard, H[enry] Clay, Jona[than] Russell, and Albert Gallatin. (*Library of Congress*)

In the end, it would be up to at least two of the commissioners in the room, along with several other American leaders across the Atlantic, to transform the Treaty of Ghent from a piece of paper into a living reality on the western frontier. James Madison and future presidents James Monroe and John Quincy Adams would bear the major responsibility for implementing Article IX; but former War Hawks Henry Clay, as the secretary of state, and William Crawford and John C. Calhoun, each serving as the secretary of war, would also play a part, and so would William Henry Harrison, along with territorial officials and Indian agents at work across the western frontier. They had all participated in a war, and now in a peace that the British had first attempted, and who then demanded the dismembering of the United States on behalf of the Indians.

Andrew Jackson—who at this moment was waiting behind the barricade between the Mississippi River and the Cypress Swamp that slaves from the surrounding plantations had just completed outside New Orleans to hold off Pakenham's army, and so prevent the loss of the Mississippi and the Far West beyond it—would also be called upon to turn back the clock to before Tippecanoe. Whether it would be possible for these men to forget what had happened remained a mystery for the future to decide. But once decided, it would affect the lives of the many tribes currently living in the state of Ohio—the Delaware, Shawnee, Seneca, Ottawa, and Wyandot—and those living farther to the north and west in the old Ohio Country—the Miami, Pottawatomi, Kickapoo, Sac and Fox, Menominee, Chippewa, and Winnebago—who for three months in 1814 had a country of their own.[65]

TWO

Starting Over at Springwells

The opening weeks of 1815 passed with a sad and unbearable slowness for James Madison. He had moved to the Octagon House with his wife, Dolly, after the British set fire to the president's mansion just months before in September 1814, and could do little more than watch and wait for the postrider to come up the road from the Potomac with the mail from New Orleans. Secretary of State James Monroe had set up a chain of express riders linking major cities to the capital in the darkest days of the British invasion of the Chesapeake. But for some unknown reason, from January to February, as day dragged into night and night gave way to day, there was still no sign of a rider bringing word of what had happened in New Orleans.[1] Had the British broken through Jackson's line of militia waiting behind the barricade outside the city? Were they even now heading up the Mississippi to take Saint Louis and all of Louisiana to the west and beyond? Or had they sailed away victorious from Lake Pontchartrain toward the Caribbean, where at this very moment they were rendezvousing with more ships and soldiers fresh from victories on the battlefields of Europe? For Madison, the future of his presidency, and perhaps the very future of the United States, was riding on the answers to these questions.

James Monroe was in even more terrible shape than the president whom he served. He had collapsed from exhaustion after holding the government together almost single-handedly after the burning of Washington. Friends who met him were surprised to see how haggard he looked and how much weight he had lost.[2] No amount of rest could turn him into the man he once was, and now he could not rest as he waited as anxiously as President Madison to hear what had happened at New Orleans and, even more important, what had happened at Ghent. Had the British walked away from the negotiating table, leaving the Americans humiliated and the negotiations abandoned? Was the dismemberment of the United States a done deal on paper, and now only awaiting a perfect execution by Britain's top generals? Or was it just the fabled Ohio Country that would be lost to the Indians? Monroe had already made contingency plans to handle every future catastrophe. First, he planned to do what his administration had failed to do in the three previous years of fighting. He would force greater support for a professional military through a reluctant Congress. By the opening of February 1815, he had won the right to incorporate state troops into the regular army, doubled the land bounty for enlisted men, and even gotten the right to recruit minors.[3] At last there would be an army strong enough to hold off the British tide once it broke over America's shores. Then he would rally a people finally united in the understanding that if they did not stand and fight, their nation would surely disappear from the face of the earth.

Both men were stunned when the postrider from New Orleans finally arrived in Washington on Saturday, February 4, with news that General Pakenham lay dead in the trap that Jackson had set for him along the Rodriguez Canal. Early on the morning of January 8, 1815, more than eight thousand British soldiers had come in wave after wave toward Jackson's men, who fired back at them from the barricade. Pakenham and his troops, three-quarters of whom were veterans of Wellington's Peninsula Campaign, were cut down by musket and artillery fire in the early morning light that filtered through the smoke and fog. Seven hundred redcoats died alongside their commander. Another fourteen hundred were wounded, and five hundred more were captured. Jackson had lost

James Madison, left, president of the United States during the War of 1812, and James Monroe, right, his secretary of state and acting secretary of war. (*Library of Congress*)

only seven men killed and six others wounded. He could neither explain nor comprehend why the British had marched so willingly to their deaths. He could only conclude that the "unerring hand of providence shielded my men."[4]

News of the victory swept through Washington, and by evening the city was ablaze with torchlight parades. Every town on the eastern seaboard exploded in celebrations when news of Jackson's victory made its way to them. Only the secretary of state seemed unable to join in the festivities. Monroe remained convinced that the British still threatened from "Detroit, along the lakes Erie & Ontario, along the St. Lawrence, & Lake Champlain, & from Maine to the Mississippi thro' the whole extent of the coast." He could not forget the news he had received months before that upwards of fifteen thousand redcoats had set sail from Ireland. Reports had just come in from Georgia about an attack on Cumberland Island and the sacking of St. Mary's. The state's legislature had sent a desperate plea to Madison begging for help.[5] Was this the beginning of a larger invasion by the Royal Navy massing in the Atlantic? Even if he had known where the British fleet was at this moment, Monroe would not be satisfied until he learned what had happened at Ghent.

He did not have long to wait. Exactly one week after news of Jackson's victory arrived in Washington, the British war sloop *Favorite* landed in New York City. On board was Anthony St.

John Baker, a representative of His Majesty King George III, carrying the official copy of the Treaty of Ghent that the Prince Regent had signed on behalf of his ailing father. The *Favorite*'s captain had meant to put in along the Potomac, but storms off the Virginia Capes had forced his ship north. New York was still recovering from the unexpected news of the victory at New Orleans when word arrived that a peace treaty had been signed. The celebrations in the city started up again, and the joy spread northward to Boston, where church bells rang, schools closed, and people took to the streets in parade after parade. St. John Baker hired a coach in New York and took the post road south through Philadelphia and Baltimore to Washington as fast as his horses could carry him. At Baltimore, he overtook members of the Hartford Convention, who were on their way to the nation's capital to threaten Madison with the secession of New England if he did not conclude the war immediately. Even with the stunning news of peace, they continued on in the wake of St. John Baker, but neither Madison nor Monroe would receive them once they arrived.[6]

Little did St. John Baker know, as he raced south toward Washington, that word of the Treaty of Ghent had already arrived in the capital. Christopher Hughes, Henry Clay's secretary, had sailed from Belgium on a schooner called the *Transit*, which had made it through the storms off the Chesapeake Bay and had arrived in Annapolis on Tuesday, February 14. Hughes hurried to the Octagon House with a copy of the treaty in hand to let the president and his secretary of state know that a peace had been concluded. "Not an inch ceded or lost" were the first details of the negotiations at Ghent that spread through the city. Bonfires were lit, and people paraded through the streets once again.[7] On the next morning, Madison delivered the treaty to Congress, then, in the midst of debates on how to finance the enormous cost of the war, urged them to act quickly:

> I have received from the American commissioners a treaty of peace and amity between His Britannic Majesty and the United States of America, signed by those commissioners and by the commissioners of His Britannic Majesty at Ghent on the 24th December, 1814. The termination of hostilities depends upon the

time of the ratification of both parties. I lose no time, therefore, in submitting the treaty to the Senate for their advice and approbation.[8]

On Thursday, February 16, the Senate approved the Treaty of Ghent by a vote of 35 to 0. St. John Baker finally made it to the outskirts of Washington on the following evening, and could not understand why boisterous Americans ran into the road and cheered on his carriage as he hurried through the city toward the Octagon House. He finally understood when he handed the official copy of the treaty, signed and sealed, to the secretary of state, who in turn delivered it to the president. It was eleven o'clock on Friday evening, February 17, 1815.[9] The War of 1812, which had nearly dismembered the United States, was over.

President Madison declared the war officially at an end on the following day when he sent a message to the House and Senate describing in the simplest terms possible how relieved and grateful he was for the peace. He looked back to the desperate hour when the Congress had declared war on Great Britain. How right the many Americans were who had dreaded this war, Madison now admitted, for the cost in lives and property proved to be high. He sympathized with the Congress as it struggled to pay the enormous debts built up during the war. Still, he acknowledged that much good had come from the conflict, for a "conscious patriotism" had swept over the land. Suddenly the United States of America, founded on the abstract principles of life, liberty, and the pursuit of happiness, had become an emotional experience for its citizens as well.

While Madison was truly humbled by the near defeat of his country, he confessed that his heart, too, swelled with pride at the memory of the many gallant young men who came forward to serve in battle after battle on land and sea. Looking ahead to the future, the president reminded the Congress that the war had taught the nation just how dangerous the world truly was. Even if the peace promised by the Treaty of Ghent proved true, the United States would still need a strong navy and a standing army in the future to protect it. Madison, sounding like he once did long before when he was a friend and ally of Alexander Hamilton, urged the Congress to continue its support for America's developing industry. Although not a deeply religious man himself, he looked forward to an era of peace and prosperity for his young nation that had been saved at the last minute by the very hand of Providence.[10]

In the next few weeks, Madison and his secretary of state scoured the Treaty of Ghent to make sure that every article was clearly understood and properly implemented. They were most amazed at how the American negotiators had been able to convince the British to give up the sine qua non of the Indian state north of the Ohio River. Letters finally arrived from John Quincy Adams and Albert Gallatin, explaining that it was the Duke of Wellington, not their diplomatic skills, that had saved the day. Their letters also spoke of their lingering doubts about the Treaty of Ghent. Neither Adams nor Gallatin was as satisfied with the document as were Madison and Monroe. Adams may have preserved the West, first won by his father in 1783, but he was disappointed in himself for failing to secure the right of Americans to fish off the Grand Banks of Newfoundland. Gallatin disliked Article IX and dismissed it as "nominal" at best. He complained to Monroe that he and the other commissioners had no choice but to accept the clause or walk away from the negotiating table. He advised the administration to consider the article merely provisional. Henry Clay agreed, and complained to anyone who would listen how miserable the treaty was. It was madness, he argued, to think that the war in the western country could somehow be forgotten, and that the Americans and Indians could go back to the world before Tippecanoe.[11]

Neither Madison nor Monroe could understand why Adams, Gallatin, and Clay were so dead set against the treaty. For them, the peace achieved at Ghent was nothing short of a miracle. They took quite seriously the requirement to turn back the clock before Tippecanoe and planned to implement Article IX with all deliberate speed. Like two men who had faced certain execution, but who were pardoned on the way to the gallows, they embraced the article as their salvation. They had come close to losing the vast Ohio Country claimed since the days when James I gave Virginia all the land west and northwest of the colony in its colonial charter. Even now, with Tecumseh's death in 1813 and the second Treaty of

Greeneville signed a year later, fighting with the Indians still continued along the Upper Mississippi. By fully implementing Article IX of the Treaty of Ghent, Madison and Monroe could finally bring peace to the western frontier. They would break the tie between the British and the Indians, forever sealing a permanent friendship with the tribes and opening the long-coveted land to settlement.

Within a month of the treaty's approval, Madison appointed William Clark, governor of the Missouri Territory, as the lead negotiator to implement Article IX of the Treaty of Ghent with the many far western tribes. Ninian Edwards, governor of the Illinois Territory, and Auguste Chouteau, a wealthy fur trader from St. Louis,

William Clark, well-known for his epic exploration with Meriwether Lewis of the Louisiana Territory, was appointed by President Madison in 1813 as governor of the Missouri Territory. (*Library of Congress*)

would assist him.[12] Clark had spent much of the last ten years in Missouri since returning from his famous exploration of the Far West with Meriwether Lewis. He had been the superintendent of Indian affairs for all the tribes in Louisiana before the War of 1812, and the governor of the territory since 1813. He had set up a fur trading business with the influential Chouteau family and Manuel Lisa, a larger-than-life Spanish entrepreneur, and thus he knew most of the tribes north of St. Louis and west up the Missouri to the Rocky Mountains. They called him the "Great Red Chief" for the color of his hair, and respected him as someone who seemed to understand them. But that had not kept the tribes from joining the British during the War of 1812. In fact, most of them were still at war in varying degrees with the United States.[13]

By Clark's latest count, thirty-seven tribes from the western Great Lakes to the Rockies had gone on the warpath against the Americans. Some, like the Sac and Fox, the Winnebago, and the Menominee, were close allies of Tecumseh. Many of their chiefs

had been with the Shawnee leader from the confederation's beginning. They had traveled with him throughout the country recruiting followers. They were at his side from the fall of Detroit to the
moment he died fighting his old nemesis, William Henry
Harrison, along the Thames River. Although their leader was
gone, they refused to give up the fight to win a country of their
own. Clark believed they would never agree to sell more of their
lands for a pittance. Nor would they stop their attacks on frontier
settlements. Every American, especially farmers with their wives
and many children who took over the land with their barns and
fences and who dreamed of a better life, was an enemy to be dealt
with mercilessly. Their determination, along with support from
British traders who came down the Red River from Lake
Winnipeg in western Canada, inspired most of the tribes on the
Upper Mississippi to keep up the fight against the Seventeen Fires.

Doubting that any treaty could ever truly bring peace,
Governor Clark duly sent out thirty-seven speeches, one each to
the respective tribes still at war with the United States. He and
Governor Edwards had already told the tribes in the Missouri and
Illinois territories that the war was over, but this had not stopped
the bloodshed along their respective frontiers. Horrible tales of
murders of whole families on isolated farms filtered into St. Louis
and Kaskaskia. British captain Andrew Bulger, who had captured
and then commanded Prairie du Chien, the American post on the
Mississippi upriver from St. Louis, openly bragged that his warriors had brought him more scalps in the last six weeks than during the entire war. When he got official word of the Treaty of
Ghent, Bulger abandoned his post, but not before he distributed
his remaining stores to the Indians, promised more supplies from
Mackinac, which he claimed his government would never surrender, and burned Prairie du Chien to the ground. When word came
back to St. Louis that Indians along the Rock River had murdered
the messenger sent to invite them to the council, Clark could not
find anyone else who was willing to carry more invitations deep
into the Indian country. Finally, a militia captain named George
Kennerly volunteered to go into the dangerous territory north of
the ruins of Prairie du Chien and along the Missouri to seek out
the Mandan, Sioux, Teton, Mahas, Kansas, and all the rest. Clark

gave him an armed gunboat, which finally convinced other men to go with him.[14]

It seemed madness to Governor Clark to start peace negotiations in the midst of war. He wrote to James Monroe, who had been acting as secretary of war since the burning of Washington, recommending that the grand council, with the far western tribes, be delayed until the warriors who had committed mayhem on the frontier were brought to justice. Stories of Indian cruelty were told throughout the Far West, and every immigrant from back east heard the same tales when they arrived. The settlers, old and new, remembered the names of all the men gunned down at their plows, the mothers scalped as they did their humble chores, and the children murdered, with their brains dashed out against rocks or tree stumps. Some of them were even thrown into boiling vats of maple sugar.[15] One need not look far in St. Louis to find dazed orphans, survivors of these horrible massacres, wandering the streets. How could the people of Missouri and Illinois turn back the clock to before Tippecanoe, when the war unleashed by Tecumseh and his followers still threatened their lives each day?

Monroe and Madison did not see it this way. As terrible as the fighting had been, and still was, along the far western frontier, all must be forgiven and forgotten if Article IX of the Treaty of Ghent was to be implemented. In fact, the president was more concerned about sending gifts to the warring tribes than bringing murderers to justice. He ordered Monroe to purchase $20,000 worth of goods to be distributed to all the chiefs and headmen at the grand council. He gave specific instructions that these gifts must be as high in quality as any British goods offered to the tribes. They must be distributed in such a way that Indians friendly to the United States did not think they were being slighted in favor of hostile tribes. Clark was told to let all the Indians know that the presents were only the beginning of more goods to come from forts and trading posts, which the government was planning to build from Chicago, down the Illinois River, and then west along the Missouri to the Rockies. Madison also wanted to rectify the damage that Captain Zebulon Pike had done some ten years previously while exploring the Upper Mississippi. Pike had stripped the chiefs and warriors he met along the way of the silver medals given to them by the British. Madison knew that the Indians cherished these objects and wore them with pride. Tecumseh himself always wore a medal with an image of King George III around his neck. The president made sure that new medals were struck and given to the chiefs, with the largest going to Indians who had lost theirs to Captain Pike.[16]

A flood of goods arrived at Clark's trading house in St. Louis in early June. Monroe had personally selected the items himself from a store in Georgetown. He sent boatloads of blankets, cotton cloth and calico, handkerchiefs, ribbons, frock coats and flags, garters, paint, tobacco, wampum, needles, and pipes, along with rifles and powder. Clark decided to hold preliminary discussions in a special council house, built near his trading post in St. Louis, before moving six miles north to the French village of Portage des Sioux for the formal signing of the treaties.[17] Thousands of Indians from eleven major tribes living on the prairies and plains of the Mississippi River valley were soon on their way to Missouri to negotiate treaties and receive the many gifts that their Great Chief, President James Madison, had bought for them.

Timothy Flint, a minister from Massachusetts who was traveling through the West, chronicled his observations of the council in his memoir, *Recollections of the Last Ten Years*. He described the breathtaking sight of so many tribes gathered with their families along the Mississippi. Tribes as far ranging as the Omaha, Teton, and Osage to the West, who set up their "tents of tanned buffalo robes," and the Pottawatomi and Piankeshaw from the East, who came in their "beautiful canoes of white birch bark," arrived to negotiate treaties of peace and friendship that would make it seem like the War of 1812 had never happened. Clark was relieved when so many Indians, by some counts as high as six thousand, set up camp in the flower-filled meadows near Portage des Sioux. He was even more relieved, however, when Madison ordered the governors of Tennessee, Kentucky, Georgia, and the Mississippi and Indiana territories to send militia straightaway to St. Louis upon Clark's request if anything went wrong.[18]

Still with grave doubts about whether any treaty could turn back the clock to 1811, Clark opened the council on July 6, with Edwards and Chouteau at his side. He explained repeatedly that peace alone, not any more land cessions, was the sole purpose of the negotiations. The war between Great Britain and the Seventeen Fires was over. The English king and the Great Chief Madison had signed a treaty promising that the British, Americans, and Indians would forget the wars of the past and live in peace forever. Chiefs of tribes living farthest to the west, who had come down from the foothills of the Rockies with Manuel Lisa, seemed willing to listen to him; but tribes along the Mississippi River and farther east in the old Ohio Country remained openly hostile. The Winnebago, Kickapoo, and Sac and Fox sent only one minor chief, who had no authority to sign treaties for his people, but who claimed that he could at least speak for them. He was an angry young Kickapoo who warned Clark that never again would any tribe sell land to the Americans. Even more defiantly, he claimed that they would never give up the land they had already signed away in treaties. The millions of acres that Clark in Missouri, Edwards in Illinois, and Harrison back in Indiana had taken from them could never be surveyed, and so would never be settled.[19]

Clark soon found that none of his complaints to the administration about insolent young chiefs or the continuing Indian attacks along the frontier could deter Madison, his secretary of state, James Monroe, or his new secretary of war, William Crawford, from proceeding with the implementation of Article IX of the Treaty of Ghent. Pushed on by their prodding, Clark was able to report back to the War Department that by September he had some success. He and his fellow commissioners had been able to conclude treaties with the Yankton, Teton, and Mahas to the west; the Sioux of the Lakes and the Sioux of the River of St. Peter's to the north; the Big and Little Osage to the south; and even the Piankeshaw to the east. The Iowa, Kansas, Fox, and Kickapoo had been reluctant to negotiate, but in the end they had signed treaties, too. Clark wrote that the Sac might be willing to come in and treat later in the fall.

Every treaty the Indians signed at Portage des Sioux was exactly the same with only the names of the tribes changing in each. First, every injury or hostile act on all sides was mutually "forgiven and forgot." Then peace as it had existed in 1811 was declared, with the implication that somehow it would be everlasting. All prisoners were to be released and exchanged at Fort Clarke, on the Illinois River. Whether Indians had taken Americans—the victims usually being women and children—or members of other tribes, it no longer mattered. They were duty bound to return them to their "respective nations." All previous treaties, including the ones that promised the surrender of land to the Americans, were to be honored.[20]

As the many tribes that had pitched their tepees and wigwams disappeared from the meadows around Portage des Sioux, Governor Clark could not help but wonder how long the phantom peace would last. He had seen so much fighting since he had come west from Virginia as a boy, following in the wake of his older brother George Rogers Clark. He had served as a lieutenant in Wayne's army with another young Virginian, William Henry Harrison, and fought with him at Fallen Timbers. He agreed that promises of lasting peace had been made at Greeneville, but he also understood how hard it was to keep the peace with so many Americans coming west. The tide of people heading to the farthest frontier would only escalate now that the War of 1812 was over.

Even as the Indians broke camp in Missouri, government surveyors were already moving into the Illinois Territory to open the country for settlement. The collision of peoples along the western frontier brought new problems each day. As Clark reported to the administration, the Piankeshaw were "extremely anxious" to exchange their land in Illinois for land in Missouri. They wanted to sell some acres back east to buy horses and plows, so that they would become successful farmers once they were safely across the Mississippi. In contrast, their neighbors, the Pottawatomi refused to move from land that the Sac and Fox had sold out from under them to the Americans. They would soon return to their winter hunting grounds nearby, and in the spring would come back to the rich black soil along the rivers of Illinois to plant corn and raise their families.

Still, tribes farther west, like the Iowa, who were just coming into contact with the Americans, were begging Clark to buy as much land from them as he wanted. They were impressed with the money and goods doled out in annuities, and for the moment did not fear the towns and farms that came with them; but the Shawnee and Delaware knew all too well what happened when the Indians made deals with the Americans. No treaty line held them back, and no amount of surrendered territory satisfied them. Members of these two tribes had come to Missouri some thirty years earlier to escape the floodtide of Americans who were just starting to cross the Ohio River at the close of the revolution. Now, in the country around Cape Girardeau granted to them by the Spanish, they found themselves threatened by Americans once again. Settlers stole their horses, broke into their homes while they were away hunting, and farmed Indian land that did not belong to them. Some of the Cherokee who had come west to Arkansas were just as desperate to escape the Americans. They begged Clark to plot out a "certain tract of country" for them somewhere in Missouri. He must then prevent the settlers from overrunning their land and so save the tribe from disappearing.[21]

How the many treaties signed at Portage des Sioux would bring peace and stability to a frontier where conditions were ever-changing was a question that haunted Clark's fellow commissioner and business partner, Auguste Chouteau. He had seen the change first-hand, having experienced it from the days when he was a sixteen-year-old boy traveling up the Mississippi River from New Orleans with his family to found the city of St. Louis. Now at sixty he was the wealthiest and perhaps the wisest man in Missouri. He had amassed a fortune in the Indian trade, and lived in a fine house with a wide, columned porch overlooking the Mississippi. He knew the tribes better than any white man in St. Louis, even better than Governor Clark, and counted many half-breed sons and daughters among the Osage as his children. But even *he* had to admit that he did not understand the Indians completely. Knowing who all the tribes were and where they lived in relation to one another was something he had never been able to determine in forty years of trading with them. Now he watched the Americans making treaties of peace and lasting friendship with these restless people, whom he believed would never give up their traditional homelands or current hunting grounds without a fight.

There were additional concerns that Chouteau would have wanted to express to the Americans, who seemed confident that they could resolve all the problems on the western frontier. For one thing, the brutal violence within and between the tribes could never be ended by signing treaties of peace and friendship with them. Whiskey, so plentiful on the frontier, may have made this violence worse, but it had not created it. One need only look at the downfall of the great Illinois to understand this. A century before the Chouteau family had founded St. Louis, the tribe had dominated the boundless prairie country on both sides of the Upper Mississippi. But wars with other Indian nations, and among its own many bands, had reduced the tribe to a mere handful of drunken men and starving women and children. By 1815, there were fewer than seventy Illinois left, many of whom could be seen across the Mississippi wandering the streets of St. Genevieve like ghosts.[22]

While Clark and Chouteau may have thought no one in Washington was listening to them, the administration clearly understood from the many messages sent to the War Department that there was trouble on the frontier, especially back east among Tecumseh's closest allies. Both Madison and Monroe originally thought that Clark's treaties would be enough to meet the requirements of Article IX of the Treaty of Ghent. But by late spring of 1815, even before any of the far western tribes had started for Portage des Sioux, they had commissioned General William Henry Harrison, now the hero of the Thames as well as Tippecanoe, along with Major General Duncan McArthur, who had served in the War of 1812, and Indian agent John Graham to meet with all the tribes in the state of Ohio and the Indiana and Michigan territories. In the summer of 1814, Harrison had already concluded a treaty with many of these Indians at Greeneville on the same spot where Anthony Wayne had negotiated the original treaty in 1795.[23] But now in order to fulfill the promises made at Ghent, he was to call back all the tribes who had made peace with the United States, along with the many chiefs still allied with Great Britain. He was to tell them that every previous treaty, including the first and second at Greeneville would be reconfirmed, but no new land cessions would be sought at this time. The leaders of the predominant tribes, including the Wyandot, Shawnee, Ottawa, Delaware, and Seneca, were asked to come to Detroit in the last week of August in 1815. Even more important, Tecumseh's brother, the Prophet, was invited to the negotiations; and while he was not a chief and therefore could not sign any treaty, his presence was crucial for the success of the negotiations.[24]

Harrison was a cautious man who had learned in more than a dozen years of negotiating with the Indians of the Ohio Country, the greatest one being Tecumseh, that winning approval for more treaties would be difficult if not impossible. He knew that the chiefs and warriors who had followed Tecumseh up until the moment of his death considered the Americans insatiable

An illustration celebrating William H. Harrison's decisive victory over Tecumseh's confederation at Tippecanoe on November 7, 1811. (*Library of Congress*)

liars. Their hatred toward the United States ran so deep that Harrison often traveled with an Indian bodyguard. A young Seneca named the Beaver had saved him before the War of 1812 by killing a Shawnee warrior who planned to assassinate him. Another Seneca warrior, Captain Tommy, slept outside his tent in the final campaign of the War of 1812 to keep him safe.[25] Harrison decided his greatest protection in the upcoming negotiations would be to have the most trusted leader of the most respected tribe at his side. That man was Tarhe the Crane of the Wyandot. While the name Tarhe meant "dog" in his own language, the French had called him the "Crane" because of his great height and slender legs. He was the head chief of the Wyandot, a remnant of the once great Huron nation, who lived along the Sandusky River in northern Ohio. The other Indians called his people the "grandfathers" for the wisdom they had gained in their long fight against the Six Nations. This struggle had driven them from Canada to the Ohio Country just south of Lake Erie by the 1740s, making them one of the first historic tribes to settle there. Tarhe kept the sacred wampum that recorded the history of the Wyandot, along with every treaty signed by their chiefs.[26]

Instead of heading directly to Detroit, where the council was to be held, General Harrison told his fellow commissioners to meet him at Tarhe's village, near the upper Sandusky River.[27] He had gone there to invite the great chief to the council personally. The two men had first met in battle more than twenty years earlier at Fallen Timbers. Harrison, then a twenty-one-year-old aide to General Anthony Wayne, fought against hundreds of warriors, one of whom was Tarhe. The Crane, then fifty-two, had already seen much fighting at the side of chiefs like Pontiac, Cornstalk, and Little Turtle. But for Tarhe the battle against Wayne in August 1794 was more terrible than any other. He watched in horror as most of the Wyandot chiefs, twelve in all, fell around him in the tall grass near the rapids of the Maumee River. With his right elbow shattered in the fight, he finally fled the battlefield. Later, with the women and children of his tribe hungry after the long winter, he headed for Greeneville to make peace. There he spoke passionately in defense of his people to Wayne and his young lieutenant, Harrison, but in the end, he made his mark on the first of many treaties that he would sign with the Americans on behalf of the Wyandot.[28]

Like other chiefs who had fought the Americans only to be finally defeated, Tarhe never went to war against the United States again. He returned to his village, called Cranetown, in the Sandusky River valley with his wife, Sally, an American woman who had been captured as a child in Virginia by horse thieves and then traded first to the Cherokee and then to the Wyandot. He was happy to marry his oldest daughter, Myerrah, or "White Crane," the child of a French woman who had been taken by the Indians as a little girl, to Isaac Zane, a member of the legendary family of American frontiersmen, who was kidnapped by the Wyandot on the frontier when he was nine. He was proud to be known as a friend of the whites, a fact that ten years after Greeneville put him in direct opposition to Tecumseh and the Prophet. The two brothers first targeted the outspoken Wyandot chief Leatherlips, who openly condemned their confederation, by accusing him of witchcraft and ordering his execution. They planned to do the same to Tarhe, but their defeat at Tippecanoe saved his life. Tarhe survived the rise and fall of the Shawnee brothers, living on annuities that came to his tribe from selling land to the Americans and still living free with his people behind what remained of the Greeneville treaty line in northwest Ohio.[29]

When the War of 1812 broke out, although some Wyandot chiefs, like Walk in the Water, went straight to Tecumseh's side, Tarhe was able to keep most of his people loyal to the Americans. It was then that General Harrison, now the commander of the Army of the Northwest, first came looking for the Crane. He found him at Franklinton, just north of Columbus, where he asked the renowned chief to help him in the final struggle against Tecumseh and the British. Although he was then seventy-one, Tarhe agreed to join Harrison. He and his black servant Jonathan Pointer, a slave from Virginia who had had been captured as a boy, fought alongside him at the Battle of the Thames. Now nearly two years later, the aged Crane mounted his horse and once again followed his old friend north to Springwells, a Pottawatomi village on the outskirts of Detroit, where the council was to be held.[30]

Harrison was disappointed upon arriving at Springwells to see that many tribal leaders, including the Prophet, were missing. The council was set to open during the last week of August, and thousands of Indians had already gathered there with their families. They demanded food and whiskey from Harrison and also told him that the Prophet and many other Indians were across the river at Fort Malden, supposedly at this very moment in a council with officials of the British Indian Department who were likewise fulfilling the requirements of Article IX of the Treaty of Ghent. Unable to contain his contempt for the British, built up over a lifetime of misery at their hands from his boyhood on the James River during the American Revolution to the long fight against Tecumseh on the far frontiers of his nation, Harrison exchanged a few pointed notes with the British commander at Malden, telling him to send the Indians back across the Detroit River for the required council. He got a curt reply from Major Edward Barrak, who informed him that "he had no control or authority whatever over Indians," they being considered as a "free and independent people—consequently, at liberty to act for themselves." Tarhe intervened to keep the peace by sending his nephew to Amherstburg with a personal invitation for his fellow chiefs to come and treat with the American commissioners.[31]

The council finally opened at Springwells on August 25, with Harrison still fretting that the Prophet had not yet appeared but praising the man at his side, Tarhe the Crane, as an "archangel." He gave the floor over to the old chief so that he might perform the ancient ceremonies and do everything necessary "to remove all difficulties and impediments to their sitting around the council fire." After Harrison took his seat, the Crane rose and thanked everyone who had come to Springwells, as well as all the Indians who were still across the river talking to the British. He looked about the council and spoke first to the Wyandot, Delaware, Seneca, and Shawnee who had remained loyal to the Americans during the War of 1812. He noticed how their eyes were brimming with tears. He then turned to the few Wyandot chiefs present who had broken with the Americans and fought alongside Tecumseh. He knew that they were even more broken in spirit than the Indians who had sided with the Seventeen Fires. Not only had they lost many of their young men, but now their women and children were starving. Something must be done, or they would perish once winter was upon them.

Taking woven strings of white wampum in his hand, Tarhe touched the eyes of all those present in the circle around him so that they might see clearly again. Then putting down the wampum, he took a white feather and touched their ears so that they might hear the truth, and let it sink deep into their hearts. Picking up the white wampum again, he now touched it to their throats, one by one, to wipe away the bitter taste of defeat and so allow them to speak truthfully and kindly to one another. Then he passed among the downcast Indian leaders a last time, touching their hearts with the white wampum, so that the meaning of this council might sink into friend and foe alike.[32]

After Tarhe had touched his fellow chiefs in the present moment, he turned to their bitter memories of the past. These, too, must be healed. He knew the pain of remembering the devastation of the war. So many men had died in battle, and just as terribly so many villages had been torched, so many fields of corn set aflame, and so many families torn apart. The bones of countless warriors lay scattered and unburied. Though no one said it, some must have wondered, perhaps even Harrison, where

Tecumseh lay buried.[33] To erase these memories, Tarhe knelt and patted the ground in front of him, as if he were collecting all the scattered bones and burying them. He took another piece of white wampum and used it to smooth over the same ground while saying that he was covering up the bones with a white board, so that they would be safe forever:

> One bunch of wampum was to clear the eyes, unstop the ears, cleanse the throat, and amend the heart; another to collect the bones, to bury them, to smooth the graves, and to secure by a board, which the sun could not harm, nor the rain moisten.[34]

Once Tarhe had completed the ancient ceremonies, Harrison was able to light the council fire that would remain burning until the treaty was signed. But since the day was late, he decided to end the council for the night and resume on the morning of August 31. On that morning, Harrison could not help but notice how beautiful this late summer day truly was. He noticed, too, amidst the wonder of this day, how anxious the Indian women were for peace. He could only hope that their men were just as eager to achieve it. Harrison then apologized to everyone for forgetting an important part of the opening ceremonies. He had not swept out the council house. So before beginning the long speech he had prepared, he asked Tarhe to take a broom and sweep out all the evil.

When everything was finally complete, Harrison began his talk that would last on and off for several days. He started at the moment in time from which he believed all relations between the United States and the Indians must be measured – the first Treaty of Greeneville. He had never forgotten this pivotal event of his youth. Harrison had come to Ohio as an eighteen-year-old boy who had run away from his family's plans for him to become a doctor, and chose instead the life of soldiering, a dream he had wanted for as long as he could remember. He carried memories of the day he arrived at Fort Washington in November 1791, just two days after the Ohio tribes decimated the army of Arthur St. Clair. Three years later he fought alongside General Wayne at Fallen Timbers, and then waited with him throughout the long winter back at Fort Greeneville for the Indians to come in and negotiate a treaty.

For Harrison, the pledge of lasting friendship made in the Treaty of Greeneville between the United States and the Indians was sacred. The hatchet, the terrible symbol of war on the frontier, had been taken out of everyone's hands and buried deep in the ground. Then the "great chief" Wayne had planted a tree over the buried hatchet, and the tree grew strong and tall for nearly a decade. But then something went terribly awry. Harrison could not bring himself to speak the name of Tecumseh, but would instead only say that a kind of "madness" swept through the young men of the tribes. They tore up the tree, took up the hatchet, and launched a war along the frontier. That war was soon swallowed up in an even greater war between the United States and Great Britain—a war that was finally over, and so the war between the United States and the Indians must now be over.

If anyone at the council expected him to say that the British had been victorious, and that an Indian state was about to be created in the western country, they were disappointed. The United States had won many battles—at Baltimore, Plattsburgh, and New Orleans—and had retained all of its territory and boundaries. But if anyone expected him to say he had come to buy more land from the Indians, as he had done many times when he was governor of the Indiana Territory, then they were wrong, too. Harrison said he was here only to explain all that had happened in the War of 1812, and to win a new treaty of peace and friendship with every tribe present. He spared none of the details about the long conflict going back some twenty-five years, which had brought England, the United States, and France into open conflict, first on the high seas and later on the North American continent. Some, like Tarhe the Crane, still had memories of fighting with the French against the British more than sixty years earlier, and Harrison explained how another war had broken out again between France and England. The United States, so young and hopeful, wanted only to trade with the world and so remain at peace with everyone. Yet she had been dragged into this war, which grew more terrible, when a leader named Napoleon took over France and vowed to attack any ship trading with England. The British countered by attacking any ship bound for France.

Soon America was caught in the cross fire. The British boarded her ships and kidnapped her sailors until finally she could bear it no longer. She declared war on Great Britain. This was the war that many Indian warriors, misled by their own madness, had joined, and this was the war that was finally over. Napoleon had been defeated, the English were victorious, and now King Louis XVIII was back on the throne of France. Harrison told the chiefs that for a time Napoleon had come back to reclaim his crown in France, but that nine kings, led by the English king, had met him in a great battle at Waterloo. By all accounts, Napoleon had lost this battle—at least that is what Harrison was hearing from the British. But whether Napoleon had fallen a second time or was again in power did not matter, for a treaty had been signed between England and the Seventeen Fires. This treaty said that all must be forgiven and forgotten between the Americans, the British, and the Indians. That was why the United States, symbolized by an eagle holding arrows for war in its left talon and an olive branch for peace in its right, was reaching out to the tribes. For Harrison, the peace offered was not a new one, but was the same peace that General Wayne hammered out in his treaty at Fort Greeneville.[35]

The council recessed for a few days in the hope that Indian leaders still hostile to the United States would finally arrive. On the morning of September 4, Harrison was relieved to see the Prophet sitting with Tarhe and the other chiefs. His presence meant that whatever dreams the Shawnee holy man still held out for an Indian homeland somewhere in the western country were over, probably dashed in his meeting with the British at Fort Malden. Harrison had not seen Tenkswatawa since the night before the Battle of Tippecanoe when he promised that his warriors would disperse, even as they planned to attack the American camp on the following morning. When he rose to speak, the Prophet never mentioned that fatal dawn, nor spoke of how his actions on that day had ruined the dreams of his brother. Instead, he mocked Harrison's long speech by making the witty comment that removing the hatchets from the hands of the Indian would make it impossible for the old women to chop enough wood to build wigwams for their people.

Yet, he had to agree with Harrison that the war was over, since he had just learned the same from the British. This was good, he proclaimed, for too many had died, too many were widows, and too many were still suffering. Now there must be peace, and all would go back to the way things were before that morning in November 1811, when he told his young men to crawl a mile on their bellies to the American camp, kill Harrison on his white horse, and launch the war on the western frontier that his brother had long planned. The Prophet seemed to recognize at last that not just men, women, and children, not just whole clans and villages, but the hope of an Indian nation lay dead and buried under the Crane's wampum. The Prophet ended his speech by saying that, while he was not a chief and so could not sign any treaty, he had to admit that Tarhe and the other leaders present had done their best in the negotiations with Harrison:

> Let us adhere to our chiefs and thank them for what they have done for us; although we are warriors, let us attend to our women and children, and cast behind the implements of war, and never look at them again.[36]

On the following morning, when the council began again, Harrison was disappointed that the Prophet had gone back across the river to Canada. But the chiefs said not to fret since the Prophet had promised he would not oppose the treaty and to let President Madison know this. The Prophet's departure had no ill effect on the council. By September 6, 1815, Tarhe the Crane and ninety other chiefs were ready to sign the Treaty of Springwells. Harrison and the other commissioners spent the day explaining the main points of the treaty to the tribes. First, all tribes that had been openly hostile to the United States, including the Chippewa, Ottawa, and Pottawatomi, were "given peace" by the United States and brought back under its protection. All their possessions, rights, and privileges were restored to them exactly as they had been in 1811. The tribes that had remained loyal to the Americans during the entire war—specifically most of the Wyandot, Seneca, Delaware, and Shawnee, as well as hostile ones like the Miami, who had made peace at Greeneville in 1814—were also brought back under the protection of the United States, and so were any other tribes that had continued to oppose the Americans after 1814. All the chiefs, headmen, and warriors would return to their prewar status and regain the property they held in 1811. Harrison added a final article, to which the tribes and chiefs readily agreed:

> Renew and confirm the treaty of Greeneville, made in the year one thousand seven hundred and ninety-five, and all subsequent treaties to which they were, respectively, parties, and the same are hereby again ratified and confirmed in as full a manner as if they were inserted in this treaty.[37]

On the following day, interpreters read the treaty in the language of each tribe present. Then on the morning of September 8, 1815, Tarhe and the other chiefs made their marks on the Treaty of Springwells. Some made an X near their names, while others drew simple outlines of the totems of their clans. By signing the treaty, they promised to return to the way things were before Tecumseh's dreams were shattered at Tippecanoe, and the whole world plunged into war. Harrison forwarded the official treaty to Washington and gave a copy to the Crane, who carried it back to his village in Ohio, where he would maintain it, side by side, with copies of the Greeneville treaties and the sacred wampum. If Harrison or the other commissioners had any doubts about the treaty, they did not mention them in the records of the council sent to Madison and Monroe.[38]

The president and secretary of state were relieved when the Treaty of Springwells arrived in the capital at almost the exact same moment that the numerous treaties signed at Portage des Sioux were also delivered. They proudly affixed the seal of the United States to each treaty and then signed their names. How different the world looked to both men in just one year. Twelve months before, they were waiting amid the ruins of their burned-out capital for news of Ghent and New Orleans. Now Madison was able to tell the opening session of the Fourteenth Congress that Americans could at last awake from the long nightmare of a world at war, which had haunted the nation since its founding under the Constitution. "In conformity with the articles in the treaty of Ghent relating to the Indians, as well as with a view to the tranquility of our western and northwestern frontiers," he explained, "measures were taken to establish an immediate peace with the several tribes who had been engaged in hostilities against the United States." Article IX had been fulfilled, and peace now reigned with the Indians, just as it did with the British. Even when Napoleon had broken free from his imprisonment on Elba in February 1814, and ruled France for a hundred days until his crushing defeat at Waterloo in the following June, Madison reminded Congress that the British had not seized one American ship, nor did they impress one American sailor.[39]

Still, if either Madison or Monroe had taken the time to read through the papers sent to them by William Henry Harrison, they might have seen that not everyone on the western frontier was as convinced as they were that peace would reign forever. A Pottawatomi chief, whose name was not recorded, had addressed the council at Springwells in its closing moments. He noticed how the Americans always began and ended their meetings by acknowledging the Great Spirit so he would thank him, too, for returning the world to the peace made long ago at Greeneville. Then the chief asked everyone to pause and reflect if that truly was such a perfect moment to return to in time. He did not want to tear up the graves or disturb the ashes of the chiefs who had signed the treaty with General Wayne. But he must pause and reflect on what his ancestors had set in motion at Greeneville.

They had agreed to give up land that the Master of the Universe had intended for the Indians. In return, they received yearly payments from the Americans, but these annuities had been determined in a "less enlightened" time, and were not enough for the tribes to live on. If only he could actually go back to Greeneville, he would then ask the chiefs to pause and reflect on the impact that signing this treaty would have on their own people. What would become of their children, still so innocent in their cradles, if the land that God had given to the Indians, and so their very birthright, was taken away from them? All the joy over peace in the past restored in the present could not answer this terrible question that would haunt the tribes throughout the coming years as the world raced all about them into the future.[40]

THREE

Boundaries Long Gone

If the British had hoped to restore peace between the Americans and the Indians by turning back the clock to 1811, then they had accomplished their goal. But if by Article IX of the Treaty of Ghent they had still hoped to shore up the boundary between the United States and the Indian country, thus creating a permanent homeland for the tribes behind it, then they had miscalculated. The line between the Americans and the Indians had given way long before 1811. By the time that the War of 1812 had broken out, numerous treaties had already been signed, which moved the tribes onto smaller and smaller pieces of ground. For the Indians in the state of Ohio, especially, the boundary line between the Americans and themselves had become an encroaching circle, or better yet, an encroaching square, given the requirements of the Land Ordinance of 1785. The law divided the West into six-mile–by–six-mile square blocks called townships, which in turn were subdivided into thirty-six one-mile-by-one-mile square sections of 640 acres each. The removal of the Ohio tribes onto township reserves was well under way before the ink dried on the Treaty of Ghent, or before General Andrew Jackson, the hero of New Orleans, had given much thought to running for the White House.

The fact that the boundary line promised at Greeneville had been slowly disappearing for nearly a decade was something that William Henry Harrison could admit neither to himself, nor to the many chiefs who had gathered at Springwells. In his mind, the Treaty of Greeneville was a sacred point in time when the Indians had promised Anthony Wayne that they would never go to war against the United States again. But he refused to recognize that it was also a point in space, a line on a map that mirrored the natural ridge across the state of Ohio from Fort Laurens in the East to Loramie's Station in the West. North of the boundary all the rivers emptied into Lake Erie, while south of it they flowed down to the Ohio. When Harrison pushed the clock back past 1811 and all the way to 1795, he meant to restore peace on the frontier forever, but not to restore the boundary that kept the Americans on one side and the Indians on the other.[1]

Perhaps Harrison could only recognize Greeneville as a moment in time, and not a point in space, because he had played a part in dissolving that same boundary. His treaties at Grouseland in 1803, Vincennes in 1805, and finally Fort Wayne in 1809 had opened the Indian country past the western end of the Greeneville treaty line to settlement. His actions had helped Tecumseh and the Prophet make a case to the tribes that the Americans, so insatiable in their demands for Indian land, would never remain behind the boundary set at Greeneville. But Harrison always maintained that the treaties he negotiated were merciful. He was not like other frontier Americans, who would only be satisfied when every Indian was slaughtered. These "violent and unprincipled men," as Harrison described them to the secretary of war in the summer of 1815, would not rest until "we . . . fall upon them and murder them all." In contrast, throughout his long career as a territorial official, he had faithfully executed the humane policy first set by President George Washington. The government recognized the tribes as the rightful owners of the land, and then convinced them to give up their claims to it in exchange for annuities, which Harrison defined as "their only resource against want and misery."[2] No better response could have been given to such an approach than did Tecumseh, who told Harrison at their first meeting in Vincennes in 1810, "Brother! When you speak to me

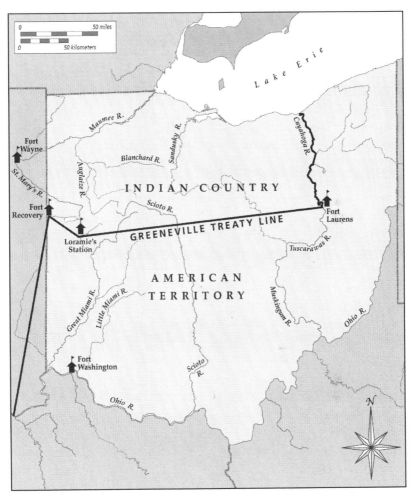

Map 1. The Greeneville Treaty Line, 1795.

of annuities I look at the land and pity the women and children.
. . . I want the present boundary line to continue."[3]

Harrison's old friend Tarhe the Crane had played an equally
important part in dissolving the Greeneville treaty line at its eastern end. Like Tecumseh, he had once believed that no man owned
the land and so none could sell it out from under another. "It
belongs in common to us all," he had proclaimed to Anthony
Wayne at Greeneville in the summer of 1795. "No earthly being

has an exclusive right to it," he argued. "The Great Spirit above is the true and only owner of the soil; and he has given us an equal right to it."[4] Still, he had been the first of many chiefs to sign the treaty, making an X and then drawing a tiny porcupine, the symbol of his clan, next to it. Perhaps at that moment he truly believed that the boundary line would hold and that he could keep his people safe behind it from the surveyors, who carefully plotted out their six-mile-by-six-mile square townships, and from farmers, who came fast behind them to fill up the carved-out country. The $1,000 in yearly goods that Tarhe's tribe would receive might keep his people well stocked with items that they had come to depend on since European traders first arrived in North America—not only guns and ammunition, but cloth, needles, buttons, coats, pots and pans, and all the other luxuries that had become necessities to every Indian family on the frontier.[5]

Tarhe had gambled that signing the Treaty of Greeneville would keep his people safe at least for a time. But in the end, it had only protected the Wyandot for ten years. By the summer of 1805, so many people from New England had poured across the eastern edge of the boundary into a place called the Western Reserve that American officials came looking for more land to buy from the Indians, promising more goods in return. On July 4, 1805, at Fort Industry, which sat on a bluff overlooking the Maumee River where modern-day Toledo, Ohio, now stands, Tarhe again made his X on a treaty that allowed the eastern end of the Greeneville line to give way. It would now move west from the Cuyahoga River, 120 miles inland from the Pennsylvania border to be exact, thus opening up half a million acres of land to surveyors and settlers. In exchange, Tarhe and his Wyandot, along with the Shawnee, Delaware, Munsee, and Seneca, would receive another $1,000 in goods each year at Detroit—$825 paid by the American government and $175 paid by the Connecticut Western Reserve Land Company. The Ottawa, Pottawatomi, and Chippewa would each receive a lump sum payment of $4,000, plus another $12,000 distributed in six annual payments.[6]

The chiefs who signed the treaty with Tarhe the Crane, like Walk in the Water and Leatherlips of his own tribe, Bluejacket and Black Hoof of the Shawnee, and Tontogony the Dog of the

Ottawa, could take some comfort in the fact that they would still be allowed to hunt and fish on the ceded land as long as it remained the property of the United States. This was important because the annuities promised at Greeneville and now at Fort Industry, were not enough to buy the many manufactured goods on which the tribes depended. If the chiefs wanted to keep the supply of goods coming from government-run "factories" or trading posts, first established by President Washington throughout the Indian

Tarhe the Crane. (*Author*)

country, and continued by President Thomas Jefferson, with more detailed regulations, then their people would have to deliver the requisite amount of furs necessary to buy them.[7]

The records of these factories that lie buried to this day in the National Archives in Washington, DC, give a clear portrait of the bind in which the chiefs were trapped. Government officials kept precise calculations of how many skins it would take to buy the goods that the Indians needed. For example, if a chief delivered 30 deer, 27 raccoons, 81 muskrats, 3 fox, and 4 minx totaling $66.34, he could buy the following goods worth exactly $66.34 for his people:

Blankets
Twill coating
Blue strouds (blankets)
Scarlet flannel
Blue cloth
Fine blue cloth
Brown linen
Calico
Chintz
Ribbon
Butcher knives
Knitting needles
Spades

Tin kettles
Pewter basin
Rifle
Powder
Salt
Corn by the bushel[8]

But if Tarhe and the thirty-one other chiefs who signed the Treaty of Fort Industry thought the new boundary would hold and so keep their people safe behind it for years to come, they were wrong. Just two years later, American negotiators were back demanding more land. President Jefferson, the master of maps and western rivers, decided his people living in the Western Reserve must be connected to his people in Detroit. To do this, the Greeneville treaty line would have to be bent out of shape and made to twist back down the Maumee River valley to the mouth of the Auglaize, and then go due north for more than a hundred miles until it met the latitude line running west, from the point where the St. Clair River emptied into Lake Huron.[9] This strangely misshapen boundary would still leave the Wyandot free to roam behind it, along with the Shawnee, Seneca, and Delaware, but the Ottawa, who had lived along the Maumee since the time of their great chief Pontiac, would see the boundary between themselves and the United States disappear. They would be made to live on the tiniest pieces of ground they had ever known within the lines that government surveyors drew around them.[10]

The treaty to accomplish all of this was negotiated at Detroit in 1807 by William Hull, then governor of the Michigan Territory who five years later would be disgraced by surrendering Fort Detroit to Brock and Tecumseh. Hull had to send out three formal invitations before the tribes agreed to the council. The last invitation came directly from President Jefferson, who assured the Indians they had nothing to fear, and should expect only continued friendship with the Americans.[11] In the final treaty, the Ottawa agreed to give up their remaining territory in northwest Ohio, as well as their lands south of Detroit, in exchange for $3,300 a year in money, goods, farm equipment, and livestock, along with another $2,400 in annuities. The government would allow the Ottawa to stay in the Maumee River valley, but only if they moved to "reservations." These reserves were measured out as full or partial townships, drawn in accordance with the Land Ordinance of 1785. If the lines around the reserves could not be plotted out as perfect squares, then the treaty specifically stated that they could be drawn as parallelograms.

The chiefs of the major bands of the Ottawa would be granted these reserves on behalf of their people. The first was a four-mile-square tract near Maumee Bay, where the villages of chiefs Meshkemau and Waugau stood. Farther upriver Chief Tontogony received an exact township reserve just south of present-day Waterville, near Roche de Boeuf, a huge outcropping of limestone in the Maumee that the French had named for its buffalo shape. While many Ottawa already lived there, Chief Tontogony would move across the river a few miles south and establish his village on the creek that still bears his name.

The tribe was also granted a three-mile square reserve at a place called Presque Isle, near the site of the Battle of Fallen Timbers; but it could never be plotted out since it was within the Twelve-Mile Reserve set aside for the United States by Anthony Wayne in the Treaty of Greeneville. In its place, the Ottawa would eventually receive a three-mile square reserve at Wolf Rapids on the Maumee, upriver from the one at Roche de Boeuf. The government promised to send a blacksmith to live among the Ottawa to repair their guns and other tools. While Tarhe was not present at the negotiations, Walk in the Water, along with Skahomet, or "Joe," and Iyonayotha, or "Black Chief," did sign the treaty, securing the same payments and annuities for the Wyandot. Several chiefs of the Ottawa's kindred tribes, the Pottawatomi and the Chippewa, did the same.[12]

Despite the restrictions imposed on them by the Treaty of Detroit, the Ottawa may have signed in the hope that they would still be able to continue their tribal life without too much interference from the relentless advance of the Americans. For them, the Greeneville treaty line might be gone, or better yet, might have collapsed around them in township lines, but the Great Black Swamp remained a natural boundary between the tribe and the westward push of the settlers. Stretching 120 miles from Lake Erie up the Maumee and then reaching back forty miles inland to the east and southeast, the tangled mass of towering trees and impassable wetlands would hopefully keep the surveyors and farmers back across the barrier.[13] If the Americans stayed put or went around the swamp to Michigan or Indiana, then the Ottawa might be protected for generations to come.

During the spring and summer months, the women of the tribe would have plenty of acres in the rich bottomland of their tribal reserves on the Maumee and Auglaize to grow corn, beans, and squash. There would be plenty of fishing at Maumee Bay and along the nine miles of rapids that ran from Tontogony's village south of Roche de Boeuf and back down the river to just below the site of the battlefield at Fallen Timbers. Even within the confines of the treaty, the Ottawa would be allowed to leave their reserves during the winter months to hunt in the surrendered territory, as long as the land remained the property of the United States. They could wander east to the Sandusky River and west to present-day Fulton and Henry counties, where they could take deer, bears, raccoons, and even lynx and fox, which were still plentiful, and bring them into the government trading posts at Piqua, Fort Wayne, or Detroit. They could exchange the fur for manufactured goods with the Americans, just as their ancestors had once traded with the English, and before that with the French.

On their return trip to their reserves in late winter and early spring, they could camp by the many streams where the sugar maples grew, and there they would make syrup for their families. Once back home, they could in turn trade their own goods with the few hardy pioneers who dared to make a go of farms and towns on the edges of the Black Swamp. Not only furs but also moccasins, baskets, hickory nuts, honey, wild berries, and plums were the top sellers. Toys made by Ottawa women were popular items for sale to children on the Ohio frontier. At an appointed time every year, the Ottawa bands would receive their promised annuities. For a little while, at least, it may have seemed as if they, too, had turned back the clock to the best of all possible worlds.[14]

But keeping up the rhythms of farming, hunting, and trading, in the face of the advancing Americans, was becoming increasingly difficult for the Ottawa and the other tribes to maintain. Although Tarhe never signed another treaty giving away land after

Fort Industry, most of the other chiefs continued to do so. They made their marks and drew their totems under the relentless pressure to maintain a boundary between their people and the Americans. By signing, they promised to stay put on increasingly smaller lots of ground, even as they knew the hunt for fur must continue over wider and wider areas. As farmers leveled the forests and turned over the prairies, animals disappeared. Many were killed off as predators dangerous to livestock, while the rest headed west into the remaining wilderness. Only by leaving their dwindling country and roaming on land still owned by the United States could the tribes take enough fur to trade for the goods they needed at the government-run factories. How they would be able to continue hunting once all the government land was sold to settlers was a problem that only the future could determine.

Still, no matter what the tribes surrendered to keep the peace promised from Greeneville to Detroit, the Americans always demanded more. One year after bending the Greeneville treaty line out of shape at Detroit, Governor William Hull was back at Brownstown in the Michigan Territory, just across the Detroit River from Fort Malden, asking for more Indian land. This time he said his people needed the land to build a road that would connect the new settlements at the Foot of the Rapids of the Maumee River to the western edge of the Connecticut Reserve. The road would be 120 feet wide and would include a one-mile strip on either side, where Americans would be allowed to settle. A second road, 120 feet wide, would be necessary from Lower Sandusky, formerly an old Indian village called Jungquendendahor, or "Place of Peace," and running south through Wyandot country to the remnant of the Greeneville treaty line. The Americans would use this road to transport lumber and other supplies needed to repair the Western Reserve Road and build bridges along the way. The fifteen Wyandot, Shawnee, Ottawa, Pottawatomi, and Chippewa chiefs who signed the treaty, among them Walk in the Water, Black Hoof, and Tontogony, received nothing in return for signing the treaty, except for the guarantee that their people would still be allowed to hunt and fish along the surrendered roadways.[15]

Tarhe, who did not sign the treaty at Brownstown, was stunned at how quickly the Americans overran his people's land once promises were made to allow roads through Wyandot territory. In May 1810, he dictated a distraught petition to Ohio governor Samuel Huntington, asking his help in getting surveyors and settlers out of what remained of Indian country. Much like his friend William Henry Harrison, he looked back to the Greeneville treaty as the starting point for understanding the relationship between the Americans and the Indians. He remembered how General Wayne had told the tribes that his own people were very greedy. If any of them came onto Indian land, trying to survey it and so take it away from them illegally, the chiefs were to tell government officials, who would in turn drive the Americans away.

What Wayne had warned about was now happening, so Tarhe asked Governor Huntington to control his people. "We would wish you to send out two papers with orders upon them for those people not to encroach upon us," he explained. "One for your Children at this place and one for your Children at Scioto to show and Convince the people that it is contrary to law to meddle settle or survey land over the line." Tarhe added that he would have come to see Huntington in person if not for rumors of smallpox running rampant in the southern part of the state. "Father[,] we your Children salute you with our Compliments and may the grate Spirit bless and assist our Father and we his Children that we may live together in peace," were the last words of the petition under which Tarhe made his mark along with eight other Wyandot chiefs.[16]

But the clash never ended, and the Americans never stopped coming onto the land left to the tribes from Greeneville to Brownstown until Tecumseh and the Prophet rose up to stop them. Their confederation tore the Ohio tribes apart, with the Ottawa joining the Shawnee brothers, and for a time breaking free from their tiny reserves, while most of the Wyandot, Delaware, Seneca, and even the Shawnee remained true to their promises of peace with the Americans. All the chiefs were soon caught in the cross fire, as the Shawnee brothers ordered the deaths of every leader who opposed them. Walk in the Water escaped by joining the cause, Leatherlips died with a hatchet buried in the back of his head, and Tarhe was spared at the last minute in the aftermath of Tippecanoe.

Yet, whether they joined Tecumseh or opposed him, they were all soon swept up in the Indian war along the western front of the War of 1812. The conflict decimated tribes on both sides. Villages, with their orderly rows of wigwams, were torn apart; horses and livestock were stolen; and women and children went hungry as their fields of corn and beans went up in flames.[17] In the end, the war brought only ruin for Tecumseh, who was shot down in the meadow alongside the Thames River. He had preserved Canada for the British, who had in turn abandoned the Indians at the negotiating table. In the end, they had little to offer their allies except Article IX of the Treaty of Ghent. The Americans had promised peace once more, a second time at Greeneville and then at Portage des Sioux and Springwells, and so seemed to say that all would go back to the way it once was behind the remnant of the Greeneville treaty line that had survived the terrible war.

If only the progress of the world and people across time and space could have been stopped at this moment, then maybe the tribes could have returned to a good life in what remained of their country behind the old "Indian Boundary." But nothing stops in history, especially along America's western frontier in the early nineteenth century. Following the end of the War of 1812, settlement that had slowed to a trickle before the war, and was pent up as if behind a dam during the war, suddenly burst into Ohio. So many people, in fact, came to Ohio in 1815, immediately after the Treaty of Ghent was ratified, that the year was nicknamed the "Great Migration." Settlers seemed to arrive overnight by the tens of thousands from New England, the mid-Atlantic states, and the Upper South. Much of the soil in New England was depleted after centuries of use. Many places that had been burned by the British in the American Revolution and the War of 1812 had never recovered. Land prices in New Jersey, eastern Pennsylvania, and New York were out of reach for most Americans. Desperate people were willing to walk west over the Appalachians toward the promised land of Ohio. Any hardship was worth it for the chance at a better life. Southerners came, too, white and black, running from soil worn out by tobacco and from a world ruled by plantation owners, who worked the best land with the most slaves. Even more would come down the National Road, an extension of the old

Cumberland Road that would stretch from Baltimore to Wheeling, West Virginia, on the Ohio River by 1818.

With the War of 1812 over and peace with England restored, settlers also came from the British Isles. Morris Birkbeck, a wealthy English farmer who was on his way to open up a settlement for his fellow countrymen on the prairies of southern Illinois, left a vivid account of the Great Migration in his *Notes on a Journey in America*. So many people were on the roads in Pennsylvania heading west to Ohio that they seemed crowded night and day. Birkbeck explained:

> We have now fairly turned our backs on the old world, and find ourselves in the very stream of emigration. Old America seems to be breaking up, and moving westward. We are seldom out of sight, as we travel on this grand track, towards the Ohio, of family groups behind and before us, some with a view to a particular spot; close to a brother perhaps, or a friend, who has gone before, and reported well of the country. Many like ourselves, when they arrive in the wilderness, will find no lodge prepared for them.[18]

The growth of the population of the state of Ohio between the ending of the War of 1812 and the decade of the 1820s was truly astounding. In 1800, there were 42,000 people living in the Ohio Territory. This was far more than the requisite number of 5,000 free men needed for Ohio to move to the second stage of territorial government under the provisions of the Northwest Ordinance. A territorial legislature could now be elected, which in turn sent William Henry Harrison to the House of Representatives. Harrison contributed to the race for Ohio and beyond by introducing a land law named after him that allowed people to buy farms on credit. By 1803, Ohio had 60,000 people, the number needed for a territory to petition the Congress for statehood. In that same year, Ohio entered the Union as the seventeenth state. By 1826, the population had reached over 800,000, with most of that growth occurring in the ten years since the War of 1812 ended. Benjamin Drake, who later authored the first biography of Tecumseh, exclaimed in his history of Cincinnati in 1826, "This increase in a single state . . . is perhaps without a parallel in the history of this or any other country."

Although the population growth in other states during the same period was not quite as dramatic as in Ohio, immigration to the West was great enough to incorporate several states into the Union. Indiana became a state in 1816, while Illinois would follow in 1818.[19]

The responsibility for ensuring the orderly settlement of the West during the aftermath of the Great Migration fell on the shoulders of James Monroe. Elected president in 1816, he would not forget the last terrible days of the War of 1812, or the promise of Article IX of the Treaty of Ghent. He considered himself duty bound to formulate an Indian policy that would keep the peace among all competing parties on the frontier. The policy he established, with the help of his secretary of war, John C. Calhoun, had two major elements. The first one called for negotiating additional treaties and land cessions with the eastern tribes, just as every president had done before him. The Indian nations would be asked to sign away hundreds of thousands of acres to the United States in exchange for lump sum payments and annuities. The surrendered land would then be surveyed and sold to American citizens and recent immigrants who were coming west in record numbers. But more clearly than any previous president, Monroe would make certain that most tribes would be allowed to stay on reserves plotted out within that same territory. There was some precedent for this in treaties with the Iroquois, especially the Seneca, who in 1797 had given up their land in western New York and Pennsylvania in exchange for $100,000 in stock in the Bank of the United States and eleven small reserves drawn around Seneca villages. A few of these reserves were more than forty square miles in size, but most were only one or two square miles. The settlement of the Ottawa on their tiny reserves in the Maumee River valley was yet another precedent.[20]

The second aspect of Monroe's Indian policy led him to request money from Congress to help the tribes survive and even thrive on their new reserves. His administration was flooded with reports from territorial governors and Indian agents detailing the state into which many tribes had fallen. Drunkenness was common everywhere, especially in tribal villages that adjoined frontier settlements. Debt was another problem, as Indians purchased manufactured goods on credit, which they needed for the long months between payments of their annuities. Chiefs were often desperate to sell more land to the government in order to pay off their debts to the traders and to buy even more goods. Violence and thievery against Indians were also major problems, with the perpetrators rarely punished.[21]

Lewis Cass, governor of the Michigan Territory, was one of the most trusted advisors to both the Madison and Monroe administrations on the state of the Indian nations living north of the Ohio River. As he once explained to Madison's secretary of war, William Crawford:

> I have frequently conversed with them about their situation and prospects and have found them deeply sensible of their forlorn condition, and anxiously desirous of meliorating it. I doubt whether the eye of humanity in a survey of the world could discover a race of men more helpless and wretched.

He had seen Indian men go from being frightening warriors on the Ohio and Michigan frontier during the War of 1812 to becoming pitiful drunkards, who were taken advantage of by all parties just a few years later. He believed that the United States must do everything in its power to treat the Indians with respect. Cass now expressed this same belief to Monroe's secretary of war, John C. Calhoun:

> The time has come when we should be known to the Indians by every humane and benevolent exertion. . . . They should be protected in all their just rights, and secured from their own improvidences, as well as from the avarices of the whites.[22]

Fearing the continuing decline and possible extinction of the Indians, Monroe asked Congress to appropriate money for missionaries to go among the tribes to "civilize" them. This was a continuation, but with more regular funding, of a policy first proposed by Henry Knox when he was Washington's secretary of war. Knox believed that Christian missionaries, living among the Indians as "friends and fathers," could "fully effect the civilization" of the tribes. The men would learn to plow fields and raise crops and livestock, while the women would work solely within the home. Eventually this would lead to the assimilation of the two peoples. President Jefferson also championed the policy of civilizing the Indians. Even as he directed his territorial governors to purchase millions of acres of land from the tribes, he urged them to show the Indians how to give up the ways of the warrior and hunter and instead settle down as year-round farmers.[23] Following in the footsteps of Knox and Jefferson, Monroe won passage of the Civilization Fund Act in 1819, which allocated $10,000 a year to help the Indians make this transition. At first, his administration sent the money primarily to religious groups working with tribes west of the Mississippi River, like the Osage and newly arrived bands of the Cherokee; but funds amounting on average to a few hundred dollars a year were soon distributed to missionaries working with the tribes in many eastern states, including Ohio.[24]

Monroe got a firsthand look at the West during his triumphant tour of the northern states in 1817. He knew how the War of 1812 had divided the country, and vowed to travel to every region of the nation, binding up the wounds of the war that had seen the capital city burnt and his own health shattered. He arrived in Detroit in the late summer of 1817 and was surprised to see that the Michigan Territory was poised for settlement. He had traveled there in 1795, and found little more than a howling wilderness that would never be settled. But now, arriving from Buffalo on his lake steamer, he was met at the Detroit River's docks by the leading citizens of the town. Crowds of people marched alongside him through the streets in candlelit parades, and later joined him for parties and dances at the governor's house. Everyone, most especially Cass, seemed anxious to get the surveyors out into the country, south and west of his capital city, to open up even more towns, more farms, and more trade. Monroe sailed back to Sandusky Bay, the site where just four years before, Oliver Hazard Perry had won his stunning victory over the British, and then took the road, laid out by the Treaty of Brownstown, that ran through Wyandot territory to the Indian boundary along the old Greeneville treaty line.[25]

The northwest corner of the state of Ohio was one of the first sites where President Monroe's twofold Indian policy would be implemented. In the ten years since the Ottawa had moved to their reserves along the Maumee, northwestern Ohio had remained relatively free of American settlement. Wolves and bears were still plentiful, especially around the mouth of the Sandusky River on Lake Erie. The land was fertile along the rivers, but the climate was wet and humid in the summers. The few settlers who came into the Black Swamp along the Maumee were met by floods, mosquitos, and fevers. But even with these problems, two small towns—Maumee and Perrysburg, on opposite sides of the rapids just below Fort Meigs, which was the War of 1812 fort built by General Harrison in 1813—had already been plotted out. There travelers from the Western Reserve to the east and Detroit to the north were welcomed for business. The area had tremendous potential for farming if the swamps could be drained. Transportation would also be an important industry once more roads and even canals were built, since the region sat at the crossroads of many east-west and north-south routes in the nation. With the rest of the state filling up, the logical alternative for ambitious farmers would inevitably lead them along the rivers and into the forests and prairies of northwest Ohio.

As fall approached in 1817, officials in Monroe's War Department decided that the time was right to negotiate with the Indians for the surrender of northwest Ohio, especially since they had heard rumors of Tarhe's death for the past year. Tarhe had not signed any treaty giving up more land to the Americans since making his mark on the one at Fort Industry in 1805. If the most respected chief of the Ohio tribes was truly gone, then younger leaders might be willing to sell their remaining territory, especially if they could be convinced that the trickle of settlers heading into their country would soon become a flood. If the government could guarantee their protection on smaller reserves and make good on promises of more annuities, then maybe they could persuade the other tribes to do what the Ottawa had done in 1807. The Wyandot, Shawnee, and Seneca, along with a handful of Delaware, might willingly move to smaller reserves, while the Miami, who lived primarily in the vicinity of Fort Wayne in Indiana, might also be convinced to give up their claims to land along the western border of Ohio.

With this in mind, Monroe directed Governor Cass and Duncan McArthur, now a land speculator and rising politician in

Ohio, to call the tribes together at the foot of the Maumee Rapids in September 1817. The two men had last served together in the final charge against Tecumseh at the Battle of the Thames. Now under the shadow of Fort Meigs, they must convince the Wyandot, Shawnee, Seneca, and Delaware to do what the Ottawa had done ten years before. The tribes must surrender their remaining land in northwest Ohio and agree to live on small reserves in exchange for more annuities. The Greeneville treaty line would disappear completely, and the tribes would now live circumscribed within the township lines drawn by the Americans.

John Johnston, among the most important American Indian agents in Ohio for the first quarter of the nineteenth century. (*Ohio Historical Society*)

They would also be encouraged to take ownership of individual pieces of property. Officials in the War Department specifically told Cass to give every head of a household on the new tribal reserves a "life estate" of one section, or 640 acres, which could be bequeathed to family members. Similar instructions were sent to Andrew Jackson, who was negotiating a comparable treaty with the Cherokee.[26]

Back in Ohio, John Johnston, the Indian agent stationed at Piqua, was given the task of calling more than seven thousand Indians to the treaty negotiations along the Maumee in the late summer of 1817. In *Recollections of Sixty Years*, his memoir of life on the Ohio frontier, Johnston recalled how the Indians were deeply troubled that this treaty would be different than all previous ones. This time they would not have their friend Harrison with them to perform the ancient ceremonies and light the council fire. He had been elected to the House of Representatives the year before and was far away in the nation's capital.[27] So the tribes asked Johnston, a friend of Harrison since he was little more than a boy himself working as a wagon master in Wayne's army, to get them tobacco and white muslin for their priests to make the necessary sacrifice before the start of the council. Johnston never

remembered the Indians preparing so fervently before treaty negotiations; but they were insistent, telling him that "the Great Spirit
would not aid them" if this sacrifice did not take place. Although
Cass and McArthur balked at the delay, and refused to purchase
the tobacco and white muslin, Johnston got them for the tribes.
The great sacrifice finally took place, and with more than a dozen
translators for all the Indians present, the negotiations, which
would take six weeks, were finally under way.[28]

The trepidation of the tribes was understandable. The boundary line between the Indians who remained in Ohio and the
United States was about to give way and be replaced by township
lines drawn in accordance with the Land Ordinance of 1785. The
Indians would be removed from a life that, despite the ties to government annuities and manufactured goods, was in many respects
still free. The tribes could go where they pleased behind the
boundary line, maintaining their customs as they saw fit. But now
the encroaching squares, which only the Ottawa had known,
would be felt by all the tribes. The Treaty at the Foot of the Rapids
would mark the halfway point between the first treaty at
Greeneville and the final removal of the tribes across the
Mississippi. By signing it, the tribes gave up any hope of turning
the clock back to a world in which they were truly independent.[29]

Given the high stakes of the negotiations, the council was anything but peaceful. At one point, Chief Meshkemau, who had
lived on his reserve near Maumee Bay since signing the Treaty of
Detroit in 1807, accused the Americans of cheating the Indians
and using "all kinds of trickery and duplicity" to get what they
wanted. He became so angry that he went up to Governor Cass
and struck him with his fist. Cass launched the greatest insult possible against a proud Indian warrior: "Put a petticoat on this
woman and take her away," he shouted.[30] But even greater resistance came from the Wyandot chief, Between the Logs. A young
man of only thirty-seven, he was known among his people for his
eloquence and his brilliant memory and so was chosen to speak for
the entire tribe. He refused to sign any treaty that forced the
Wyandot to give up hundreds of thousands of acres in exchange
for their imprisonment on a township or two.

Both Cass and McArthur were at a loss on how to respond to
the defiant chief until the Ottawa made a counter proposal.

Already trapped on three small reserves for the last decade, they demanded that every Ohio tribe meet a similar fate. Along with the Pottawatomi and Chippewa, the Ottawa threatened to sell northwest Ohio out from under the Wyandot and the other tribes, pocketing all of the annuities for themselves. Cass quickly responded that he would take the deal. Faced with the total loss of their country, the Wyandot agreed to sign the treaty, but Between the Logs warned that he would head to Washington immediately after the council was concluded, with or without the approval of the commissioners, and speak of this injustice directly to Monroe.[31]

In the treaty, which was finally signed on September 29, 1817, the Wyandot, Shawnee, Seneca, and Delaware surrendered their claims to all of their remaining land in northwest Ohio in exchange for annuity payments of several thousand dollars per tribe to be paid in hard currency. More money would be paid to tribes who had "improved" their land in some way. Specific reserves were laid out under the control of the major chiefs of each tribe by "patent" or deed and by "fee simple," which meant they could be passed on to their "successors." Nine Wyandot chiefs, led by the new headman, Deunquod, or "Half King," received a twelve-mile square reserve equal to four townships, soon known as the Grand Reserve, with the village of Upper Sandusky at its center, along with another one-mile square plot for their tribe's use in a cranberry swamp near Broken Sword Creek, the exact location of which the chiefs would decide later. As in every treaty with the Ohio tribes going back to Wayne's treaty at Greeneville, the tribes would still be allowed to hunt on the surrendered land as long as it belonged to the United States. The Indians were also guaranteed the right to make sugar from maple trees on government land if they "committed no unnecessary waste upon the trees."

Of the 144 sections laid out on the Grand Reserve, each a one-mile square block made up of 640 acres, two sections apiece would go to Deunquod and his six councilors—Between the Logs, Warpole, Mononcue, John Hicks, George Punch, and Matthews. Since several of the Wyandot councilors had just converted to the Methodist faith, three sections of land would be set aside for a missionary and a school. Three sections would also support a blacksmith, who would work for the tribe. The remaining land,

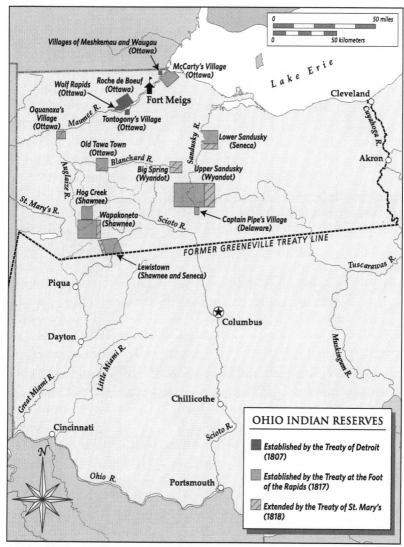

Map 2. Ohio Indian Reserves, 1807–1818.

about 80,000 acres, was to be subdivided among the 176 Wyandot men and women listed by name in the schedule attached to the treaty. The people who received the allotments, one of whom was the widow of Tarhe the Crane, would be allowed to pass the property on to their descendants with the permission of the president of the United States.

The Wyandot also made sure that they took care of the Americans who had been living with them since they were captured on the frontier when young. The list was a long one and included men and women, some of whom were fully white and others who were mixed bloods. Elizabeth Foulks had been taken on the Pennsylvania frontier when she was only nine. Later she married another prisoner named James Whitacre, who had been kidnapped in his early twenties in western Virginia. After the Wyandot set them free following their marriage, they decided to remain with the Indians. They set up a trading post and farm on the west side of the river at Lower Sandusky. Elizabeth Whitacre, now a widow with six children to support, was famous for her devotion to the Wyandot and the Americans. She once nursed William Henry Harrison back to health during the War of 1812, and warned the soldiers at Fort Stephenson on the Sandusky River when Procter and Tecumseh were about to attack. The Wyandot made sure that Mrs. Whitacre got two sections of land, drawn carefully around her family's farm and trading post. Some twenty other heads of households—including a daughter of the Shawnee chief Bluejacket; the Wyandot chief Cherokee Boy; and Peter Manor, or "Yellow Hair," the adopted son of the Ottawa chief Tontogony, each received one or two sections of land that legally defined the property on which they currently lived.

The Seneca were granted thirty thousand acres on the eastern side of the Sandusky River, which was to be subdivided among eighty-three individuals listed in the treaty. A group of Shawnee chiefs, led by Black Hoof, got a ten-mile square grant, with the council house at Wapakoneta at its center. Another group received an adjacent twenty-five-square-mile tract at Hog Creek. Both were granted by patent and fee simple, which would pass to the "successors" of the original chiefs named in the treaty. Another group of Shawnee and Seneca chiefs, led by the Shawnee Colonel Lewis, received a forty-eight-square-mile tract, equal to 1 1/2 townships, at Lewiston, in between the sources of the Miami and Scioto rivers. The Delaware agreed to give up several small tracts in the state, including a piece of ground in western Ohio, where many of the tribe had fled from Indiana during the War of 1812, in exchange for a three-mile square, or quarter-township tract, around Captain Pipe's village just south of Upper Sandusky. Each of these reserves was to be subdivided for the use of the dozens of heads of households listed by name in a schedule attached to the document. None of these tracts would be subject to tax.

The treaty also resolved several long-standing issues for the Ohio tribes. Any Indians who had remained loyal to the United States in the War of 1812, and who had seen their villages or other property destroyed, would be paid for the loss. In the end, this amounted to a few hundred dollars per tribe. The Ottawa's claim to a tract along the eastern shore of the Maumee that measured thirty-four miles square, laid out in a parallelogram around Chief McCarty's village, was affirmed. Many Ottawa still lived on their reserves near Maumee Bay, and also at Roche de Boeuf and Wolf Rapids, which had been granted to them by the Treaty of Detroit in 1807. But still more had settled farther south in the Auglaize River valley and in its tributaries. The Treaty at the Foot of the Rapids granted these Ottawa the use, but not the ownership, of a three-mile square reserve around Oquanoxa's village on the Maumee at the mouth of the Auglaize, and a five-mile square reserve at Lower or Old Tawa town on the Blanchard River, also known as Blanchard's Fork. Several of the Ottawa, along with members of their brother tribes, the Pottawatomi and Chippewa, were Catholic. During the treaty negotiations at the Foot of the Rapids, they asked that land be given to a parish in Michigan, where a Catholic college would be built to educate their children; the request was granted. Finally, all the tribes agreed that taverns, inns, and ferries could be operated on their land where needed.[32]

The negotiations were particularly humiliating for the Wyandot. They clearly understood the shift that occurred with this treaty. As the "grandfathers" of the other Ohio tribes, and with Between the Logs as their spokesman, the Wyandot were keenly aware of the history of their people as the keepers of the wampum and all the treaties signed by the Ohio tribes. John Johnston recalled the pain they now experienced, having to give up their land and move to smaller townships. He wrote the following about the final decision of the Wyandot to sign the treaty along the Maumee Rapids: "The attachment of the Wyandot was ardent for their native country. The night they agreed to give it up many chiefs shed tears." He long remembered a related incident that occurred a few years later when the Wyandot chief Cherokee Boy came to him in great distress. Cherokee Boy had lived among the Wyandot since being taken from his tribe in Georgia when he was just four. He was now a chief of the Wolf Clan of the Wyandot. His family was buried on land now owned by a white man in "Sandusky country," who was preparing to clear the ground and plow over his dead relatives. Johnston wrote to the farmer asking if the dead could remain undisturbed until the upcoming winter, when Cherokee Boy could remove them to a safer burial ground. The farmer agreed.[33]

Even the Ottawa, who had bullied the other tribes into signing away their land at the Foot of the Rapids, were distraught over their actions, knowing the Indians had renounced their proud warrior past once and for all. Perhaps this was why they brought an aged woman named Kantuckeegun to the treaty negotiations along the Maumee River. She was the niece, and most probably the third and last wife, of the great chief Pontiac, having married him shortly before his death when she was little more than a child. As the mother of Otussa, the last of Pontiac's sons, she was greatly respected among her people. But even with this deep respect, the Ottawa chiefs had to drag her forward against her will at the closing of the council and force her to sign the treaty. She finally shrugged off the young men who held her fast and, with a defiant look at the crowd, made her X alongside the name "Pontiac."[34]

In contrast, Governor Cass was overjoyed at the acquisition of so much strategic and valuable territory made possible by the treaty signed at the foot of the Maumee Rapids. "We may in fact consider this purchase," he exclaimed, "as the greatest connecting link which binds together our Northwestern frontier." He described the significance of the treaty in a letter to President Monroe, saying, "This is by far the most valuable cession which has been made to the United States at any one time since the treaty of Greeneville."[35] Monroe was just as convinced that the Treaty at the Foot of the Rapids proved the benefits of his twofold Indian policy for his nation. In his first message to Congress, given when he returned to Washington in December 1817, he explained that by further purchases of Indian land:

We shall be enabled to extend our settlements from the unin-
habited parts of the State of Ohio along Lake Erie into Michigan
Territory, and to connect our settlements by a state of degrees
through the State of Indiana and the Illinois Territory to that of
Missouri.[36]

There were also benefits for the tribes, as Monroe explained to
Congress early in 1818, when he announced that the Ohio
Indians were now officially individual property owners. Hundreds
of them had been granted their own tracts of land within the
wider reserves set aside for their people. Surely this would ensure
their transition to civilization and with it, their salvation when the
American tide swept over them.[37]

Convinced he had helped craft a humane Indian policy,
Secretary of War Calhoun was surprised when Between the Logs
arrived at his office in the nation's capital. He told the chief and
the Indians who accompanied him that he had not been informed
of their trip from any agent out west. Between the Logs answered,
"We got up and came ourselves. We believed the great road was
free for us." He explained to Calhoun that the treaty signed at the
Foot of the Rapids was unfair and demanded a new one. The eloquent Wyandot went on to make his case before Congress and
even directly to President Monroe. He said his people feared they
had signed away rights to all their land, that they would be per-
mitted to live on their remaining land only temporarily, since the
Americans would one day take this away from them, too. The
Wyandot wanted more land set aside for their tribe, along with
more annuities. Between the Logs convinced the government to
call for new treaty negotiations set for September 1818 in St.
Mary's in western Ohio.[38]

The promise of a new treaty provided some relief to Between
the Logs and his fellow chiefs, but could not allay the awful feeling that the tribes had made a terrible mistake by signing away so
much of their land at the Foot of the Rapids. The shock of what
they had done, along with the sheer weight of the change that
would come upon them now that they must move to smaller
pieces of territory within their once vast holdings, became even
more frightening in light of the death of the Tarhe the Crane.[39]
His passing seemed like a door closing forever on a past that the

tribes could never get back. A future might be coming in which the encroaching squares of the township lines that now surrounded them would increasingly inch closer until they swallowed them up entirely. The tribes would simply disappear in the flood tide of the Americans.

Tarhe, more than any other chief, was a tie to their past. After signing the Treaty of Springwells, he had returned to his favorite village, Crane Town, about 4 1/2 miles northeast of Upper Sandusky. There he lived peacefully in a small cabin with his wife, Sally, and his black servant, Jonathan Pointer. The lay of the land around his cabin told the story of a world that was fast disappearing for the Wyandot and the other Ohio tribes. An orchard of apple trees, probably planted by John Chapman, better known as "Johnny Appleseed," grew nearby. Just south of the cabin, clear signs remained of the "old gauntlet ground," where prisoners once ran for their lives, and more often to their deaths, at the center of the village. When Tarhe died, sometime late in 1816, he was buried about a half mile southeast of his cabin, on land that would eventually be purchased by an American settler named John Smith.[40]

After the death of Tarhe the Crane, the Wyandot's principal village moved back to Upper Sandusky, at the center of the tribe's twelve-mile-by-twelve-mile square reserve. This town, located on the Great Trail halfway between Pittsburgh and Detroit, had long been an important site on the western frontier. During the last days of the American Revolution, Colonel William Crawford had led his army against Upper Sandusky in the late spring of 1782. A few miles northeast of the town, Crawford met a horrible death at the hands of his Indian captors. Now the most respected chiefs of the tribes of the old Ohio Country gathered there in the autumn of 1818 to mourn Tarhe's passing. The great Iroquois chief Red Jacket came all the way from New York to honor his memory.

John Johnston, who had helped to negotiate the treaty that removed the Wyandot to this spot, long remembered the council that occurred near the spring just north of the town. He watched as the "head men and the aged" sat facing each other on two rows of benches that ran down the center of the bark council house. They bent their heads low and moaned in successive waves that started at one end of the seated figures and then moved down the other. These waves of moaning came every few minutes and lasted for hours. Johnston had never seen anything like it, and was told that this honor was only given upon the passing of a very great man. When the men had finished their "monody," the council got under way. Johnston was surprised at the animosity between the Delaware, Seneca, Shawnee, Ottawa, and Wyandot. For a time, Johnston even feared for his life. As he later explained in his memoir:

> I had attended many councils, treaties, and gatherings of the Indians, but never in my life did I witness such an outpouring of native oratory and eloquence, of severe rebuke, taunting national and personal reproaches.

Each tribe blamed the other tribes present for selling land to the Americans. The harangues started when Red Jacket accused the Shawnee of surrendering the most land, even though they were the last tribe to settle in Ohio. In fact, because they came so late, Red Jacket said they had no right to sell anything. Then Black Hoof, the aged Shawnee chief, rose from his place and blamed the Seneca, Red Jacket's own tribe, and the Wyandot for selling even more land. The insults reached a fever pitch when one chief, who had been handed a wampum belt as a symbol of peace, refused to touch it. Instead, he picked up a stick and used it to pass the wampum on to the next man. The angry chiefs broke up the council for the night. On the following morning, Black Hoof took the lead in restoring the peace, saying they had all acted like children. The wampum was passed around the council, with every chief taking it by the hand before passing it on. They then admitted they had all sold land to the Americans, and must now accept the consequences.[41]

Although calm was restored, the awareness that much had changed forever remained. Tarhe the Crane's death and the council at the Foot of the Rapids truly marked the passing of one era and the beginning of another—the outcome of which no one could foretell. Now that their people were removed to small reserves in Ohio, the chiefs knew that much in their traditional way of life would have to change. If there was any turning back the clock, then maybe it was to the time when Washington's secretary of war, Henry Knox, and later President Jefferson, first recommended that the Indians live exactly like the Americans.

Black Hoof of the Shawnee knew this would require changes, but he had already lived through so many with his people. Known among them as Catahecassa, he remembered growing up somewhere in the South, probably in Florida, where he bathed in saltwater as a boy. He recalled how his people believed they had come to America from across a great sea. Every year they held a ceremony thanking the Great Spirit for their safe journey. But once the last treaties were signed that removed all the tribes onto smaller reserves, they never performed the ceremony again, perhaps fearing that the protection they had long enjoyed from the Great Spirit had disappeared. Black Hoof, like so many other chiefs in Ohio, was wary that moving onto smaller pieces of ground, and promising that Indian warriors would farm and raise livestock, might still not be enough to satisfy the Americans. Perhaps someday they would remove the Shawnee and the other tribes from these same reserves. He did not want to leave Ohio, but would go wherever his tribe wanted. Echoing the sentiments of Tecumseh, whom he had once bitterly opposed, Black Hoof put the dilemma his people faced this way to Johnston:

> We will go anywhere you please, if you will afterwards let us alone, but we know from past experience, you will keep driving us until we reach the sea on the other side of the Rocky Mountains, and then we must jump off.[42]

FOUR

A Race Against Time

When treaty negotiations opened at St. Mary's in the late summer of 1818, Between the Logs and the other chiefs who had guided the Wyandot since the death of Tarhe the Crane, along with several Seneca leaders who had traveled with them to Washington, could be proud of the fact that they had convinced the American government to rectify the injustices in the treaty signed at the Foot of the Rapids of the Maumee River. They had met with President James Monroe and his secretary of war, John C. Calhoun, and had even addressed members of the Senate's Committee on Public Lands in December 1817. Between the Logs had explained to everyone he met in the nation's capital that a twelve-mile-by-twelve-mile square piece of ground, four townships to be exact, was simply not enough for the remaining one thousand Wyandot to live on.

Wyandot men would now have to plant crops and raise livestock to feed their families, and continue to hunt to help pay for manufactured goods, but the reserve granted to the tribe in the recent treaty did not provide enough land. With households averaging six people, the estimated allotment of 480 acres per family was too small a tract on which to survive. The Seneca grant was also insufficient and needed to be redrawn to include land south of their current reserve, where the tribe had already established working farms.[1] Neither the Wyandot nor the Seneca opposed the great changes that had come upon their tribes since the end of the War of 1812. Both were more than willing to "settle down," as the white man was so fond of saying, to a "civilized" life. Both understood better than anyone else that they were in a race to support themselves exactly as the white man had before the tide of American settlement made it to the edges of their reserves. But they also knew that they would be off to a terrible start and would never be able to win the race if the treaty that removed them to these reserves was so unfair.

Calhoun listened to the eloquent complaints of Between the Logs, as well as to the recommendations made by the Senate Committee on Public Lands, and ordered Lewis Cass and Duncan McArthur to go back to a grand council in western Ohio and set things right between the tribes and the United States. The Committee on Public Lands had specifically reported that the Wyandot should be recognized for their willingness to give up the lion's share of the remaining Indian lands in Ohio. Specifically, of the nearly 3,700,000 acres ceded to the United States at the Foot of the Rapids in 1817, 3,360,000 had once belonged to the Wyandot. Thus it seemed only fitting that if the government were now willing to cede land back to the Indians, most of it should go to the same tribe.

Senators on the Public Lands Committee were equally concerned about what would become of the individual land patents that had been granted by fee simple to various Indians in the schedule attached to the original treaty. While they agreed that this was a good idea since the tribes would be learning the value of privately owning land, the senators feared that their own people would take advantage of this clause in the treaty. They would literally overrun the Indian reserves and buy land right out from under the individuals named in the document. Before anyone knew what was happening, every reserve would be broken up and handed over to the white man. Fearing this, the committee recommended amending the 1817 treaty with language that made it clear that an Indian could only give or sell land on an Ohio reserve to another Indian with the approval of the president of the United States.[2]

While the Wyandot and Seneca chiefs had won much in Washington, it must have been disconcerting for them to see so many other tribes from Ohio, and even from farther west, gathered at St. Mary's when they arrived there in September 1818. The Ottawa, along with the Shawnee who had also agreed to move to smaller reserves as a result of the Treaty at the Foot of the Rapids, were present, but so were the Miami, Pottawatomi, and Wea, who still lived on hundreds of thousands of acres along the Wabash River and its tributaries in Indiana. The Delaware, who now lived mainly along the White River in Indiana, had also arrived in St. Mary's. As Between the Logs and his fellow chiefs prepared to negotiate a treaty that would include their own recommendations and those of the Senate, they wondered what more the Americans were planning to ask of the many Indians that had come to council. Would the removal of the Ohio tribes to tiny pieces of ground, hopefully to increase soon by an extra 100,000 acres, be enough to satisfy the Americans? Or would they demand even more land from tribes living farther west? What could be done to hold back a people so driven to take every last acre for themselves? If nothing could be done, then what was the point of working so hard to give up their traditions in order to become respectable property owners just like the Americans?

In the face of such questions, and with the press of settlers all around them, the chiefs of the Wyandot and Seneca agreed to a special "supplementary treaty," signed on September 17, 1818, that modified the Treaty at the Foot of the Rapids. The American government promised that the newly marked-out township reserves would belong to the Indians and to their heirs "forever." Governor Cass, the lead negotiator for the United States, agreed that the individual Indians named in the previous year's treaty could only transfer their lands to their chosen heirs with the president's approval. The Wyandot reserve at Upper Sandusky was increased by an extra 55,680 acres, or eighty-seven sections, with the new acreage laid out south of the section already granted to Cherokee Boy. Members of the tribe living in villages at Solomon's Town and Blanchard's Fork would receive 16,000 acres, or twenty-five sections measured in a perfect square. This land would be known as the Big Spring Reserve, since it sat at the headwaters of the Blanchard River. The tribe would also receive an extra $500 a year in annuity payments. The Seneca would receive 10,000 more acres, or nearly sixteen sections laid out directly south of their current reserve on the Sandusky River. The tribe would also see a $500 increase in their annuities.[3]

Between the Logs and his fellow Wyandot chiefs—Deunquod, Warpole, John Hicks, George Punch, Matthews, Scoutous, Quoqua, and Cherokee Boy—along with eight leaders of the Seneca, had won thousands of acres and hundreds of dollars for their respective peoples. And still they were not satisfied with winning concessions for their tribes alone, but had also demanded more land and money for other Indians in Ohio whose chiefs had joined them in signing the supplemental treaty. The Shawnee reserve at Wapakoneta was increased by an additional 12,800 acres, or twenty sections, while the Shawnee and Seneca at Lewistown received an extra 8,960 acres, or fourteen sections. The forty-eight-square-mile reserve at Lewistown would be divided by an east-west line running through its middle, with the Shawnee living to the south and the Seneca to the north. Annuities went up by $1,000 for the Shawnee and Seneca of Lewistown and by $1,500 for the Ottawa.[4]

Still, the chiefs were not completely successful in controlling the negotiations at St. Mary's. The American government had returned over 100,000 acres to the tribes, but not without demanding something from the Indians. Just three days after winning concessions in the supplementary treaty to the one previously written at the Foot of the Rapids, Between the Logs and seven other Wyandot leaders signed away their rights to the tribe's traditional council grounds at Brownstown and Maguaga. In exchange for giving up this land (now Trenton, Michigan), the Wyandot received all or part of seven sections of "Township Four," just south of the Huron River in the Michigan Territory.[5]

It was ironic that the government demanded the Brownstown site, where in 1812 Between the Logs, at only thirty-two, had spoken forcefully against Tecumseh and in support of the Americans. He had spent a year living with Tenkswatawa before coming to the conclusion that the Shawnee holy man was a fraud, just as he had earlier concluded that the Seneca prophet Handsome Lake could

not be trusted.[6] The young chief, who had been named the official speaker for the Wyandot nation because of his amazing memory, recited a speech on behalf of the aged Tarhe, who could not
attend the council. He urged the tribes to see the danger in
Tecumseh's plans and to recognize the sheer madness of trying to
stop the Americans by yet another war:

> Why would you devote yourselves, your women, and your chil-
> dren to destruction? Let me tell you, if you should defeat the
> American army this time, you have not done. Another will come
> on, and if you defeat that, still another will appear that you cannot
> withstand; one that will come like the waves of the great water, and
> overwhelm you, and sweep you from the face of the earth.[7]

But whether they opposed Tecumseh, like most of the
Wyandot, or supported him, like many of the Miami,
Pottawatomi, and Wea, it did not seem to matter. Either way, the
tribes met the same fate: removal to small reserves laid out in
accordance with the official township lines of the Land Ordinance
of 1785. In a separate treaty signed at St. Mary's in early October
1818, the once-great Miami, who had struck terror in the hearts
of American soldiers and settlers for generations, relinquished millions of acres in Indiana, approximately a third of the state, and
land on the western edge of Ohio in exchange for all or parts of
seven townships. Twenty-three sections were set aside for specific
individuals named in the treaty, including Richardville, the tribe's
current headman. For their lands, the Miami received an extra
$15,000 in annuities, along with a sawmill and a gristmill.
Furthermore, the government promised to hire a blacksmith and
a gunsmith for the Miami and send 160 barrels of salt to the tribe
each year. The Pottawatomi also signed a treaty ceding their
remaining lands south of the Wabash in exchange for a seven mile
by seven mile square reserve on Raccoon Creek near the mouth of
the Wabash and $1,500 more in yearly payments to the tribe. The
Wea agreed to surrender their claims to land in Indiana for annuities totaling $3,000, to be paid in silver coins. For $4,000 a year,
also payable in silver coins, the Delaware agreed to give up all of
their remaining territory in Indiana.[8]

While the chiefs who had signed the many treaties of St. Mary's
could now take their people home down the ancient traces to what

remained of their once vast holdings in the old Ohio Country, there could be no going back to the way things were before the Americans' arrival. Perhaps in a few weeks, after they had harvested their corn and celebrated the festivals for their dead, they could go off on their winter hunt. Even if government surveyors came quickly into their country, a season or two might pass before settlers actually opened up farms and towns on the surrendered land. The men could lead their families, one by one, into the surrounding forests to chase the last few bear and other animals that still remained. They could harvest enough pelts to buy the manufactured goods that their annuities would not afford. Maybe for another spring, they could go back to their villages, where the women and girls would plant the corn, beans, and squash again, and for just a moment everything would be the same as it had been for generations.[9]

But the old cycle could not go on much longer, since the chiefs had promised, by signing the treaties at St. Mary's, and before this at the Foot of the Rapids of the Maumee, that they would give up their old ways of hunting from fall to winter, and of farming from spring to summer. The X, or totem, that each chief made alongside his name was a pledge that the men of his tribe would become tillers of the soil. They would do what Washington, Knox, and Jefferson had once asked of them before Tecumseh and the Prophet led their revolt, before the British recruited and abandoned the tribes, and before the Americans came west, not by the hundreds or thousands, but by the hundreds of thousands. They would turn away from the path of the warrior and hunter and follow the course of American civilization, which demanded the private ownership of land. How they would have enough money to buy the things they needed, once they gave up hunting completely, was not something that anyone at the moment could comprehend.

Although much had been lost at the Foot of the Rapids, still much remained. With the Wyandot at 1,000, the best estimates of the local Indian agents placed the number of Shawnee at 800 and the Seneca at 400. There were a few hundred Ottawa and at least 45 Delaware.[10] While their numbers were small in comparison to Ohio's population of nearly 500,000, the tribes had managed to hang on to over 300,000 acres. Their small township reserves had all been laid out in good country. The Shawnee, and the Seneca who lived with them, remained in the rolling prairie country, where many of their ancient "chalahgawthas," or principal towns, once stood. The land was well irrigated with many streams. The Auglaize ran through it, and here, too, were the headwaters of the St. Mary's, the Great Miami, and the Scioto. The soil in the bottomlands of the many rivers and streams was deep and black.

Similarly, the Ottawa were still in the valley of the Maumee, where their greatest chief, Pontiac, had once lived. Their villages stood alongside the river's rapids, which were stocked with fish and lined with elm trees. The soil was sandy but still good for raising corn and other crops. The Wyandot held the country they had known since the days when they had fled from Canada, with the Iroquois close behind. The sites of their villages were the same as they had been for nearly a hundred years. They had kept their cranberry bog, surrounded by willows, and had continued to maintain the stands of sugar maples that they loved so well. Finally, they could take some comfort in the fact that their villages still lined the old trace from Pittsburgh to the Maumee Valley, and then north along the lake to Detroit. The Seneca and the Delaware, who lived north and south of the Wyandot, had kept their land in the rich soil of the Sandusky River valley.[11]

But while their reserves were in good country, much would have to change if the tribes were to hold onto them. They might still be able to retain their identity as a people, but only if they transformed their customs enough to be acceptable to the Americans who were heading their way. They could probably hold onto their language, their law, their government, their ancient tales, and maybe even their religion, but the way that they managed their property and worked among themselves would have to change. Their tribal lands, where fields were once tilled in common, must now give way to family farms with fences all around them, to keep the cattle, hogs, and horses safe. The warrior life, which had ended for some at Greeneville and the rest at Springwells, was gone forever. Now the men must truly become breadwinners, like the whites who were coming closer to them each day. They would need to chop down trees and open up enough acres to grow corn, wheat, and hay for their families and their livestock. While they could receive aid at the government-run sawmills and gristmills, they must build cabins for their families and barns for their crops and animals. At least for a while, the men and boys would still be able to go on winter hunts for furs to trade for manufactured goods; but this would be a side occupation compared to their true vocation as farmers, carpenters, and even mechanics.

As the men took on these new chores, the women would leave the fields and become homemakers. They would no longer farm, build wigwams, or transport goods, but would now spend their days in the cabins built by their husbands and sons. There they would prepare the food that the men raised and sew clothes from the goods that their husbands purchased. Even the children would have to change. Instead of following their fathers and mothers into the woods or fields, they would have to attend school and learn to read and write English and do arithmetic, thus learning record keeping among other things, like other American pioneers. Rather than learning from their parents and grandparents, they would instead have to learn from the white man's books. A new cycle would replace the old, as the boys grew up to be farmers and the girls grew up to be housewives.

If they wanted to survive and remain in this beautiful country long ago named Ohio, then the tribes reasoned that they would have to do what the government had been recommending for a generation. They must become just like the farm families whom they had fought for so long on the western frontier. Hopefully, once the Americans arrived at the edges of the Indian reserves, and marked out their farms and towns, they would respect the hard work of the tribes and agree to live in peace with them. To agree to make such a great change so quickly, however, was a gamble. There was no guarantee that once the tribes had succeeded in transforming themselves, the Americans would honor their promises and remember that they had demanded such a change as the price for peaceful coexistence.

The transformation would also be challenging because it must take place under the daunting pressure of another demand, first raised around the council fire at St. Mary's. Even as the chiefs of the Ohio tribes negotiated for more land in order for their people to succeed as farmers, Governor Cass had suggested that maybe they would be better off leaving the state for good. Instead of trying to live like the white man, perhaps they should head west across the Mississippi River, and there carry on their ancient ways as if nothing had ever happened. This, in fact, was the only way for the Indians to survive. The Delaware took Cass up on his offer, promising in the treaty they signed at St. Mary's to leave for a new home in the West sometime within the next three years. In contrast, the leaders of the Wyandot, Seneca, Shawnee, and Ottawa were stunned that Cass, a man most of them respected as a friend, would propose such a terrible idea, which they rejected completely.[12]

For the chiefs of the Ohio tribes who had signed the supplemental treaty at St. Mary's, such a proposition meant banishment, not survival. They had taken the chance that the Americans would hold to the bargain, which was offered to them by earlier presidents, and which was proposed again by James Monroe. The Shawnee especially remembered visiting President Jefferson in 1802, before Tecumseh and the Prophet launched the war that tore the western tribes apart. They still cherished a golden chain he had given them. "I send you by your beloved Chiefs, a Chain," he had said in a letter written to them on his behalf by his secretary of war, Henry Dearborn: "It is made of Gold, which will never rust, and I pray the Great Spirit to assist us in keeping the chain of our friendship (of which this gold chain is meant as an emblem) bright for a long succession of ages."[13]

If they were to survive on their township reserves in Ohio, then the tribe would hold onto the golden chain, and take as much help in the present as possible. The Shawnee, in fact, had already asked for help from the Quakers. They had known the Quakers since the time of William Penn. Older members of the tribe, like Black Hoof, who had been born in the 1730s or perhaps even earlier, remembered how much their parents and grandparents respected Penn. There was something about this man that was different from the other white people who were arriving by ship daily from Europe. He seemed to want the same things that all the others wanted, land and furs especially; but when asking for these things, he honored the wishes of the Indians who already inhabited the colony he was about to establish in Pennsylvania. In April 1682, several Shawnee chiefs and their people were among the hundreds, perhaps even thousands, of Indians who met the young Englishman under the Great Elm Tree at the tribal council ground where Philadelphia now stands. They remembered how their people came armed to the teeth, but William Penn came without weapons. He wore "no crown, scepter, mace, sword, halberd, nor any insignia of office," only a sky-blue sash made of purest silk tied around his coat, the outfit of a common soldier. He carried no sword or gun, but instead came in the company of his fellow Christians, whom he called his "friends."[14]

The Shawnee had a way of sizing up a man's character when they met him for the first time, which determined their future relationship. An ancient Shawnee king named Wapatha was the first chief to negotiate a treaty with Penn on behalf of his people. He judged him to be a good and decent fellow, as well as the other members of the Society of Friends, or the Quakers, as their enemies called them. The treaty signed between the Shawnee and the Quakers promised eternal peace and friendship between the Indians and the "Christians." Both peoples pledged to deal fairly with each other. They would leave the doors of their homes open to white and red alike, and would never rob, harm, or in any way slander their "brethren."

From this time forward, whenever Penn wanted Shawnee and other tribes' land, he would buy it outright with gifts, always making sure he kept a neutral middle ground between the Indians and his settlers. The goods that Penn offered in exchange for the pelts and skins of beaver, deer, buffalo, bear, and other animals were of the highest quality, and never included rum, wine, or whiskey. Just like Thomas Jefferson would later pledge, Penn offered the symbol of a golden chain, which would never rust or decay, as a sign of the love and harmony between the tribes and the Quakers. The chain would last "while creeks and rivers run, and while the sun, moon, and stars endure." The Shawnee, for their part, held onto a copy of the treaty that Wapatha had signed with their friend William Penn for years to come.[15]

The ties between the Shawnee and Penn's colony did not last, but instead disintegrated shortly after he departed for England in

1701, never to return. After several bloody skirmishes with local settlers, the tribe left Pennsylvania for good, heading first to the Carolinas and then even farther south to Florida, where Black Hoof remembered swimming in the ocean as a boy.[16] The Shawnee next made their way back up through the Appalachians, heading into Kentucky, and finally crossed north of the Ohio River, just as the great war was about to break out between France and England in 1754. While the tribe lost touch with the Quakers, the Society of Friends remained concerned about the Shawnee and the other Indians, and even maintained detailed records of late eighteenth-century tribal history and movement on the North American continent.[17]

As they kept a watchful eye on the Indians from a distance, the Quakers became increasingly concerned about the rising bloodshed between the settlers, with their voracious appetite for land, and the Indians, with their ruthless attacks on frontier outposts. The violence seemed to grow worse after the American Revolution ended. The Quakers were especially troubled by the fighting between the Ohio tribes and the American armies sent to their country in the early 1790s. In 1794, the annual meeting of Friends, held in Philadelphia, set up a committee to try and stop the continuing war between the Indians and the United States. They made recommendations for peace to President Washington, which were in turn sent to General Anthony Wayne. At the opening of the treaty negotiations at Greeneville in August 1795, Wayne read a letter from the Philadelphia Quakers, in which they offered to come west at their own expense and help the Shawnee and their brother tribes. Wayne assured the Indians that the Quakers, whom he had known growing up in Pennsylvania, were good people. Take their gifts, advised Wayne, and any other help they might offer to make the transition to a more civilized life a smooth one.[18]

In 1802, he went to Washington with several Shawnee and Delaware chiefs to see President Jefferson, and Black Hoof stopped in Philadelphia to meet with members of the Society of Friends. He was pleasantly surprised that the descendants of William Penn's original followers were as kind to the Indians as their ancestors had been. They loaded down the chiefs with money and gifts, along with promises that they would come to Ohio and teach modern farming techniques to the Shawnee. Upon learning of this, the Miami chief Little Turtle sent word to the Quakers that he needed their help, too, in "civilizing" his people. By 1806, the Quakers were regularly purchasing plows and farm equipment for several western tribes, but most especially for the Shawnee. In that year alone, they sent goods valued at more than 11,000 pounds sterling to the tribe.

One year later, Black Hoof returned to the nation's capital seeking additional help for his people, especially in learning better ways to farm. Jefferson's administration authorized William Kirk, a Quaker originally from Baltimore, to set up a mission and a model farm at Black Hoof's village of Wapakoneta. Already working successfully with the Miami near Fort Wayne, he went immediately with several followers to Ohio, and by spring of 1808 helped the Shawnee put more than 500 acres under cultivation. They grew traditional crops, such as corn, beans, and squash, as well as planted new ones, like cabbages, turnips, and potatoes. Many Shawnee continued to grow food on communal farms, while others followed the American example and fenced off individual plots to raise crops for their families. The Quakers also taught the Shawnee animal husbandry and how to build sturdy cabins with windows and chimneys. A grateful Black Hoof wrote a letter to Jefferson thanking him for sending the Quakers. "They are a good people," the chief explained, "and concerned for our welfare and have done a great deal for us in instructing our young men in a good way and how to use the tools we see in the hands of our white brothers."[19]

Sadly for the Shawnee, the government dismissed Kirk from his position after hearing rumors about his bad behavior. Despite the Shawnee's defense of Kirk as a good man, the Quakers shut down their mission at Wapakoneta in 1809. No Quakers came to help Black Hoof's people during the War of 1812; but once the conflict ended, they returned to work among the Shawnee on their own and not at the government's request. They raised funds to build a dam across the Auglaize River. Then they erected a gristmill (for grinding corn and wheat) and sawmill, and sent a superintendent and his family west to teach the Shawnee their operation.

Sometimes Quaker pioneers who were heading to the south-western part of the state, or who were passing through Ohio on their way to Indiana or Illinois, stayed for a time among the Shawnee to help them at the mills. They showed the men how to use teams of horses and oxen to work their farms. They made boards and smaller pieces of wood at the sawmill on the Auglaize, also teaching the men how to build houses and barns, stake up fences, and even make furniture. The Quakers showed the Shawnee women how much easier it was to grind corn at a grist-mill, where a large stone used the power of the river's falling water to crush the grain, rather than doing this by hand.[20]

In 1819, the year after the many treaties were signed at St. Mary's, a Quaker woman living in Cork, Ireland, sent thirty-six iron plows, valued at over 16,000 pounds sterling, to the Shawnee at Wapakoneta. Settlers in the region reported that the Shawnee were slowly learning how to use them, even though the Quakers did much of the work at first. Before long, the Shawnee men were in the fields raising acres of corn, beans, and pumpkins. The Quakers were proud to say that the tribe was more and more devot-ed to a settled life, especially the raising of livestock. The Shawnee had upwards of 125 head of horned cattle and 200 hogs. They also regularly used their annuities to buy more cows and calves.[21]

In the same year that the plows arrived from Ireland, a Quaker family by the name of Harvey came to Wapakoneta. Isaac Harvey, the father of the clan, took over running the mills for the tribe, while his son Henry helped his parents in their work with the Shawnee, and later wrote the first history of the tribe. The Harvey family clearly understood the trying position that the Shawnee were in after signing the Treaty at the Foot of the Rapids, and then the supplemental treaty at St. Mary's. Calling the tribe the most "kind-hearted people" they had ever met, the Quaker missionaries openly sympathized with the plight of the Shawnee. Once, they had roamed free, thought young Henry Harvey, and were the lords of the forest. Anywhere they settled was their home, and they feared no man nor owed allegiance to any earthly power. Then the Americans came, first as colonists of Great Britain and later as cit-izens of the United States, with their endless demand for more and more land, which in turn led to one war after another.

Not even the great Tecumseh, with all his eloquence, was able to stop them. The Shawnee were now facing the dilemma of having to become exactly like the enemy they had fought for so long if they were to survive. This would be a difficult challenge for any tribe, but for a people as proud and sensitive as the Shawnee, it was a "severe trial indeed." Although he and his parents worked to help the Shawnee make the transition to the ways of their "oppressors," Henry Harvey could not help think that "to exchange an Indian life for the life of a white man, is nothing short of a thorough, radical change out and out."[22]

Despite the trials of making such a transition, the Shawnee could count on the Harvey family to urge them not to lose heart. They were most discouraged when they looked ahead and feared that despite their best efforts, the government would take back their land. Young Henry often heard the complaint that "if they improve their lands the whites would want it, and persuade the government to drive them off." The Harvey family, along with other missionary Quakers who came to help the Shawnee on their Ohio reserves, promised that the United States would not be "so intolerably hard." They were certain "after the solemn pledges so often made and repeated, that if they would improve their lands and be at peace, that they never should be asked for their land."[23]

The Harvey family could make this confident pledge because, after working with the tribe for a few years, they believed that the Shawnee were well on their way to becoming a success story on the Ohio frontier. Their homes were well built, their barns well stocked, and their fences offered sturdy protection for crops and livestock. The Quakers, however, believed there was one area in which they had failed the Shawnee, and that was in religion: they were unable to make any converts among them. John Johnston, who was the Indian agent of the tribe for many years, often said that no tribe hated the white man's religion as much as the Shawnee.[24] While they respected the Quakers, as well as the Shakers, believing that both denominations actually practiced what they preached, the tribe mocked the rest of the Christians whom they had met while living on the western frontier; they dismissed them as hypocrites.

Tecumseh best expressed his tribe's contempt for Christianity when he reminded William Henry Harrison, in their first meeting in Vincennes in the summer of 1810, that the whites had waited for centuries for their savior, only to have then murdered him. "How can we have confidence in the white people?" he asked Harrison. "When Jesus Christ came upon the earth, you killed and nailed him on a cross." He added sarcastically, "You thought he was dead, but you were mistaken." Tecumseh seemed to imply that just as Jesus's followers failed to anticipate the resurrection, the white man failed to foresee that the Indians would rise again under his leadership.[25]

Even after the Quakers had proved that there were good Christians among the whites, the Shawnee remained "bitterly opposed" to the faith. God had given Christianity to the whites, they often explained to John Johnston, just as he had given the Indians their faith in the Great Spirit, the Good Grandmother, the Thunderbirds, and all the other divine forces in the natural order. To them, the Shawnee faith was one of joyful prayer to their Creator, practiced through song and dance. They would keep their religion and their own festivals, like the Green Corn Dance in summer, the Festival of the Dead in autumn, and other celebrations, and had no need of the white man's God or his downcast rituals.[26] Because of their contempt for Christianity, the Shawnee resisted every attempt to establish a school on their reserves, where their children would be taught to read, write, calculate, think, and, most terrible, pray like a white man. When the Shawnee finally relented and let the Quakers build a school, they were allowed to teach manual arts, like husbandry and carpentry, and reading and writing, but not religion.[27]

Much like the experience of the Shawnee with the Quakers, the Ottawa, who had returned from St. Mary's to their reserves along the Maumee River, received help from the Presbyterian Church. The only difference was that the Presbyterians came to help the Ottawa, without their being asked. They, too, headed west, believing that if they could teach the Ottawa the civilized arts of husbandry and homemaking, then the tribe would be able to live on their remaining reserves at peace with the whites who surrounded them. In 1808, the Virginia Synod of the Presbyterian Church sent missionaries, led by Reverend Joseph Badger, to minister to the Indians of northwest Ohio and southeastern Michigan.

Badger and his fellow Presbyterians were stunned at the condition to which the Ottawa living along the Maumee had fallen. Many were constantly drunk; they had no domesticated animals, with the exception of a few emaciated dogs; they begged for food, and when not given enough, they stole all they could get their hands on. The missionaries did not fault the Ottawa for their behavior, but instead blamed their condition on the fact that they had met the worst possible white men on the frontier. Even though he had won few souls to Christ, Reverend Badger recommended that a mission be established in the Maumee River valley for the purpose of converting the Indians, most of whom were Ottawa, to the Christian faith. He decided his energy was better spent ministering to the Indians along the Sandusky River. He also later served as the chaplain of Major General William Henry Harrison's army during the War of 1812.[28]

There was no further missionary activity to the Ottawa until October 1822, when a small company of Presbyterian missionaries made their way in a schooner across Lake Erie from New York to the Maumee River valley. Led by Reverend Isaac Van Tassel and his bride, Lucia, the daughter of Joseph Badger, the missionaries had been sent west by the Presbyterian Mission Society in Pittsburgh.[29] The society followed Reverend Badger's recommendation and purchased 687 acres of land near Chief Tontogony's village, about twelve miles upriver from Fort Meigs, for establishing an Indian mission. It was to this site that the Van Tassels, along with Reverend Samuel Tate, his wife and son, Reverend Alvin Coe and his wife, and two "maiden" ladies who had come west to teach the Indians—Miss Sabina Stevens and Miss Hannah Riggs—were heading in the fall of 1822. The waters of Lake Erie were so rough that Lucia Van Tassel remembered years later how she laid in her berth "praying that He who stills the deep" would bring them "safely to their work." After running into storms off Maumee Bay, the schooner capsized, but the missionaries swam to shore with no loss of life. Van Tassel told his followers to stay behind and recover from their ordeal. He and Mr. Barnes, another missionary who had joined them, would go ahead to the mission site called Ebenezer, at the mouth of Tontogony Creek.[30]

Reverend Van Tassel and his assistant, Mr. Barnes, found the land purchased for the mission in an excellent location on the east side of the Maumee. It sat high on a bluff overlooking a bend in the river. Chief Tontogony's village was just to the south along the creek bearing his name. There was another Ottawa village, named Nawash, on a nearby river island, and still another directly across from the mission on the opposite shore, called Kinjoano's Town.[31] Van Tassel and Barnes worked clearing the ground and built a large log cabin that measured 60 by 16 feet. The rest of Van Tassel's party, which now included a farmer and his wife, a carpenter, and a blacksmith, arrived a few days later and worked on the rest of the mission. They quickly constructed the main building, a clapboard house that stood two stories high and measured 30 by 80 feet. A large annex, some 20 by 100 feet, was attached behind it. The missionaries also dug a well and even planted an apple orchard.[32]

On November 26, 1822, just one month after coming into Ottawa country, the Maumee Indian Mission officially opened. At first many parents refused to send their children to the school. The Van Tassels understood that this reluctance came from the mistreatment that the Indians had received at the hands of the white man. Some local whiskey traders, worried that the teetotaling Presbyterians might interfere with their business, even paid mothers and fathers to keep their children away from the school, but soon several parents brought their reluctant "scholars" to the mission. The Van Tassels reported that the first class had 32 children, including 17 Ottawa, 10 Wyandot, 3 Shawnee, 1 Chippewa, and 1 Munsee. The students were expected to attend class six hours a day from Monday through Saturday. On Sunday, they were expected to attend services that consisted of hymn singing, scripture reading, and listening to at least two sermons. They learned reading, writing, and the basics of the Christian faith, along with farming for the boys and homemaking for the girls. Additionally, missionaries taught the children how to graft fruit trees, and grow mulberry trees as a way to start the manufacture of silk. Students also helped out on the farm that the missionaries opened up on an island in the Maumee.[33]

Sometimes the children of settlers whose families had just arrived in the Maumee Valley joined the scholars at the mission. One such boy, Dresden Howard, arrived from New York with his

family at the same time that the
Van Tassels headed west to open
their school. His grandfather,
Thomas Howard, a veteran of
the Continental Army, bought
land a few miles upstream from
the mission, near Wolf Rapids
(now Grand Rapids, Ohio). The
Howards built their house on
the east side of the river, facing
another Ottawa camp on the
opposite shore. There Tontog-

The Maumee Indian Mission was still
standing in the late nineteenth century.
(*Historical Collections of Ohio*)

ony's adopted son, Peter Manor, or Yellow Hair—who had been
granted a section of land in the Treaty at the Foot of the Rapids—
operated a sawmill for the local Indians and the growing number
of settlers. Here, too, was an important council ground for the
Ottawa, situated under a huge white elm tree that stood on the
west side of the river, and measuring five feet across and rising fifty
feet before its branches began. Young Howard remembered what
a quiet place it was to sit under the Council Elm and listen to the
rapids running over the river's rocky bottom. The Indians had
truly chosen the perfect place for their councils.[34]

Much like Henry Harvey, who probably sympathized more
with the Shawnee's dilemma than did his parents, Dresden
Howard understood more clearly the Ottawa's painful transition
than did his own family. He considered life along the Maumee
River in the 1820s nothing short of heaven on earth. He made
friends among the Indian children and ran wild with them in the
woods and fields like a "turkey or a partridge." In the summer,
they fished in the river, or hunted small animals and birds with
bow and arrow. Then in the fall, they headed through the woods,
stealing shellbark hickory nuts from the bears and raccoons.

Winter was the best season, especially when the snow lay deep
on the ground. The Indian boys made sleds out of elm bark measuring about one foot wide and three or four feet long. Tying pieces
of string to the front of their sleds, they would stand and wait for
as many other boys and girls as could fit on the strips of bark to
pile on behind them. When Dresden Howard was an older man,

and had become a respected farmer and even a state representative, he could still remember the joy and terror of racing down an embankment toward the river on an Indian sled over the bright snow that was as smooth as glass. "You can imagine that it was almost death to shut us away from all these pastimes," Howard later wrote, and to be "shut up in a school-room . . . , where long prayers were said morning and evening, and not a smile or whisper allowed."[35]

If it was nearly impossible for a frontier child like Dresden Howard to sit in the mission school week after week, then it was even more unbearable for an Indian boy or girl. Many came and left after only a few days. Their parents were never able to coax them back, and many fled into the woods at the mere suggestion of their possible return. Howard empathized with these children and wanted to join them. He hated the mission school so much that he planned to run away and hide in an Ottawa village; but then he thought better of it, remembering that the Indians were simply too honest and would have to tell his parents where their son had gone. Yet, as he grew older, he came to understand the mission's purpose. The traditional Indian way of life was passing away. Although not all Ottawa understood the change coming into their country, certainly not as well as the Shawnee, some of the children's parents who brought their children to the school did, and realized that new skills, like farming and carpentry for the boys and weaving and sewing for the girls, would be needed, since the old ways inevitably gave way to the new.[36]

The Ottawa came to love Reverend Van Tassel, his wife Lucia, and the other missionaries who lived among them for their kindness and generosity. They were especially fond of Reverend Coe and called him "Tender Heart." The missionaries looked optimistically at the progress that the Ottawa were making toward civilization. Unlike his young pupil Dresden Howard, Isaac Van Tassel saw the Indians as quite willing and even anxious to adapt to the ways of the white man. While they generally seemed to resist lessons in the Christian faith, they were very interested in learning how to read in their own language. After another minister, named Sidney Brewster, arrived from Geauga County in 1824 to help out at the mission, Isaac and Lucia Van Tassel had more time to master the Ottawa language, which they rightly identified as a dialect of Chippewa. The couple became so fluent that they were able to translate the Our Father, the Ten Commandments, several hymns, and spelling lessons into Ottawa. They had them printed in Hudson, Ohio, for use at their mission school. Brewster's help also gave Reverend Van Tassel more time to travel to other Ottawa reserves in the Maumee River valley. He was able to open a school at one of them, and even won some converts to the faith.[37]

There was another area where the Van Tassels and their mission family were justly proud of helping the tribe. They were able to convince many of the Ottawa chiefs to develop a plan for ending the whiskey trade on their reserves. The missionaries often complained to their governing board that the Indians were "surrounded by fraudulent, corrupting white men" and so "enslaved by habits of intemperance." After three years of working diligently with the Ottawa, Van Tassel was overjoyed when the chiefs finally called a council to address the problem of drunkenness among their people. They agreed to ban whiskey and other spirits from their reserves, and enforced their decision by appointing several young men to destroy any liquor brought onto their land, either by a white man or an Indian. By 1828, Reverend Van Tassel could happily report to the Presbyterian Mission Synod in Pittsburgh that when the Ottawa had given up drink, they were better engaged in the civilization process, planting more acres of corn and building sturdier houses, and some even joining the Presbyterian Church.[38]

Benjamin Stickney, the Indian agent who served the Ottawa during the early 1820s, reported similar progress among the tribe to the American government. He observed that the Ottawa had many domestic animals, including hogs, cattle, and chickens, which they took with them on their winter hunts. While learning how to farm with iron plows, they asked Stickney, in the spring of 1824, to buy several of them. They were extremely careful with their annuity payments, monitoring them down to the last cent, and kept a watchful eye on the exact sections of land they owned in the Maumee River valley. The Ottawa were equally protective of the rights of the whites who lived among them. For example, they demanded that Peter Manor be given clear title to the land that had been awarded to him in the Treaty at the Foot of the Rapids. Manor did not want to lose his mill or his farm because he did not have a proper deed. The Ottawa also asked Stickney to find a blacksmith to repair their guns and farm equipment and to shoe their horses.[39]

Agent Stickney did his best to obtain everything the Ottawa needed as they made the transition to a new way of life. He was impressed with their history, especially their language, and like the Van Tassels, he did his best to master it. As the Ottawa tried to work their reserves, just like the American farmers did, Stickney was most amazed that they were still able to keep up many of their ancient customs, most especially their dances. He watched as they built walled enclosures for these dances, most of which took place in the summer, and he was convinced that the many Indian mounds throughout Ohio had once been enclosures for similar dancing grounds. "I have seen one thousand persons," he wrote to Governor Lewis Cass in 1824, "in motion at once performing the circuit of the dance, in single file between these walls." Having resigned themselves to life on their reserves in Ohio, which totaled close to 30,000 acres, and accepting the help of Presbyterian missionaries, families like the Howards, and government annuities that came by way of their Indian agent, the Ottawa seemed to have struck a delicate balance between themselves and the Americans that would keep them safe in Ohio forever.[40]

For a time, after signing the Treaty at the Foot of the Rapids, and the treaties at St. Mary's one year later, the Wyandot were able to maintain a similar balance between their traditional way of life and the demands of the future. In the spring and summer, they planted their crops in the deep black soil of their reserves. After the fall harvest, they still left their villages to hunt in small groups in the surrounding countryside. They went as far as twenty-five miles beyond the borders of their reserves in the wintertime, with Hardin County, still mostly empty of settlers, being their favorite spot. There they took hundreds of pounds of wild game and collected the highly prized bear fat, which they would use throughout the year. In February and March, they headed back to their reserves, stopping at the stands of sugar maple trees on the way.

The women tapped them, collected sap, and boiled it into syrup for use as the only condiment in Wyandot cooking.[41]

Much like the Ottawa and the Presbyterians, the Wyandot at first received help from the Methodists without the asking. Many older Wyandot were Catholic and had been so since the days when the French ruled the Great Lakes. They could be seen carrying rosary beads and wearing crucifixes. In 1803, when Joseph Badger opened a Presbyterian mission at Lower Sandusky (now Fremont, Ohio), the Wyandot who were Catholic protested, even murdering some of the converts. The Presbyterians finally withdrew from the area right before the War of 1812.[42] But in 1816, the year before the tribe signed the Treaty at the Foot of the Rapids, a young Methodist preacher by the name of John Stewart had arrived in Upper Sandusky. He had followed his parents, who were both former slaves, from Virginia to Marietta during the year of the Great Migration. Stewart had many adventures on his way north, including his conversion to Christianity. At one point, while in prayer or perhaps even in a dream, he heard God tell him to go to the "north." Eventually he found his way to the Wyandot reserve at Upper Sandusky. Jonathan Pointer, the black man who lived with Tarhe, befriended him and helped him minister to the Wyandot. Stewart had a beautiful singing voice, and some Wyandot converted after listening to him sing while preaching.

Stewart's most influential supporter was William Walker Sr. He was a white man who had been kidnapped by the Delaware in Virginia when he was eleven. Walker always remembered the bright sunny day when he was riding a horse, with his uncle plowing a field behind him. No one had been taken by Indians in this part of Virginia for some time, so they were surprised when shots rang out, and the cry of "Indians!" went up from their settlement. William and his uncle ran for the fort and almost made it; but at the last minute his uncle was shot dead, and he was snatched away. Young Walker was taken across the Ohio River, where he lived for a time with the Delaware until a white man who knew his family ransomed him. Walker remained among the Indians and married Catherine Rankin. Her mother was the daughter of a French trader and a Wyandot woman of the Big Turtle Clan. Her father, James Rankin, was an Irish trader who worked for the Hudson

Bay Company. Now known as Catherine Walker, she was greatly beloved by the Wyandot and was frequently used as an interpreter at important councils. She supported Stewart, even though many in the tribe, both the Catholics and the traditionalists, opposed him. With help from the Walkers, Stewart won a few converts to the faith and tried his best to deal with the growing problem of drunkenness among the Wyandot.

Real success finally came for Stewart in February 1817, when he preached on the Last Judgment. Standing in a wooden shed with one side open to the bitter wind, and facing a small group of Wyandot huddled in front of him, he preached so eloquently that many Indians swooned and shouted to be saved, fearing a life of eternal damnation. Others begged him to stop speaking and to end this awful commotion. Then a Wyandot woman jumped to her feet, clasped her hands before her and fell to her knees, thanking Jesus for saving her from her sins and rescuing her from the everlasting flames of hell. The experience of the Holy Spirit moving like this through a crowd might have been common enough in a camp meeting among American settlers on the western frontier, but the Wyandot had never known anything like it.[43]

Many chiefs, including Between the Logs, Mononcue, Squire Grey Eyes, Matthew Peacock, and John Hicks, were converted on the spot. They remembered this night as the great dividing line between the old world and the new. For Between the Logs, especially, his Christian faith brought an inner peace like nothing he had ever experienced. He had been a highly emotional young man who was able to control his feelings when acting as the principal speaker of the tribe, but not when dealing with troubles in his private life. When a Wyandot "wretch" spread rumors that Between the Log's wife was a witch, the young chief, so drunk that he did not know what he was doing, stabbed his wife to death. Still suffering from deep guilt for this senseless act, his newfound faith brought a meaning and purpose to his life that the ancient beliefs of his tribe could no longer satisfy. He also embraced the call of the Methodist faith to give up liquor of all kinds. Temperance would bring his people salvation in this world, while their faith would secure eternal life for them in the next. It would also help them cope with the trauma of Tarhe's death, and face the many trials that lay before them, including the humiliating Treaty at the Foot of the Rapids and the tribe's removal to two small reserves.

Between the Logs became so certain of the good that Christianity could do for the Wyandot that he set out for Zanesville, Ohio, hoping to convince more Methodist preachers and teachers to come and help Reverend Stewart build a church and mission school on the Grand Reserve. He told them that the Wyandot had chosen a section of land for the school on high ground west of the Sandusky River, with a spring

Between the Logs, a Wyandot chief and Christian convert in an 1827 engraving. (*Author*)

flowing nearby. There the children would be safe from the spring rains and have fresh water to drink. Between the Logs knew this was a good location because Governor Return Jonathan Meigs had chosen this same spot as his camp for the Ohio militia in the War of 1812. The chief added that the Wyandot would give $200 a year to support a church and a mission school.

The Methodists heard the call, sending first another minister, Moses Heckle, to help Stewart, and then, in early 1821, Reverend James Finley and his mission family. Finley went to Upper Sandusky somewhat reluctantly, thinking he had neither the patience nor the training to open a school for Indian children. But his local bishop in Kentucky, Reverend Thomas McKendree, who had long been interested in ministering to the Indians as well as to the settlers, thought otherwise. So Finley yoked his oxen, loaded a wagon with household goods, and headed down the old trail from the town of Warren in eastern Ohio with his wife, two hired hands, and a young teacher named Harriet Stubbs. It took them eight days in October 1821 to travel 150 miles to the Grand Reserve.

As soon as they arrived, Finley went to work building his mission. From four in the morning until nine at night every day of the week but Sunday, he chopped down trees, hauled logs to the sawmill, and then brought the lumber back to Camp Meigs. The work was so hard that his hands bled as he labored and one of his workers deserted him. Yet he pressed on with building a school and homes for his mission family, along with clearing ground for a farm nearby. On the Sabbath, he rested from his labors and took time to preach to the Wyandot in their old council house. Sometimes John Stewart helped him by holding weekly prayer meetings, but he was suffering from consumption and so grew weaker day by day.[44]

As hard as life was, Reverend Finley and his company continued on through the end of 1821 and into 1822. He made sure never to ask the Wyandot for help, considering this a sign of respect for the tribe. He had come to serve the Wyandot, and did not want them working for him as common laborers. Finley did ask several chiefs to serve as administrators on the board of directors for the school. The little mission family soon won the love and respect of many of the Wyandot, with Harriet Stubbs becoming the favorite. She had given up a comfortable life in the home of her brother-in-law, Judge John McLean, to teach the Wyandot children. Even before the mission school was finished, the girls followed her about the Grand Reserve from sunup to sundown. They quickly learned the alphabet from their young teacher, whom everyone called "Red Bird" because the red cape she wore reminded them of the beautiful cardinal.[45]

Finally, in the summer of 1823, just about a year and a half since Finley and his followers had arrived in Upper Sandusky, the Wyandot Indian Mission opened for business with sixty-nine "scholars." At first some Wyandots vowed they would never send their children to school; but that changed once the respected Chief Squire Grey Eyes led his daughter Margaret by hand to the mission. Then many of the other chiefs decided to bring their children to the school. Since all the students boarded there, some children came from as far away as Canada. Later, even a few children of local white settlers enrolled at the school.[46] Missionaries first made sure the Indian children were free of lice and fleas. They washed the bear grease out of their hair and taught them how to brush and comb it. The children were allowed to keep the leggings and moccasins their mothers had made for them, but they were also given new linen clothes made from the flax that the missionaries grew. These linen clothes included shirts, belts for their hunting knives, and bandanas for the boys, and smocks dyed with bright colors for the girls. Ribbons were used to tie the girls' hair in braids.

In the morning, the students and their teachers prayed and ate together. Then they had their lessons. The boys learned farming, carpentry, and animal husbandry, while the girls learned how to cook, clean, spin, knit, and sew. Finley noticed early on that the boys had a much tougher time settling into the school routine than the girls. He decided to divide them into teams so they could compete against each other. This made a big difference and soon the boys were learning as easily as the girls. Everyone took lessons in reading, writing, spelling, arithmetic, and the fundamentals of the Methodist faith. They also worked side by side on the mission farm. Fifty of the 140 acres that belonged to the mission were planted in corn, while vegetables like turnips, cabbage, and potatoes were raised on the rest. Animals were kept in pens made from logs from Fort Feree, built in Upper Sandusky during the War of 1812. On the weekends, the students were encouraged to go home to their families so they could worship side by side. Only children who had come all the way from Canada remained over on Sundays.[47]

The greatest problem remaining for the Wyandot Indian Mission was the lack of a church. Finley continued to preach in the old council house covered with elm bark, even though it lacked a fireplace and had a dirt floor. He often complained that the place was hot in summer and cold in winter. He could not use the school as a church because it was too small to hold the growing numbers of Wyandot parents and their children who came for services on the weekend. In order to raise money for the mission, Finley set out for Washington, where he was able to meet first with President Monroe and later his secretary of war, Calhoun, whom Finley believed showed a remarkable concern for the Indians. When many of the Wyandot chiefs complained about the tribe's subagent, Calhoun dismissed him and appointed Reverend Finley in his place. After Finley explained the need for a church at Upper Sandusky, he offered him $1,333 from the Civilization Fund to build it. Finley asked if this was an appropriate way to use the government's money. He never forgot the secretary's response, and recorded it years later in his memoir of his time among the Wyandot. Calhoun said yes and added his profound hope that "it might remain a house of worship when both of us are no more."[48]

When Finley got back to the Grand Reserve, he did not have to build his church alone. This time the Wyandot men came without being asked. They hitched their horses to wagons and headed for the shallow bottom of the Sandusky River, where they dug out the blue limestone that had formed eons before and hauled it back to the place where their house of worship was to stand. Soon the thirty-by-forty-foot building with wooden floors and limestone walls rose not far from the school. Finley was so proud of his church that he predicted "it would stand if not torn down for a century to come."[49]

When John Johnston paid a visit to the Wyandot as their agent, he was impressed with the progress that the tribe had made at the mission. The children were better behaved in their classes than any frontier children he had ever seen, and the same could be said for the way the Wyandot conducted themselves at Sunday services. "A better congregation, in behavior, I have not beheld," wrote Johnston to Bishop McKendree. He noted that the spirit of industry seen at the mission and its school seemed to be working its way throughout the whole of the Grand Reserve, heading out amid the fine log cabins with brick and stone chimneys that the Wyandot had built, amid the cornfields enclosed by sturdy fences, and amid the well-kept herds of cattle, horses, and sheep. Everywhere he looked, a "spirit of order, industry, and improvement" prevailed.[50] If a stranger had come upon the farms of the Grand Reserve, he might have thought he stumbled onto a thriving community of American pioneers.

Many other visitors who made their way through northwestern Ohio in the late 1820s and early 1830s saw much the same thing that Johnston had observed. The Indians were making the transition from the life of the warrior and the hunter to one more like the white man. Travelers who passed through what remained of Indian country commented on the happiness and prosperity of the tribes they met along the way, especially the Wyandot under the tutelage of the Methodists. Others noticed the success of the

Seneca, who had "settled down" on their reserve just north of the Wyandot with no help from Christian missionaries.

One such visitor was an Englishman named William Bullock. In 1827, he traveled from Cincinnati to Urbana, Ohio, and then headed to Sandusky, on the southern edge of Lake Erie. As he made his way north, he was most impressed with the beauty of the Seneca reserve. He noticed its park-like setting, in which the woods had been carefully cleared. Bullock was struck at how much the reserve looked like the gardens of the English nobility back home. "We wished to enter some of their houses, which were well built, with sash windows and shingle roofs," he later wrote in a memoir about his trip, "but we were told in general they avoided receiving the visits of white strangers." Bullock was convinced the Indians were quite comfortable as evidenced by the "cultivated fields" and "large herds of cattle and horses." The Indians who did approach him deeply impressed him:

> Near one village, we met a young Indian driving a handsome wagon, drawn by four remarkably fine oxen, which would have done credit to any English gentleman; the youth was well-dressed, and passed our carriage with a look that sufficiently marked his consequence. . . . We also conversed with several Indians, some of whom were on horseback, armed with rifles; they were civil, and seemed pleased that we took notice of them. A squaw, with her son behind her, accompanied us some miles. Her dress was a loose blue cloth coat, with scarlet pantaloons, black beaver hat and feathers, and her face was painted bright red.[51]

Surely the Seneca had a deep and abiding sense that they had won the race laid out for them by the Americans. In only a dozen years, they had given up the ancient round of hunting and farming in order to become year-round tillers of the soil and respectable property owners. The Indians could take comfort in the certain hope that when visitors to their country gave way to farmers who settled on land near the remaining reserves, they would be so impressed with the progress of the tribes that they would let them live in peace, not just for a little while, but forever.

FIVE

On the Edge of Eternity

As the Shawnee and Wyandot were becoming success stories of surviving and even thriving on their reserves in Ohio, questions arose among the Indians themselves about the value of this experiment. These questions centered on the purpose of the removal of the tribes to smaller pieces of ground within their former territory. What had this type of removal actually meant to accomplish? Had the tribes agreed to live on these reserves so that they could follow the ways of the white man? As they headed down the path toward becoming farmers and housewives and, for some of them, Christians, would they have to give up all their ancient customs? If they did, would they simply merge into the wider American population inching closer to the boundaries of their reserves each day? Or had the tribes agreed to this removal so they could preserve their customs while adapting the best that the white man had to offer on their own terms, and so prepare for the inevitable arrival of the encroaching Americans and at the same time remaining true to themselves?

For James Finley, Methodist minister to the Wyandot, the answer to all these questions was clear: removal of the Indians to smaller reserves helped the tribes make a successful transition to civilization in this world, while it prepared them for an even better life in the next. At Upper Sandusky and Big Spring, he watched as Christianity grew and thrived among the Wyandot. Finley would carry stories of the wonder of this transformation with him throughout his life. Even when he left his work with the tribe to minister first to frontier farmers and later to prisoners in Ohio's new state penitentiary, he was haunted by memories of the faith of the Wyandot. He saw it best at summertime camp meetings, when hundreds of Indians gathered to pray in open fields to "Shasus," the Wyandot name for Jesus. They would leave their ponies, each tied with a bell around its neck, in the tall blue grass nearby, and then cross the open meadows to pray under the trees. The campground was lit by candles that had been set up on posts all around. The ringing of the bells and the voices of the Wyandot singing the old Methodist hymns in their own language, all in the twilight of a summer evening on the Ohio frontier, made it seem that Finley and the whole tribe had crossed over to heaven while still living on this side of the grave.[1]

He saw the wonder of it all in the winter, too, especially on a dark afternoon in January 1822, when he traveled fifteen miles from Upper Sandusky into the surrounding woods to a long funeral train. It was New Year's Day, and snow clouds lay heavy in the sky. Finley and his companions among the tribe were taking an old woman, known in his memoirs simply as the "mother of Jaco," to her final resting place. Finley had made the coffin for the woman himself. He now looked around him and saw the Wyandot wrapped in their blankets leaning against the bare trees in deepest sorrow. All was silence, with only a few women weeping, until Chief Mononcue cried out, "Farewell, my old and precious aunt! You have suffered much in this world of sin and sorrow." Then he thanked her for the good example she had set and for looking after her family. "That hand that fed us will feed us no more," cried the chief. "We weep not with sorrow, but with joy, that your soul is in heaven." Finley remembered how they had gone back home with snow falling all around, but comforted in the knowledge that there was a purpose to their lives beyond this world: "Blessed are the dead that die in the Lord from henceforth," Finley later wrote in his *History of the Wyandott Mission*.[2]

According to Finley, it was more than the rhythm of the seasons that had changed for the Wyandot. The very rhythms of the lives of the men, women, and even children had changed as well. He often recalled how the Wyandot children would go off on their own in small groups into the fields to pray. The young girls especially seemed more willing to talk about their faith when they had become Christians. The same new boldness could be seen in older women who prophesied for Christ. Finley often told the story of a woman greatly opposed to the new faith, who one night had a dream similar to the Shawnee Prophet's vision many years before but with a decidedly Christian undertone. The woman saw two paths laid out before her. One was a smooth road to the left, which was crowded with moccasin footprints, while the other was a steep hill on the right, which few were traveling. She woke from her dream with a start after realizing that the crowded road led to perdition, and the less trodden path to heaven. She became a Christian immediately and did her best to convert others in her tribe.[3]

Finley remembered that warriors, too, were just as deeply affected by the new faith. His first convert was Big Tree, an aging Wyandot who complained that he was always tired and ached all over, probably from rheumatism. He was a big man, like his name implied, who still dressed in the ancient style of the tribe, with his long hair wrapped in a silver tube and a silver-encased jewel in his nose. Big Tree had been a great warrior since the days when the French and English fought for his country. But the time of the warrior was now passed, and Big Tree could no longer find any purpose to his life, so he spent most of his waking hours drinking whiskey. One day alone in the woods, he lay down on the ground, crying out to God and asking him why he was still alive? Why must he go on when there was no hope? It was then that the peace of God descended on him. "I felt young again," he later told Finley. He was amazed at how he could now communicate with an all-loving God every moment, and the experience of prayer changed him for the good. He had the will to live again and face whatever came his way. He would endure, just as Christ endured every suffering and yet triumphed in his Resurrection. No misery in this world was so great that the promise of eternal life could not lift the burden.[4]

But perhaps most of all, Finley remembered how many of the chiefs, most especially Between the Logs and Mononcue, had become ministers themselves and were better preachers than he. He brought them to speak to other tribes, like the nearby Seneca, and even the Chippewa, who lived far to the north in the Michigan Territory. He also took them to camp meetings, where the Indian preachers exhorted the settlers to live their faith, not merely to recite from the Bible or a catechism by rote. They may have spoken in broken English, but had more than made up for this by their powerful sermons. Having been trained through years of speaking to Indian councils, sometimes including many tribes, the chiefs were able to express themselves in a manner that most white people had only seen played out on stage.

Mononcue was one of several Wyandot chiefs who traveled east to raise money for the Wyandot Indian Mission. (*New-York Historical Society*)

The chiefs traveled with Finley to the quarterly meetings of the Ohio Methodists in Columbus, and in 1826, they joined him on a speaking tour through the eastern states to raise money for the Wyandot Indian Mission, and visited New York, Philadelphia, and Washington. Mononcue was most impressed with the great sea turtle he saw in a museum in New York City. Even though he was now a devout Christian, he called the creature his "grandmother," remembering the Wyandot tale of how long ago the world had been built up on the back of a giant turtle and how he was himself a member of the Big Turtle Clan. "I have seen many of her children," he exclaimed, "but never have I seen *her* before."[5]

Why was this new faith important to so many Wyandot, and why, after some resistance, did they embrace it on their new reserves so willingly? In a trying time, a belief in Christ gave meaning to a world that was collapsing all around them, along with bringing the certain hope of an eternal reward from God in the next. But just as important, it helped the Wyandot overcome the worst parts of the traditional Indian way of life that survived the disintegration, most especially the day-to-day violence that was so common among families and villages. Christianity taught a new

discipline of controlling one's emotions and forgiving one's enemies, both within and outside of the tribe. How many Indian
homes, not only the family of Between the Logs, had been torn
apart by murders committed in a moment of rage or because of
the need for revenge? The coming of Christianity to the reserves
transformed them from mere geographic areas or lines drawn on a
map, as the Americans understood them, into new worlds with
inner dimensions of law and order. This was most apparent within families, in which the Christian belief in the sanctity of marriage as a covenant, in other words "till death do us part," ended
casual divorce common among Indians and helped stabilize the
rearing of children.

Between the Logs understood the powerful transformation
occurring on the Ohio reserves better than any other Wyandot
chief. He had seen the men of his tribe go from being feared warriors at Fallen Timbers, where at only fourteen he fought alongside Tarhe the Crane, to becoming a "nation of drunkards" after
the War of 1812 ended. In between, he and his people had looked
to Tenkswatawa and Handsome Lake to help them find a way out
of their suffering, but both proved to be "imposters." He, along
with most of the Wyandot, sided with the Americans in the final
war against Great Britain, only to see their country whittled down
to less than a handful of townships. In the aftermath of so much
loss, the Wyandot turned against each other, and even a chief as
eloquent as Between the Logs could do little to stop them. The
chaos had entered his own household when he murdered his wife
in a drunken rage. Although he never took another drink again,
and later married the widow of Tarhe the Crane, he still found no
way out of the terrible condition into which he and his people had
fallen.[6]

Many Wyandot finally found the peace they were seeking on
that bitterly cold night in February 1817, when John Stewart
preached about the Last Judgment in the little shed standing open
to the wind on the Grand Reserve. "The work broke out,"
Between the Logs remembered, and God went on to do "great
things for us." The chief always described his conversion as a passage from darkness to light. The darkness included many things
from the ancient round of rituals and sacrifices to the modern

addiction to whiskey. Once in the bright light of the Christian faith, the Wyandot experienced a prayerful relationship with God, and relief from the senseless misery that came from all of the traumatic changes in their recent lives. Now spouses remained faithful to each other, and understood their primary duty was to protect their children, feed and clothe them, teach them right from wrong, and correct them when they made mistakes, but always to do it in a spirit of love. Christianity brought a certain order to families, and this soon worked its way to the entire tribe. The chiefs now saw a more profound aspect in their role as tribal leaders, who would perform their duties faithfully and watch over their people, making decisions about what was best for everyone in this life and ultimately what would be best for them in the next.

For the Wyandot, temperance was perhaps the greatest gift the Methodist faith brought them. Reverend Finley, like every other circuit rider on the western frontier, demanded that his new converts formally pledge to give up drinking forever. This made perfect sense to the Wyandot, who had long recognized the destruction that liquor brought. Men and women wanted whiskey, rum, and wine so badly that they would abandon their children and even kill each other for it. The whole tribe sank into debt, owing money to traders for whiskey and other goods that they could only pay for with furs. Thus, at the very time when they were trying to make the transition to a more settled way of life, they were forced to go hunting, not only for the purpose of feeding their families, since they were now farmers, but also to pay for items that they had used long before. Soon the money that came as part of their annuity payments was not enough to pay off their mounting debts. "I can compare whiskey to nothing but the devil," explained Chief Mononcue at a camp meeting, "for it brings with it all kind of evil." He then went on to give a litany of the miseries that the whiskey trade had brought into his country: it destroyed happiness and made the Indians poor; it deprived wives and children of food and clothing; it made men and women lie, steal, cheat, and even kill to get more drink. "It is a great curse to your own people," argued Mononcue. "Why not cease making it?"[7]

The order that pervaded the inner lives of the Wyandot was expressed in their outer lives as well. Even the most embittered traditionalists recognized that the old cycle of hunting in the fall and winter, and farming in the spring and summer, was dying. As the Americans moved closer, the ancient forests of elm and sycamore were brought down, and the bears and panthers were disappearing. When the tribe went on winter hunts, they had to go as far west as the White River in Indiana. Even there the country was filling up with the farms and towns of the Americans. The choice before the Wyandot was clear: change or die.

Property ownership was the most important change for the tribe. Like other Indian tribes, the Wyandot had always held their land in common. In the spring the women planted crops, and in the fall they harvested them. In accordance with the Treaty at the Foot of the Rapids, they had moved away from common ownership of the land by listing every Wyandot who was to receive a section of reserve land; but they did not immediately implement this provision. Ten years later, in 1827, the tribe decided to give 160 acres to every family on the Grand Reserve. If a family was large, they might receive additional acres. Families could retain their land and pass it on to their descendants as long as they remained on the Grand Reserve. No Wyandot could sell land to another Indian or to a white person, since this might lead to only a handful of families owning most of the reserve. However, they could exchange land among themselves. All the land not given to specific families would be held in reserve by the tribe as common pasture lands, or as grants for future generations.[8]

In an important sense, the Wyandot had become pioneers like their American neighbors. The people who visited the Grand Reserve, including Bishop James McKendree, commented on the rapid improvements that the tribe was making. Everywhere they looked there were well-built log houses with stone and brick chimneys; glass windows with sashes; wood floors; fenced-in fields of grain and hay; herds of horses, cattle, and sheep; and acres of apple and peach orchards. They saw children respectful in their lessons in school and pious congregations to match any seen on the frontier. Compared to the ruin that the tribe had sunk to little more than a decade earlier, the transformation was nothing short of miraculous. Truly the Wyandot had come close to achieving a heaven on earth.[9]

For chiefs like Between the Logs and Mononcue, along with respected leaders like Squire Grey Eyes, John Hicks, and Matthew Peacock, the Wyandot were living a better life on their small reserves than they had ever known previously in their former territory. They retained their tribal identity and government, even as they took on new customs from the whites, including better ways to farm and raise livestock, educate their children, and practice religion. In the end, they saw the process as beneficial—one that they were able to control by themselves. Yet there were other members of the tribe who viewed removal to the Grand Reserve and Big Spring in a totally different light. While they, too, had agreed to live on smaller pieces of ground, they did not believe that this meant they were to become pale copies of the Americans. Their most ancient customs, especially their spiritual ones, must be maintained at all cost. If Reverend Finley was right that the township reserves were somehow on the edge of eternity, then it must be that the Wyandot could preserve the beliefs they had held since time immemorial.

Deunquod, head chief of the Wyandot and leader of those who opposed the Methodists, expressed this position in a variety of ways. One of his favorite methods was to harass Reverend Finley during church services. He and his followers, who represented perhaps half of the tribe, often came fully dressed in traditional garb with their faces painted. Deunquod made sure he was covered in silver from head to toe. He wore bands of the shining metal around his head that were decorated with feathers and dyed horsehair, and wrapped silver around his arms and legs and hung silver half-moon shapes on his chest and down his back. Animals were painted on his clothes, while snakes were drawn up and down on his arms. Around his ankles, he tied deer hooves that rattled as he walked. His followers were dressed in much the same way, and made a terrible clacking noise as they marched into the council house. They sat at the front on the ground and puffed their pipes, blowing smoke at Finley.[10]

After Finley was finished preaching, Deunquod proceeded to argue the finer points of the faith, especially where Christianity and the Bible were contradictory. He learned about this from the local whiskey traders, who knew the Bible well enough to discredit the preacher and make sure their trade continued. Were there really so many rules and regulations in the Bible? Had not Moses come down from the mountain with God's laws written on stone tablets, only to smash those same tablets when he saw the Israelites worshipping idols? If the tablets were gone, then surely the law was gone. Even if Finley could find a few remaining rules, Deunquod argued that the God of the white man had made laws for the white man, while the God of the red man had done the same for his people. He knew for a fact that in the days of their grandfathers the two gods had met far to the west to determine once and for all whose religion would rule this continent. They decided that whoever had the power to move a mountain would win. The god of the white man opened his Bible, and got down on his knees and shouted at the mountain, but nothing happened. Then the god of the red man struck his stick on the turtle shell of the earth, and the mountain crumbled. Surely this was proof that this continent belonged to the red man and his god, not to the whites and their god.[11]

For Deunquod and his supporters, the Wyandot tale of Aataentsaic, the Woman Who Fell from Heaven, made more sense than the biblical story of Creation. When the woman tumbled from the sky, the animals worked together to make a home for her. They built up dirt on the back of a giant sea turtle, just like the one Mononcue had seen in the museum in New York City. Later, the woman had a daughter who gave birth to twin sons, Tsestah, the "Man of Fire," and Tawiskaron, "the "Man of Flint." The battle between these two brothers began all the conflict in the world, which created a kind of tension that was necessary for everything to function properly. Again, this seemed a more reasonable explanation of the realities of this life than did a good God fighting a fallen angel named Lucifer. In the end, after the struggles of this world were done, the Wyandot believed all would be well: there would be no final judgment of people's souls, as the Christians preached, with some going to heaven and others condemned to hell. Instead, the Wyandot would go to a paradise below the earth, which the animals had made for them as their eternal home. There they would forever enjoy the ancient cycle of life that the tribe had known on earth, from spring to summer and from fall to winter.

They would farm and fish and hunt, and live in villages with their families. There would be no want, no hunger, and no death, only endless happiness.[12]

Living at Lower Sandusky, just north of the Big Spring reserve, the Seneca rejected Christianity even more completely than did Deunquod and his followers. They saw life on their new reserve quite differently from the Wyandot who had become Methodists. Here was a place where they could live outwardly like the white man, but inwardly remain true to their own identity. The tribe followed the *Gaiwiio*, or "Good Word," of Handsome Lake, the Iroquois prophet who had visited their villages along the Sandusky River in 1806 and 1807. Handsome Lake taught them that, like devout Christians, they must practice a strict morality, and give up bad habits that were destroying their people, especially witchcraft, drinking, and disregard for family life. Husbands and wives must be faithful to each other, and should welcome children and care for them, just as they must cherish their elders. The prophet also told them to live in peace with the Americans who were steadily moving closer. They could adopt the white man's ways to make their lives better, but they need not go to the white man's schools. They should not follow Christianity, a religion intended by the Creator for the whites, but must instead practice their own traditions, which Handsome Lake urged them to simplify so as not to upset the whites.[13]

The Seneca generally agreed with the teachings of Handsome Lake, but sometimes ignored his recommendation to keep the peace with the whites by modifying their traditions. The most important custom they decided to maintain with no changes was the White Dog Sacrifice of midwinter. Handsome Lake told them to perform the ancient ceremony with deer, not with dogs, since the white man cherished them. For a while, the tribe acceded to his request before using dogs once again. Amid the orderly farms and well-built homes of their reserve along the Sandusky, they gathered outside the tribe's main council house at dawn in early February to perform the rite. Just as the first rays of the morning came up over the horizon, the tribe took two spotless white dogs, one male and one female, strangled them, and then hung them on crosses. Each one was decorated with red and white ribbons, which were tied about their muzzles, eyes, ears, and front and back paws.[14]

A man named Samuel Crowell witnessed the last White Dog ceremony held in Ohio on February 1, 1830. He remembered that a young Seneca named Good Hunter told him why the tribe had gone back to using dogs instead of deer. They did so after Good Hunter himself had a terrible dream. In it, he was being chased by some unknown power, and no matter how fast he ran, the awful thing kept following him. He was terrified that it would chase him all the way west to the distant ocean. Then suddenly, Good Hunter came upon a canoe and paddled it safely home. When he awoke and described his dream to the Seneca at Lower Sandusky, they tried to interpret its meaning, but none saw it as the obvious reflection of the white man's relentless pushing of the tribes westward to the point of driving them into the sea, as Tecumseh had predicted so long ago. Instead, they thought the dream portended that the Great Spirit was angry at his people for stopping the White Dog Sacrifice. They had become too much like the white man, both within as well as without.

When they renewed the ancient festival of midwinter, the tribe used it as a chance to reflect back on the life they had lost, but still could not forget. In the first light of a day chosen in February, the month of the Hunger Moon, they gathered around their head chief. He spoke of all that he had accomplished as a warrior, of his bravery, and the number of scalps he had taken. Despite all the changes that had come upon the Seneca, he vowed that he would remain a warrior forever, even if the Americans pushed him into the Rocky Mountains. Then he ordered the young men to take the dogs down from their crosses and bring them to him. After the dogs were placed in his arms, the chief carefully laid them on the pile of burning logs near the council house. He continued to pray over them, throwing sweet-smelling tobacco on the fire, until they were completely consumed like a biblical holocaust. Everyone then entered the council house, where they first sat in a circle, feasted on corn, bread, and game, and later danced and sang old melodies long into the night. All was as it had been before and would be for all time.[15]

The Wyandot who were now Methodists thought their Seneca brethren to the north had gone mad for clinging to ancient super-stitions, even as they tried to modernize their way of life. They thought the same of Deunquod, and openly confronted him. Between the Logs told the chief to take his supporters and go. The tribe would simply have to split in two. But Deunquod backed down, vowing he would do his best as the head of the tribe to keep the Wyandot together. In keeping with his promise, he stopped coming to church services, to mock the faith and spar with Finley; however he ended up supporting the mission school, and converted to the faith in 1825.[16]

But the Seneca were not as easily convinced, despite frequent meetings with Methodist preachers from the Wyandot nation. In these encounters, Mononcue led the way in condemning the killing of dogs and all the other ancient practices. Drawing from the opening chapter of Genesis, he asked, "Do you suppose the great God that spread out the heavens, that hung up the sun and moon, and all the stars to make light, and spread out this vast world of land and water, and filled it with men and beasts, and every thing that swims or flies, is pleased with the smell of your burnt dogs?" Then, echoing the words of the Prophet Joel, he said, "Rend your hearts, not your garments." He went on to proclaim, "I tell you to-day, that his great eye is on your hearts, and not on your fires." Mononcue's challenge to the Seneca was clear: Change yourselves. Grow more merciful and less vengeful. Live in accordance with the law that God had written on your hearts for a better life in this world and a still better one in the next. In this way, he seemed to imply, their tribal reserves would be transformed from a prison to a paradise.[17]

The Seneca could not agree, and more and more chafed against the confinement on their reserve at Lower Sandusky. The pressure to remain and become like the white man was revolting to them. Many other Indians agreed. No one hated the changes that had come upon the tribes more than Tecumseh's brother, the Prophet. His long fall from grace, which began with the loss at Tippecanoe, had continued throughout the War of 1812. No longer respected for his supernatural powers, he had stayed on at Prophetstown when Tecumseh left to fight with the British. Even though he later sent Pottawatomi warriors to attack Fort Harrison and Fort Wayne, the Prophet never participated directly in any battle. He followed his brother on his final retreat into Canada, but stood back from the fighting along the Thames in October 1813. Sitting astride his horse at the side of General Procter, he watched as Harrison's men cut down Tecumseh and his followers in the meadow near the river. Fearing for his own life, he fled with the British toward Hamilton, Ontario, and did not stop until he was safely out of Harrison's reach.[18]

With Tecumseh dead, Tenkswatawa lost what little influence he still had over their shattered confederation. Only his immediate family, which included Tecumseh's son, Paukeesaa, along with some Shawnee and Kickapoo warriors and their families, stayed with him. The loss of his power was almost unbearable for the Prophet. He demanded respect from the British and tried with all his might to convince them that he was now the leader of a still-great Indian confederation. He told them that he had been chosen as the war chief of all the combined tribes, while his nephew was the village chief. "I am now put in the place of my Brother!" he proclaimed. "I expect to be listened to as he was!" The British were willing to feed and supply the Prophet's followers as long as their ships could still make it across the Great Lakes.[19]

Until the bitter end, which finally came in the fall of 1814 during the treaty negotiations at Ghent, the British were willing to pretend that someone in Tecumseh's immediate family might be able to assume leadership of an Indian nation somewhere south of the Great Lakes and north of the Ohio River. Governor General Prevost, who tried to rebuild the tribal confederation shattered at the Thames River, presented Tecumapease, the older sister of Tecumseh, with silver, cloth, and wampum. For a time, he thought that Tecumseh's seventeen-year-old son might be the next leader of his people.[20] But the Treaty of Ghent, which ended any possibility of an Indian state, also ended the need to find someone to lead it. By the summer of 1815, British authorities in Canada were finally done with the Prophet, and did everything in their power to send him back across the Detroit River to the Americans. Like all the Indians of the old Ohio Country, the Prophet had outlived his usefulness to the British, who now sat securely behind the borders of Canada outlined at Ghent.[21]

The Prophet drifted back and forth between settlements in western Ontario for the next decade. He was late in coming to the negotiations at Springwells in September 1815 because the Shawnee in Ohio, who still considered the Prophet a dangerous fool, had cared enough about him to send a warning that Harrison was determined to take him prisoner and kill him. While the rumor proved false, the Prophet came to the negotiations a somewhat humbled man. He agreed that the war was over, and the cause for which he and his brother fought so long was truly dead. He also knew Harrison would not allow him to sign the treaty. In Harrison's eyes, the Prophet, like his brother, was merely a usurper, not a true chief. When Tenkswatawa demanded the right to settle along the River Raisin, where American troops had been massacred in the winter of 1813, Harrison denied his request. The Prophet then sent some of his followers ahead to his abandoned village along the Tippecanoe Creek with orders to rebuild it. He planned on joining them up until Governor Cass told him he was no longer welcome in the United States. Even if he were allowed back into the country, Cass explained, angry settlers along the western frontier would most certainly hunt him down and kill him.[22]

Returning to Canada, the Prophet could only watch as his reputation was permanently eclipsed by the growing legend of his brother. Tecumseh was quickly becoming a hero on both sides of the Great Lakes. The British considered him the savior of Canada. Americans who had fled from his wrath now named their towns and children after him. In contrast, the Prophet was ridiculed by everyone. Friend and foe alike gave him no credit for building the Indian confederation that had nearly dismantled the United States on the western frontier—all credit went to Tecumseh.[23] The Indians who had followed Tecumseh to Prophetstown never forgave his younger brother for the disaster of Tippecanoe, a loss from which they never fully recovered. Tribes that had stayed faithful to the United States reminded everyone of what they had always believed: the Prophet was an imposter. In the midst of near total condemnation, Tenkswatawa survived by begging provisions from the few Canadian officials who still had the patience to deal with him. He continued to receive help as late as 1823, when the British awarded £388 to the Prophet, his nephew Paukeesaa, and their six dependents for losses they had suffered during the War of 1812.[24]

The Prophet's wish to return to the land of his birth finally came true when Lewis Cass had a change of heart. Like other young men who had made their fortune on the American frontier, Cass had watched Indian warriors, once bent on destroying the United States on the western frontier, turn into the drunkards that Between the Logs bemoaned. In 1800 he had come west to Ohio from New Hampshire with his family when he was only eighteen. In those days, Indians were a terror who could strike from the edges of a settlement at dawn, or at a lonely farm at twilight, murdering the men and infants and carrying off most of the women and children. By the time Cass was a grown man, the tribes were still strong enough to forge a confederation under the charismatic Tecumseh. He had witnessed the Shawnee's power firsthand when he served as a colonel of the Ohio militia in the army of General Hull. He was horrified when Detroit fell to the British and Indians, and refused to give up his sword, smashing the weapon instead and throwing the pieces to the ground.

Cass never forgot this humiliating experience. While Tecumseh and his followers were ultimately defeated, they had terrorized settlers along the entire frontier, halted the westward migration of Americans, if only for a moment, and served as faithful allies of the British in a desperate bid to save what remained of their country. So many chiefs and warriors had died in the struggle that Governor Cass now spent much of his time feeding their widows and children. Whole clans and villages had disappeared. In the end, whatever chance the tribes had of holding onto their once vast territory disappeared, not just at the Thames River and Ghent, but at Springwells and finally at the Foot of the Rapids.[25]

But over time, Lewis Cass came to sympathize with the plight of the very tribes he had helped to defeat and then remove to small reserves throughout the old Ohio Country. Suddenly the loss of whole peoples who had been so fierce and independent troubled him. As he met more and more drunken Indians and their starving families in the streets of his capital at Detroit, he came to doubt whether those who survived would ever be able to make the transition to the civilized ways of an American farmer. Even if they could, why should they have to? He suddenly felt a deep nostalgia for the defiant and arrogant warriors he knew as a boy. Perhaps

Indian men were destined for the life of a warrior and a hunter. If the Americans forced them behind plows on farms laid out by government surveyors, then maybe they were actually interfering with God's will for the tribes.

Even if the Indians were able to make the transition, wouldn't the Americans simply overrun them someday, taking their farms and the last acres of their township reserves away from them? Maybe the tribes belonged in an unchanging world, where the boys grew to be warriors and hunters and the girls followed after them as wives and mothers. The ancient cycles could continue in such a place. Governor Cass was soon convinced that the reserves carved out for the tribes throughout the old Ohio Country were unsuitable for the Indians. He came to believe that they belonged in the endless prairie country west of the Mississippi, where they could live the life that God had intended.[26]

As he clarified his ideas about removing the tribes, which he first proposed to the Indians at the treaty negotiations at St. Mary's, Cass was determined to record as much about their traditions as possible before they disappeared, either by being overrun by the Americans or by moving far away to the West. He sent questionnaires to every Indian agent on the frontier, including John Johnston and Benjamin Stickney, who were working with the Ohio tribes, and to William Clark, who was still serving as superintendent of Indian affairs at St. Louis. He interviewed Indian chiefs, too, asking them to recall their ancient traditions, from how they raised their children to what they believed about the afterlife. He soon had officials throughout the West joining him in documenting Indian customs before they completely disappeared. Henry Schoolcraft, a young engineer who joined Cass on his travels to treat with Indian tribes at the far western edges of the Michigan Territory, compiled enough information to write one of the first comprehensive histories of the American Indians ever published.[27]

In the midst of such nostalgia, Cass decided that even the Prophet could be useful. Surely he knew more than almost anyone else about the frontier traditions of the Shawnee and the other tribes in Tecumseh's confederation. Cass invited the Prophet, who was still living with a handful of followers in western Ontario, to come to Detroit and share his memories of the old ways. Tenkswatawa was barely surviving on handouts from the British and was anxious to find a way to support his small family. He was determined to make an impression on Cass when he crossed over from Canada to meet with him in the spring of 1824. Close to fifty, he still stood tall and strong, dressed in a bright blue coat over a white cotton shirt. He wore silver all over, from the ornament in his red turban to the long earrings that dangled to his shoulders, and from the half-moon piece that circled his neck to the bands around his powerful arms. He was suspicious at first about Cass's motives, and revealed little. But then, impressed with the kind reception he received, he opened up and told him as many stories as he could remember.

The Prophet came back and forth from Canada several times to meet with the governor, wondering if he would ever be allowed to return to the United States permanently. Cass finally told him he was free to go back to Ohio, but he would have to live for a time under the authority of the aged chief Black Hoof, an outspoken critic of Tecumseh and his confederation, at his village at Wapakoneta. Tenkswatawa wondered how this could be allowed. Cass explained that he hoped the Prophet would still have enough influence over the Shawnee to convince them that their rightful place was not in Ohio but west of the Mississippi. For the Prophet, the prospect of removal seemed nothing short of a miracle. In fact, at this late hour, it was the only way of fulfilling the dream that he and his brother had once shared of establishing a permanent homeland for their people.[28]

For many Indians who had lost their lands in Ohio, and who were now slowly losing their traditions and their very identity, the possibility of moving west of the Mississippi River suddenly made sense. Until this moment, their choices appeared to be limited to settling down on their remaining reserves and slowly learning to live like the whites, or staying on those same reserves and retaining their identity. But what if Governor Cass was correct that there was another way? Why did they have to stay confined on tiny reserves in the East when the prospect of preserving their traditional way of life beckoned from the West? If Cass was right, then there was no reason why the tribes had to remain in Ohio. They could just as easily exchange their lands for new territories west of the Mississippi.

This was not a new idea. Both the Shawnee and the Delaware had been leaving Ohio for the far western country since before the American Revolution. The Spanish had sought out the Shawnee as allies since the 1760s. Pierre Laclede, founder of St. Louis and stepfather of Auguste Chouteau—the renowned fur trader who had helped negotiate the many treaties at Portage de Sioux—started trading with them in 1769. A decade later, after American colonists arrived from Virginia and set fire to tribal villages throughout Ohio, hundreds of Shawnee left their ruined towns and headed for the peace and freedom of Missouri. Tecumseh's mother, Methoataaskee, was one of the refugees. She went west in 1779, just five years after her husband, Pukeshinwau, had died at the hands of the Americans. She left behind her son Tecumseh, then only eleven, and the Prophet who was even younger, and headed to a place called Apple Creek, near Cape Girardeau. By 1812, at least twelve hundred Shawnee were living across the Mississippi in Missouri, far from the bitter memories of the Ohio Country.[29]

While the Shawnee who remained behind in Ohio survived for two more generations, most of the Delaware had already left. John Johnston, who knew the Indians well, said no tribe hated the white man quite as much as the Delaware. For two centuries, the white man had pushed the Lenni Lenape, as the tribe called themselves, from the Atlantic shore westward over the Appalachians. After signing the Treaty of Greeneville in 1795, which took away the tribe's land in southern Ohio, the Delaware settled on the West Fork of the White River in the Indiana Territory. Their great chief Buckongehelas, who set up a town in Indiana for his people from Ohio, often told them not to trust the whites, and never to give up their own customs. If they were tempted to do so, they should remember Gnaddenhutten, the site of the massacre of the Christian Delaware by the Americans during the revolution. Even with their deep distrust of the Americans, the Delaware had rejected the teachings of the Prophet and refused to follow Tecumseh in the War of 1812. Many fled back across the Indiana border to Piqua, in western Ohio, where the American government gave them a small tract of land and placed them under the protection of William Henry Harrison and Indian agent John Johnston. The tribe later surrendered this tract in exchange for a small piece of ground around Captain Pipe's village, near Upper Sandusky in the Treaty at the Foot of the Rapids.[30]

It was their new leader, Captain Anderson, one of the signers of the treaties at St. Mary's, who decided the time was right to lead most of his tribe across the Mississippi. A few Delaware, listed by name in the 1818 treaty, would stay in Indiana on half and quarter sections of land allotted to them. Still more would remain behind in Ohio at the village of Captain Pipe, the aged son of the more famous Captain Pipe who had orchestrated the torture and death of Colonel Crawford in the last days of the American Revolution. But the main body of the tribe would head west.

The government had promised to provide a new home for the Delaware "upon the west side of the Mississippi" in the treaty signed at St. Mary's. The American government would provide 120 horses, transport them to their new home in Missouri, and make a one-time payment of $13,312.35 to pay off the tribe's debts. The Delaware would continue to receive $4,000 each year added to their other annuities, all paid in silver coins. The Delaware would also get a blacksmith in their new home. Captain Anderson told a New York immigration society scout, David Berdan, that one of the reasons for the move was the ever-present problem of whiskey on the frontier. The whites brought whiskey to his people, and there was continuing trouble because of it.

As promised, in 1821, Captain Anderson, not a young man any more, led eight hundred Delaware, mainly on horseback, down the old buffalo trace from the White River to Vincennes and then on to Kaskaskia. John Johnston, who served as agent for the first leg of the trip, miscalculated how much food and supplies the tribe would need. Many Delaware had become sick and died by the time the tribe reached the Mississippi. The agents who oversaw the rest of the tribe's journey also ran short of supplies. Despite the hardships of this first "trail of tears" for a tribe that still held land in Ohio, Captain Anderson and the Delaware made it to their new home along the James Fork of the White River in southwestern Missouri. Eight years later, the chief negotiated a new treaty that took his people farther west to a reserve south of the Kansas River. When Captain Anderson died in 1831, the Delaware could say that while their new home across the Mississippi was not as plentiful as the land they left behind in the Ohio Country, they had at least retained their own identity.[31]

The Shawnee chief Colonel Lewis, better known among his people as Quitewepea, was soon convinced that following the Delaware west might offer the best possible future for his tribe. Even before Governor Cass recruited the Prophet to help remove the Shawnee from Ohio, Colonel Lewis had taken the lead in trying to convince his people to head across the Mississippi; but many Shawnee did not trust Colonel Lewis. While he was a decent man when sober, he became a frightening brute when drunk. Reverend Finley remembered him as a "handsome man, well built, of an open and free countenance," but a "savage" once he tasted liquor. Colonel Lewis was especially infamous among his own tribe for committing a murder when "well corned." He had been drinking with some Shawnee and Delaware when he started to brag that he could kill a man without shooting him. When a drunken Delaware sitting next to him on a barrel asked him how this could be done, Colonel Lewis drew out a knife from his belt and stabbed him in the heart. The man died instantly. On the next day, the Shawnee held a council in which they determined that Colonel Lewis was at fault and ordered him to pay the blood price of a horse to the dead man's widow.

There were more reasons why so many Shawnee disliked Colonel Lewis. They questioned how he had managed to get a township set aside for himself and his followers at Lewistown during treaty negotiations at the Foot of the Rapids in 1817. They also accused him of stealing annuities meant for the entire tribe, and then using them exclusively for his own people.[32]

When the Shawnee threatened to strip him of his title of chief, Colonel Lewis decided that now was the time to follow the Delaware west. He headed first to Missouri and then south to the Arkansas Territory, where he was amazed at what he saw there: instead of Indians hemmed into tiny reserves and trying their best to act like the white man, he met Delaware, Shawnee, Wea, Kickapoo, Piankeshaw, and Peoria, all under the leadership of the

Cherokee, living as their ancestors had back east in villages between the Ozarks and the Ouachita Mountains. The Cherokee had first crossed the Mississippi some forty years earlier, seeking better winter hunting grounds and fleeing from the Americans, whose settlements were rapidly spreading after defeating the British in their revolution.

By the early nineteenth century, they were also heading west to escape from those of their own who were becoming too much like the white man. The split between the Cherokee of the Lower Towns along the Tennessee River, who wanted to go west, and those of the Upper Towns, who wanted to stay east, became so deep that in 1808 a deputation of chiefs headed to Washington, seeking help from President Jefferson. He assured the tribe that the government supported both factions. The Cherokee who wanted to continue down the path toward civilization, at least as the Americans defined it, in their traditional homeland should be allowed to do so; but those who wanted to maintain their tribal customs and adopt only the white man's ways as they saw fit should be allowed to go west.[33]

As Jefferson explained in his official response to the delegation in January 1809, the Cherokee who stayed behind would be "assured of our patronage, our aid and good neighborhood"; but those who headed west would also have the support of the United States. The president urged the latter group to explore the valleys of the Arkansas and White rivers, avoiding the Mississippi altogether because the Americans would probably settle along it someday.

Once the Cherokee had found a home in Arkansas, Jefferson asked them to return and treat with the American government. In the new treaty, the Cherokee would exchange a portion of their tribal land back east for the new country that they had chosen out west. "We shall still consider them as our children," Jefferson said of the Cherokee who would move to Arkansas. "Give them the benefit of exchanging their peltries for what they will want at our factories, and always hold them firmly by the hand."[34]

By the War of 1812, nearly five thousand Cherokee lived in Arkansas. They had traveled west by flatboats along the Tennessee, Ohio, and Mississippi rivers. They brought their livestock overland, crossing the Mississippi at Choctaw Bluffs (later Memphis). Originally the Cherokee built several towns along the St. Francis River, but after these were destroyed by floods following the New Madrid earthquakes, they moved farther west along the many tributaries of the Arkansas River. Visitors to the region noticed the fine homes of the Cherokee, their fenced-in fields full of corn and cattle, and the beautiful cloth woven by the women. Many commented on how much more civilized the Cherokee were than the few whites who lived near them; but they also noticed that the men of the tribe were still hunters, especially of the buffalo, which roamed in huge herds along the western end of the Arkansas River and out onto the Great Plains.

In 1817, Cherokee chiefs living in Arkansas had negotiated the treaty recommended by Jefferson nearly a decade earlier. By this treaty, the tribe promised to exchange millions of acres in Tennessee, Georgia, and North Carolina for a comparable amount of land in Arkansas. Any "poor warrior" who wanted to go west, but who had no worldly goods of his own, would receive a gun, ammunition, a blanket, and a brass kettle or a beaver trap from the American government. Members of the tribe who wanted to stay on the ceded ground could apply to the government for individual reserves of one section, or 640 acres, as a fee simple, which could be passed down to their heirs. They could also become citizens of the United States. About fifty Cherokee, living mainly in North Carolina, obtained individual reserves and American citizenship in accordance with these provisions. Finally, the government promised to conduct a census of the tribe. Annuities would be allocated according to the Cherokee population in Arkansas and back east.[35] Eastern Cherokee leaders negotiated another treaty with the government in 1819, which determined the boundaries of tribal land in eastern Tennessee, western North Carolina, northern Georgia, and Alabama, along with the borders of the Arkansas reserve. Ultimately, the Cherokee agreed to surrender five million acres in the East in exchange for three million in the West.[36]

By the time Colonel Lewis made his first trip to Arkansas, a third of the Cherokee lived there. Known as the Western Cherokee, the borders of their tribal reserve ran from Point

Remove Creek to the White River on the east, and from Fort Smith to present-day Harrison on the west. Colonel Lewis found the country in between these borders to be rich in bear, deer, and buffalo. The men hunted the full length of the Arkansas River, and even followed game west across the plains to the Rocky Mountains. The women stayed behind raising acres of corn, beans, and pumpkins in the rich bottomlands. Colonel Lewis saw, too, how the tribe's cattle thrived in the reserve's rolling hills. While there were a few slaves, there were no large cotton fields worked by gangs of blacks, like some Cherokee owned back east. In fact, the Western Cherokee scoffed at members of their tribe who were trying so hard to open up plantations in Georgia and work them with slaves. They had no desire to be part of the world-wide cotton boom, or prove to the Americans that they could succeed as plantation owners.[37]

But what most impressed Colonel Lewis was that Cherokee men in Arkansas were still warriors. Shortly after arriving across the Mississippi, they organized a confederation with local tribes like the Quapaw and Caddo, along with bands of eastern Indians that had followed them west. Together they fought the Osage, masters of the plains' eastern border, who had themselves come long ago as refugees from the Ohio Valley fleeing the Iroquois.

The Western Cherokee even made a case to the American government that Arkansas should become an Indian territory fully under their control. Their main argument was that they were "civilized," meaning that they farmed and lived in stable villages, unlike the "uncivilized" Osage, who were year-round hunters. President Monroe agreed, and ordered William Clark to negotiate a treaty with the Osage in 1818 to remove them from their land in eastern Arkansas. The Cherokee, however, were not satisfied, and continued to demand a treaty that completely removed the Osage from their remaining land in Arkansas as well as from Missouri.[38]

Two years before such a treaty was negotiated, in the summer of 1823, Colonel Lewis participated in a grand council with the Western Cherokee. The leading force behind the council was Takatoka. He was a war chief who had moved to Arkansas in 1819 and had assumed leadership of the tribe upon the death of their former head chief, Toluntuskee. More than anything else, he hated the transformation under way among his people back east. They were "getting to be neither white nor Indian," but some strange combination in between. Takatoka especially disliked their grow-ing reliance on slave labor, which he considered a "repugnant fea-ture of white American civilization." He also despised the mission-aries, who came among his people to teach them the white man's ways hidden beneath the mask of Christianity. He mocked Cherokee converts to the Christian faith as the "breeches and pan-taloons party," and opposed every attempt to set up mission schools on the tribe's Arkansas reserve.[39]

Much like Tecumseh, Takatoka dreamed of building a united Indian nation, not in the old Ohio Country, so long coveted by the white man, but in the Arkansas Territory on the edges of the western plains, where the "old ways" of the Indians, which were deemed superior to the customs of the whites, could be preserved. On behalf of the many chiefs gathered at the 1823 council, he asked Colonel Lewis to call a larger council in Wapakoneta, where all the eastern tribes would meet with the western tribes to discuss the advantages of joining the Cherokee on their Arkansas reserve across the Mississippi. Acting as Takatoka's ambassador, Colonel Lewis headed first to St. Louis, where he told William Clark of the troubles the Indians were experiencing in Ohio. Then he described the promise that the West held for the survival of the tribes. He did not say that in Arkansas and on the plains beyond the young men could become warriors once again, but instead spoke of the advantages of incorporating the white man's civiliza-tion at their own pace and on their own terms.

Clark, in turn, told Secretary of War John C. Calhoun what Lewis had relayed concerning why the great council of eastern and western tribes was being called:

> First, the Indian settlements in Indiana, Ohio and New York had become surrounded and hemmed in by a dense white popu-lation, leaving no lands to hunt on, and affording too great a facil-ity for the introduction of ardent spirits, so destructive to the Indians; and secondly, to give the Indians forming the council of a settlement by which they might enact and enforce their own laws and regulations to promote an agricultural life, which they

are extremely anxious to exchange for that of hunters which has become a precarious dependence; and thirdly, to receive among them teachers, and husbandmen to prepare themselves in every way to enjoy the same blessings which they see industry and agriculture extended to the white man, and endeavor to enjoy those blessings themselves and extend them to other nations under their influence.[40]

He promised to send John Graham, the Indian agent who had helped William Henry Harrison negotiate the treaty with the tribes at Greeneville in 1814, along with Colonel Lewis to Ohio to discuss the tribes' move. Takatoka wanted to come east to talk personally with the Shawnee and other Ohio tribes, but he was delayed by the continuing war against the Osage. Finally, in the fall of 1824, he headed for Kaskaskia, where members of the Shawnee and Seneca tribes who had come all the way from Ohio were waiting for him. He never made it, as he died along the way; but on his deathbed he urged his companions to continue the mission. They traveled to St. Louis, where they bid farewell to William Clark, who sent Graham and Pierre Menard—the Indian agent at Kaskaskia—to accompany them to Ohio.

Colonel Lewis led a party of sixteen chiefs back to Wapakoneta, where they hoped to make their case for an Indian nation west of the Mississippi. They carried strands of white and blue wampum as symbols of the peace and unity that the western tribes were offering to the eastern. Colonel Lewis planned to present the wampum to the Ohio tribes, specifically to the Shawnee and the Ottawa, but would also send the beads west to the Sac and Fox, south to the Creek, and east to the Iroquois. From Wapakoneta, Colonel Lewis and the other chiefs planned to travel to Washington, where they hoped to arrive by February 1825.[41]

The thought of a new life in the far western country ran counter to everything the Ohio tribes had been trying to accomplish since the War of 1812. Most of them had rejected Tecumseh, turning their backs on his dream of a joint Indian homeland. In exchange for their loyalty, the government had removed them to reserves, no bigger than a handful of townships, in their once vast territory, where the Americans convinced them that time was running out. The tribes must learn to settle down permanently, becoming farmers and housewives, like the Americans who were steadily coming their way on the frontier. If they acted like the Americans, there would be peace.

For some, like the Delaware, the price for this transformation was too high, and they sold most of their remaining land in the east for an unknown future in the West. For others, like the Seneca, they could accept the change if they were allowed to live in two worlds. The first consisted of whitewashed homes and fenced-in fields; the second was communion with their traditional beliefs. Finally, at least for the Wyandot, the transformation allowed them to experience a peace and prosperity that they had never known before, even as they prepared for eternal happiness in the next life.

The future seemed set until Colonel Lewis arrived at Wapakoneta with one more possibility. He knew a place where the Indians would not have to stay locked in tiny reserves, and would not have to transform themselves into the white man, nor choose between a good life in this world or the next. Follow me west to a land of freedom, beckoned Colonel Lewis, where the old ways could survive along with the new, and the dream of Tecumseh could at last be realized. Eternity would have to wait, he seemed to say, for there was still a great deal of living for the Indians to do in this world.

SIX

The Future Unravels

C olonel Lewis had a plan that made sense to many Indians on
reserves in the East and to frontier officials, like Lewis Cass
and William Clark. But to others, like the Christian Wyandot at
Upper Sandusky, the plan could be summarized in one word:
madness. It ran counter to the flow of history and memory and
seemed to reverse the order of time itself. After generations of
resisting the Americans, the majority of the Indians who remained
in Ohio had agreed to take up a life almost identical to them.
They had signed the treaties at the Foot of the Rapids of the
Maumee and at St. Mary's, which removed them from countless
acres to pieces of ground measured in a handful of townships. Like
many pioneers, they harvested acres of corn and wheat, raised livestock, and set up schools to educate their children. Having accomplished all this in less than a generation, they were now told by one
of their own to abandon the plow and the prayer book, to trek
west of the Mississippi to Arkansas, and cross vast plains beyond
stretching to the Rocky Mountains, and there start over again
down the path of the warrior and the hunter.

There was no greater opponent of Colonel Lewis than Black
Hoof. He hated him as much as he had once hated Tecumseh.
While no longer a young man, he was determined to use whatever

strength he had to stop the growing movement to send the tribes west of the Mississippi. He was furious that a disgraced chief chose to negotiate with the Cherokee, the traditional enemies of the Shawnee, and was on his way to treat with the president of the United States. Black Hoof told the Shawnee what local traders had relayed to him—that is, that the Far West was full of hostile Indians who did not want eastern tribes coming their way. They also warned him that the government would not be able to pay annuities to tribes once they moved across the Mississippi. Lastly, he reminded the Shawnee that they had refused to surrender their traditional beliefs; even the Quakers, whom they respected, had not been able to change their minds. Surely the Great Manitou had "assigned" this land to the Shawnee. If they headed west of the Mississippi, he would withdraw his protection from the tribe, and they would be given over to the power of Manitee, the evil force at work in the universe.[1]

Colonel Lewis ignored the objections of Black Hoof and headed straight for Washington. He arrived in February 1825, when President Monroe had just reversed his long-standing Indian policy, recommending instead that the tribes be removed west of the Mississippi. Monroe had taken nearly a decade to come to this conclusion. In the last dark days of War of 1812, he had seen the near dissolution of his nation at the hands of the British and their Indian allies. The final Treaty of Ghent had avoided this catastrophe, and Monroe, in his final year as Madison's secretary of state, had completely implemented its Article IX. Later, as president, he crafted his own Indian policy that resembled those of Washington and Jefferson; but in several ways improved upon them. Like Washington, he sent negotiators into the western country to write treaties that gave Indians annuities in exchange for their land. But Washington's policy had made no provision as to where the Indians were to live once they had surrendered their country. Monroe corrected this oversight by negotiating the removal of the tribes onto reserves within their former territory.

Similarly, both the Washington and Jefferson administrations had advocated teaching the finer arts of civilization to the Indians who signed treaties with the Americans, but they had failed to secure regular funding for this effort. In contrast, Monroe had won passage of the Civilization Fund, which made $10,000 available annually for the tribes as they made the transition to a new way of life. They could use the money to buy livestock and farm equipment, teach their children how to read, write, and do arithmetic, and even build Christian churches. This fund had provided the money for Reverend James Finley to build the Wyandot Mission Church in Upper Sandusky. Although small by modern standards, the sum encouraged missionaries to come west and help the tribes. Congregations back east collected even more money to be used to aid the tribes' transformation on their new reserves. The pace of change picked up, with hundreds of thousands of settlers moving west to find a better life, and the tribes would learn to adopt the settlers' lifestyle. When they were ready, the two strands of the national experience would merge peacefully together.[2]

Monroe had found an able assistant in constructing his Indian policy in his secretary of war, John C. Calhoun. Upon assuming office, Calhoun was certain he could help the president implement a reasonable approach to the settlement of the West, which hopefully would be acceptable to all sides; but the president found that other appointed officials often opposed him. One of his loudest critics was General Andrew Jackson, who served as the government's chief negotiator with the Choctaw, Chickasaw, Creek, and Cherokee. Jackson had also led the war against the Seminole in Florida during Monroe's first term. He questioned every principle upon which the nation's Indian policy had rested since the days of President Washington. Above all else, he did not believe that the tribes should be treated as the rightful owners of land, nor should the Indian nations be recognized as sovereign. They were instead subject peoples who had finally been defeated in the War of 1812.

Before he negotiated a treaty with the Cherokee in 1817, Jackson told Monroe that continuing such outdated policies was simply "absurd." Maybe this charade was necessary in former times, when the tribes were truly a threat to the United States, but now "circumstances have entirely changed." Since the American people needed more land, the strong "arm of the government" should take it away from the Indians. He even recommended that the government accomplish this by the right of eminent domain

Colonel Lewis, left, was an advocate for eastern tribes to relocate west of the Mississippi, while Black Hoof, right, the most respected chief of the Shawnee in Ohio, vehemently opposed leaving their traditional homelands. (*Library of Congress*)

granted in the Constitution. His views were shared by many commissioners who helped him negotiate treaties with the southern tribes during Monroe's presidency, including Governor Isaac Shelby of Kentucky; Return Jonathan Meigs Sr., the agent to the Cherokee; and Tennessee's governor Joseph McMinn.[3]

McMinn, in fact, had been calling for changes to the government's Indian policy since James Madison was president. He had worked tirelessly to remove the Cherokee from millions of acres in his state and then open the land for settlement by whites. He had first recommended his idea of encouraging tribes to give up their remaining land in the East for new territory across the Mississippi to Madison's secretary of war, William Crawford. Heads of households who stayed behind would be given 640 to 1,000 acres each and granted the same rights of citizenship that free blacks had in the United States. Crawford examined this proposal, but decided in favor of continuing the route of "civilization" and "assimilation" laid out since Washington's day. Still, Crawford could not help but fear that this process would move too slowly, and land-hungry pioneers would take the country away from the Indians before they had time to transform themselves.[4]

Lewis Cass, one of the top negotiators with the northern tribes, also called upon President Monroe to make the removal of the tribes the cornerstone of his Indian policy. He had concluded before most other frontier officials that the tribes belonged in the

West, as much for their own good as for the interest of the United States. He mentioned the possibility of exchanging Indian land back east for new lands in the West at the negotiations at St. Mary's in 1818, much to the horror of the chiefs. While only the Delaware had accepted his suggestion, Cass's vision of the Indians losing their very souls on their dwindling reserves later helped him recruit the Prophet to his cause. Cass also tried to convince Monroe administration officials that the tribes' removal to across the Mississippi was the most humane Indian policy possible. In all that he proposed, he had the full support of Indians, like the Western Cherokee, and chiefs, like Colonel Lewis, who saw removal of the tribes across the Mississippi River as the only way for the Indians to survive.

While the president and his secretary of war had held fast to the decision to shift the tribes to smaller pieces of ground and oversee their transition to the white man's ways—especially through Monroe's first term—they did allow commissioners to offer tribes the option of trading land in the East for land in the West during treaty negotiations. Indians wanting to maintain their traditions could head across the Mississippi, while those who wished to become civilized, according to the standards of the white man, would be allowed to remain in the East. Generally negotiators in Ohio, like Lewis Cass, did not offer an exchange of land in their treaties since resistance to removal among the tribes was so strong. However, southern negotiators, like Andrew Jackson and Governor McMinn, regularly included such exchanges in their treaties. The 1817 treaty with the Cherokee, which sent a branch of the tribe to Arkansas even as the majority stayed back east, was an example of the implementation of the dual policy on the southern frontier, as was the Treaty of Doak's Stand, which Jackson negotiated with the Choctaw three years later, in which the tribe agreed to relinquish most of their lands in Alabama for a huge reserve in Arkansas near the Western Cherokee.[5]

By allowing this option, Monroe and Calhoun strove to maintain the difficult balance between the demands of their own citizens, who wanted even more land, and the Indians, who often disagreed on the best future for their tribes. However, in one key area, they lost the fight. Halfway through Monroe's second term, private traders demanded the right to control all commerce with the Indians. Congress agreed and took the government out of the business of the Indian trade. George Washington had first recommended the establishment of government-run trading houses in 1793, and an Indian trade system was organized three years later. The purpose of these trading houses, or "factories," was not primarily to make money. Instead, they were meant to tie the tribes to the United States and break the bond between the Indians and the British.

As the 1796 law stated, the factories would "render tranquillity with the savages permanent by creating ties of interest." Six years later, following the passage of the Trade and Intercourse Act, which consolidated all previous laws on government factories, President Jefferson told Congress that these establishments would encourage tribes to pursue agriculture, manufacturing, and civilization, thus "bringing together their and our sentiments." Government officials—which included Secretary of State James Monroe on one occasion during the Portage des Sioux negotiations—purchased goods in eastern cities like Washington and Philadelphia, and shipped them to western Indian agents who oversaw the factories, where eastern tribes brought the skins and pelts of deer, fox, bear, raccoon, and even buffalo and panther, and exchanged them for the many goods on which they depended. From guns and iron tools to needles, thread, cloth, and buttons, Indian families relied on the American government to make high-quality goods available to them.[6]

But as soon as the War of 1812 ended, many private traders argued that the government-run system was no longer necessary. The British had cut their ties with the American tribes as the Treaty of Ghent had promised, thus there was no need to use the factories as an arm of the nation's foreign policy. Businessmen were certain that high profits could be made in the Indian trade, and they wanted to control those profits themselves. Madison's secretary of war, William Crawford, had objected mightily to the transfer of the Indian trade from public to private hands. He did so primarily on the grounds that unscrupulous traders would head west and set the tribes against each other in a battle for the best goods. The result would be continual warfare among the Indians, which would lead to the "expulsion of the aboriginal inhabitants of the country to more distant and less hospitable regions." As Crawford explained in a report to the Senate in 1816: "The correctness of this policy cannot for a moment be admitted. The utter extinction of the Indian race must be abhorrent to the feelings of an enlightened and benevolent nation."[7]

Secretary Calhoun, Crawford's successor in the War Department, agreed completely and made similar reports to the Senate during his time in office. If the government simply opened up trading to all comers, then the worst examples of American greed would head to the Indian country. Traders would come west with one sole motive: profit at any cost. They would sell whatever could make them the most money, including whiskey. In contrast, government traders would continue to seek only moderate profits and would adhere to the government's prohibition against selling spirits of any kind to the tribes. The positive effect that government traders would have on both the Indians and the overall peace of the West far outweighed any possible profits made in the fur trade. Calhoun also argued that if government trading posts were allowed to continue, even for just a little while longer, then Indian villages would spring up around them. In such an environment the tribes would learn the value of private property, and slowly become more lawful, and hence more peaceful. Americans would forget the horror of frontier Indian warfare, and the tribes would settle down as responsible farmers. In just one more generation, there would be a permanent and lasting peace among the two peoples. If this process were not allowed to proceed, and unscrupulous traders and greedy farmers headed west, Calhoun worried that "those who were once the proprietors of this prosperous country" would face "annihilation."

Calhoun made sure that western Indian agents who oversaw the factories and the annuities distribution were well paid. In 1818, upon his recommendation, the Senate approved a pay scale for Indian agents and subagents. The agents, or "factors," who were to be appointed by the president with the advice and consent of the Senate, received anywhere from $1,300 to $1,800 annually, while all of the subagents received $500 yearly. There were fifteen agents, distributed among the Cherokee, Creek, Choctaw,

Chickasaw, and Seminole, as well as agents in the Illinois Territory, Prairie du Chien, Natchitoches, Chicago, Green Bay, Mackinac, Vincennes, Fort Wayne and Piqua, the Lakes, and St. Louis. Calhoun told the Senate that it would be beneficial to the western frontier if officials were allowed more time to complete their work among the tribes.

But by the start of Monroe's second term, Calhoun's approach to the Indian trade seemed outdated, especially to private traders, like John Jacob Astor, as well as to many settlers on the frontier. Americans were heading west at the same record pace set during the Great Migration. It took them only five years since the Treaty of Ghent was signed to settle all the way to the Mississippi. In the process, not only had Indiana and Illinois joined the Union, but so had Mississippi in 1817 and Alabama in 1819. The growth occurred peacefully, with no interference from many Indian nations who were now living on reserves within their former territory, nor from the British, who remained true to the promises made at Ghent.

In the midst of such peaceful growth throughout the West, traders could make the case that the nation's oversight of the Indian trade was no longer necessary. Congress agreed, and on May 6, 1822, the system of government-run trading houses, which had been in place for nearly thirty years, was officially abolished over the objections of both the secretary of war and the president. The fifteen agents serving all the way west to St. Louis were ordered to bring their remaining stores, which included both trade goods purchased by the government and furs brought into the factories by the Indians, to a warehouse in Georgetown in the District of Columbia, where all the items would be sold at a public auction, and the profits would go to the government to settle any debts against the various agencies.

In 1824, partly in reaction to the bill, Calhoun created the Office of Indian Affairs within the War Department under the direction of Thomas McKenney, former superintendent of Indian trade. From this office, agents would still be sent out to man stations in the West. While they would no longer oversee Indian trade, they would continue to distribute annuities and act as intermediaries between the tribes and the government. John Johnston remained the Indian agent for the Ohio tribes under the new system. Calhoun also recommended that superintendents of Indian affairs be appointed to oversee agents and subagents. Lewis Cass, still serving as the Michigan Territory governor, would act as Indian Affairs superintendent for tribes north of the Ohio River, James Miller would do the same for those in the Arkansas Territory, and William Clark would serve the remaining tribes west of the Mississippi.[8]

Still, by the close of Monroe's presidency, no amount of government reorganization could stem the rising tide of complaints pouring into the administration regarding the nation's Indian policy. Many territorial officials, especially in the North, were convinced that the meeting of the tribes and the settlers was ultimately damaging to the Indians. Drunkenness, violence, and debt seemed everywhere the rule. The tribes were dwindling in numbers and generally quite miserable surrounded by whites. They could only be saved by removing them across the Mississippi. Indian agents in the South, like Return Jonathan Meigs, who worked with the Cherokee, saw another destructive pattern at work. He witnessed a growing nationalism on both sides. The tribes on their eastern reserves were becoming more aware of their sovereignty and had no desire to blend in with whites. The Americans were increasingly nationalistic and refused to welcome Indians into their ranks. A separation of the two peoples, with the Mississippi in between them, might be the only way to keep the peace. Finally many Americans, especially in the southern states, saw no value in civilizing the Indians once they moved onto smaller reserves within their former territories. Instead, they wanted all the tribes, whether they lived liked white men or retained their ancient customs, banished from the eastern states and sent west across the Mississippi.

Much like government trading houses, the idea of civilizing Indians now seemed to many a worn-out concept from an older world; it made more sense in a time when warriors swooped down on frontier settlements and murdered Americans with British guns. But now in a more peaceful time, waiting for the Indians to "civilize" simply meant allowing former enemies to hang onto valuable territory. Eventually, after all the wars and all the treaties, the tribes were still in possession of millions of acres of black soil in both the Middle West and the Deep South—first-growth forests of oak, hickory, and sycamore—and trails that connected growing towns to major waterways. Many Americans now demanded that the country be opened for settlement. The Indians, no matter how fast they were racing toward civilization after the War of 1812, must go. There would be no setting the clock back before Tippecanoe, or waiting for another generation for two streams of life, one red and one white, to catch up with each other. The Indians must be sent into the country called the Great American Desert, and the settlers must follow in their wake, taking every township out to the Mississippi and just beyond.

James Monroe, seen by many of his contemporaries as the last survivor of the founding generation, watched as history seemed to pick up speed in the last months of his presidency. The old conflicts that had haunted the United States since he was boy serving in Washington's army appeared to be over. The Indians were no longer seen as a threat on the eastern side of the Mississippi River, but were instead considered a nuisance. Americans who believed this often reminded the president of how the tribes were struggling on their reserves even as they ignored the many ways they were succeeding. To them, the Indians were primarily a drunk and disorderly lot, and prone to violence, not so much against the white man anymore but against each other. Stories of the senseless murders of one Indian by another were told all along the western frontier. Even a chief as civilized as Between the Logs, who was now known throughout Ohio as a devout Christian and an eloquent preacher, awoke one morning to find his own brother, still a "heathen," holding a knife to his throat, threatening to kill him and his entire family if they did not renounce their Christian faith. Incidents like this seemed to prove that there was a wild streak in the Indian spirit that could never be fully tamed. If this was the case, then waiting for the tribes to become successful farmers and property owners seemed futile.

But even more tragic for the future of the tribes, none of this seemed to matter anymore: the United States was swept up in the dissolution of the old and the rapid creation of the new. The old was the world that had led up to the War of 1812. The trauma of facing an endless Indian war on the western frontier and the fear of the British dismembering the nation back east had disappeared a decade before. Napoleon had been defeated at last, and the world war that had gone on for twenty -five years was finally over. Through it all, the United States had held together and had gone on to experience a wave of patriotism unparalleled in its short and lively history. James Monroe, the harried secretary of state and acting secretary of war who had done his best to save his country in the last days of the War of 1812, had gone on to become a popular president—so popular, in fact, that no one ran against him in his bid for a second term. With its greatest leaders gone and its opposition to the War of 1812 a disgrace, the Federalist Party dissolved. For just a moment, in this "Era of Good Feelings," it seemed that James Monroe and his Democratic-Republican Party would reign forever.

However, few things remain permanent in a democracy, least of all who holds power. By 1824, the year when Colonel Lewis first brought his case to the tribes in Ohio for an Indian country west of the Mississippi, the United States was swept up in the wildest presidential election to date. The same men who had worked together to defeat the British in the War of 1812, both at the negotiating table and on the battlefield, were at each other's throats as candidates for president. John Quincy Adams and Henry Clay had been the top negotiators at Ghent, William Crawford had served as the ambassador to France during the fall of Napoleon, and Andrew Jackson had smashed the British in the last battle of the war at New Orleans.

As Colonel Lewis worked to remove his people from Ohio, these four men went after each other in a head-to-head battle over who could best lead the American nation into a growth spurt that would have seemed impossible just a decade before. Adams and Clay promised roads and canals and other internal improvements that would make their infant nation into a great one. Crawford, a former secretary of the treasury, promised common sense management of the nation's finances, and was for a time the front-runner until a stroke took him out of the race. Jackson had proven at the Battle of New Orleans he could command men and turn the very direction of history. In the turmoil of such a wild campaign over the country's future, the older debate over the civilizing of Indians seemed behind the times.

In fact, the rising issue of the day was no longer the future of the Indians east of the Mississippi, but the future of slavery west of it. When the United States was struggling to survive against the combined threat of the Indians and the British—from Fallen Timbers to the Thames and Horseshoe Bend—the slavery controversy had been muted. But almost from the moment that peace finally came at Ghent and New Orleans, the problem of slavery, still existing in a nation founded on the principle that "all men are created equal," reared its ugly head. Although no one spoke the question as eloquently as Abraham Lincoln would a generation later, it was already in the whirlwind of the nation's political life: Could the United States continue to go on half slave and half free?

The debate over this question erupted when Missouri petitioned to enter the Union as a slave state in 1820, the same year that President Monroe ran unopposed for reelection. Slavery had been banned in the old Ohio Country north of the Ohio River as a result of the Northwest Ordinance. Americans now debated if the ban should be continued across the Mississippi to the Rocky Mountains. Should Missouri, lying north of the point where the Ohio River met the Mississippi, enter the Union as a free state, just like Ohio, Indiana, and Illinois had done? Or should Missourians be allowed to continue to be slave owners even after their territory became a state? Henry Clay, currently Speaker of the House of Representatives, saved the day by proposing a compromise that allowed Missouri to enter the Union as a slave state, while all future states lying north of Missouri's southern border would be free. So the issue seemed to be resolved for the moment, but how it would ever end, especially since the cotton raised by hundreds of thousands of slaves in the South was a top export of the United States and a staple of countless factories sprouting up in the North, remained a mystery.

As Colonel Lewis made his way east from Wapakoneta with a small party of supporters early in the winter of 1825, he might have been surprised to learn that no one knew who the next president of the United States would be. Andrew Jackson had received the most popular votes with 41 percent of the total, but no candidate had won a majority of the electoral votes, thus as prescribed by the Constitution, the election would go to the House of Representatives. The only sure thing was that John C. Calhoun would be the next vice president. He had announced his candidacy after his own state had failed to nominate him for president. His name was on the ballot in every state; but in some states he was listed as Clay's running mate; in others, Jackson's; in others, Crawford's, and still others, Adams's. He had won the vice presidency in an electoral landslide, but for which president?

Amid the chaos over who his successor would be, James Monroe had undertaken a final review of his Indian policy. Less than a year earlier, when James Finley had visited Washington and won the promise of money to build his church at Upper Sandusky, both Monroe and his secretary of war seemed committed to the course they had set for the Indians from the start of their administration. The tribes would be allowed to remain on their reserves east of the Mississippi, where they would learn to become good farmers, law-abiding citizens, and maybe even Christians. But sometime during the following year, which saw the wildest American election to date, Monroe and Calhoun changed their minds. Right after the New Year in 1825, they had come to the conclusion that it would be better for the tribes and the Americans if the Indians living east of the Mississippi exchanged their remaining lands for new territory west of it.

Pressures coming from the South, especially Georgia, had been growing every day. The Georgia legislature reminded the president that the state had surrendered its western lands to the nation in 1802 upon receiving a firm promise that the federal government would eventually remove the Cherokee. Governor George Troup was now threatening to take control of the rich Cherokee lands in the northern part of his state if Monroe failed to act. He also demanded the right to negotiate a treaty to remove the Creek from another five million acres in Georgia. The situation had become so volatile that the Senate had spent much of 1824 debating what should be done, but could come to no agreement, thus made no recommendations to Monroe.[9] Complaints and concerns had also continued to mount from territorial officials and Indian agents along the entire frontier. Many of them described the sad conditions of drunkenness and debt into which so many Indians had fallen. Finally, hearing news from William Clark that tribes from Ohio had come to him with the specific request to join the Western Cherokee in Arkansas made a powerful impact on the administration. Monroe directed Calhoun to write a report detailing the exact numbers of Indians by tribe living in the East and what the most reasonable order of their removal to the West should be.

On January 24, 1825, Calhoun delivered his report on Indian removal to the president. He first explained that tiny remnants of tribes that had lived on reserves in Maine, Massachusetts, Connecticut, Virginia, and South Carolina since colonial times should be allowed to stay there. They numbered only 2,000, but the other 92,000 Indians living from Michigan to Florida should be readied to move west. The president should meet with tribal leaders to explain why removal was necessary for their peoples' survival and to strengthen the United States. Indians in northern Illinois and Indiana, Michigan, and New York, along with the Ottawa along the Maumee River valley, would head to new lands in the Wisconsin Territory. Calhoun noted that tribes from New York were already moving there. Indians in southern Illinois and Indiana, including the Kaskaskia, Miami, and Eel River, along with the remaining Ohio tribes—the Wyandot, Shawnee, Delaware, and Seneca—would head onto the plains west of Missouri and Arkansas. They would be joined by the four major southern tribes, the Cherokee, Choctaw, Chickasaw, and Creek. Soon the Seminole would go, too, but not until their land in Florida was surrounded by settlers.

Calhoun added that perhaps the Chickasaw could live with the Cherokee, and the Creek could live with the Choctaw on their reserves in Arkansas. The government would have to obtain land from the Osage and the Kansas, who would in turn migrate farther west toward the Rocky Mountains. The United States would have to protect all these tribes from each other and make sure no harm came to any of them. Government funding of mission schools should also be continued in the new Indian territory. Calhoun concluded by reminding Monroe of the great evil to which the tribes had been long subjected, referring to the "incessant pressure of our population, which forces them from seat to seat." The government must give the tribes the "solemn assurance that the country given them should be theirs as a permanent home, for themselves and their posterity, without being disturbed by the encroachments of our people," which, as Calhoun explained, was "so fatal to the race."[10]

Monroe presented Calhoun's ideas to the Senate in a special message just three days after receiving the report. In order to promote the "security and happiness of the tribes within our limits," he proposed that eastern Indians be given lands "west and north" of the United States and its territories. Why was Monroe advocating this? He explained that his new policy was in large measure a response to Georgians' complaints. They were demanding that the government remove the Cherokee from their state in accordance with the compact signed between the United States and Georgia in 1802. The pressure had been mounting for some time, so much so that Monroe worried the people of Georgia would soon take matters into their own hands, driving the Cherokee from their lands and exterminating Indians. This, along with the continuing concerns coming from the western frontier that many Indians were not making the transition to civilization but were instead sinking into poverty and ruin, hence into ultimate destruction, led him to conclude that it was best for the tribes to head west.

The president explained that the Indians, surrounded and pressured by the whites, were having an increasingly difficult time sustaining "their kind of government." In this situation, they were exposed to "frequent disturbances" from which the government was always trying to rescue them. Soon their tribal government of chiefs and councils would "lose its authority and be annihilated." This would have devastating consequences, since in the long run "the moral character of the tribes will be lost." All this could be avoided if the tribes consented to move across the Mississippi. Monroe described the far western country as "equally good and perhaps more fertile" than the land the Indians currently held back east.[11]

Just days after Monroe and Calhoun officially proposed their new policy, Colonel Lewis and his party arrived in Washington. The Shawnee chief met with Calhoun and reminded him of the treaty signed at the Foot of the Rapids eight years earlier, which had plotted township reserves for his people and even granted patents to individual Indians. He now held out his patent before him, saying that the government had told him if he ever wanted to sell his land, then he was to bring the document back to Washington. "I am determined to move to the west of the Mississippi," he explained, "and have brought back the platt [*sic*] and patent which you gave me." He told Calhoun that he had called a grand council in the spring for all the eastern tribes, and that he would do his best to convince every Indian present to head for a new life across the Mississippi. Colonel Lewis asked only one thing from Calhoun: let him send an "upright man" to the council who had the best interests of the Indians and the government at heart. This man would negotiate the treaties exchanging tribal reserves back east for a joint Indian homeland in the West.[12]

Two days after meeting with Colonel Lewis, an overjoyed John C. Calhoun dictated three letters to Indians across the country. The first was addressed to Colonel Lewis and his followers still visiting in Washington. He told them that both he and the president agreed completely with their plans for a grand council and the eventual removal of the eastern tribes to the West. "Your determination is a wise one," he explained to the Ohio Shawnee. It made perfect sense that the Indians would want a country of their own, assuring them that they would maintain the land "forever." He promised to send Governor Cass, a "friend of the Red Man," to Wapakoneta to write treaties that would make removal possible. Calhoun would also make sure the government paid the tribe for any improvements made on their reserves. Anthony Shane, a half-breed who had grown up with Tecumseh, would be sent along as interpreter.

The same enthusiasm came off the pages of Calhoun's second letter written to the Shawnee in Missouri. You are the "children" of the American president, he explained, and he "wishes you to be prosperous and happy." In his final letter, addressed to the Cherokee in Arkansas, he spoke of his deep sorrow upon hearing of the loss of Takatoka. But even though their great chief was gone, the tribe must carry on the work he had left for them and unite all the tribes. "Red men should especially be the friends of red men," Calhoun asserted, "and they should all unite in one family as brothers." He gave them practical advice on how to determine the exact borders of their new country across the Mississippi. Above all else, he urged them to set its eastern boundary as far back as possible. By so doing, they would achieve what they most wanted and so desperately needed—"separation from the whites."[13]

Calhoun entertained Colonel Lewis and his party for an entire month before sending them back to Wapakoneta with presents and the promise of better land for everyone in the far western country. He was certain that the administration's plan for Indian removal would be welcomed in the Senate, which had spent much of the previous year debating what should be done about the Cherokee in Georgia without reaching a conclusion. Calhoun believed the new policy would be implemented quickly, especially after winning the support of influential congressional members, like Missouri senator Thomas Hart Benton. Benton advocated removal, since he wanted the Shawnee and Delaware, who lived in his state, sent farther west. But Calhoun soon discovered that most members of Congress opposed his plans for removal, being horrified at the new policy and calling it hypocritical. It reversed the course of civilization and assimilation laid out for the Indians since the founding of the republic, and was little more than a land grab. If there was any dissolute life in the country to worry about, then it could be found in the broken promises of the American government to the Indians—not among the tribes themselves.[14]

During his final days in office, Monroe could take some comfort that he was not the first president to recommend removal as the official government policy. Thomas Jefferson, in fact, had originally proposed the idea when he was negotiating approval for the purchase of Louisiana, and worried about the constitutionality of acquiring it. Since he had questioned the constitutionality of the Bank of the United States when he served in Washington's cabinet, he felt duty bound as president to question the constitutionality of a major land acquisition that would nearly double the size of the United States, so he drafted an amendment that would create an Indian territory in the new purchase north of the thirty-first parallel. Tribes west of the Mississippi would be recognized as the rightful land owners until they abandoned the territory or surrendered it to the American government.

Tribes living on the eastern side of the Mississippi would be allowed to "exchange" their current lands for new land west of the river. The government would be authorized to build forts, control salt springs and mines, explore the geography, set up roads and navigate the rivers, and regulate trade in the Indian Territory. Jefferson envisioned the Indian Territory near modern-day Oklahoma, where the tribes would band together, still with the support of the United States and regular annuities, to act as a buffer protecting the nation

Lewis Cass, appointed governor of the Michigan Territory by President James Madison in 1813, a position he held until 1831. (*Library of Congress*)

from the Spanish. Finally, with the encouragement of Federalists like Alexander Hamilton, Jefferson decided to purchase the Louisiana Territory without a constitutional amendment.

In the end, James Monroe would not be the president to decide whether the Indians should be removed to the far western country. The question would fall to John Quincy Adams, who won the presidency over Andrew Jackson. As Monroe's secretary of state, Adams oversaw the resolution of issues left unfinished in the Treaty of Ghent. He had chosen Albert Gallatin, his fellow commissioner at Ghent and now Monroe's ambassador to France, to negotiate the Convention of 1818 with Great Britain. The treaty restored the right of Americans to fish off Newfoundland and Labrador. The British also agreed to pay for slaves taken during the War of 1812. But most important, the western border between the United States and Canada was set at the forty-ninth parallel, from the Lake of the Woods to the Oregon Country, which would be jointly occupied by both nations for the next decade. One year later, Adams and Don Luis de Onís, Spain's minister in Washington, negotiated the Transcontinental Treaty, which gave Florida to the United States and set the nation's southwestern border from the Gulf of Mexico to the Pacific.

As secretary of state, Adams had been no stranger to Indian affairs. He had, in fact, signed every treaty negotiated with the tribes by Calhoun's War Department. He was well aware of the struggles of the tribes to survive on ever-smaller pieces of ground, while others sought refuge across the Mississippi. He also knew that every president from Washington to Monroe had failed to stop the dissolution of many of the tribes or to restrain the relentless push of Americans for land. While he had greater sympathy for the tribes than either Andrew Jackson or his own secretary of state, Henry Clay, who did not think them "as a race . . . worth saving," he was just as anxious to establish a policy that would settle the Indian problem once and for all and let him get on with the business of fulfilling his dreams for his nation. No man, in fact, had come to the presidency with greater plans for his country than John Quincy Adams. Even before the March 1825 inauguration, Adams had concluded that removal west of the Mississippi was the only solution to the plight of the eastern Indians.[15]

But the new president was soon confronted by his own secretary of war, James Barbour, a former governor and senator from Virginia, who was not so certain that this was the correct policy. A dedicated follower of Thomas Jefferson, he was troubled by the willingness of President Adams to abandon the government's promises to protect the tribes if they agreed to live like American farmers. How could the War Department tell the tribes to move west no matter how far they had come down the road toward civilization, all the while promising them that their new lands across the Mississippi River would remain theirs forever? As he would explain to John Cocke, chairman of the House Committee on Indian Affairs:

> They see that our professions are insincere; that our promises have been broken; and the happiness of the Indian is a cheap sacrifice to the acquisition of new lands; and when attempted to be soothed by an assurance that the country to which we propose to send them is desirable, they emphatically ask us, "What new pledges can you give us that we shall not again be exiled when it is your wish to possess these lands?" It is easier to state than to answer this question.[16]

From the moment he assumed office, Secretary Barbour was willing to help Indians move west if this was their wish, and he continued to support the Western Cherokee in their bid to establish a permanent homeland for eastern tribes in the Arkansas Territory. In response to a long-standing demand from the tribe, he instructed William Clark to open negotiations with the Big and Little Bands of the Osage, along with the Kansas, for their remaining lands in Arkansas and Missouri. In the spring of 1825, sixty Great and Little Osage chiefs ceded territory along the Arkansas, Kansas, and Red rivers; in

James Barbour, secretary of war in the John Quincy Adams administration. (*Library of Congress*)

return, they received a new reserve stretching one hundred miles down the Kansas River, plus $7,000 annually for the next twenty years. They also received more than 2,000 farm animals, including cattle, hogs, chickens, and oxen, plus wagons, farm equipment, and the services of a blacksmith. Many of their "half-breeds," who included several children of the great Choteau family, were each granted 640 acres on the new reserve. All tribal debts, including "depredations" against their neighbors, were settled. The twelve chiefs of the Kansas signed a nearly identical treaty. While Clark was negotiating these important treaties, Barbour ordered Governor Cass to Wapakoneta, where he was to help Colonel Lewis in his bid to remove any Indian from Ohio who wanted to go west. Cass was given authority to negotiate treaties in which the tribes exchanged Ohio land for a new homeland across the Mississippi, preferably near the Cherokee in Arkansas.[17]

By supporting individual Indians wishing to relocate west, Secretary Barbour failed to consider the potential problems that might arise if the tribes split in two, mainly the matter involving annuities. Which part of the tribe, the one back east or the one out west, would receive the annual payments? Just as important, who would be the head chief of these divided tribes? Would they be older men, respected as the traditional leaders of their peoples, who stayed behind, or would they be younger men, who had little experience as chiefs, but who were daring enough to go west? Barbour did not comprehend the bitter rivalry among Indian leaders as they struggled to answer these questions; but Colonel Lewis's plans were about to be crushed under the weight of them.

When he returned to Ohio in the spring of 1825, he was certain that the tribes were already on their way to the Wapakoneta council set for the middle of May. But as time for the council approached, the Seneca and Wyandot sent word that they would not be attending. John Johnston would also not be present, claiming it was because the legislature had appointed him, without his knowledge or consent, to the state's canal commission, and that he would be away at a board meeting. Colonel Lewis worried that Johnston's absence meant that he was working against him behind the scenes. He was relieved when Governor Cass arrived from Detroit, but troubled when he saw Tenkswatawa at his side. Would the Prophet support or oppose his efforts to remove the tribe, or would he try to lead the Shawnee desiring to head west?

By the time the council finally got under way on May 18, 1825, only the Shawnee were present. Cass opened the proceedings by speaking directly to the chiefs, especially to the younger ones, who seemed anxious to leave a world where their very manhood had been stripped away from them. Look about you, Cass argued, and see how the white man surrounds your reserves on every side. See how the whiskey traders destroy your young men, the very fiber of your nation. There is only one solution to prevent the Shawnee's inevitable destruction: the tribe must sell its three remaining reserves in northwest Ohio and cross the Mississippi River onto the prairies beyond the state of Missouri. There the government would give them more and even better land than they had ever known before. In the Far West, in the rolling country along the Kansas River, they could live the same life that their ancestors once lived. Here the white man with his voracious appetite for land and profits would never bother them. How exactly the American farmers and whiskey traders would be held back, Governor Cass did not say.[18]

After Cass finished speaking, Colonel Lewis was not offered a chance to talk about his recent meetings with the president and his secretary of war. The council broke up for the day so the Shawnee could gather around Black Hoof and discuss the governor's proposal. Younger men, like Cornplanter, William Perry, and Big Snake, agreed with what Cass had said and wanted to hasten to the western country as soon as possible. Even though the Shawnee had been successful on the Wapakoneta reserve, at least from the American's point of view, they still wanted to migrate across the Mississippi. Cornplanter, in fact, was one of the wealthiest men on the reserve. He had a log house with wooden floors and a chimney, vast acreage of corn behind hand-built wooden fences, apple and peach orchards, and many horses; yet he desired to live like his forefathers had before the Americans arrived in the Ohio Country.[19]

For Cornplanter and other young leaders, life on their tribe's reserves, hemmed in by township lines, meant abandoning hope of achieving the freedom and honor that their fathers and grandfathers once knew. This was the kind of life that they had barely experienced before it ended forever at Springwells and the Foot of the Rapids. If only they could head west across the Mississippi to Kansas, they could be warriors and hunters like their ancestors. The only thing that might stop them from heading into so promising a future was the determined resistance of their aged chief, Black Hoof. He steadfastly opposed removal, and younger Shawnee feared expressing dissent once the council reconvened. The Prophet also understood this; for the moment, with the wind blowing against removal, he, too, would oppose it.[20]

When the council reconvened on May 23, Black Hoof rose to speak first. The Shawnee present knew that the old chief's words would carry the most weight. He was furious that Colonel Lewis, who had no authority to speak for his tribe, had attempted to maneuver the government into relocating his people. "We did not want any other person to do it for us," he complained. And unfortunately, the rogue chief had negotiated with the Cherokee, the long-standing enemies of the Shawnee, who were trying to swallow the tribe in their bid for an Indian nation.[21] He threw a bitter challenge at Colonel Lewis. If he wanted to leave Ohio, then he was free to go, and no one would stop him. Black Hoof was not angry that some of the Shawnee wanted to leave with Colonel

Lewis, but he would not go with them. In support of his decision, he laid before them the many treaties that he had signed with the Americans in the past decade. He reminded them of the promises that William Henry Harrison had made at Greeneville and Springwells, and Governor Cass's at the Foot of the Rapids and St. Mary's. The government had promised peace and marked out reserves in Ohio that would belong to the tribes forever. So here at Wapakoneta, Hog Creek, and even Lewistown, he would stay.

Black Hoof was so deeply respected among his people that none dared to question him. Only the Prophet was brave enough to speak, but merely to add that he agreed with the chief. He told Colonel Lewis not to grow anxious or lose heart. Listen to the old chief, he argued, and go west to a better country if that is your wish. Colonel Lewis was furious, not at Black Hoof or the young men who stood by silently, but at the Prophet, who proved himself to be a two-faced liar. The humiliated chief left for the west on the second "trail of tears" out of Ohio with forty followers. By September, they had made it as far as Kaskaskia, where Colonel Lewis told the local Indian agent Pierre Menard that he would have brought more people with him, nearly all of the Ohio Shawnee in fact, but the Prophet had stopped them. He also blamed the Indian agent John Johnston, whom he believed had secretly interfered with his plans. He said that ten more Shawnee families, or about fifty people, had stopped along the Wabash to hunt and would soon be on their way to Kaskaskia. He then departed for the Cherokee country along the Arkansas River valley, where he would die one year later.[22]

Colonel Lewis's attempt to remove the Shawnee from Ohio might be forgotten if not for remnants of his story left behind in the letters of the Office of Indian Affairs. But still we can take one last look at his face before he leaves us since Thomas McKenney had the presence of mind to have the chief's portrait painted during his final trip to Washington. It was done at the studio of the artist Charles Bird King. The painting shows him proud but somewhat downcast. His white hair comes out from underneath the red print cap on his head. He wears a ruffled cotton shirt, with a cape around his shoulders. A silver medal of Thomas Jefferson, presented to him by Secretary of War Henry Dearborn when

Colonel Lewis, along with Black Hoof, visited the nation's capital in 1802, hangs down around his neck. He seems to be looking off into the distance, perhaps remembering one last time what the white man had done to drive his people into near extinction before he, too, disappears into the vast spaces and uncounted time of history.[23]

Despite the failure of Colonel Lewis's plans in Ohio, Secretary Barbour remained committed to supporting any Indians, whether Shawnee or Cherokee, wanting to go west. But at the same time, he was just as dedicated to defending any Indians who wanted to stay in the East. If Barbour had failed to understand how deeply divided the chiefs and their tribes were on the first question, he was even more unaware of how many of his fellow Americans stood ready to oppose him on the second one, especially the citizens of Georgia. In February 1825, the state of Georgia negotiated the Treaty of Indian Spring with several lesser Creek chiefs, who surrendered all the tribe's land in the state. For this action, their nation's top chiefs promptly ordered their execution.[24] Even though President Adams and Secretary of State Clay signed the treaty within days of assuming office, Barbour convinced them to disavow the agreement and write another treaty with the tribe's true leaders, which would pay the Creeks for surrendering most of their land in Georgia and also allow them to remain there on a small reserve. The secretary of war negotiated the new treaty himself with Creek leaders who met with him in Washington in January 1826.[25]

Certain he had won an acceptable compromise with all parties, Barbour was stunned when Governor Troup and politicians throughout Georgia condemned the Treaty of Washington. At first they complained that the chiefs planned to keep all the money for the surrendered land for themselves. But even after Congress modified the treaty to include distribution of funds from the land sale at a tribal council, they still opposed it. As Troup explained in letters to the War Department, the people of Georgia would only be satisfied with the complete removal of every Indian from Georgia. Caught between memories of the "tomahawk and the scalping knives" and federal troops' "bayonets," which Barbour was threatening to send against them, Troup vowed to defy federal law in his state and oust the Creek nation himself at the head of the Georgia militia. Armed conflict was averted only when Barbour, who considered Troup a "mad man," agreed to negotiate another treaty with the tribe that gave them new land in the west in exchange for their remaining land in Georgia.[26]

Throughout the growing crisis in Georgia, Barbour had spent every spare moment in the archives of the War Department, trying to unravel the history of the nation's Indian policy in order to create a better one. He studied every treaty back to 1789, along with correspondence and reports from territorial governors, local officials, Indian agents, missionaries, and the tribes themselves, and concluded that the nation's Indian policy from Washington to Monroe had been largely humane. The government had tried to save the tribes by allowing them to remain in their own country, while also giving them time to transform themselves from warriors and hunters into farmers. However, the transformation to a more settled way of life was proceeding slowly in parts of the nation, and in the process, many Indians were suffering. The clash of two civilizations along the western frontier had brought many tribes to ruin. Disease, violence, misery, debt, and above all else drunkenness seemed everywhere the order of the day. While trying to blend the two civilizations, the government had been unable to protect the Indians from the ills that came with contact between the tribes and the settlers. Time was running out because many Americans were growing impatient with the problems associated with civilization and assimilation, and public opinion was shifting in favor of sending the tribes across the Mississippi River as the only way to solve these problems.

Before this happened, Secretary Barbour made one last attempt to craft a policy that protected Indians who had successfully made the transition to a new life on their eastern reserves while allowing those who were intent on maintaining their traditions to head west. He enlisted the help of Thomas McKenney in the Office of Indian Affairs, and also had the support of the president, even though Adams believed it was too late for such benevolence to work. Barbour's final plan, submitted to the House Committee on Indian Affairs in January 1826, stated that the most "advanced" Indians who wanted to stay in the East would be allowed to do so; but a point would come when their tribal government would dissolve and they would become citizens of the states in which they lived. For those who needed more time to become civilized, as Americans defined the process, the United States would open up two new Indian territories west of the Mississippi River. One would be in the Central Plains while the other would be in the Wisconsin Territory. There Indians would learn to live as respectable property owners, and pass through the three stages of territorial government outlined in the Northwest Ordinance. Eventually the territories would enter the Union as new states, and tribal identity would disappear as the Indians became assimilated.[27]

The House had been working on a bill that would strengthen the current policy of encouraging tribes to become civilized on their eastern reserves, but took Barbour's ideas into consideration, primarily because of the eloquent report he attached to his proposal. The document provided one of the most honest appraisals of American Indian policy ever written. While on the surface the nation's approach to the Indians seemed benevolent, it rested on the principle of "power as the only standard of right." From the discovery of America to the present day, the white man was driven by the desire to acquire Indian land and to use whatever means necessary to take it. The tribes had slowly but inevitably been pushed back from the Atlantic to across the Appalachians, and were now heading into "inhospitable recesses," where they would continue to waste away.

In the process, Americans, who prided themselves on their good government, had ignored the very principles that make a government good, namely justice, moderation, and humanity. There was, in fact, "but little on which the recollection lingers with satisfaction" in the sad history of the relationship between the American nation and the Indians. The final chapter was in many ways the most depressing. The United States had prevailed on the tribes to give up their ancient ways and settle down as year-round farmers on small reserves. But while the Indians had done everything asked of them—"reclaimed the forest, planted their orchards, and erected houses, not only for their abode, but for the administration of justice, and for religious worship"—this still was not good enough for the Americans who must have every inch of Indian land. Once again they must surrender their country to the white man and prepare to face "some new desert."

While members of the Committee on Indian Affairs incorporated Barbour's proposals into their legislation, the House rejected the bill after a short debate in February 1826. For the moment, the majority of congressmen wanted to continue the nation's original Indian policy of allowing the Indians to stay in the East and slowly assimilate into white culture. Barbour believed this approach, like his own attempt to craft a new policy, would soon go down to defeat once the cries for Indian removal grew louder. In his discussions with people in Washington, both in and out of the administration, he was shocked at how many believed that the Indians were fit for removal at best, extinction at worst. Nearly everyone agreed with Secretary Clay that the Indians were an "unimprovable breed," whose "disappearance from the human family . . . would be no great loss to the world."28

For his part, during his remaining time in office, Barbour was still determined to support Indians who wanted to head west and to defend those who wanted to stay in the East. This would not be easy since the call for Indian removal seemed to be reaching a fever pitch. Barbour's office was inundated with pleas from tribes, like the Choctaw, Chickasaw, and Seminole, begging for help against states that were demanding their land and threatening to force them at gunpoint from their homes. When the Eastern Cherokee took matters into their own hands in 1827—writing a constitution, similar to the United States of America guaranteeing their sovereignty as an independent nation—Barbour heard once again from the citizens of Georgia who were just as determined to maintain their sovereign right to control all the land in their state. Barbour worked as hard as he could to maintain a middle way, knowing all the while that it was probably only a matter of time before removal became the nation's official Indian policy. In crafting his middle way, Secretary Barbour still envisioned a time when the Indians would be fully incorporated into the American nation. Tribal government would dissolve, either in the East when the Indians became citizens of their states, or out west when their territories entered the Union. He never understood how many

Indians favored removal so that neither alternative would ever happen.

Back in Ohio, after Colonel Lewis left for Arkansas, the Prophet became the leader of the Shawnee who were determined to head west. He had settled with his wife and a few relatives, including Tecumseh's son and his family, at Wapakoneta, where he now became a thorn in the side of Black Hoof. Tenkswatawa condemned the old chief for trying to turn their people into pale copies of the Americans under the watchful eye of the Quakers. He was horrified at the way his tribe now lived,

The Prophet, Tenkswatawa, painted in 1830 by George Catlin. (*National Museum of American History*)

not just at Wapakoneta but at Hog Creek and Lewistown, too. The Shawnee had turned their backs on the dreams he and his brother had once had for them. The men were no longer warriors—a fact that was particularly painful for the Prophet as a member of the Kispoko division of his tribe. He might never have participated directly in battle like his older brothers, but he at least understood that the Kispoko, or "war division," a band from which many war chiefs had come, had lost its purpose in Shawnee society.[29]

Instead of practicing the art of war, Shawnee men were learning to work their donated iron plows and waiting for corn and wheat to be ground in mills, which the white man had built for them. At first the Prophet seemed powerless to stop these changes; but he realized that he could at least persuade the Shawnee to root out the many half-breeds from the tribe. Breaking all ties between the Indians and the whites had been a hallmark of Tecumseh's confederation. John Johnston often said that no Indian he ever met hated the white man as much as Tecumseh. He and the Prophet had ordered their followers to abandon all things white. They even demanded that Indians who were married to whites leave them and send their children back to their white relatives.[30]

Remembering all this, the Prophet focused his attention on the family of Richard Butler, the American officer who had died fighting at St. Clair's defeat in 1791. Butler had served in the Pennsylvania Line during the American Revolution and was a close friend of Anthony Wayne. He had come west at the end of the war on behalf of the Confederation Congress to negotiate the Treaty of Fort Stanwix in 1784, and the Treaty of Fort MacIntosh a year later. By the first treaty, the Iroquois had agreed to give up all claims to the Ohio Country, and by the second, Ohio's historic tribes, now confined on their small reserves in the state, agreed to the boundary that would later be confirmed at Greeneville.

The Shawnee hated Butler for another treaty he won in 1786 at Fort Finney. In bitter negotiations held with the tribe at the mouth of the Great Miami River, Butler forced the Shawnee to agree to give up all claims to their lands in southern Ohio. Even though he later fathered a son, Thomas, and a daughter, Polly, with a Shawnee woman, the tribe never forgave him. They marked him for death and made good on their claim in November 1791, when Butler's men left him wounded on the battlefield along the Wabash River and fled with their commander, General Arthur St. Clair, through the meadows and woods back to Fort Washington on the Ohio. The Indians found Butler where his men had left him, sitting against a tree. They stuffed dirt down his throat, scalped him, and finally cut out his heart.[31]

The Prophet accused Polly Butler of witchcraft, claiming she had made a man sick almost to death, and convinced many Shawnee at Wapakoneta to kill her. She ran to the house of Quaker missionary Isaac Harvey with her ten-year-old daughter and begged him to save them. He took the woman and her child to an upstairs bedroom, where he pulled two beds together, and made them lie on the bedsteads between the two mattresses and covered them. When the Indians rushed into the room to search, they saw only one bed and did not suspect that Polly Butler and her daughter were hiding there. The Indians went on to search the rest of the Harvey property. They hunted for the witch in the house, in the saw and gristmills that the Quakers had constructed for the tribe, in the stables, and even in the meat-house, but Polly was nowhere in sight.

Convinced that Isaac Harvey knew more than he was saying, a chief named Captain Wolf returned and asked him to come to the council house, where the chiefs, deeply under the Prophet's sway, were planning Polly's death. They only relented when Harvey and Captain Wolf arrived and offered to die in the woman's place. While he had convinced the Shawnee to spare the lives of Polly Butler and her little daughter, Harvey was furious that the tribe had allowed the Prophet to go this far. He had come to Wapakoneta to oversee the operation of the mills for the Shawnee, whom he and his family still respected deeply, but he now threatened to leave if they did not abandon their outdated superstitions.

His protest had some effect. The tribe never again put a woman to death for witchcraft. But the Prophet refused to halt his efforts to rid the tribe of white influence. If he could not do it on this side of the Mississippi, then he would do everything in his power to remove the tribe west of it. He headed from village to village on his tribe's reserves, trying to convince his people to come with him. He also stayed in contact with Governor Cass, traveling back to Detroit to meet with him in person in the fall of 1825. At the same time, a disgusted Isaac Harvey moved his family to a farm five miles south of Wapakoneta, and later started a school for any Shawnee still willing to learn the white man's ways.[32]

By early 1826, John Johnston reported to Governor Cass that at least 100 Shawnee were ready to leave Ohio and move across the Mississippi. Although several younger chiefs, who had previously refused to confront Black Hoof openly, held leadership roles in the group, Johnston noted that the Prophet was clearly "at the head of the emigrating party." In September, he informed Cass that the size of the group had nearly doubled. Many of them were quite well off by American standards. They had cabins, orchards, and fenced-in fields, along with horses and livestock. With the exception of their horses, they were willing to leave the rest behind. They were certain that the government would pay them for the improvements they had made on their farms, and were ready to head west, even before their land in Ohio had been formally exchanged for land in the West, or their Indian agent had secured funding for the trip across the Mississippi.

Johnston fully supported the Prophet and his followers in their bid for a new homeland. While he had opposed Colonel Lewis, considering him untrustworthy and an interloper in tribal affairs, he was nevertheless in favor of removal. Like many officials on the western frontier, he was deeply troubled by the mistreatment of the Indians at the hands of the settlers who surroundeded them. If a Shawnee did any harm, intentional or otherwise, to the property of a white man, then Johnston had to pay for the damages out of the tribe's annuities; but if the same was done to a Shawnee, which was far more frequent, there was no restitution. Johnston was most upset that the Shawnee and other Indians could be murdered at will, and the perpetrators of these crimes were rarely brought to justice.

He finally concluded that the only hope for this people to live in peace and to escape certain destruction was for the tribe to move west. Johnston often said that if he was not in such poor health, he would take them there himself. But he agreed with Black Hoof that any such removal must be done on the Shawnee's own terms. It could not be forced upon them by a chief like Colonel Lewis, who had been stripped of his authority by his own people, or by an enemy tribe like the Cherokee, who hoped to dominate the Shawnee in the new Indian nation west of the Mississippi. If the Shawnee could go west and pick out a good place to live, then Johnston thought they would surely see the wisdom of removal and head across the Mississippi with no complaints.[33]

Convinced he knew the Shawnee better than any other official, Johnston organized the removal of the Prophet's party completely on his own. He used money allocated to his Indian agency at Piqua to hire two local men, Joseph Park and William Broderick, as "conductors" for the trip. They were to take the Shawnee as far west as St. Louis, where Johnston assumed that William Clark would take over the responsibility of caring for them. He also bought pork and ten barrels of flour for the Shawnee. He did not purchase any fodder for the horses, since he believed there would be plenty on the route west from Wapakoneta through central Indiana and Illinois. For some reason that Johnston never fully explained, he told only Governor Cass that the Prophet and his party were on their way to Missouri. He may have been planning to accompany them himself right up until the very moment the Shawnee left for the western country. But when no money arrived from the Michigan Superintendency, the War Department, or the

Office of Indian Affairs, he decided to stay behind. After all, he wrote to Cass on September 9, 1826, "I cannot go without money." Yet he saw nothing wrong in sending the Shawnee on ahead without any cash. For his part, Governor Cass had also failed to inform either William Clark or Secretary Barbour about the departure of the Prophet's party.[34]

Two and a half weeks later, on September 26, 1826, the long line of Shawnee wagons and horses left Wapakoneta for some unknown place in the Far West. Johnston kept no records on the exact number of people leaving, but estimated it was two hundred, the Shawnee later claiming the number was closer to four hundred. The Prophet, astride a prized white horse that Cass had given to him, led the way, certain that his people would be in St. Louis in little more than a month's time. Johnston told Cass that it would probably take six weeks for them to get to Kaskaskia, where they would have to spend the winter due to the lateness of the season. Not to worry, he assured the governor, for he would meet up with them next spring when he brought a Shawnee "exploring party," which had stayed behind in Ohio, out west to pick out a new home for the tribe across the Mississippi.[35]

Sadly, Johnston failed to communicate his plans to the Shawnee and as a consequence what resulted can only be described as a tragedy. Although it did not begin as a "trail of tears," it quickly turned into one. From the very moment that this third party of emigrants left Ohio, things started to go wrong. Instead of heading due west, Park and Broderick decided to escort the party through the hilly country along the White River in southern Indiana. The terrain was marked by steep ravines and thick woods, and the Shawnee had to spend time morning and night rounding up their horses, which had wandered off. To complicate matters, the clear weather of early fall did not last long, as rain started falling right after the Shawnee left Wapakoneta, and downpours were steady throughout October and November, clogging the roads and fields. Many of the Shawnee were soon sick from dysentery, which swept through their camp. With little fodder for their horses, they, too, became weak and began to die off.

It should have taken a week to get across the state to Vincennes, but instead it took two months. The local newspaper, the *Western*

Sun, noted their arrival and reported that "the celebrated Indian Prophet and a son of Tecumseh were in the company."[36] Just fifteen years earlier, both the Prophet and his charismatic older brother had paid visits to Governor Harrison at his mansion beside the Wabash in Vincennes. How the world had changed since then. Harrison, the hero of Tippecanoe and the Thames, had gone back to his farm at North Bend, just west of Cincinnati, and started his slow but steady rise in national politics. He had been serving in Washington, as a senator from Ohio since his election in 1824, and in May 1828 he would be appointed as the minister plenipotentiary to Simon Bolivar's new nation of Gran Colombia. Tecumseh, long dead and buried in a secret grave, was already a legend among his own people, and his legacy was growing among the Americans. His younger brother was left to lead a remnant of their tribe west into an unknown future. Many Shawnee complained to him that they wanted to go back, but back to what? The Prophet still had enough influence to urge them to travel on.

Once the Shawnee left Vincennes, things went from bad to worse. At the Embarrass River, just across the Wabash in Illinois, William Broderick decided to leave for home. He was being paid by the day, and once the money ran out, so did his time of service. Joseph Park stayed with the tribe an additional three days until they made it to present-day Flora, Illinois, before he, too, headed back for Ohio. The Shawnee were now abandoned and alone, out of food and out of money, with their families and horses sick and dying. With the exception of John Johnston and Lewis Cass, no one was aware they were on the road. Even if they had known, there was little anyone could have done, since no treaty had been negotiated with the Shawnee in Ohio that exchanged their land in the state for land in the Far West. If the Prophet understood any of this, he did not seem to care. He pressed on and led his dwindling party, now down to less than three hundred Shawnee along with one Seneca family, to Kaskaskia, on the western edge of Illinois, in January 1827, four months after they had left Wapakoneta.

Here the Shawnee finally received help when the Indian agent Pierre Menard stumbled upon them. He had no idea that they were coming west and was stunned at their condition. He was used to seeing immigrants trekking across Illinois to the far western frontier, but none had arrived in as bad a shape as the Shawnee. He counted 271 of them, hungry, weak, and some almost naked. He asked them what had happened to their clothing. They told him that once the pork and flour that Johnston had given them ran out, they had to sell the clothes off their backs to buy food for their families. Much of what they had not sold, including their saddles and calico, was stolen, and all they had left was a letter from Johnston saying that "they should be well-treated." Menard used his own money to buy them more meat and flour along with tobacco and salt. He passed out blankets to the poorest among them, but he had no fodder for their horses, many having weakened and died. Even the beautiful white horse of the Prophet lay dead somewhere in the Illinois prairie country. Menard directed the tribe to head twenty miles south of Kaskaskia to a place called Big Bottom. There was enough grass in the bottomland along the Mississippi to feed the horses that had survived the harrowing trip west. He also promised to send a blacksmith to repair their guns.[37]

William Clark was just as surprised as Pierre Menard when he learned about the arrival of the Prophet's party in Illinois. He was in the midst of negotiating the removal of the Shawnee in Missouri to new reserves either within the state or along the Kansas River, but he had gotten no word from anyone in Ohio or Washington about the Shawnee coming west from Wapakoneta. He urged them to stay at Big Bottom and even rounded up replacement horses. He sent food, too, after word came back to him in St. Louis that the desperate Shawnee were killing livestock stolen from farms near the Big Bottom just to survive. He then sent his subagent, Richard Graham, to meet with the Prophet in April 1827.[38]

When Graham arrived at the Shawnee camp at Big Bottom, he was just as stunned as Menard at the Shawnee's "miserable condition." Somehow they had survived the winter on the Illinois prairie, but they were now weaker and hungrier than ever. "The suffering of these poor people are really distressing," he wrote back to Clark. Their horses, especially, were in such terrible shape that

Graham decided the tribe must stay at Big Bottom to keep the remaining animals alive. He counted 227 people in the Prophet's camp, with 203 being Shawnee and 24 Seneca. While the Prophet thought 17 people had died, no one could give agent Graham an exact count, or of how many people were lost on the way or how many had turned back for Wapakoneta. He did notice that 80 of the survivors were "young men," who were not "first-class" chiefs but were nevertheless "distinguished men in their nation." Many of the others were very old men, warriors of the last generation and earlier, and the Prophet was in his fifties.

Graham listened as the Shawnee holy man loudly condemned the tribe's agent in Ohio for failing to supply the emigrants properly for their journey west. He said that his people had done what John Johnston, as well as Lewis Cass and President James Monroe, had asked them to do. We came west, he said, where we "might live happy and grow to be a great nation again." All they wanted was land across the Mississippi River where their families could "grow up and be happy." "You see us now here before you, in great want, and ask you to take pity on us," he cried. Graham listened and wondered if any Indian would come west from Ohio after hearing what had happened to the Prophet and his people. For now, at least, he got them food, nine ounces of salt meat or one pound of fresh meat, plus one pound of flour or cornmeal per person per day. He would keep them safe in Illinois and wait for further instructions from Clark as to when to send them to St. Louis.[39]

Clark worried that the Prophet might disrupt negotiations under way to remove the Shawnee from Missouri. Pressured by the people of Missouri who wished to rid their state of Indians, and responding to Shawnee complaints regarding continuing abuse from local settlers, Secretary Barbour had authorized Clark to find a new home for the tribe.[40] Clark now offered the Prophet and his followers the chance to go out to the proposed reserve of the Missouri Shawnee, past the western edge of the state along the Kansas River, with a party of local Shawnee and Delaware. The Prophet went with great hopes about this new land, but was at first quite shocked and even disoriented at the sight of the country along the Kansas. It was like nothing he had ever known in Ohio or Indiana or even Upper Canada. The horizon opened up for miles of windswept grassland, sometimes growing taller than the height of a horse and always moving in the constant wind.[41]

The scouting party was especially worried that there were so few trees. A local trapper they met along the way assured them that there were some, mostly oak and hickory, a way up the Kansas, but a point would come where there would be only empty country all the way west to the Rocky Mountains. Yet there was plenty of game, deer, elk, and so many buffalo, which had disappeared from Ohio a generation before. The bottomland along the rivers and streams seemed rich and would be good for the women to raise corn, beans, and squash. Perhaps in the end, no matter how different this land was from the beautiful Ohio Country, the Shawnee might be able to make a better life for themselves here than in the one they currently knew, where they were imprisoned on their reserves back east.

As the Prophet and the other Indians explored the far western country, William Clark wrote to the secretary of war asking him what to do about the newly arrived Shawnee. Barbour answered Clark that he did not know to which Shawnee he was referring. He said quite honestly that he had no idea Indians from Ohio were on their way west. There had been no treaty negotiations with the Ohio Shawnee for the exchange of their reserves in the east for new lands in the west. But no matter who they were or from where they had come, the government had no money allocated for them. Barbour told Clark that he would have to find the funds to help them himself in the reserves of his own agency. Luckily, Thomas McKenney in the Office of Indian Affairs did have some money available and sent Clark $2,321.60 to take care of the Shawnee.[42] But Clark soon had an even bigger problem on his hands. The Shawnee in Missouri along with the Delaware, who had emigrated from Indiana a few years earlier, hated the Prophet. Captain Anderson was still alive and remembered the damage that Tenkswatawa had done in his witch-hunts among the Delaware before Tippecanoe. He and his fellow chiefs wanted no part of the troublesome Shawnee holy man in their country. Even more humiliating for the Prophet, the three younger chiefs who had come with him—Cornplanter, William Perry, and Big Snake—all chafed under his leadership and wanted to strike out on their own.[43]

It was not until August 1827 that the Shawnee finally left Big Bottom and made their way to St. Louis, where on the twenty-ninth William Clark finally met the man who, along with his older brother Tecumseh, had helped launch the War of 1812 in the western country. The younger Shawnee chiefs had already visited him in St. Louis, assuring him that their problems with the Prophet were over, and that they were all now of "one fire." "We are anxious to start and as soon as we can get off, we want to go," they had told him. But Clark could still see the strains within the Ohio Shawnee when the angry Prophet confronted him and demanded that he be addressed as the principal chief. In that role, he asked for $750 to pay his people's way west to the new homes that he had chosen for them in Kansas. Clark explained that since no one knew they were coming west, no money had been set aside for them. He suggested that the tribe borrow funds against their annuities, which they would then have to pay back to the government. The Prophet agreed and told Clark to take $1,000 and buy needed supplies for the Shawnee. If they tried to buy these same goods, the white man would surely cheat the poor Indians.[44]

On September 8, 1827, three weeks shy of the one-year anniversary of their departure from Wapakoneta, the Shawnee headed west out of St. Louis. They followed the southern side of the Missouri to the mouth of the Osage River and then traveled southwest along the Osage to where it joins the Niangua River, where they spent the winter. It was a happy time for the Shawnee and for the few Seneca who had come with them since leaving Ohio. They had plenty of grass for their horses and plenty of game to feed their people. On April 25, 1828, they packed up their winter camp and headed west into the valley of the Kansas River. They arrived at the Shawnee reserve that had been carved out along the southern edge of the river, the same land that Clark had purchased from the Osage and the Kansas, on May 14. Now they broke apart into separate villages, with the younger chiefs and their families spaced equally apart from others some twenty miles along the river, in order to have enough room for their families to survive by hunting and farming.

For a time, at least, everyone seemed content with their new life in Kansas except for the Prophet. He had been shamed by his own people when they refused to recognize him as their principal chief. Even Tecumseh's son, Paukeesaa, finally deserted him, taking his wife and children to live in a village farther west along the Kansas River. The Prophet withdrew, first to the hills just south of the present-day neighborhood of Argentine in Kansas City, and then east to a place called White Feather Spring. He called these settlements "Prophetstown," and in both he sank deeper into poverty and despair, remembering that he had tried to win for his people what his brother had once sought—a "large piece of land for their own . . . where they would have room for their families to grow up, where they would always be happy." He would die alone, sick and emaciated, except for a few family members, in the last Prophetstown, in November 1836.[45]

Despite the near disaster that had befallen the Prophet's party on its journey west, many Indians back in Ohio now regretted that they had not left with him. The remaining fifty or fewer Delaware in the state were the first to demand that the government buy their land and send them west. They were living on their small reserve near Upper Sandusky under the leadership of old Captain Pipe. Their neighbors to the north, the Seneca, who were apparently successful on their reserve at Lower Sandusky, were even more anxious than the Delaware to leave, and were certain that the few members of their tribe who had joined the Prophet had the right idea. They were extremely unhappy living in a part of the country filling up with so many Americans. In 1820, Sandusky County was organized around the northern end of their reserve, while in early 1825 the southern portion of their land became part of Seneca County. In the meantime, the population of the entire state continued to rise. By 1830, it had reached 938,000, a 400 percent increase over the 1810 population of 231,000. It would increase another 60 percent to 1,519,000 by 1840. During the same ten-year period, the National Road would make it to Columbus, just about fifty miles south of the Wyandot's Grand Reserve, by 1833, and to Springfield, a little over fifty miles southeast of the Shawnee reserve at Wapakoneta, by 1838.[46]

The Seneca, who numbered only 550 in the late 1820s, complained of their plight to Governor Cass and later directly to President Adams. They explained that they were "now surrounded by a dense white population, which has brought so many evils upon us that we can no longer reside here." They tried on three separate occasions during the late 1820s to win government approval for an exchange of their reserve back east for new land in the West. On their fourth try, when they sent their local subagent, Henry Brish, directly to Washington, the Seneca finally got a positive response from the government. It was now early 1831, and there had been a sea change in Washington with Andrew Jackson's inauguration two years earlier. The new administration had ended the debate over what the nation's Indian policy should be and had instead committed itself to removing the Seneca, the remaining tribes in Ohio, and the rest of the Indians living east of the Mississippi River to some point west of it.[47]

SEVEN

The Exodus of the Seneca

Like the many other tribes still living in Ohio, the Seneca had come into this beautiful country long ago as refugees. They called themselves the Onondowagah and were the keepers of the western door of the great Haudenosaunee Confederation. The Delaware called them the "Mingo," or "treacherous," much like the Algonquin tribes used the name "Iroquois," or "snakes," for the Haudenosaunee.[1] No one knows for certain when the Seneca came to Ohio, but it may have been before the French, under La Salle, claimed the country for themselves. The Seneca remembered living for generations along the Sandusky River. In the lagoons and forests circling the southernmost shore of Lake Erie, they had found a country teeming with bear, wolves, and deer, and streams rich in otter and fish. The country was full of game, and the bottomland perfect for growing corn and beans, so much so that other Indians came and settled among the Seneca. Iroquois, like the Cayuga, bands of the Munsee, and maybe even survivors of the defeated Erie Nation, had lived side by side with the Seneca in the Sandusky Valley for nearly two centuries. They had come in the wake of tribes who arrived hundreds and maybe even thousands of years before leaving behind mounds filled with pottery and arrowheads. Now, in the late 1820s, it would not be an easy thing for the Seneca to leave this country and become refugees once again.[2]

It would also not be a simple matter for the Seneca to cut their ties with the rest of the Iroquois, even though these bonds had been unraveling for some time. Living at the far western end of the confederation, they had more often than not allied with the Ohio Indians rather than with the Haudenosaunee, especially since the American Revolution. When the Iroquois signed treaties that surrendered the Ohio Country to the United States, the Seneca living along the Sandusky sided with the new confederation formed to oppose the advance of settlers into their country. They rejected all offers of compromise and instead agreed with the Delaware, Shawnee, Ottawa, and Wyandot, along with the Miami who lived at the headwaters of the Maumee, that the Ohio River must be maintained as the border between the Indians and the United States. Most of the Iroquois living farther east had already given up the fight against the Americans right after the revolution. One by one, the nations of the Haudenosaunee surrendered their territory to the United States, settling down on small reserves in New York and Pennsylvania or heading across the St. Lawrence to Canada, where the British government gave them land.

In 1797, by way of the Treaty of Big Tree, the Seneca of New York became the last of the Iroquois in the East to give up their country. They sold millions of acres west of the Genesee River to the American government in exchange for stock in the Bank of the United States and eleven small reserves. Handsome Lake was a signer of this treaty, and he aided his people's transition to their new life and also tried to restore the frayed ties between the Ohio Seneca and their New York relatives by teaching a middle path in which traditional customs could be maintained even as the ways of the white man were adopted. When twenty years later, they moved to their own small reserve along the Sandusky River, they were already prepared to make whatever changes were necessary to survive in Ohio.[3]

The thirty-thousand-acre reserve granted to the Seneca at the Foot of the Rapids in 1817, which was increased by another ten thousand acres at St. Mary's in 1818, was excellent country. If the Indians assimilated into white civilization, the United States would allow the Seneca to stay here for many more generations to come. When the Americans plotted the Seneca reserve map, including intersecting township lines and county borders, they started at its northwest corner, where Wolf Creek emptied into the Sandusky River. The northern border of the reserve then ran due east through Ballville and Green Creek Townships in Sandusky County. The eastern border turned south through Adams and Scipio townships in Seneca County. At a point between sections 9 and 10 of Scipio Township, the southern border of the reserve headed west until it hit section 8 of Clinton Township in the same county, and from there, the western border of the reserve ran up the Sandusky River to the mouth of Wolf Creek.[4]

This was the reserve on which the English traveler Matthew Bullock encountered so many proud young Seneca in 1827. The men were well dressed, with their rifles strapped across their shoulders and their wagons drawn by fine oxen, and were living in comfortable houses with sash windows and shingled roofs. There the Seneca mother with her face painted bright red and with her little son close behind her had ridden alongside him for miles and miles. As far as Bullock could see, the removal of the Seneca to a forty-thousand-acre reserve in Ohio was a success: the Indians had become "civilized" and now lived a life in keeping with the rhythms of the white man. Their Indian agent, John Johnston, fully agreed with Bullock's assessment; and in his view, no tribe transitioned as successfully as the Seneca.[5]

Bullock, however, might have been surprised to learn how unhappy most of the Seneca actually were. Living a life so outwardly "settled," yet inwardly committed to the ancient ways of their people had taken its toll. They tolerated endless harangues of Methodist preachers, both red and white, but remained unmoved. They were baffled why Christians spent so much time arguing over the Bible when the Great Spirit had laid open the book of creation for all to see. Even more troubling, the Seneca could not understand why the Americans sent so many missionaries, or "blackcoats," among them, rather than teachers of the "arts of agriculture," who would instruct them on plowing, sowing, and reaping. Why were the Americans so obsessed with spreading their religion? If the Seneca did the same and wandered among the whites preaching about Nowanet, the Good Spirit who ruled the universe, or proclaiming the *Gaiwiio* of their prophet Handsome Lake, the outraged Americans would put a stop to it immediately.[6]

Unfortunately, prayers to the Good Spirit had not been able to save the Seneca from the encroaching whites. In 1822, the same year that the government closed its many trading houses, the local land office moved from Delaware to Tiffin—a distance of about fifty miles south—and then to Bucyrus, where it would stay open until 1842. Both the United States and Ohio had banned the sale of liquor to the Indians, but local officials often turned a blind eye to people who came among the tribes selling whiskey. Even worse, the private traders who had replaced the government agents lived for profit only and so more skins and pelts than ever must be taken in order to purchase goods. Sacred rituals could not keep the game from disappearing. Not even the White Dog Sacrifice of winter was powerful enough to prevent the Seneca from turning against each other amidst their growing anxiety and despair.

The situation had become so unbearable that in 1826, a year before Bullock arrived at the Seneca reserve, the tribe's headman, Coonstick, and two of his brothers, Steel and Cracked Hoof, had crossed the Mississippi in search of better hunting grounds and so a better place for their people to live. Coonstick left two other brothers, Comstock and Seneca John, in charge of the tribal reserve back in Ohio. The party would not return to the Sandusky River for at least two years. When they did return in 1828, they found their people in worse shape than when they had left them. Comstock had died under mysterious circumstances, and Seneca John was suspected of murdering his brother through witchcraft. Supposedly, he had asked a medicine woman to make a poison that killed Comstock, for which she had been burned at the stake. If Seneca John had been found guilty, then Coonstick would have had to carry out the execution himself in accordance with the customs of the tribe.[7]

Accusations against Seneca John only made matters worse between the tribe and surrounding whites. White settlers in the nearby Huron River valley had taken a liking to the big chief who stood well over six feet tall. Every fall, he and his family passed by their farms on his way east to hunt bear and deer, and they would stop and barter baskets, deer hams, and trinkets for bread, flour, and cornmeal. Years later, pioneer families still remembered seeing Seneca John carrying white children high on his shoulders. They loved him so much that they would run toward any Indian party coming their way hoping the tall chief was among them. Seneca John would return to their settlements again in the spring on his way to the stands of sugar maples near Vermillion, where his wife and children would make sugar, while he hunted raccoons and made traps to sell to the whites. Once the weather warmed and summer was upon the land, he would return to his village on the Seneca reserve, where his wife and daughters would plant corn, while he hunted and fished and waited for the yearly round of travel to start up again in the fall.[8]

The settlers were so fond of Seneca John that on at least two occasions they intervened on his behalf against their fellow Americans who were taking advantage of him. Once, when they worried that Seneca John was drinking too much, they were determined to find the white man who was selling him whiskey. Reverend James Montgomery, the first subagent to work among the Seneca, suspected a fellow named Broughton. To catch him in the act, the preacher and two of his friends dressed up like Indians and went with Seneca John to Broughton's cabin. When Broughton poured them whiskey, Montgomery threw off his blanket and confronted his host. Broughton was so frightened that he promised never to sell whiskey to Seneca John or any other Indian again. Another time a settler named Blanchard sold a horse to Seneca John, but then stole him back for himself. Seneca John went to Blanchard's farm asking for the return of his horse, only to hear that the sale had never occurred. He turned to his friend Daniel Sherman, one of the first settlers of Sherman Township in Huron County, for help. Sherman wrote a note and told him to take it to Reverend Montgomery. In turn, Montgomery promptly rode out to Blanchard's farm, got the horse, and returned him to Seneca John.[9]

For being a friend of the whites, Seneca John was suspect among his own tribe, most of whom had no use for the settlers and their encroaching towns and farms. His brothers Coonstick and Steel had been deeply fond of their brother Comstock, and now turned a deaf ear to Seneca John's pleas that he did not kill him through witchcraft. "I loved my brother Comstock more than I love the green earth I stand upon," he told the tribal council. "I would give myself, limb by limb, piecemeal by piecemeal. I would shed my blood, drop by drop to restore him to life." The council found him guilty, and his two brothers told him to prepare to die at their own hands. Seneca John asked that he be allowed to live one more day so he might see the sunrise and look out across the green earth one final time, to which Coonstick and Steel agreed. Seneca John went to the cabin of his friend Hard Hickory and asked if he could spend his last night on earth on his front porch. He chose this spot because it was far enough away from his own cabin so that his wife would not see the execution, and because it faced east toward the dawn. Seneca John would be able to see the sunrise for the last time on the next morning. He also wanted his friend Hard Hickory to be a witness to the fact that he died a brave man.

Hard Hickory heard approaching footsteps toward his cabin just after dawn on the following morning. He peeked out through the door to see Coonstick, Steel, and another Indian, named Shane, standing over Seneca John, who was still asleep in his blanket on the porch. They woke him, and he unshrouded himself from his blanket and stood up. Then he removed a handkerchief that was tied around his head. Hard Hickory noticed how Seneca John's long hair fell down around his shoulders. The doomed chief looked toward the sunrise and at the beautiful country of his birth one last time. Then Coonstick and Shane took him by his arms, and when they had led him about ten steps from the porch, Steel buried a tomahawk in the back of his skull. The chief fell to the ground. They dragged his lifeless body under a nearby peach tree certain he was dead. But his long hair had prevented the fatal blow, and he soon revived. Seneca John looked up at his brother Coonstick and asked, "Now, brother, do you take your revenge." Before Coonstick could save him, Steel reached down and slit his brother's throat from ear to ear. On the next day, they buried him not more than twenty feet from where they had killed him, placing a small picket fence around his grave.[10]

The settlers along the Huron River who loved Seneca John were horrified at his execution and considered it an act of cold-blooded murder. One of them swore out a complaint against Coonstick and took him before a justice of the peace, who promptly remanded him for trial before the Ohio Supreme Court. Traveling north from Columbus on the circuit, the magistrates decided the case in a log schoolhouse in Lower Sandusky. After weighing the evidence, they ruled that the chief, acting on behalf of his tribe's ruling council, had full authority to mete out justice to Seneca John, and that Ohio had no right to interfere with tribal customs within the confines of the tribe's reserve along the Sandusky River. Much to the horror of the Americans who had brought charges against Coonstick, the court let the chief and his fellow executioners go.[11]

The arrest and trial of their head chief before the white man's court was the last straw for the Seneca. They had pleaded with local Indian agents to get them out of Ohio, and begged Governor Cass to tell the government that they were ready to exchange their traditional homeland along the Sandusky River for a new land in Kansas or beyond. In desperation, they wrote an official petition demanding that they be removed west of the Mississippi. What were their reasons? First, the game was nearly destroyed on their lands in Ohio. The buffalo were long gone, and now the bears and panthers were fast disappearing. Soon there would not even be enough deer or raccoons to trade for the manufactured goods they needed. Even the many wolves who had given their name to Wolf Creek, the starting point for measuring the Seneca reserve, were nearly gone.

But even more important, white people were crowding around the Seneca's main village at Green Spring, bringing the dreaded whiskey that few Indian men or women seemed able to resist and that corrupted their young. Give us a new country "beyond the Mississippi," the Seneca asked, and "there [we will] have some hope of reclaiming" our children who have fallen into bad habits and of preventing younger ones from acquiring them. The tribe specifically requested that an agent be sent to Ohio to oversee the exchange of lands and help the Seneca make the move west. If this was not possible, they would come in person to Washington, to negotiate with government officials face-to-face. When the petition was complete, and every chief had made his mark on it, they sent it to the newly elected American president, Andrew Jackson.[12]

Needless to say, the Jackson administration was delighted when word arrived in Washington that the Seneca were asking to exchange their reserve in Ohio for land west of the Mississippi. Not that Jackson understood or cared to understand the conditions that drove them to write the petition. In his mind, he already knew them. The Indians had been placed in the unenviable position of being forced to settle down as farmers at the same time that the American government was demanding more and more land from them. Faced with such an impossible situation, the tribes had remained savages, refusing to give up hunting as their main livelihood and heading deeper and deeper into the forests that were disappearing as fast as the animals they were chasing.

The fact that many of the eastern tribes, not only the Cherokee in Georgia but also the Shawnee, Wyandot, and, most especially, the Seneca, had already made great strides in farming and raising livestock, and were continuing to hunt to pay off debts and buy manufactured goods, was something that Andrew Jackson refused to consider. No reports to the contrary could convince him that Indians living east of the Mississippi had given up their "savage habits." In his opinion, all the northern tribes, including those still in Ohio, were "miserable remnants" of once great nations. Surrounded by whites, who daily pressed closer, they lived a "wretched existence, without excitement, without hope, and almost without thought."[13]

Like many who had grown up on the frontier, Jackson looked back into the memories of his youth and saw the Indians as he had known them long ago. Even more than the brutal warfare they practiced, he remembered how the tribes had allied with foreign powers from generation to generation to oppose the westward advance of the Americans. He was especially proud that the United States had finally defeated the Indians and taken its place among the nations of the world. His speeches to Congress were filled with details of every treaty negotiation with England, France, Spain, Portugal, Denmark, and Russia. But the triumph of his beloved homeland, to which he had devoted so much of his life—from the time he was confronted with a British sword as a defiant boy in the Carolina backwoods to the moment he defeated Pakenham's redcoats high atop the barricade along the Rodriquez

Canal—spelled tragedy for the Indian nations. If things continued on as they had since the ending of the War of 1812, then the "12,000,000 happy souls," now living in twenty-four states, would simply crush the Indians.[14]

Many Americans living on the frontier that was settled between the revolution and the War of 1812, especially in the Deep South, agreed with Jackson. They could not forget the brutal wars that had left thousands dead and many more scarred for life. Their experiences were best expressed in a petition that the General Assembly of Georgia sent to Congress in 1824 demanding the

President Andrew Jackson oversaw the removal of the tribes from the eastern United States. (*Library of Congress*)

removal of the Cherokee. According to the petition, the people of Georgia still remembered the "war-whoop of an approaching foe" descending on their cabins in the middle of the night. Even now, in their mind's eye, they could see their homes and farms "ablaze" in the distance as they fled from them in the dark. Like Jackson, they were impatient to put this story behind them. Instead of moving in "quick-time" with the rest of the nation, they remained trapped in a "protracted infancy." Everywhere else, Americans raced toward the future, settling all the way out to the Mississippi and beyond; but in Georgia the people seemed locked in the past. They still lived with a "long line of frontier exposed" to "savages," who at any time might swoop down and wreak havoc and vengeance upon them.[15]

Though Jackson might have agreed with the citizens of Georgia, he was also motivated by more than dark memories of the past. He was a charismatic political leader who had staked his fortune on providing opportunities for the average man against the wealthy elites who had run the country since colonial times. People at the bottom of society had only one way up, and that was through the acquisition of property. For white men in the early nineteenth century who were farmers or who hoped to become farmers someday, this property was government land acquired from the Indians and sold in small parcels for a few dollars an acre. Jackson appealed to these voters, a fact that was clearly shown when he won every midwestern and southern state in the election of 1828. Removing the Indians from their remaining land in the East would open up nearly 100 million acres for sale and settlement. Jackson never doubted that the people who voted for him, especially the many farmers in the Middle West and South, would support him in his quest to remove the Indians, knowing in the end he was doing this for them. He could also help keep his campaign promise to run a more efficient federal government, since after deducting the cost of Indian removal from future land sales, the government would still make enough profit to reduce the national debt, a goal that Jackson had set for himself as president.

To anyone who might argue that the Indians should not be forced off land that rightfully belonged to them, Jackson made the same argument that he had once made to President Monroe. The land belonged to the United States, not to the Indians. Most of the tribes that had been in treaty negotiations with Jackson knew this argument well. Unlike William Henry Harrison, who often started his negotiations with the Indians by allowing them to perform sacred rituals, Jackson frequently began with a description of the laws that governed the ownership of America. As he understood it, the Indians had lost control of the continent the moment the English set foot on the Atlantic shore. From that time, the English king owned America and granted portions of it to the original colonies in their charters. After the Americans defeated England in their revolution, ownership of the country passed from the king to the United States by way of the Treaty of Paris in 1783. Later the former colonies, now states, surrendered their claims to land beyond their western borders back to the national government. According to Jackson, pretending that the Indians had somehow maintained any right to the millions of acres that stretched from the Atlantic to the Mississippi was simply a waste of time. The American people had waited long enough. They had fought and bled for this land, losing many battles, but in the end winning every war against the Indians for control of this country. Since the War of 1812 ended, they had anticipated the moment when they could transform the last remnant of Indian land into something of value—farms and towns rather than hunting grounds.[16]

For all these reasons, Andrew Jackson proposed offering a simple "exchange" of land now occupied by the tribes in the East for comparable territory in the West, from the time he was a candidate in 1824, only to be robbed of the presidency in the "corrupt bargain" a year later, until he was finally inaugurated in 1829. On a strictly voluntary basis, the eastern tribes would be able to exchange their last eastern reserves, which they had won after the War of 1812, for new lands in the West. Where exactly these lands would be, Andrew Jackson did not say, but it would probably be on the vast plains that stretched west from Missouri to the Rockies, which no American farmer wanted. This would have to be a voluntary exchange because even an old Indian fighter like Jackson claimed he could not bear the thought of forcing the tribes to abandon the graves of their fathers without their consent. Once the tribes were across the Mississippi, they could continue in their traditional ways, even hunting all the way to the Rocky Mountains. No settlers, soldiers, missionaries, whiskey traders, or politicians would bother them there. They could make alliances among themselves as they saw fit, and maybe even establish an Indian commonwealth.[17]

By proposing such a plan, Jackson was making a common practice of the administrations of both James Monroe and John Quincy Adams the official Indian policy of the United States. On the one hand, Monroe had placed the tribes onto smaller pieces of ground within their ceded lands, and had secured funding for missionaries to help the tribes make the transition to a life similar to the Americans. The stone church that stood on the Wyandot Grand Reserve in Upper Sandusky was a testament to this policy. But Monroe had also sent a third of the Cherokee nation west to Arkansas in 1817, along with some Choctaw in 1820. By the end of his second term, he had concluded that removal was the only way to appease settlers' demands for more land and to protect the tribes from the degradation and violence that came from contact with the whites.

Monroe's successor, John Quincy Adams, agreed. While he supported James Barbour's efforts to protect tribes on their current reserves, his administration frequently gave in to settlers' demands for the removal of local Indians. After supporting the Western Cherokee in their bid to establish a permanent homeland for the eastern tribes in Arkansas, even having moved the Osage and Kansas west in 1825, Secretary Barbour succumbed to pressure from the citizens of Arkansas to remove all the Indians from their territory. Their settlements had grown around the Cherokee reserve, completely surrounding it. They wanted the tribes out of Arkansas before they applied for statehood; and on May 6, 1828, just three weeks before Barbour left his job as the secretary of war to take up a diplomatic post, he personally negotiated a treaty with the Western Cherokee to surrender their reserve in Arkansas for land farther west along the Neosho River. The promise he placed in the opening lines of the treaty, namely that this new country would "remain, theirs forever—a home that shall never, in all future time, be embarrassed by having extended around it the lines, or placed over it the jurisdiction of a Territory or State"—did not alter the fact that power had once again triumphed over justice.[18]

In his quest to remove the Indians, President Jackson had the full support of territorial officials, most especially Governor Lewis Cass. A longtime supporter of removal, he was ready to do whatever was necessary to implement the new policy. One week after Jackson's inauguration, Cass wrote to Thomas McKenney, who had also come to the conclusion that the Indians must be sent west for their own preservation, with specific recommendations on how the removal of the Ohio tribes should be handled. The process should start with the Seneca of Sandusky, who were anxious to emigrate. Cass was aware of their desire, since he was the frontier official and had forwarded the tribe's petitions to the president requesting their removal. He could invite a few of their chiefs to come by steamboat to meet him in Detroit. The expense would be minimal, and a treaty could be quickly negotiated.

Once that treaty was concluded, the government should next convince the Wyandot living at the headwaters of the Sandusky and the Shawnee of Wapakoneta living at the headwaters of the St. Mary's to give up their lands. Cass again offered to negotiate with the head chiefs at Detroit. Lastly, the Ottawa scattered throughout the Maumee and Auglaize river valleys could easily be convinced to give up their lands, since they were surrounded by impinging white settlements. Cass was certain that the Ottawa would not have to be sent west. Instead they would happily move across Lake Michigan to live with other Ottawa or with their Pottawatomi and Chippewa relatives. But no matter what happened or what order the government chose to remove the tribes, "very little expenses need be incurred," Cass assured McKenney.[19]

William Clark also supported Jackson's plans for Indian removal. He had advocated removal of the tribes throughout the presidency of John Quincy Adams and continued to do so once Jackson was president. But he usually made his recommendations with greater sympathy for the Indians, in part because he had witnessed the dissolution of so many tribes since the days when President Jefferson sent him and Meriwether Lewis on their famous expedition to the Far West. Clark watched as the power of the Indians was broken in two, and their "warlike spirit was subdued." He believed their downfall began with Wayne's victory over the Ohio tribes at Fallen Timbers in 1794, and ended with Jackson's defeat of the Seminole in 1818. Having done "everything in our power to crush them," Clark wrote to Secretary of War James Barbour, "humanity cries out that we help them." The greatest aid must be given to the Indian warrior as he made the difficult transition from hunting to farming. As Clark explained to the War Department:

> In the transit from the *hunter* to the *farming* state, he disintegrates from a proud and independent savage to the condition of a beggar, a drunkard, a thief, neglecting his family, suffering for foods and clothes, and living the life of a mere animal.

To prevent greater dissolution of the Indian character, the eastern tribes must be taken to the rolling prairie country and the land of well-watered streams west of Missouri and Arkansas. There they could be taught how to farm, build houses, lay out their fields and orchards, raise livestock, and even master the rudiments of reading, writing, and "cyphering." With the full protection of the United States, especially the army, which would establish military posts on the frontier's edges, and staff them with enough soldiers to keep the white man and his evils away, the Indians, especially the chiefs, would finally stop killing each other and live together under one government. Tribes even farther west, like the Sioux, could be helped if their young people were brought together in common schools intended to culturally assimilate the Indians; if not done, this would portend doom for the Indians, since they would be caught between two worlds. This could be prevented, Clark argued, if the United States, after two centuries of fighting the tribes, would only "cherish and befriend them."[20]

Much like Governor Cass, who would eventually be called to Washington as secretary of war, Jackson wanted the removal of the eastern tribes done in an orderly way. But unlike Cass, who pitied the Indians for how far they had fallen, Jackson felt no nostalgia for the tribes. Like Clark, the president agreed that the eastern Indians had finally been defeated. But unlike Clark, he could not forget what powerful warriors they had been. Somehow Article IX of the Treaty of Ghent, which required peace between all parties, never quite struck a chord in Andrew Jackson. Turning the clock back to before Tippecanoe belied the fact that many of the eastern tribes had joined Tecumseh in his efforts to destroy the small farmers on the western frontier who were the very backbone of Jackson's political base. After he smashed the Red Sticks at Horseshoe Bend, he continued fighting the Seminole in Florida for another four years—to him, their resistance proved that the Indians were still savages, who would never make the transition to civilization. It was simply too late to wait longer.[21]

In fact, in Jackson's eyes, the more they tried to become "civilized," the more dangerous they became. The Eastern Cherokee in Georgia were a case in point. In their bid to remain in Georgia, they had written a tribal constitution, which in essence created a state within a state. Jackson may have been considered an uneducated fool by his enemies, but he was a practicing attorney before he became a national hero, and he knew his Constitution well. He was especially fond of quoting Article IV, section 3, which mandates that "no new States shall be formed or erected within the Jurisdiction of any other State." For Jackson, an Indian reserve within a state that wrote its own constitution—that is, set up a government and passed tribal laws, not merely old traditions but new statutes—was anathema to the future of the United States. What he thought about the Seneca winning the approval of the

Ohio Supreme Court to hold trials and perform executions on their reserves, he never said, probably because he never knew. But in his opinion, tribes that wanted to practice their own law on their remaining reserves would be just as potentially destructive to the unity of the American nation as Tecumseh's confederation had been a generation earlier. If the Indians wanted to practice their own law, they must go west; if they chose to remain east of the Mississippi, then they must submit to the laws of the state within whose limits they resided.[22]

Jackson had said all this as he made his way to the White House. He let everyone know that if he became president, he would end the debate over the nation's Indian policy that had plagued Adams's administration. Instead, the removal of the tribes would be a top priority of his presidency. If nothing else, Jackson was a man true to his word.

In his first inaugural address, in March 1829, he called for the removal of the eastern tribes to west of the Mississippi. This was necessary, he argued, since efforts to civilize them had largely failed. Surrounded by whites, they were sinking deeper into destitution. Later that same year in his first annual message to Congress, he again called for Indian removal, and, from then on, discussed the matter in each annual message he delivered, often in detail. Neither the cautious steps of John C. Calhoun, who was now Jackson's vice president, nor the careful reasoning of Adams's secretary of war, James Barbour, would be tolerated. The tribes would be removed for their benefit, which in turn would prevent them from disappearing, and for the good of the American nation, which would be preserved from the establishment of countless Indian nations within its borders.[23]

In April 1830, Jackson's supporters in Congress introduced a bill calling for an "Exchange of Lands with the Indians Residing in any of the states or Territories of the United States, and for their removal west of the river Mississippi," first in the Senate and then in the House. In eight simple sections, the president's vision for the removal of the tribes was clearly laid out. Jackson was also given near total authority to oversee the process. "As he saw fit," the president could exchange land that tribes held in the East for new territory in the West. He could authorize an evaluation of improvements that the Indians had made on their reserves and pay the tribes for them. The improvements would become the sole property of the United States. The president would then oversee the removal of the Indians, funding the trip west and helping the tribes financially for one year in their new homes. All previous treaties, and thus all the annuities promised in them, would still be honored. Jackson believed that $500,000 would be enough to cover the removal of all the tribes. The Indians would retain their new land in the West as long as they desired. If things went badly on the other side of the Mississippi and the Indians disappeared, the land would revert to the government. Jackson hoped to prevent this by promising to protect the tribes heading west from other Indians already living across the Mississippi, as well as from any other person who might harm them.[24]

Jackson might have been convinced that Indian removal was the best policy for the nation to follow, but Congress was not so sure. The House of Representatives had defeated James Barbour's plans, which included removal as an option for the tribes, and before that, Congress had refused to consider Monroe's proposal on Indian removal, made during his last days in office. In both instances, Congress had preferred to continue the longstanding policy of civilizing and assimilating the Indians. To have an even bolder plan suddenly placed before them was a shock to many members, especially to those from the Northeast. Opposition to the bill was quite bitter in the Senate. Theodore Frelinghuysen, a junior senator and anti-Jacksonian from New Jersey, spoke first against the bill for six hours over a three-day period. He reminded President Jackson that the Indians were human beings with rights that must be honored. They had already surrendered over 214,000,000 acres to the United States. Surely this was more territory than even the most ambitious Americans farmers would ever hope to cultivate.

Forgetting the trauma that Tecumseh's confederation had caused in the War of 1812, both in the old Ohio Country and the Deep South, Frelinghuysen argued that the tribes had done everything the government asked of them. They had become successful husbandmen, most especially the Cherokee in Georgia, who were at the current center of the storm over Indian removal. Beyond the sheer injustice of it all, Frelinghuysen also raised the issue of the abuse of executive authority embedded in the act. The president and the Senate had always made treaties together with the tribes, but now all power over the eastern Indians had been handed to the president to do whatever he willed with them as they made their way west. Peleg Sprague of Maine and Ascher Robbins of Rhode Island, who both hated Jackson as a power mad demagogue, echoed many of Frelinghuysen's arguments when they, too, rose to condemn the bill on the Senate floor.[25]

While the South largely supported the bill—especially Georgia—Ohio's two Senators, Benjamin Ruggles and Jacob Burnet, opposed it. Ruggles had moved from Connecticut to Ohio in 1807 and had opened a law practice in Marietta. He was elected to the Senate in 1815 as a Democratic-Republican, but could not follow his party's tilt toward General Jackson a decade later, preferring instead to support William Crawford and then John Quincy Adams. His hatred of "King Andrew" would eventually lead him into the Whig Party. Jacob Burnet particularly disliked Jackson, especially his attitude toward the Indians. He had come west to Cincinnati in the late 1790s as a young man from New Jersey. He had seen the Indians go from being fierce warriors who terrorized pioneers on the Ohio frontier to determined farmers trying to survive on their shrinking reserves. He supported their right to exist as a separate people on the few reserves that still belonged to them. As a justice on the Ohio Supreme Court, he made an important ruling in the case of Nimble Jemmy, a Seneca Indian who sued a man named McNutt for stealing a valuable piece of land from him. Burnet and his fellow justices restored the land to the Indian. When his friend William Henry Harrison was appointed special minister to Colombia in 1828, Burnet took his place in the Senate, where he opposed everything Jackson stood for, from his unreasonable opposition to the Bank of the United States to his cruel and arrogant demand for Indian removal. But in the end, when the Senate roll call was finally finished on April 24, 1830, the opposition of Ohio's two senators did not matter: Jackson's supporters prevailed by a vote of 28 to 19.[26]

The debate was even more heated in the House of Representatives. Six future Whig congressmen—Connecticut's

Jabez Huntington, William Storrs, and William Ellsworth, Maine's George Evans and Isaac Bates, and Indiana's John Test—condemned the Indian Removal Bill on the House floor. Their arguments ran from defending the tribes as the original inhabitants, and therefore the rightful owners, of the remaining eastern reserves, to warning that any forced removal of the Indians would lead to their destruction, not their salvation. A few of the representatives said they might support removal if it was strictly voluntary, or if the Indians posed a real threat to the United States, but neither seemed probable. In speeches given on Indian removal in May 1830, the tribes still living in Ohio were mentioned only in passing, with the debate centered on the plight of the Cherokee in Georgia. Not one defender of the Indians described how far the Ohio tribes had come on their remaining reserves in setting up prosperous farms and educating their children in the ways of the white man. The final speaker, Representative Test of Indiana, concluded with a warning that the entire nation, not just the Indians, would suffer if this terrible act were passed. Power would be stripped from Congress and placed in the president's hands. The mechanism of "checks and balances" so famously placed at the heart of the Constitution would be destroyed.[27]

When four representatives, all from Georgia, rose in turn to defend the bill, each denied that the Indians had made any progress toward civilization. As Richard Wilde explained, "In the long interval which has elapsed since their first knowledge of the whites, it would be difficult to find a single improvement which has taken place, in their principles, habits, or condition." He made the claim for all the tribes, not just the Cherokee, even though he had never seen the fine homes and fields of the Shawnee and Seneca, or heard the Wyandot praying to "Shasus" in their camp meetings on summer evenings in Ohio. In the end, none of this mattered. Wilde and his fellow supporters of Indian removal turned the remaining debate into a defense of the citizens of Georgia and their rightful claim, under the government's 1802 agreement, to the Cherokee land in their state.[28]

On May 18, 1830, Congress voted on an amendment to the bill written by James Hemphill, a Jackson supporter from Pennsylvania, to delay Indian removal for a year. During that time, a three-man commission would visit the eastern tribes and determine if they really wanted to move west. Then they would cross the Mississippi and investigate whether the new homeland proposed for the Indians was worthy of settlement. The Hemphill amendment went down to defeat after Speaker of the House Andrew Stevenson, a devoted supporter of the president, broke the 98 to 98 tie. Eight days later, on May 26, 1830, when the roll call was finally completed on the proposed Indian removal bill with no amendments, the bill passed, but barely, by a vote of 102 to 97.[29]

Only two of Ohio's fourteen representatives in the House, James Findlay and James Shields, voted for the Indian Removal Act. Both were staunch Jackson men. Findlay represented the First Congressional District in Cincinnati, while James Shields came from the Second Congressional District, which stretched along the Ohio from Cincinnati to the Scioto River. Four other Democrats broke with Jackson in this first crucial test of his presidency and voted against the bill. They were William Russell of the Fifth District, which included Ottawa and Seneca counties, William Stanberry of the Eighth District near Piqua, William Irvine of Toledo's Ninth District, and William Kennan Jr., whose Tenth District included Parma. Seven other congressmen, who all identified themselves as anti-Jackson men, voted against it, too. Only one congressman, John Milton Goodenow of the Eleventh Congressional District, which took in Cleveland and Shaker Heights, did not vote. He had resigned a month earlier to become an Ohio Supreme Court justice and would not be replaced until after the vote on Indian removal. In the end, every Ohio congressman representing a district with Indians still living on tribal reserves voted against Jackson's bill. If they had been able to convince Findlay and Shields to join them, and kept Goodenow in Washington long enough to support them, then the bill would have been defeated in the House by a tie vote of 100 to 100.[30]

Back in Ohio, tribal members who had done everything the government asked of them were stunned that their efforts had come to nothing. The Shawnee who had stayed behind at Wapakoneta, refusing to follow Colonel Lewis or the Prophet, were shattered, as were the many Wyandot who had made such progress toward a new life in Upper Sandusky. The missionaries who supported the tribes, like the Harvey family living with the Shawnee, the Methodists working with the Wyandot, and the Van Tassels at Ebenezer on the Maumee River, were outraged. They protested to anyone in or out of the government who would listen that the tribes were not disappearing into the forests in a desperate bid to maintain their old ways, but were instead making rapid progress toward civilization through "exemplary conduct." They had the support of newspapers, like the Cincinnati *Chronicle*, which condemned Jackson's bill. The *Chronicle* argued that removal was "expensive and not conducive" to civilizing the Indians. The paper also recommended that the reserves be subdivided into individual allotments so that all Indians would have land and thus transform more quickly into "ordinary farmers." The citizens of Brown County along the Ohio River signed a petition against the removal of the Indians and promptly forwarded it to Congress in Washington.[31]

The most moving defense of the Indians against Andrew Jackson and his supporters came from the "Ladies of Steubenville." Sixty-two women in one of Ohio's oldest towns, which was founded as a fort in 1787 to protect the first government surveyors who were laying out township lines from Indian attacks, did their best to prick the consciences of the men who held high office in their country. Admitting they were merely women and therefore could "not presume to direct the general conduct" of their husbands and brothers, they went on to "*advise* and *persuade*" them to have mercy on the Indians, who were clearly their fellow human beings. Many of them, in fact, were their fellow Christians. "May we not hope," they asked, "that even the small voice of *female* sympathy will be heard?" Like the Indians, the women admitted that they had no power. But unlike the tribes, they at least had the respect of white men who claimed they were doing everything they could to protect the weaker sex. How different it was for the Indians. They had no power and no one to look out for them. How could the government ignore the "solemn treaties" signed with these "hapless people" and push them west into a "distant and dreary wilderness," where they would be annihilated? This would be a travesty, not just for the many eastern tribes but also for the American people, who would be denounced for all time for their cruelty. It would bring dishonor upon the nation that could never be overcome.[32]

But there were others in Ohio who did not see it this way, most especially the Seneca who wanted to go west. The tribe stood by the concluding remarks of their most recent petition to Andrew Jackson: "Father; your red children know that you are a Great Warrior. They know that you are just and wise in council, and they believe that you love your red children, and will give them a kind answer." They wanted to exchange their reserve in Ohio for land across the Mississippi. "Your red children will wait patiently until their father will send them word. . . . Father, your red children sincerely wish that you live very long and be always well and may the Great Spirit now and always bless you."

Many white men who were neighbors of the Seneca supported the tribe in their desire to go west. Seventy-eight citizens of Seneca County sent a petition to Jackson demanding that the Seneca be "removed to a country better adapted to their habits of life." Seemingly unaware that the tribe had stopped planting corn in hopes that the president would send them west as promised, the men complained that the tribe's lack of farming proved how backward and uncivilized they truly were. They were also jealous of the annuities that the tribe regularly received. They complained that these payments gave whites who intermarried with the tribe an unfair advantage over the average American pioneer who had no ties to the Indians.[33]

While some Americans complained that the government was spending too much on annuities, more realized there was a great deal of money to be made in Indian removal. The president and his War Department would have to hire people to negotiate the treaties, pack up the tribes and send them west, and guard them in their new homes for at least a year. Indian property back east would have to be sold, with possibly some of the profits going into the pockets of the agents who negotiated the sale. One Ohioan who wanted in on the opportunities opening up by way of Indian removal was an ambitious office seeker and Jackson supporter by the name of Colonel James B. Gardiner. He came to Washington in 1830 to take full advantage of the spoils system as it applied to Indian removal. A two-term senator in the Ohio legislature and a former newspaperman from Greene County who had reported on the friendship between Harrison and Tarhe during the War of 1812 in his paper the *Freeman's Chronicle*, Gardiner offered himself as the best person to negotiate treaties of removal with his state's many tribes. The Jackson administration agreed and appointed him the special commissioner to the Indians of Ohio for removal and the special commissioner and agent for the emigration.[34]

Although he had no experience dealing with Indians, Gardiner was assigned the task of negotiating a treaty with the Seneca of Sandusky, who had arrived in Washington in early February 1831. In the treaty, signed on the twenty-eighth, Coonstick, Seneca Steel, Hard Hickory, Good Hunter, and Small Cloud Spicer, the very men who had condemned Seneca John to death, agreed to give up their land in Sandusky and Seneca counties, which had been granted to them in the treaties at the Foot of the Rapids and St Mary's, in exchange for 67,000 acres in the Indian Territory, which would soon be known by the Choctaw name of Oklahoma. Their new reserve was to be north of the one that Adams's secretary of war, James Barbour, had plotted out for the Western Cherokee along the Neosho River. The Seneca would be the second tribe sent west, preceded by the Choctaw, after the approval of Jackson's Indian bill. Gardiner's success came neither from a special skill nor any luck on his part, but from the deep desire of the Seneca to leave Ohio. Many in the tribe, in fact, were baffled at the American opposition to Jackson's offer to exchange tribal lands in the East for new land in the West. To them, the president was their savior.

On the surface, the Seneca seemed to have gotten a good deal. The government promised to build them a gristmill, a sawmill, and a blacksmith shop on their reserve. Also, the government would advance them $6,000 for improvements made on their reserves in Ohio; the treaty stipulated that they would have to reimburse the government for this money from the sale of their lands. Similarly, the president would appoint an agent who would sell property that the tribe could not carry with them. While the agent was to hand over the profits to the individual Indians who owned the property, a fair market value for goods sold off as part of Indian removal would be hard to come by especially since the owners of those same goods would have already gone west.

The government also promised to pay for the tribe's move across the Mississippi, but did not explain in the treaty that funds for this would be taken out of the profits from the sale of the Seneca reserve in Ohio. In the end, on the long trip west, the tribe would get little for free besides 100 rifles, 400 blankets, and 50 plows, hoes, and axes "to assist them in commencing farming." Henry Brish, the subagent who had come with them from Ohio to the negotiations in Washington, sometimes paying himself for things they needed along the way, would get 160 acres of land on their surrendered reserve. Five chiefs would each get $100 for the long journey back home to Ohio, but they would have to pay it back from the initial land sale of the tribe's eastern reserve.[35]

Gardiner had help in negotiating this first treaty with the Ohio Indians from Jackson's secretary of war, John Eaton, who sent him detailed instructions on how to proceed. Eaton saw the treaty with the Seneca as the first step in a process that would remove all the tribes from Ohio. The Seneca, in fact, would be the first Ohio tribe to head west, followed quickly by the Shawnee, the remaining Delaware, the Ottawa, and finally the Wyandot. As the national debate concentrated increasingly on the wisdom or folly of removing the Eastern Cherokee from Georgia, Jackson's War Department planned to pressure the Ohio tribes to sell their land and head west. There would be no voluntary removal for these Indians. They would instead be convinced of the necessity of moving across the Mississippi and to pack up for the journey. Like the president he served, Secretary Eaton maintained that this was for the tribes' benefit, who would surely disappear if the administration did not step in and save them. "Experience and observation" clearly showed, as he explained to Gardiner, that as long as the Indians remained in Ohio, and for that matter in any eastern state, "collisions must be looked for," with "injuries" to the Indians resulting.

For this reason, Gardiner was told to head to Ohio with the Seneca treaty in tow, and to determine the other tribes' willingness to move west. He was to work closely with John McElvain, another Jackson supporter who had been appointed as the new

Indian agent for the Ohio tribes, much to the consternation of John Johnston, who was let go from his post at Piqua for being a member of the opposition. McElvain had already concluded the sale of Captain Pipe's village, the small Delaware tract south of the Wyandot Grand Reserve to the government, for $3,000 in August 1829. "Caution is essential," Eaton explained, probably because the Indian Removal Act was supposed to be "voluntary." Gardiner was to go quietly among the chiefs and see what they were thinking. He was to assure them that the government meant no harm to their people and was only doing this for their benefit. Above all else, he was to convince the Indians that they were about to be inundated by waves of white settlers. The latest census had counted only 2,350 Indians in Ohio, with totals for the tribes listed as 800 Shawnee, 551 Seneca, 542 Wyandot, 347 Ottawa, and 80 Delaware. Their only hope for survival was to go west beyond the Mississippi as soon as possible. There they would receive land that was comparable to the land they were giving up in Ohio. Once Gardiner had signed a treaty with one tribe, he was to move on to the next.[36]

Confident that the removal could be accomplished in weeks, Colonel Gardiner arrived at the Seneca reserve in May 1831. The Seneca had pledged that they would call a grand council in which he would be able to treat with all the Ohio Indians. As promised, the chiefs of the many tribes were waiting for him, but not to sign any treaties. Instead they were furious that Jackson had sent him to force them off their land. Gardiner became so frustrated trying to deal with the chiefs in the council that he decided to speak privately with as many Indians as possible. He would try to get each one of them to sell their land to him, and once this had been accomplished he would send them all west as tribes. The chiefs were outraged when they learned of his plans and reminded Gardiner that, according to the treaties they signed at the Foot of the Rapids and St. Mary's, they held their land as individuals, and could only sell it as a tribe. A frustrated Gardiner wrote to the War Department for help: "I am very badly in need of a book on Indian treaties," he demanded.[37]

As he struggled to convince the Ohio Indians to move west, he quickly found out that he would get little help from either John

McElvain or Henry Brish, since the two men despised each other. McElvain was angry that he had been completely cut out of the plans to remove the Seneca. He agreed that the Seneca were ready to head west along with the Delaware, a once "noble" tribe that had fallen into a truly "dissipated" state. The Ottawa would probably be the next tribe to go, since so many settlers were crowding around them in the Maumee River valley, but the Shawnee and Wyandot would most certainly refuse to move anywhere.[38] However, none of these observations, which he made frequently to government officials, seemed to matter. Instead, Jackson's administration had placed its trust in Henry Brish, his subordinate. Brish went about making plans to sell all the property of the Seneca and take the tribe west without consulting McElvain. When McElvain asked if he could fire Brish for insubordination, the War Department said no, claiming that the Seneca trusted him and were relying on him to oversee their removal.[39]

There was an even more important problem facing Gardiner than dissension between Ohio's Indian agent and his subagent. From the time that the Seneca had signed the treaty, the chiefs regretted their decision. They were certain they had made a terrible mistake and did everything in their power to delay the departure of their people. First, they promised to depart by June 1831, but then decided to wait until the "roasting-ear time," when the corn was ready to harvest in August. But when the time arrived, they told Gardiner that they could not go, since most of their chiefs were in New York to surrender the wampum belt that tied the Ohio Seneca to the rest of the Iroquois Confederation. In their absence, and over the protest of John McElvain, subagent Brish decided to move forward with the sale of property that the tribe would be unable to carry when they were finally forced west. He threw himself so completely into his work that he resigned as the subagent of the Seneca. He could now devote all of his energy to the tribe's removal.[40]

Brish announced the sale of the tribe's property in a broadside distributed in towns that had sprung up around the Seneca reserve. The sale was set for ten o'clock in the morning on September 22, 23, and 24. The first day's sale would be held at the home of the Seneca chief Samuel Cloud Spicer, the second day at the Seneca council house on the Sandusky, and the final sale at the tribe's council house near Green Creek. All the livestock, farm equipment, and chattel property that the Seneca could not take with them would be sold for cash only. The sheer amount and type of goods up for sale proved the claim false that these Indians still lived as wandering hunters rather than substantial farmers.

Plows, wagons, and guns went quickly along with shovels and hoes. So did household items such as tables, bureaus, dishes, skillets, and even butter churners. The tribe sold cows, hogs, and especially horses, including older mares, blind animals, and yearlings, with the promise that they could take their best horses across the Mississippi. Farmers who came to the sale took away bushels of corn, beans, squash, and potatoes. Seneca reserve improvements, including cleared fields, cabins, fences, stables, and apple and peach orchards, were also up for sale. In his determination to move the tribe west as soon as possible, Brish sold off everything for far less than it was worth. When all transactions were complete, the sale of personal property yielded only $2,587, while the improvements garnered a mere $6,000.[41]

Meantime, Brish and McElvain argued over the best way for the tribe to travel to their new reserve. McElvain wanted them to go west by steamboat, while Brish favored an overland route; but either way, Brish planned to accompany them to St. Louis and then to the Neosho River. Gardiner was little help in deciding which route to take since he had moved on to treating with the Shawnee and Ottawa and could no longer be bothered with the Seneca. In the end, McElvain and Brish agreed to allow for both routes, with half the tribe boarding steamboats in Cincinnati, while the rest would head west along a route similar to the one the Prophet's party had taken.[42]

By late October 1831, a panic set in among the Seneca. Agent McElvain arrived on the reserve with more than two dozen wagons to start loading up the tribe. He admitted it was terrible for them to leave their "ancient home," but he believed their sudden change of heart stemmed more from the deep divisions within the tribe than any nostalgia. The Seneca were not really one people, he explained to Governor Cass, but were instead remnants of the many nations of the Iroquois. The tribe had at least 30 chiefs.

They vied bitterly for the position of principal chief and were not averse to murdering each other to achieve their ambition. To show the chiefs there was no turning back, McElvain sent a doctor from house to house to vaccinate everyone against smallpox.

The chiefs spoke openly of heading for New York, or even better for the safety of Green Bay or Canada, but it was too late. Time was moving forward too fast. McElvain made the case that it would be better for the tribe to head west across the Mississippi, because then they would be able to stay together. He ordered the families to board the waiting wagons for the fourth "trail of tears" out of Ohio.[43]

On November 5, 1831, 340 Seneca, along with a party of 58 Delaware, including the aged chief Captain Pipe, who had sold their land in 1829, started down the long road to the far western country. The caravan stretched seventy-five miles alongside the Sandusky. McElvain soon found the exodus to be a more difficult task than he had originally imagined. He complained to the War Department of many things, including the fact that the Seneca and Delaware had to stop at every Ottawa and Shawnee village along the way to "bid farewell to their friends." Costs were mounting, and he knew he would have to explain this to Jackson's penny-pinching administration. He had told the War Department that the Seneca and Delaware could be moved west for only $12,500, but one week into the removal, costs were climbing past his original estimate. At best, Indian removal was a "difficult, tedious, disagreeable," business, made worse by "designing[,] wicked men," like his subagent. As his last act as the subagent of the tribe, before resigning his post, Henry Brish had rented out the Seneca's sturdy homes, according to McElvain, in order to line his own pockets.[44]

Brish complained, too, to the Office of Indian Affairs. He saw himself as the Seneca's protector, who was doing his level best to protect their interests as they headed west. He had sold off all the Seneca property that could not be taken west. He had put his friends in charge of protecting the Seneca cabins until he could return from across the Mississippi and sell these off, too. However, even before the tribe left Ohio, the "work of destruction" had commenced. His friends could not stand guard over the Seneca homesteads round the clock, and soon settlers were taking away all they could carry, including windows, doors, brick and stone chimneys, and floorboards. They even tore down the fences, dug up apple and peach trees, and hauled everything away. In his own defense, Brish said he had no more control over this than he did over the weather that would plague the tribe on its long journey westward. The weather in November was already bitterly cold, and the rain never stopped. At times the roads were nearly impassable, and the Seneca wagons could only travel five miles a day.[45]

Shortly before the Seneca reached Dayton, the "land party" of 110 Seneca along with the Delaware, led by Captain Pipe, broke away from the "water party" and headed west out of the state. They would go overland to St. Louis. Brish, who had demanded a land route, decided to stay with the water party, though he worried it was too late in the season to travel west by wagon; but McElvain disagreed. He believed the tribes were good hunters and would be able to support themselves without any extra supplies beyond the tents he had provided for them. He did not seem to realize that Indiana and Illinois were no longer territories in a wilderness loaded with game but states in the Union filled with farms and towns of American settlers. The War Department had allocated funds for him to purchase new blankets for every member of the tribe, but he decided not to buy them because the British had given the Seneca blankets the summer before, when the tribe made its annual visit to Fort Malden. Nor did he purchase fifty new rifles, which the government had authorized.[46]

The land party departed with no further instructions than to head for St. Louis, where William Clark would be waiting for the emigrating Seneca and Delaware to send them to the Neosho River valley. The rest continued to Dayton, where they were to travel on the Miami and Erie Canal to Cincinnati. As they prepared to board the canal boats, they were told to leave their finest horses behind. McElvain had promised that if they sold their broken-down animals before leaving the Ohio reserve, they would be able to take their best horses and ponies with them across the Mississippi. But now, with the cost of their removal steadily rising, the heartbroken Seneca could only stand by and watch as their beloved animals were sold away from them for pennies on the dollar.[47]

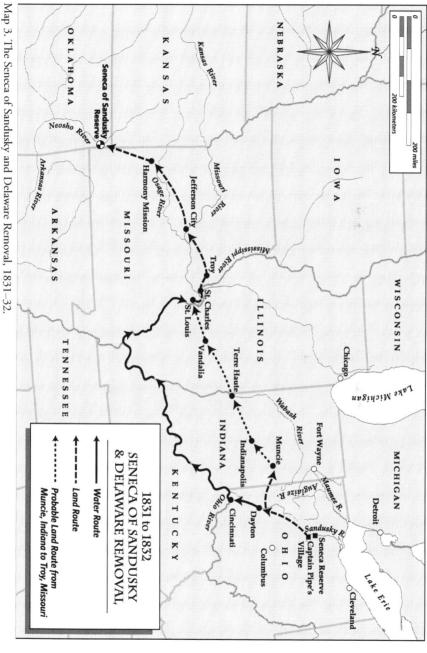

Map 3. The Seneca of Sandusky and Delaware Removal, 1831–32.

On November 5, the water party, numbering 231 Seneca, boarded a steamboat named the *Benjamin Franklin* in Cincinnati, and eleven days later they arrived in St. Louis. William Clark was surprised to meet people traveling with so much property. They had boxes full of everything they would need to establish new farms along the Neosho. Clark was astounded when, amid all the farm implements packed so carefully, he found peach stones, tucked away in hopes of planting orchards on the distant plains. The Seneca were obviously not degraded warriors, struggling to transform from self-sufficient hunters to sedentary farmers. They were, instead, successful pioneers who had somehow been caught in the cross fire of the national debate over Indian removal. Clark told Brish to have them store their belongings in a warehouse on the Mississippi and then head for a temporary camp seven miles outside the city. Brish was suddenly shaken at the prospect that the Seneca, who had come from such comfortable homes and farms, were about to be "thrown in the wilderness, in the midst of winter."

Even though it was still autumn, the weather felt like the dead of winter. Clark secured blankets for every Seneca, along with rifles, axes, hoes, and plows, before sending them to a camp eight miles outside of St. Louis. Brish remained behind collecting even more supplies, including wagonloads of pork and flour, which the Seneca would need if they were to survive until spring. He railed against McElvain for failing to supply the Indians with enough food and blankets before leaving Ohio. His preparations took so long that he was not ready to lead the Seneca to their new reserve until early December. When the wagon train finally reached St. Charles, where the tribe was to cross the Missouri River, many Seneca were so sick they had to be left behind.

Those who headed across the Missouri stopped at the town of Troy, some fifty-five miles northwest of St. Louis. Neither they nor their horses could go any farther in the terrible weather, since wherever he looked, Brish saw people "frost-bitten, sick, and some dying." The children were suffering the most—not only from the cold but from an outbreak of the measles. In their despair, the Seneca demanded whiskey and turned on each other in drunken rages, killing their enemies to settle new and old scores. Brish wrote home requesting three friends to join him in Missouri, just to keep the "dissipated" and "bloodthirsty" Seneca from destroying themselves. He was tempted to abandon them and go home to Ohio, but the distraught Seneca begged him to go back and find the land party lost somewhere in Indiana or Illinois.[48]

Coming to his senses, Brish purchased still more supplies for those stranded at Troy, and then headed back across the Mississippi to look for the Seneca and the small party of Delaware who had taken the overland route. They were camped just outside of Muncie, Indiana, about eighty miles east of the Ohio border. The weather had been as cold in Ohio and Indiana as it was in Missouri. Four people had already died, along with at least eighteen horses. Most of the rest were too weak to travel onward, especially after John McElvain stopped supplying them. They had only survived because their interpreter, Martin Lane, used his own money to buy them food. They had written a desperate petition to William Clark telling him of their troubles. They included a letter to Brish telling him that they were in Indiana, where they would wait until spring to come west, but the letter arrived after he left Missouri and was on his way back east. He finally found the Seneca and Delaware near Muncie, and decided to stay with them through the winter. In the spring of 1832, he brought them west to Troy, Missouri, where he finally reunited both parties. He then led them across the state, struggling through rain, cold, flooded streams, more cases of the measles, and finally through an attack of flies that made life so miserable for the oxen that they could only travel at night. It took five days just to make the ferry crossing at Jefferson City on the Missouri, and another month to reach Harmony Mission in the southwestern corner of the state.[49]

On July 4, 1832, after nearly eight months of travel, the first group of Indians to be officially removed from Ohio finally arrived in their new home on the Neosho River. Among the survivors, Henry Brish counted 352 Seneca and Delaware along with some Cayuga who had come west to live with their relatives. At least 30 people had died on the long trek, while others were still along the trail making their way toward the tribe's reserve in the northeastern corner of the Indian Territory. Brish would regret for the rest of his life forcing these people to go west at the wrong time of the year and without proper provisions: "I charge myself with cruelty in forcing these unfortunate people on," Brish confessed to William Clark, "at a time when a few days delay might have prevented some deaths, and rendered the sickness of others more light."[50]

The Seneca who had survived the trip west were disappointed to learn that the government had plotted out their reserve on land promised to the Cherokee. In late December 1832, at the Seneca Agency near the headwaters of the Cowskin River in Oklahoma, the tribe's chiefs signed a treaty exchanging 67,000 acres west of the Neosho for 60,000 acres east of the river, directly adjacent to the Missouri line.[51] Meanwhile, back in Ohio, a government surveyor, with the ironic last name of "Christmas," headed across the Seneca reserve carefully plotting out six-mile-by-six-mile square townships. He marked the trees that the Seneca had once used to identify the property lines of their own farms as the corners for the thirty-six sections within each township. By the end of the year, all 40,000 acres of the rich soil of the Seneca reserve, except where the tribe's empty and decaying villages stood, and a 160-acre plot at the lower rapids of the Sandusky that the tribe had set aside for Henry Brish, had been surveyed and thrown open for settlement.[52]

EIGHT

The Shawnee Exile

According to their own legends and tribal memories, the Shawnee had migrated many times. They remembered in ages past crossing over water and coming into a new country. Where they had come from to get to this place or what body of water they had passed over during their migration, they could no longer remember but they knew it was long ago. After a time of wandering, they came to settle in a place that the French and the Americans later called Ohio. Here they made allies with the Delaware and enemies of the Iroquois, who pushed them out of their new homeland. They traveled south to a warmer, mountainous country with swamps and marshland, where the other tribes called them the Shawnee, or "Southerners." Wherever they went, whether past the town of Savannah or along a river called Sewanee, they left their name behind them. Along the way they made friends with the Muskogee, or Creek, Confederation and enemies of the Cherokee and Choctaw. In the south, they first encountered a people they named the Shemanese, or "Long Knives." They were the colonists from Virginia who always spoke of peace even as they placed the bright shining sword of war before the Indians. The Shawnee later used the term for all the Americans.

It was hard to escape these people. Hungry for land for their farms and plantations, they moved up the eastern rivers in the thirteen colonies strung along the Atlantic. To escape from them, the Shawnee returned north across the Belle Rivière of the French, called the Oyo by the Seneca, and settled in their former homeland along the Great and Little Miami rivers and their tributaries. Like other tribes who came to Ohio in the eighteenth century, the country seemed a refuge from the fierce fighting elsewhere on the continent, but the promised peace proved to be elusive. A bloody war broke out between the French and the Americans for control of the Ohio River and the land that lay north of it. The Shawnee, like most of the other tribes, sided with the French. When they were defeated, the tribe joined Pontiac. When he was defeated, they went on to fight Lord Dunmore and the Virginians, who wanted to settle across the Ohio River. The Shawnee kept Ohio, but lost Kentucky and were soon swept up in another war, being British allies against the rebellious colonists in the American Revolution. When the war was lost and Great Britain surrendered Ohio to the United States, the Shawnee refused to recognize the treaty that gave up their country to the Americans. Under the leadership of their great war chief Wawayapiersenwaw, better known as Blue Jacket, they held off the armies sent against them until Anthony Wayne finally defeated them at Fallen Timbers. A year later at Greeneville, they relinquished the country along the Great and Little Miami rivers, where they had lived for two generations, and most headed north and west, with some going even farther across the Mississippi.

A decade later, the tribe broke apart even more completely when Tecumseh and the Prophet put their confederation together. Many younger chiefs and warriors joined the charismatic brothers, but older leaders, most notably Black Hoof, opposed them and remained loyal to the United States. But whether they supported Tecumseh or fought against him, it did not seem to matter to the Americans. While the animosity between the Indians and the Americans was forgotten at Springwells in 1815, so was the loyalty. Two years later, the Ohio tribes, whether they had sided with the British or the Americans in the War of 1812, saw most of their territory taken away. By way of the treaty signed at the Foot of the Rapids, they were placed on township reserves in northwestern Ohio with promises that the strife was over and that this land would be theirs forever.

From this point forward, the Shawnee who remained in Ohio, much like the Seneca and the Wyandot, did everything in their power to meet the demands of the Americans. Even the proudest warriors in the tribe became farmers, learning how to raise livestock and build barns and fences to protect their crops and their animals. They had watched as Colonel Lewis and the Prophet, who for all their differences could not tolerate such a life, headed across the Mississippi. The Seneca, who had just sold their land, would soon follow them. Many Shawnee feared it was only a matter of time before negotiators arrived at Wapakoneta, Hog Creek, and Lewistown, demanding their removal, and forcing them to give up their land in Ohio in exchange for an unknown country and an unknown future in the grassy plains west of the Mississippi. Even as rumors swirled through their villages in the late spring of 1831 that Colonel Gardiner was on his way to take their land, most Shawnee could not believe that the Americans would force them into exile.[1]

Gardiner finally arrived among the Shawnee in late June or early July. He laid out the government's plans for the tribe's removal as an ultimatum and not as something that was up for debate. First, he made sure to get the French fur trapper Francis Duchouquet, the tribe's most trusted interpreter, drunk, so that he could not help in the negotiations. Then for a full day and a half, he browbeat the Shawnee into believing that their situation was hopeless. It must have been disconcerting to hear a white man make the case that the Shawnee must leave Ohio, because the settlers who surrounded them were so evil. Look how they trample your fields and steal your cows and horses, Gardiner reminded them. They sell you whiskey and murder your young men knowing they will never be brought to justice. Surely, he chided the Shawnee, you have seen how untrustworthy the white man is. From William Penn, an imposter who "acted no better than a thief," to the greedy Georgians of the present age, the story was always the same: the whites took what they wanted, and the Indians were left with nothing.[2]

But now the situation was different. President Andrew Jackson had devised a plan to make the Shawnee rich. He would give them a 100,000-acre tract near their kinsmen from Missouri along the Kansas River. They could head west with a surveyor and pick out the land for themselves. Before they left for their new home, the government would pay them for the improvements they had made on their Ohio reserves. The Shawnee would receive cash for every barn, fence, orchard, field, and cabin sold before starting west. Gardiner assured them that the flow of money would not end there. It would continue with the government contributing thirty cents for every acre sold, which would earn 5 percent annual interest in the US Treasury. The Shawnee could make yearly withdrawals from the fund or take a lump sum payment.

Gardiner closed the council by assuring the Shawnee that they would live next to their kinsmen from Missouri who had already settled on a new reserve in Kansas that was rich in buffalo, elk, and deer. The tribe's old friend William Clark had negotiated the deal six summers before on behalf of the entire tribe. Gardiner also promised that the Shawnee would have all the guns they ever needed along with a sawmill, gristmill, and tools of every description. But he added that if they refused to move west, Ohio's government would simply incorporate the tribe's remaining reserves into the state. The president would no more stand in the way of Ohio taking control of Shawnee land than he was standing in the way of Georgia robbing the Cherokee of their territory. Once the reserves were part of Ohio, the Shawnee would have to pay taxes on their land. Their young men would be forced to build roads for the state without any payment. The whites would overrun their villages, killing their people, trampling their crops, and stealing farms and livestock without fear of prosecution. Gardiner left with a warning that he would be back within the month to hammer out the details of the removal treaties. The first would be negotiated with the Shawnee and Seneca of Lewistown, while the next would be with the Shawnee of Wapakoneta and Hog Creek. Gardiner also planned to negotiate a treaty with the Ottawa who lived at Oquanoxa's village and at Old Tawa town along the Auglaize River, in the hope that they would be sent west with the Shawnee and Seneca.[3]

After Gardiner left, the world seemed to come undone for the Shawnee. Local traders descended on the tribe demanding immediate payment for their debts before they departed for the West. This put even more pressure on the Shawnee to give up their reserves in Ohio. Most saw no way out except to sign whatever treaty Gardiner placed in front of them when he returned. They could use the money from the sale of their lands to pay off their debts and then head west as quickly as possible. Only Henry Harvey told the Shawnee not to be intimidated and urged them instead to hold their ground. Now a grown man with a family of his own, he had been at the treaty negotiations and did not like the tactics that Gardiner used to frighten the tribe. If the Shawnee refused to sell, he argued, the government would back down and let them stay in Ohio. But few were listening to Harvey anymore, especially after a tragedy more terrible than their possible removal across the Mississippi struck the tribe. Sometime in the middle of July 1831, their beloved chief Black Hoof died.[4]

Black Hoof was well over 100, maybe even closer to 120, when he passed away. He had been a warrior for his people since the days of the French and Indian War when he joined in the ambush of General Edward Braddock south of Fort Duquesne. Black Hoof went on to fight against Anthony Wayne at Fallen Timbers and negotiate peace with him on behalf of his tribe at Greeneville. Like all the chiefs who signed the Treaty of Greeneville, he never went to war against the United States again. In 1802, he met with Thomas Jefferson and from then on guarded the golden chain the president had given his tribe as a symbol of the enduring friendship between the Americans and the Shawnee. He also cherished a letter from Jefferson's secretary of war, Henry Dearborn, in which he relates that the president would "pay the most sacred regard to existing treaties between your respective nations and ours, and protect your whole territory against all intrusions that may be attempted by white people."[5]

During the War of 1812, Black Hoof had kept most of his people from joining Tecumseh. After the war ended, he negotiated for the tribe at Springwells and at the Foot of the Rapids. Once the Shawnee were settled on their remaining reserves in northwest Ohio, he oversaw the process of teaching his people how to farm year round with the help of Quaker missionaries. He had opposed the two great proponents of removal to the West, Colonel Lewis and the Prophet, arguing that neither man had the authority to speak for the tribe. He was especially angry at Colonel Lewis for attempting to negotiate a future for the Shawnee with the Cherokee, the traditional enemies of the tribe. Even worse, he considered the Prophet a disgraced madman.

Black Hoof, however, had seen much in his long life and knew when the future was no longer possible but instead inevitable. The Americans seemed determined to take every last inch of Indian land in the East, especially since the election of Jackson. Perhaps the Shawnee should move west on their own before the government forced removal on them. Black Hoof informed Indian agent John Johnston that he would be willing to take the remaining Shawnee across the Mississippi, but only if he could go there himself and choose the best land for his people. Johnston relayed the message to Lewis Cass, still governor of the Michigan Territory. But before the government could take Black Hoof up on his offer, Jackson had become president, John McElvain had replaced John Johnston as the agent of the Shawnee, and the Indian Removal Act had been signed into law. By the summer of 1831, the Seneca of Sandusky had already sold their land, and the Shawnee were next on the list for removal. Suddenly the future seemed more troubling than ever to the Shawnee. What would happen to the tribe now that their beloved chief was no longer with them? Should they try to stay in Ohio? Or was removal as inevitable as Black Hoof believed it to be and so they must go west?[6]

Henry Harvey remembered how terrible the loss of Black Hoof was to the tribe at this difficult time. He and his family hurried from his farm near Wapakoneta to the cabin where the dead chief was laid out. In front of the cabin door, the tribe's best hunters had piled up wild game, including twenty deer and numerous turkeys, while the women had brought bread. All this would be eaten at the feast that would follow the burial. Inside the cabin, the chief's body, which was wrapped in a new Indian blanket, lay on a stone slab. Around him were all the gifts his people had brought for him, calico, leather belts, and ribbon. They had carefully placed his prize possessions, including his gun, tomahawk, knife, and pipe, nearby. Harvey later recalled the awful silence among the Shawnee as they kept their eyes firmly fixed on the dead chief who lay motionless before them. "Not one word was spoken for hours," he later wrote in his history of the tribe. The Shawnee seemed like children who had lost their only parent and now had no one to look out for them.

When the time came for the burial, four young men carefully lifted the chief's body and carried him out of the cabin. The new head chief John Perry, the aged father of the younger Perry who had gone west with the Prophet, came next with the other chiefs following behind him in single file. Then Harvey and his wife followed without their baby who was left behind with a Shawnee woman. She would make sure that the child did not cry out and disturb the burial. Finally, the rest of the Shawnee came along behind them. Together they stood in silence at the burial site.

Once the chief had been laid in the ground with wooden planks placed around him like a coffin, John Perry took out a bag of tobacco seeds. Starting at the chief's head and walking around the grave, he cast the seeds on the body. Silently and in single file, the Shawnee and the Harvey family headed back to Wapakoneta. Before leaving for home later that evening, Henry Harvey tried to reassure the tribe that the government would not take their land away from them. No matter what Colonel Gardiner had said, the Shawnee had done everything the Americans asked of them since the ending of the War of 1812. The United States would honor its treaties with the tribe and let the Shawnee stay in Ohio.[7]

What Harvey did not know was that the decision to remove the Shawnee had already been made, not just in the broad strokes of the president's vision, but right down to the last penny as planned by John Eaton, Jackson's close friend and his first secretary of war. With the Seneca treaty acting as the "foot in the door" for the remaining negotiations in Ohio, John Eaton had given Gardiner even more detailed mathematical calculations to follow when negotiating treaties with the remaining Ohio tribes, including the Shawnee. There would be no "exchange" of territory, as the removal act had mandated. Instead, the tribes would sell their land to the government, which would then open the land to Americans for sale and settlement. Once a tribe's land was sold, the govern-

ment would deduct anywhere from 62.5 to 70 cents for every dollar made for expenses related to settling the Indians in their new
home across the Mississippi. The remaining 30 to 37.5 cents
could be given immediately to the tribe, but more likely the
money would be placed in the sinking fund that Gardiner had
described to the Shawnee. The government would then have thirty years to pay back the principal to the tribes. According to
Eaton's formula, the tribes could sell hundreds of thousands of
acres and receive not one penny in the process. He assured
Gardiner that all this was being done "at the pleasure of
Congress," and so reminded himself that, under the Constitution
of the United States, the House of Representatives and the Senate
would have to be involved in Indian removal, even though the act
gave full power to the president to oversee the process.[8]

Eaton and his staff in the War Department had carefully chart-
ed out for Gardiner how many people and how much land would
be involved in the removal of the Ohio tribes. They plotted out all
the information so carefully that Gardiner need only look at the
charts he carried with him as he headed for the Shawnee reserves
to know what was at stake.

Tribe	Souls	Acres	To be given West of Mississippi River
Wyandots	500	163,000	165,000
Shawnees	600	117,000	150,000
Senecas	200	40,000	50,000
Ottawas	300	50,000	70,000
	1600	370,000	435,000

The charts also listed blankets, plows, hoes, axes, and guns,
which the Shawnee and the other tribes would receive. In the end,
the tally of goods required to transfer the Indians west of the
Mississippi came to $10,000. Another $60,000 would have to be
added to the total for daily rations on the long trip west. Eaton
estimated this cost based on $30 "per head," an amount that
Jackson thought fair and often warned his War Department never
to exceed.[9]

Since the government would have the added expense of negotiating the treaties that removed the tribes, Eaton calculated

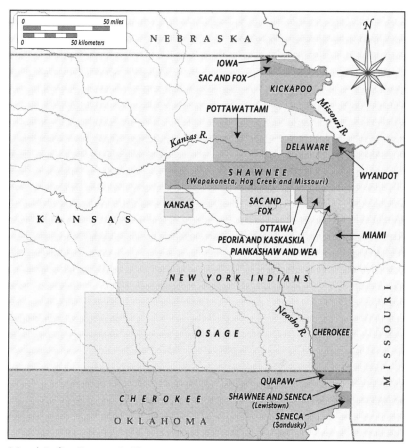

Map 4. Indian Reserves in Kansas.

another $74,000 would be necessary, at a rate of 20 cents per acre. This brought the total of removing the Ohio tribes to $134,000. The War Department had also promised Gardiner $5 per diem plus another $3 for every twenty miles he traveled. Giving him a last warning to practice "strict economy," Eaton told Gardiner that he could draw up to another $2,000 from the War Department. This would boost the cost of the removal of the Ohio tribes to at least $136,000. With only $500,000 allocated for removal of all the tribes in the Indian Removal Act, Eaton had already granted close to 37 percent of the appropriated funds to send only 1,600 "souls" west from Ohio. If someone in Jackson's administration was paying attention to the cost of removing the Ohio tribes as the test case for overall removal, they would have seen that the bill for sending the larger southern tribes west, most specifically the Cherokee, would climb into the millions of dollars. Still in the end, the government hoped to recover any losses accrued from removing the tribes from Ohio and elsewhere by selling their surrendered reserves at one to two dollars per acre. When all the balance sheets were tallied, the tribes would have paid for their passage west, and the president would be assured of making a tidy profit for his nation.[10]

Not long after the death of Black Hoof, Colonel Gardiner arrived back at Lewistown, determined to write a treaty with the Indians there before moving on to Wapakoneta. He promised the Shawnee and Seneca a 60,000-acre tract along the Neosho River lying near the tracts of the Seneca of Sandusky and the Cherokee. On July 20, 1831, thirteen chiefs, headmen, and warriors of the "Mixed Band," as it was commonly known, made their marks on a treaty giving up their land in Ohio forever. Out of the proceeds of the sale of their reserve at Lewistown, the government would furnish a sawmill and a gristmill and hire a blacksmith for the Shawnee and Seneca on their new reserve. The government would also use the profits to pay for the move and support both tribes for one year. Supplies, including blankets, plows, hoes, axes, rifles, horse gear, and tents, would likewise be provided out of the sale of their land back east. They would also receive $6,000 for improvements made on their Ohio reserve, but this, too, would be taken out of the profits from the sale of their land. Once they arrived in their new home, they could take possession of the reserve, knowing that it belonged "in fee simple to them and their heirs forever" as long as they remained a tribe. They could never sell the land to individuals, but instead could only sell it in total to the government.

The Shawnee and Seneca demanded only a few things during the negotiations. One was to honor their Indian agent and interpreter, Colonel James McPherson. He had been captured during the American Revolution and lived among the Indians for over fifty years. He was married to a white woman who had been raised as a captive of the Seneca, and both were much beloved by the local tribes for their generosity to the Indians at their trading post in Lewistown. This was the main reason why the Shawnee and Seneca asked that Colonel McPherson be given a half section of land at Lewistown in the treaty that removed them from Ohio.[11] An adopted son, Henry McPherson, of the Mixed Band got 160 acres. Finally Martin Lane, the interpreter who had helped the Seneca and Delaware on their trip west and who was married to a quarter-blood Seneca woman, would be granted 160 acres, the exact location of which would be chosen by President Jackson.[12]

Colonel Gardiner headed next to Wapakoneta, where on August 8, 1831, twenty-one chiefs of the remaining Shawnee signed a treaty nearly identical to the one just signed by the Mixed Band. One of the major differences dealt with where the Shawnee would be going. They would give up their two reserves in exchange for 100,000 acres within the fifty-mile square grant given to the Missouri Shawnee along the Kansas River. If this land was already settled, then the president would choose another 100,000 acres right next to the Missouri Shawnee. Another difference included an advance of $13,000 for improvements made at Wapakoneta and Hog Creek, along with the promise of specific types of tools for building and proper scythes for harvesting wheat. The Shawnee also requested that Francis Duchouquet be granted the land assigned to him in previous treaties and that Joseph Parks, a quarter-blood Shawnee who had been the tribe's interpreter, be given 640 acres of their surrendered land in Ohio. They asked that money be set aside for their relatives living near the Huron River in Michigan in case they ever wanted to come west. Like their kinsmen at Lewistown, the Shawnee of Wapakoneta and Hog Creek would be granted land in Kansas as a fee simple, meaning they could hold this land "forever" as long as they remained a tribe. They, too, could not sell their land to any individual, but only to the government.[13]

Gardiner headed next to a council with the Ottawa at Maumee Bay. He was particularly interested in removing the Ottawa from their two reserves along the Auglaize River valley just north of the Shawnee in Wapakoneta. Gardiner knew that many Ottawa were intermarried with the Shawnee living farther south and would hopefully want to go west with their relatives. On August 30,

1831, twenty-four Ottawa chiefs agreed to surrender the three-mile square tract at Oquanoxa's village on the Auglaize and the five-mile square tract at Old Tawa Town on Blanchard's Fork, whose use they had been granted by the Treaty at the Foot of the Rapids in 1817. In exchange, the tribe would receive a 34,000-acre tract south or west of the reserve of the Shawnee from Missouri and Ohio on the Kansas River. It would be granted "by patent in fee simple" and belong to the Ottawa as long as they remained a tribe. The chiefs also agreed to give up their reserves at Roche de Boeuf and Wolf Rapids in the Upper Maumee River valley in exchange for 40,000 acres right next to the reserve of the Ottawa from the Auglaize River. Gardiner promised that the Ottawa would receive a profit from the sale of the 21,760 acres that they had just surrendered after seventy cents per acre was deducted from the total to pay for the tribe's removal to the West and to settle all debts with local traders listed in the treaty. They would also receive blankets, rifles, axes, plows, horse gear, and tents as gifts from the government.

For the moment, only the Ottawa living at the two villages on the Auglaize promised to move west. The rest of the tribe would remain on their reserves near the mouth of the Maumee or at three temporary reserves set up by the removal treaty where they would be allowed to stay for three years. One reserve was a section of 640 acres granted to Chief Waubegakake near the mill of the tribe's friend Peter Manor; the second was a section and a half of 960 acres set aside for Muckquiona, also known as Bearskin, below Wolf Rapids. The third reserve was a river island, near where Bearskin was growing corn. Whether the Ottawa living on these temporary reserves would be forced to go west in three years was not mentioned in the treaty.[14]

While Colonel Gardiner was working out the deal with the Ottawa, Henry Harvey convinced the Shawnee that the treaties they had just signed were fraudulent. He was certain that Gardiner had lied to them and that the government would overturn the agreements if the Shawnee brought the facts to the attention of Jackson's administration. John Johnston agreed and wrote an angry letter to Lewis Cass complaining that the tribe had not realized what they were signing. He accused Gardiner of failing to pay the Shawnee for the many horses stolen by settlers and offering them far less for their improvements than they were actually worth. In the fall of 1831, with the encouragement of both Harvey and Johnston, the tribe gathered in a council in Richmond, Indiana. They chose a delegation to present their case before the president. In the first week of December, John Perry and several other chiefs along with Henry Harvey arrived in Washington and met with the new secretary of war, Lewis Cass, who had replaced John Eaton just one day after the treaty with the Shawnee of Wapakoneta and Hog Creek had been signed.[15]

Cass had been getting reports from Ohio that Gardiner was incompetent and often arrived at treaty negotiations completely drunk. Charges of corruption and drunkenness had plagued Gardiner's political career for some time. In 1825, the Ohio House of Representatives denied him a seat after a challenger claimed he made improper campaign promises. Right after Jackson's election, Gardiner had been nominated for a position in the land office in Tiffin, but after several Ohio politicians complained of his excessive drinking, he was not confirmed. John McLean, then the postmaster general and later a justice of the Supreme Court, described Gardiner as "frequently drunk" and on one occasion so inebriated that he fell off his horse and had to ride in a wagonload of corn. Both the *Scioto Gazette* (Chillicothe, OH) and Columbus *Ohio Monitor* censured Gardiner's character and his methods. Secretary Cass urged the president to review the treaties, but Jackson answered that the Shawnee should "fare no better" than any other tribe. The Senate did review the treaties and the charges against Gardiner. A leading force behind the investigation was Ohio's newly elected senator Thomas Ewing, a dedicated anti-Jacksonian. However, the Senate, firmly under the control of Jackson's followers, decided that while Gardiner might have been a bit overzealous, the treaties were still valid.[16]

The Shawnee might have turned again to Lewis Cass for help if they had not found their old friend greatly changed. The man who had negotiated the treaties to win them their last reserves in northwest Ohio and who had studied their culture so diligently was now the leading architect of their removal. Cass had come to the conclusion that the Indians would never survive surrounded by the white man, who brought drink, debt, and many other miseries to the tribes. They must go west to the country past Missouri, where hundreds of thousands of acres of bountiful land would provide a good life for them. He dismissed the accomplishments of the many tribes living on their reserves in the eastern states, including Ohio, as the work of mere half-breeds. The pure-bred Indian had a resistance to the civilized life, which must be recognized and fostered. Once the tribes were across the Mississippi, the Indians should be allowed to continue in their old ways while slowly learning new ones from the white man, such as farming cash crops, raising livestock, and educating their children. Cass had ignored any evidence to the contrary that the eastern tribes were well on their way to a "civilized" life just as Jackson had done. There would be no turning back on the issue of removal for either man.[17]

Since he had assumed office, after most of Andrew Jackson's cabinet had resigned over Peggy Eaton, the scandalous wife of the former secretary of war, Cass had crafted detailed plans to make the "emigration" of the tribes, the word the president preferred to use rather than "removal," run like clockwork. Jackson had chosen Cass in part because he was an excellent writer who could lay out the case for the administration's Indian removal policy to the public—and, even more important, to the courts. He also knew Cass was an able administrator from his long service as the governor of the Michigan Territory. At first, Cass asked the president specific questions about Indian removal in the hopes of discussing the administration's plans before implementing them. But Jackson grew impatient with his new secretary of war. He expected Cass to work out the details of the policy that he had pushed through Congress and then move the tribes westward as quickly and economically as possible without further discussion.[18]

Cass got the message and went to work in the late summer and early fall of 1831, restructuring all matters dealing with the Indians in the War Department. The Congress had done away with the position of superintendent of Indian trade when it closed down the government trading posts. Thomas McKenney, the last superintendent, had stayed on in the Office of Indian Affairs to oversee dealings with the tribes until 1830. Secretary of War John

Eaton, who preferred making all the decisions related to the tribes himself, had replaced McKenney with Samuel S. Hamilton, a former clerk in the War Department. When Cass took over as secretary of war from Eaton, he recommended that Congress appoint a commissioner of Indian affairs. Congress agreed, and in July 1832 Elbert Herring, a lawyer and former judge from Connecticut who happened to be a close personal friend of Secretary Cass, became the first commissioner of Indian affairs with a salary of $3,000 per year.[19]

In an effort to win greater support for removal, especially after the disastrous first round of the emigration of the Choctaw, a tribe that would eventually lose 2,500 people, or one-sixth of their nation, Cass established a commission to explore the country across the Mississippi River, where the Indians would live. He chose Governor Montfort Stokes of North Carolina to head the commission. Stokes was the father-in-law of William B. Lewis, a close friend of Jackson since their days fighting together against the British and Indians on the southern frontier. Cass also chose Reverend John Freeman Schermerhorn, a Protestant minister from New York known for his missionary work among the tribes, and Henry Ellsworth, the twin brother of Congressman William Ellsworth of Connecticut who had fought so valiantly to defeat the Indian Removal Bill in the House. Cass picked the last two men specifically because they were from the North, where opposition to Indian removal remained high. Cass hoped that the commissioners would return with glowing reports of the western country, thus turning public opinion in favor of removal.[20]

Yet Cass put his best efforts into creating a more precise organization for Indian removal. He was fully aware of the suffering endured by the Choctaw and the Seneca, the first two tribes to head west since the Indian Removal Act was approved. He believed that better planning at the start would make removal easier for everyone. Above all else, the Indians must be supplied with everything they needed on the long trek to their new homes. For this reason, he placed the commissary general of subsistence, the chief officer in charge of purchasing and issuing all supplies for the US Army, in charge of Indian removal. Below him, "special agents" would be appointed to manage the emigration of specific tribes. These officials would be responsible for determining the route west for their charges, making sure they had a "just regard to economy and the health and comfort of the Indians." They must also keep perfect records of each decision made, especially regarding expenses.

Next, a "disbursing agent" would be appointed. He would be a US Army officer responsible for paying the bills from funds drawn directly from the commissary general's office. A "conducting agent," usually referred to as the "conductor," would then be chosen to organize removal in the field. He would call the Indians together at a specific time and place, instructing them in "punctuality" and giving them up to two weeks to get organized. He would then hire an "enrolling agent," who would keep a record of heads of the Indian households along with their age and sex. The conductor would also keep a diary of his own, called a "Journal of Occurrences," which would begin on the day he left with his tribe for the western country and end on the day he arrived with his tribe in their new home across the Mississippi.[21]

After Secretary Cass had set up the management hierarchy, he went on to organize details of the tribes' actual removal. The special agent in charge of removal would be given power to hire even more people, including property appraisers, interpreters, and "collectors," who would be paid per diem to help round up stray Indians. He would also inform the Indians under his charge about the goods they could take west. While the government would provide wagons for the journey, each one could only carry five hundred pounds of goods, calculated at ten pounds each per fifty people. Clothing, bedding, and small cooking utensils would be the only items allowed west. Everything else, like wooden furniture or heavy farm equipment, must be left behind. These items would be sold at a public auction along with any "improvements" that individual Indians had made on their land. This, too, would all be calculated in advance, with asking prices set at the current market value for all their cleared and fenced-in fields, apple and peach orchards, and finally cabins, barns, and other buildings. All livestock, such as horses, cows, and pigs, would be sold as well. Once everything was packed, only people "too young or too infirm" would be allowed to ride in a wagon or on a horse. Everyone else would be required to walk hundreds of miles west to their new homes across the Mississippi. They would be fed along the way, with the government providing 1 1/4 pounds of fresh meat or 3/4 of a pound of salted meat and 1 pound of flour or 3/4 of a quart of cornmeal per person each day.[22]

Before Henry Harvey and the Shawnee leaders arrived back in Ohio from their trip to Washington, the Lewiston band had sold all their goods in anticipation of moving west. They had already left their reserve and were camped just north of their old village, hoping to start their journey as soon as possible. But when they learned from the Wapakoneta band of the tribe that a Senate investigation was under way, which left the recent treaties with the Shawnee in limbo, they worried about how they would feed themselves. Where could they plant corn to live on if their removal to the West was delayed until the spring of 1832 or even later? They would have to survive the approaching winter on handouts from the Shawnee of Wapakoneta or their old friend John Johnston.

Gardiner did not receive further instructions from Lewis Cass until May 1832, when he was told to take immediate steps to remove the Shawnee, Seneca, and Ottawa from Ohio. He was ordered to get the tribes ready for departure sometime in late summer or early fall. They must definitely leave before the winter set in. As the special agent in charge of the "emigration," Gardiner was to pay close attention to which bands were leaving and in what order, what routes they would be taking west, how many men would be needed to move them, and above all else, how much the trip would cost. As Cass explained, "Economy in all arrangements and disbursements is indispensable and a strict attention will be required to the instructions."[23] Gardiner did as he was told, but as he went among the tribes preparing them to rendezvous at Lewistown by September at the latest, he increasingly sympathized with them. After all the pressure he had put on them to sign the removal treaties, followed by the humiliation of a Senate investigation into his behavior, he now took their side in every disagreement with Jackson's administration. In contrast to the correspondence of other agents working at the same time to remove the southern tribes, Gardiner's letters to the War Department were filled with increasing demands made on behalf of the Shawnee.[24]

First, Colonel Gardiner defended the Shawnee's request to go west by land and not by water. He carefully laid out the reasons why the tribe wanted this for Secretary Cass. The Shawnee were worried that their children would fall overboard and drown in the Ohio River. They also knew how dangerous steamboats could be, so they had no desire to "move by fire." The boilers that ran round the clock to make the steam that turned the big paddlewheels could explode and skin everyone alive. Passengers on deck would die in the same way "the white man cleans his hogs." Gardiner added there was yet another more delicate reason why the Shawnee refused to go by steamboat. As he explained, "their native modesty revolts" at the thought of using public toilets right out in front of everybody on deck. But most of all, the Shawnee would not go by water because they would not leave their horses behind them. The memory of the misery experienced by the Seneca of Sandusky, who just a year prior had watched as their beautiful stallions, mares, and ponies were sold off for pennies on the dollar, still haunted the Shawnee. The tribe had over five hundred horses, and they were determined to take them along.[25]

When Gardiner relayed their demand to travel overland, the War Department and the office of the commissary general both objected. Secretary Cass was worried that the Shawnee wanted to go west on horseback in order to join the uprising of Chief Black Hawk in Illinois. George Gibson, the commissary general of the US Army, worried about rising costs and the fact that the president was adamant that the Shawnee travel by water. Gardiner again defended the tribe. He told Cass that the Shawnee were loyal to the government and would even fight for the United States if called upon against the Sac and Fox. He made the case to the commissary general that traveling by land would be just as economical as traveling by water. Gibson answered that the president would have to make this decision himself, and at the moment he could not be reached since he was on his way back to Tennessee. Gardiner waited for the answer. At the last minute, Jackson changed his mind. This was in fact the only time in the long story of the removal of the eastern tribes across the Mississippi that he ever decided in favor of a request from the "emigrants," as the Indians were now called. Writing from the

Hermitage in Tennessee, the president agreed that the Shawnee could go west, down the fifth "trail of tears" out of Ohio, on horseback, as long as the overall cost of their removal remained twenty dollars a head.[26]

After Gardiner finally got Jackson's approval to take the tribes west by land, he planned to send the Mixed Band of Seneca and Shawnee first, letting them get a day or two ahead of the rest. Then the Ottawa and finally the Shawnee of Wapakoneta and Hog Creek would follow after them. By stretching the Indians out in this way, he hoped there would be no problems arising from rivalry among the tribes. But laying out the actual route that was best to take was much more difficult for Gardiner. At first he thought simply in terms of going from Lewistown to Indianapolis, down to Evansville on the Wabash, back up to Vandalia in south central Illinois, and across the Mississippi to St. Louis. But then he plotted out a more careful route, county by county, through Indiana and Illinois. The long caravan would still start at Lewistown, but it would head southwest to Greeneville, the place where Black Hoof and so many other chiefs had formally given up the fight against the Americans one year after Fallen Timbers, and then head some ten miles across the state line into Wayne County, Indiana.

The tribes would continue southwest into Rush County, and after that into Shelby County, where they would cross the Big Blue River. From there they would head through Morgan County until they met the White River. The many bands of Indians, stretching out for some eighty miles, would follow the White River southwest through Owen County. Once they made it to Johnson County, they would then head due west, crossing first the Eel River and then the Wabash into Illinois. Reaching Crawford County, they would pass through the state to Vandalia, where they would pick up the National Road and follow it through Bond and Madison counties toward the Mississippi. Once there, they would board ferries that would take them over to St. Louis. William Clark would then step in and direct them to their new homes along the Kansas or Neosho rivers.[27]

As he struggled to determine the best route to the West, Colonel Gardiner also worried that the Indians might run out of food for themselves and fodder for their horses before they got there. He knew that the administration had calculated the cost of rations down to the last penny. Convincing the president or his secretary of war to allocate more money for food would be difficult. He had already received many War Department letters reprimanding him for going into too much detail about his decision making. Government officials were only interested in how quickly and cheaply he could move the tribes west and nothing more.

With all this in mind, he turned for help to Colonel McPherson, whom he had come to know at his trading post at Lewistown. McPherson thought the rations proposed by the government were more in keeping with what soldiers usually got. He reminded Gardiner that during the War of 1812, Indians were given much more food than soldiers. In fact, they were given as much food as they wanted. For the long walk to Kansas and Oklahoma, he guessed they would need 1 1/2 pounds of flour, 1 1/2 pounds of fresh meat or one pound of salted meat, and one quart of corn per person each day. Gardiner detailed this in a letter to Secretary Cass, hoping the information would be forwarded to the president. But while Jackson had changed his mind about going by horseback, there would be no change about rations or anything else. The Indians would have to make do with the rations already allocated to them and their horses would have to find extra fodder in the cornfields along the way.[28]

Gardiner found his troubles multiplying as the time for the Indians' departure drew near. As he explained to the commissary general, "The whites are at times worse than the Indians." He was astounded at the local traders, who descended on the tribes like locusts coming upon fields of ripe grain. They demanded immediate payment of all debts, which in turn led Gardiner to ask the government to pay the tribes their yearly annuities before they left for their new reserves across the Mississippi. The whiskey traders who came into the Indian villages, hoping to make big profits from the tribes, were even worse. Gardiner complained that if he dispersed them on one day, they would be back on the next. He knew they would follow the wagon trains west, and that every night, once the tribes had made camp, the traders would be selling their homemade brew. They would not be satisfied, he complained, unless they could "filch" the Indians out of their last dollar. He assured the War Department that he would get the Shawnee, Seneca, and Ottawa safely out of Ohio, but he would need additional supplies and manpower, such as wagons with better horses and oxen, and more men, especially experienced wagon masters and strong workers who could build roads and clear paths to the West. He even demanded a doctor, explaining that the Indians were anxious for a "medicine man" to accompany them. Every request that Gardiner made, after his first request for the tribes to go on horseback, was turned down.[29]

As he finalized the last details of the removal of the tribes, Gardiner came into open conflict with Colonel John F. Lane, the US Army officer who had been appointed disbursing agent. Lane could not accept that Gardiner had won the right for the Indians to go west on horseback. He let the War Department know that he considered this foolhardy. He complained that the tribes had failed to plant crops, so they would be bringing no extra supplies with them. He also said they might not be able to find much more food by hunting on the planned route west. He worried that Indiana and Illinois were just as settled as Ohio, and that little game would be found there. Finally, how could all these people, especially old women, some of whom were over a hundred years old, and children, be expected to ride to Kansas on horseback? How would their horses, especially mares and colts, find enough fodder to survive? Going by steamboat, even if this meant selling off the horses at the docks, would have been more sensible.[30]

When Lane finally accepted the fact that the Indians were determined to go by horseback, he demanded that Gardiner call a council in Wapakoneta, so he could propose his own overland route to the West. Gardiner gathered the chiefs together and let Lane speak to them at length about the "better" way to Kansas. They listened patiently to his "flowery" speech that outlined a route starting at Bellefontaine and continuing through Urbana, Xenia, Lebanon, and Lawrenceburgh. As they passed through these "fine towns," they would see many "fine homes" and meet "many white people." The chiefs listened politely and asked for another council on the next day. This time Lane sat quietly, waiting for their response to his speech. Chief Wayweleapy, speaking for the whole group, reminded Lane, who was only twenty-two, that all the chiefs were old men. They had been in councils with the likes of Governor Lewis Cass and their old friend John Johnston. "Tell the President," he concluded, "we don't do business with boys." The crowd burst into laughter, much to the shame of Lane, who did not say a word, but left immediately for Lewistown to the "great merriment" of the chiefs.[31]

By the third week of September 1832, Colonel Gardiner was finally ready to lead the Mixed Band of Shawnee and Seneca from Lewistown, the Ottawa from the Auglaize River valley, and the Shawnee from Wapakoneta and Hog Creek west to their new homes across the Mississippi. As a final precaution before the journey, he made sure all the Indians were vaccinated against smallpox. He also spent whatever funds were necessary to outfit the wagon trains with enough food for the people and fodder for the horses hopefully to make the long trip to Kansas and Oklahoma. He spent so much cash, in fact, that the caravan would probably be out of money before reaching its final destination. He did not seem to mind and continued to send demands to the administration for help that would make the trip easier for the tribes, all of which were promptly ignored. A good party man, Gardiner never complained about Jackson's treatment of him and instead looked upon his assignment as a reward for his loyalty to the president. He often boasted that hundreds of other office seekers tried for his post, but he got the job because Jackson had such confidence in him. Daniel Dunihue, Gardiner's twenty-one-year-old nephew who had been hired as the assistant conductor for the Shawnee and Seneca of Lewistown, was fond of saying that his uncle was a "whole-hog" Jacksonian, right down to the sows and little piglets.[32]

In contrast to Gardiner's determination to get the caravan moving, the Indians, especially the Shawnee of Wapakoneta, did everything in their power to delay their departure, which was now set for September 18. Sometimes the chiefs went hunting and did not come back for days. At other times, they decided to get drunk, with most of the men and many women joining them. Even when Gardiner and his assistants could keep the whites out of their camp, the Shawnee went off on their own to buy whiskey from local farmers and traders. Funerals were another way that the

Indians delayed their departure. The ceremonies now extended for many days as the tribes remembered their dead.

One of the saddest funerals came right before the planned departure date. Mrs. McPherson, the wife of Colonel McPherson, had come down with the measles and died suddenly of an "apoplectic fit" in mid-September. The shock was great for the Shawnee and Seneca, who mourned her passing, and was even worse for Colonel McPherson, who resigned his post as conductor for the removal of the Lewistown band. Gardiner hired Daniel Workman, McPherson's son-in-law, and Judge John Shelby, a local politician who had moved north from Kentucky, to take over as the conductors for the Lewiston band. Then he waited for the tribes to finish their mourning, reminding them that they must leave soon or face the prospect of traveling on the western prairies in winter.[33]

As determined as he was to get the tribes moving, Colonel Gardiner had come to understand the ways of the Indians as time went on. He was especially sympathetic when they took time to go among the many graves of their dead, taking down the wooden fences and leveling the ground around them, so that no sign would be left behind once they had departed for the West. But the many assistants Gardiner had hired to help him were less sympathetic, at least at first. They especially did not understand why the Indians had to spend so much time dancing. For young American men on the western frontier, dancing was a pleasant pastime; but for the tribes, it was the most important way of expressing their beliefs as a group. What churchgoing was to the whites, dancing was to the Indians, and all ancient dances must be performed one last time before leaving Ohio.

First came the war dance, which the warriors always performed before leaving their villages to go fight. They stripped down to their breechcloths, and painted their bodies with fantastic shapes of monsters and serpents. They whooped and howled to the delight of the Indians, but at the cost of frightening the conductors, who were waiting to take them west. Next was the victory dance, performed when warriors returned to their villages. The women joined in the dance, singing about the bravery of their men. As beautiful as this dance was, the conductors learned that

the Dance of the Dead was the most important. It was tradition-
ally done every year in the fall, but now must be done in mid-
September, right before the tribes left Ohio. Long into the night,
they sang of everyone who had died, remembering their best qual-
ities and hoping these traits would be passed on to the living
members of the tribe.[34]

On the morning of September 18, 1832, the dances were done.
All the wooden houses built over the graves were dismantled and
the burial mounds leveled. Even if the Indians were far away in
Kansas and Oklahoma, no one would trample down the resting
places of their relatives and ancestors. Now it was time to set off on
the eight-hundred-mile trek west. The Mixed band of Seneca and
Shawnee, numbering about 250 people, would lead, with about
100 Ottawa following next, and the 450 Shawnee of Wapakoneta
would come last. The Shawnee of Hog Creek, around 80 people,
mainly women and children who were devoted to the Quaker missionaries, refused to go with the band from Wapakoneta, saying
they were all drunkards. They promised to go west in the following
spring under the leadership of John Park. He had acted as their
interpreter during the treaty negotiations with the Americans, and
would eventually become the tribe's head chief.[35]

David Robb, one of the conductors for the Shawnee of
Wapakoneta, remembered when the Indians were signaled to
leave. A very old man carrying a large gourd with a deer's leg bones
tied around its neck, whom Robb called a "high priest," mounted
his horse and rode to the front of the long line of wagons. The
priest gave out a blast on a large shell, the kind that Ohio's tribes
once used to call their people to the council houses at the center
of their villages, and then the horses and wagons, stretching eight
miles, headed toward Piqua and Greeneville. The chiefs followed
behind the old priest at the front. Most rode horseback, including
a 105-year-old white woman who had been kidnapped by the
Shawnee a century earlier in Green Briar, Virginia. Some of the
younger women and children walked beside the wagons, while
only the sick and very old rode inside the wagons.[36]

Colonel Gardiner, along with his conductors and assistants,
rode horseback beside the chiefs. They planned to rouse the
Indians by five o'clock every morning. Breakfast, prepared by the

women, would consist of meat and bread, and then the caravans would move out along the roads west until three or four in the afternoon, when they would stop and make camp, and the men would set up tents while the women cooked meat and bread for supper. Colonel Lane, the disbursing agent, would deliver daily rations of beef, bacon, and flour, and buy or arrange for fodder for the horses while on the caravan route. By nine o'clock, the camp retired in order to wake early. At this pace, Colonel Gardiner hoped to make about twenty miles a day, thereby arriving in Kansas and the Indian Territory before winter set in.[37]

The Shawnee made two sad stops along their route. The first came at Henry Harvey's farm, the Quaker missionary who had tried so valiantly to save them. Harvey found it almost unbearable to say good-bye to his friends he had known since childhood. He was haunted by one simple question: How could these people, who "reared up dwellings with their own hands, planted orchards and raised cattle, horses, and hogs," just as the government had long demanded, now be forced, "contrary to their will," into the barren West? The Indians had many questions for him: How would they survive, especially their women and children, on the long march west? Even if they arrived safely in Kansas and Oklahoma, how would they survive their first winter on the plains? And since the Americans took their Ohio land, which they had worked so hard to improve, wouldn't they do the same across the Mississippi? Harvey could answer none of these questions, but promised to follow the Shawnee west to Kansas in the following year and build a mission on their new reserve. The second stop came south of Lewistown at Piqua, where they said good-bye to John Johnston and his family one last time. Johnston's farm was laid out on the site of an old Shawnee town where Tecumseh once lived. There was a cool spring here, and Johnston had built a small cabin over it, where people could come and rest in the heat of summer. Leaving the scenes of their youth and the places where many of their dead lay buried brought the Shawnee and Colonel Johnston to tears.[38]

The fears that the Indians had about the long trip ahead of them came true right after they left Lewistown. The weather changed dramatically, with the clear days of late summer giving way to the driving rains of early autumn. The conductors, who were required by Secretary Cass to keep daily journals, recorded the misery that came with the rain. Wagons broke down and people became sick, some at first with bad colds and dysentery, but later with terrible coughs that turned out to be consumption. The conductors noticed that one group of "emigrants" bore their hardships better than the rest. Buoying everyone's spirits, remarkably, were the Indian women who gave birth along the way. One day they would climb into wagons to have their babies, and the next they were walking beside the wagons, smiling at their newborns in their arms.

The conductors were struck at the cheerfulness of the Indian mothers and commented that white women would not be so pleasant under similar circumstances. When death came among the Indians, though the conductors might grumble that the caravan would be delayed westward for an hour or so to make time for burials, they were moved at the sight of tears rolling down a mother's face as her "angel" was laid in the ground along with as many small gifts as could be spared. As Judge Shelby explained in his journal, this was a "melancholy spectacle," seeing the tribes scatter the bones of their children along the way just as they had left the bones of their fathers behind.[39]

Just as troubling was the drunkenness that plagued the wagon train. If the chiefs wanted whiskey, they got it from any town they passed, taking most of their people with them. But just as frequently settlers came out from the towns and farms along the way to sell whiskey to the tribes. Right after the Indians set up their tents and were cooking supper, the "locals" would arrive at the edges of the camp with whiskey for sale. Colonel Gardiner was stunned when even some Quakers showed up to sell whiskey. Night after night, he rounded up the white traders and threw them and their whiskey out of the camp. By the time the caravan crossed into Indiana, Gardiner enlisted several young Shawnee to act as guards around the camp. Their job was to send the whiskey traders packing as soon as they emerged from the surrounding woods. This did some good, but if the chiefs decided they needed whiskey, they still left their camps at night and headed with their people into the nearby towns to buy some.[40]

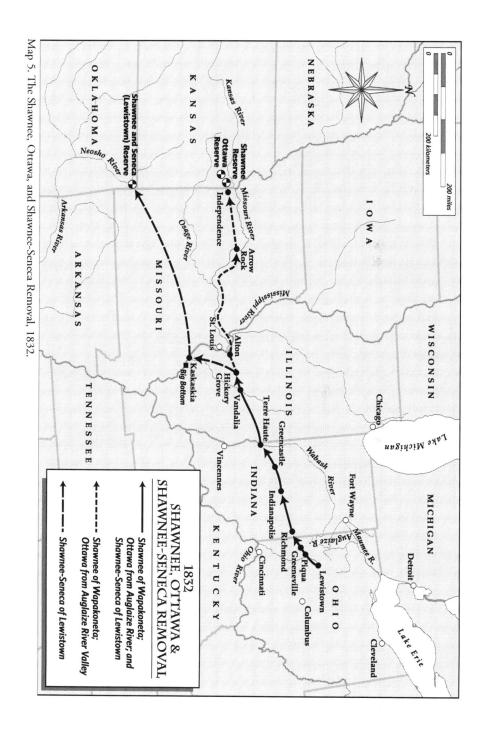

Map 5. The Shawnee, Ottawa, and Shawnee-Seneca Removal, 1832.

Things went from bad to worse when the caravan traveled from Richmond, Indiana, to the state capital, Indianapolis. The roads in Indiana were particularly bad and the rain seemed never to stop. Gardiner ordered that four horses, not the usual three, should pull every wagon through the ruts and the mud. On some mornings, the chiefs refused to move, saying they would wait for good weather so their people and their horses would have a chance to recover from the downpours. They also halted the caravan if the wagons were too far apart on the trail. This gave families a chance to catch up with one another. The Ottawa were usually a day behind the Shawnee and Seneca from Lewistown while the Shawnee from Wapakoneta were yet another day behind them. There were times when the wagons were so strung out that people went without food for a day or more waiting for Colonel Lane's supply wagons, loaded with meat and flour, to make the rounds to the many encampments.

When the Indians settled down for the night and started to prepare their evening meal, the native guards, who had gotten better at keeping the whiskey traders out, struggled to keep the curious away. As Judge Shelby described in his journal, every person from infant to "hoary age," male and female from purest white to darkest black, made their way to the Indian camp. From Richmond to Indianapolis and every town in between, local citizens had come out to gawk. The conductors, who now had a grudging respect for their charges, hated the intruders more than the Indians did. One time they told a young Shawnee to speak loudly in his own language to the crowd, which the conductors translated as meaning that the Indians were becoming very angry. Horrified, the townspeople went running for their lives, certain the Indians would attack.[41]

More trouble came once the tribes arrived in Indianapolis. Gardiner had already spent $10,000 to outfit the wagon train according to the specifications of Jackson's War Department and the desires of the Indians. He found that he was now completely out of money. Strapped for cash, he knew the government had paid the Indians $19,000 from the sale of their land right before they left Ohio.[42] So he borrowed enough money from the chiefs to buy meat and pumpkins, and paid farmers to open their cornfields to the hungry horses of the Indians. Colonel Lane was so angry at Gardiner for his mismanagement of funds that he came close to striking him, only stopping himself when he realized hitting an older man would be dishonorable. Lane blamed Gardiner for giving the Indians anything they wanted, especially the best horses and most expensive saddles, and was still angry that they were traveling by land rather than water. Furthermore, he was furious that nightly encampments averaged thirty miles apart, making for prolonged travel time while he visited each bivouac, handing out food and helping where needed, like repairing guns and attending to horses. Sometimes the fresh meat he had ready for the next encampment rotted in the wagons before he arrived there.[43]

Gardiner viewed Lane as an inexperienced upstart just out of West Point who thought he was the superintendent of the removal rather than simply the disbursing agent. He complained to his nephew, Daniel Dunihue, who was traveling with the Lewistown band, that Lane was a "vain, proud," and "self-sufficient" man. The colonel had begged Gardiner for a position while in Washington, only to turn into an arrogant monster once he arrived in Ohio. Lane let Gardiner know right from the start that he would "manage his own affairs . . . according to his own judgment" and would not take advice from anyone. Even though Dunihue knew that his hot-tempered uncle could be a taskmaster, he agreed with him wholeheartedly about Lane.[44]

The chiefs, who had come to respect Gardiner, still thought of Lane as a foolish boy and paid no attention to his complaining. Gardiner finally ordered Lane to return to Cincinnati and draw on funds that the War Department had deposited in the Bank of the United States. Lane headed instead to St. Louis, where he borrowed $3,000 from William Clark to buy more meat and flour for the Ohio Indians. Both men wrote letter after letter complaining about the other to Secretary Cass and Commissary General Gibson. The administration decided to send Lieutenant Colonel John J. Abert, an older, more experienced officer, to keep the peace. After graduating from West Point in 1811, Abert had worked for a time as a lawyer before rejoining the army in the closing months of the War of 1812. Hopefully his experience as an attorney and a soldier had given him the skills needed to end the quarreling between Gardiner and Lane. Abert was to depart Washington, find the wagon train somewhere between Ohio and St. Louis, and attempt to reconcile the two men. If this was not possible, then he was to assume command of the removal himself.[45]

After Colonel Lane left, another problem hit the wagon train, now poised to head down the National Road out of Indianapolis toward Greencastle. Colonel Greenup, the Superintendent of the National Road, warned Gardiner that people traveling east from Missouri brought frightening news that the cholera epidemic sweeping the nation had reached St. Louis. Cholera, a bacterial infection of the small intestine, caused severe vomiting and diarrhea. People who contracted the disease became dehydrated and often died within hours. The disease had long been known in India, but had only recently spread to Russia and then across the European continent to the British Isles. A ship loaded with immigrants brought the disease to Quebec and Montreal, and from there cholera spread down Lake Champlain to Albany and finally to New York City in the spring of 1832. Cholera may have remained in the East for some time, if not for the fact that in July 1832 American soldiers heading west to fight Black Hawk brought the disease to Detroit, Chicago, and then Prairie du Chien. From Iowa, cholera spread downriver to towns along the Mississippi.[46]

No one at the time knew what caused cholera, only that the dreaded disease was often fatal. Gardiner decided that the Shawnee of Wapakoneta along with the Ottawa should head for Alton, Illinois, just north of St. Louis, cross the Mississippi, continue overland around the infected city and proceed down the trail toward Kansas. The Shawnee and Seneca of Lewistown should head from central Illinois toward the Mississippi, cross the river at Kaskaskia, about eighty miles south of St. Louis, and then travel southwest through Missouri to the Neosho River. Gardiner hoped more detailed instructions from Jackson's administration on how to proceed would be waiting for him at Vandalia, the capital of Illinois and an important mail stop on the western highways.[47]

When the tribes crossed into Illinois, things seemed to improve, most especially the weather. It was now late October and the rain had finally stopped. The air was cool and the sky was blue.

When the long caravan of horses and wagons reached the prairies that stretched all the way west to the Rocky Mountains, the lay of the land was so beautiful that the chiefs made the decision to remain here throughout the winter. Young Daniel Dunihue was just as mesmerized by the grassy plains. He recorded in his diary that you could see a deer a mile or two away. He wrote home about the wonder of the sky and earth meeting in the distance. The horizon seemed to go on forever. Even the fires that burned across the prairies long into the night were a sight to behold. Dunihue was happy to leave the wagon train and head off to hunt with young Indian men. But no matter how hard he tried, he could never hit anything, much to the amusement of the Shawnee and Seneca who had no trouble bringing deer and turkeys back to camp each night. Yet Colonel Gardiner would not let them stop for long. The Illinois prairie country might be welcoming in the late fall but would become a terrible place in the bitter winds and deep snow of winter. The Shawnee, Seneca, and Ottawa must be safely along the Kansas and Neosho rivers by early December at the latest.[48]

Even amid improved conditions in Illinois, Gardiner continued to worry about cholera in St. Louis. On October 21, he rode along with his nephew Dunihue some thirty miles ahead of the caravan through a rain shower to Vandalia, hoping that letters from the War Department would be waiting for him. But there were none. He knew the letter carriers were about to leave for Louisville, Kentucky, and then head to Washington, so he dashed off a letter to Lewis Cass, telling him that the Indians would be crossing the Mississippi by November 1. He did not ask for more money or supplies, nor did he complain about his disbursing agent. Instead he spoke of the "800 souls," at least half of them women and children, whom he was shepherding through Illinois. What would become of them if, after everything they had already endured, they headed into a cholera epidemic in St. Louis? He told Cass of his plans to avoid the city, and since he had not heard from anyone back east, he said he would write to General William Clark for help.[49]

Gardiner rode toward the head of the line of wagons and caught up with the Shawnee and Seneca of Lewistown at a place called Hickory Grove, about twenty-eight miles west of Vandalia. They told him that the Ottawa were about a day away, and the Shawnee of Wapakoneta were another day or two behind them. Gardiner was surprised to find two other people in the camp, Lieutenant Colonel Abert and Colonel Lane. Abert had been trying to find him for some time. He had arrived in western Ohio just after the tribes' departure and had finally caught up with the front of the caravan just past Vandalia on October 27. Colonel Lane had wagons loaded down with pork and flour. Gardiner now realized that neither Cass nor Gibson had sent letters, because they had decided to let Abert be their eyes and ears.

After listening to both men's complaints about the other, Abert realized that reconciliation was impossible, so he would take over as special agent of the emigration of the Ohio tribes. He asked Gardiner to remain with the Shawnee of Wapakoneta and the Ottawa until they crossed the Mississippi River at Alton. He also allowed Gardiner to continue to communicate with Secretary Cass and General Clark. Gardiner wrote Clark immediately, informing him that despite all the Indians has suffered, their numbers held steady with births making up for the few deaths. Even with the terrible weather and bad roads, everyone remained cheerful. Colonel Lane announced that he would stay on, too, but would head out of Vandalia with the Shawnee and Seneca of Lewistown. As Gardiner had planned, this group would cross the Mississippi at Kaskaskia, and Lane announced that anyone who wanted to ride in a wagon from this point forward would be allowed to do so.[50]

The long wagon train, which had only been a day or two apart since leaving western Ohio, now parted company. The Shawnee of Wapakoneta and the Ottawa continued due west for Alton. Once there, they took two days to cross the Mississippi River. When they were safely on the other side, Colonel Gardiner bid them farewell and headed home to Ohio, where he completed reports required of him by Jackson's administration with a careful eye on accounting for the cost of the trip right down to the last penny.[51] Lieutenant Colonel Abert was now in charge of the removal of the Shawnee and Ottawa. He soon found removal as difficult as it had been for Gardiner. In fact, the journey became more difficult since the mood of the Indians changed dramatically once they crossed the Mississippi. A door seemed to have closed forever on the past, and the future looked more frightening than anyone had imagined.

The misery of the Indians grew as they continued along the northern edge of the Missouri River toward Arrow Rock, where the caravan would cross to the south side. The pleasant October weather and beautiful Illinois prairies had given way to the rain and cold of November, and the unpleasant Missouri countryside filled with an unwelcoming people. The citizens of Missouri had supported efforts to rid the state of Indians, pushing eastern tribes like the Shawnee and Delaware farther west to Kansas. They were not interested in helping "emigrants" pass through their state, especially if they brought cholera with them. The *Missouri Intelligencer* made note of the Indians' "fantastic appearance" as the long train of prairie schooners rambled by. These "sons of the forests" were dressed in "clothing and ornaments . . . of almost every color and description"; yet the reporter admitted that all were well dressed, with nearly all on horseback except for the children who rode in the wagons. Lieutenant Colonel Abert knew how unwelcome his party was in Missouri. He considered the Americans who treated the Indians so badly almost laughable. In most places "doors are slammed in our faces," and "some are bold enough to peep at us through the windows." Sadly, the only whites who did come out to greet the long Indian wagon train were whiskey traders. The Ottawa were especially susceptible to them. As Abert explained, the Ottawa, when sober, "are by far the most orderly and manageable of the whole detachment," but when drunk, he could not control them. "But drunk, sober, or sick," he added, "we will move them along."[52]

True to his word, Colonel Abert kept the wagon train moving, averaging twelve to thirteen miles a day. He led the Shawnee and Ottawa through rain and mud until November 13, when they halted their caravan, refusing to go any farther. The chiefs said their people must rest and their women must be given a chance to wash everyone's clothes. Abert soon had them on the move again toward Arrow Rock, but when they arrived they found the Missouri clogged with ice. They had to wait two days before ferries could carry them across the river. Once on the other side, the countryside cheered them again for a little while. Beautiful prairies broadened before them, swaying in the warm wind. But overnight the temperature plunged. On November 19, the Shawnee and Ottawa awoke to find snow on the ground. Everything was frozen, including the tents in which they had been sleeping. If this was what Kansas was like, then they could only imagine what misery must be awaiting them.[53]

As the wagon train headed into western Missouri, the weather grew steadily colder. The conductors recorded the horror of what the Shawnee and Ottawa were passing through in their daily journals. Dusk was especially terrible, because the night came on so quickly. The Indian women stumbled about in the darkness, digging through snow to find sagebrush to use as firewood. Luckily they still had meat to cook, but there was no flour, therefore no bread to bake. The remaining three hundred horses suffered, too, since there was only twenty bushels of corn to feed them. The daytime was no better. Icy wind whipped snow into the Indians' faces, and the cries of freezing children huddled in wagons were terrible to hear. People died at an alarming rate, not just from bad colds, dysentery, and consumption, but from cholera once it struck the Ottawa camp.[54]

Also troubling to the conductors were the frontiersmen they met along the way. Were these people truly the leading edge of American civilization? They seemed shiftless and lazy. Even the Mormons, who were living on orderly farms in the western part of Missouri, seemed odd and strangely out of place in this starkly empty country. By the time the wagon train reached Independence, near the state's western border, all were anxious to get out of Missouri and enter Indian country along the Kansas River.[55]

By November 30, they were only fourteen miles from the first settlement in the tribe's reserve. Misery gave way to excitement. The chiefs rose before dawn and loudly cried to their people to get up and make ready for the day's journey. The wagon masters long remembered that this was the first and only time that they did not have to rouse the Indians. Instead the Shawnee and Ottawa were urging *them* to get up and get moving. By early afternoon, they could see the first Shawnee village at the eastern edge of the tribe's reserve. This was called Cornstalk's Town and consisted of sixteen houses sitting high on a bluff above a creek that ran into the Kansas River. Everyone could see the village ahead of them through the misty rain that fell all day.

The conductors swore the Indian population had held steady, meaning that just as many children were born as people had died, yet out of 440 Shawnee who left Wapakoneta, only 334 were accounted for when Abert delivered them to their new reserve. Likewise, of the 100 Ottawa from the Auglaize River valley who joined them on the long trek west, only 72 arrived in Kansas. Since their reserve was some distance away, the Ottawa decided to stay with the Shawnee at least through the winter. No one could say for certain who had died, how many had been born, and who exactly had made it to Kansas. They only knew that the long migration of these two bands from Ohio was over.[56]

The Shawnee and Seneca who left Vandalia for the crossing at Kaskaskia arrived at the Seneca Agency on the Cowskin River two weeks later. Their journey was better than the one Abert's Indians had taken, at least when they passed through the prairies of south-western Illinois, and the weather stayed sunny and warm. Distant fires in the night were still a wonder to see, and the conductors and Indian men spent many a late afternoon and early evening hunting for deer and wild turkeys. Daniel Dunihue filled his diary, not with tales of misery, but with the beauty of the country-side. He tried his best to describe the land as if he were James Fenimore Cooper. However, the experience of being able to see for miles in all directions was simply beyond words, and he regretted he could not capture the wonder of it all in his letters home. Dunihue was also disappointed that he still could not shoot any game, while the Shawnee and Seneca brought many deer back to camp each night, giving their people venison to eat, along with the pork and flour that Colonel Lane had brought from St. Louis.[57]

But the mood of the travelers changed as they approached the Mississippi. Once the caravan came to Kaskaskia, the Indians were reluctant to cross the river, and the conductors found the town depressing. Dunihue remarked that Kaskaskia could be as prosper-ous as St. Louis if the French settlers living there had more drive. The wind in Kaskaskia blew so strong out of the west that at first the ferry boat captains refused to take anyone across the "Father of Waters." Finally, when the gusts died down, it took three days to get the Indians, their horses, and the many wagons over to the other side. Dunihue traveled back and forth twenty times, bringing about two-thirds of the Shawnee and Seneca across on the first day and most of the remaining third on the next.

On the final day, Dunihue found one last unhappy chief unwilling to take his people and their ponies onto the ferries. Somehow he coaxed all of them across the Mississippi, and to his surprise, once everyone was in Missouri, they seemed happy again. The Shawnee and Seneca did not complain or demand whiskey, but instead decided to dance. They started promptly at seven o'clock on the evening of November 9. They asked Dunihue to join them and then went looking for Colonel Lane to join them too. Dunihue forgot for a moment how much he hated Lane and was even "tickled to death to see what 'antic shines he cut up.'" The men danced in a circle facing each other, with Lane being one of them. This was a courtship dance, so the women danced in an outer ring behind the men. They danced for three hours until ten o'clock, when everyone went off to sleep.[58]

As they continued traveling southwest through Missouri, the conductors reported few incidents out of the ordinary. The long caravan stopped once so the Indians could do another dance to ward off witches in their new homeland. The wagons traveled steadily on through late November and early December. The men hunted in the late afternoon and early evening, just as they had done in Illinois. Dunihue finally aimed his gun at a "fat doe" and hit her, much to the delight of the Indians. But their happiness turned to despair when several Seneca from Sandusky, already living in the Indian Territory, rode out to greet the emigrants. They led them toward the valley of the Neosho, but had to turn back because the river was swollen from the autumn rains, and there were no ferries in this part of the country to carry them across. The Shawnee and Seneca from Lewistown, who were supposed to live north of the Seneca from Sandusky, were even more disappointed when they learned that the government had plotted out their reserve on Cherokee land. They would have to join in the upcoming negotiations with the government to move both reserves east of the Neosho River.

Everyone headed back to the Seneca Agency on the Cowskin River, where, on the afternoon of December 18, three months to the day since leaving Ohio, the conductors officially handed over the Shawnee and Seneca of Lewistown to the government. While they, too, claimed that births had kept pace with deaths, thus keeping the numbers in the course of the eight-hundred-mile trip west steady, of the 250 Shawnee and Seneca who left Ohio on September 18, only 220 were accounted for. For the moment, no one knew for certain who had died along the way, the number of children born, or the names of the people who had actually made it across the Mississippi. The conductors were also not certain where the Shawnee and Seneca would be living. This was not decided until December 29, when their chiefs, along with the Seneca of Sandusky chiefs, negotiated a new treaty with the government that moved their reserves back across the Neosho. Three years later, when an official count of the Shawnee and Seneca was finally taken, there were 211 Shawnee and Seneca from Lewistown and 251 Seneca from Sandusky living on reserves north and south of each other between the Neosho River and the western border of Missouri.[59]

The men who had brought the Shawnee and Seneca west were now anxious to get back home. Daniel Dunihue estimated that they had been gone for nearly a hundred days. The journey east would be a quick one. They would cross the Mississippi at St. Louis and then head straight back through Vandalia, Indianapolis, and Richmond to western Ohio. They should arrive by New Year's Day at the latest. But before they left, they made sure to leave the Shawnee and Seneca with as much help as possible, giving them all the public horses, gear, and every tent brought from Ohio. The Shawnee and Seneca would have to live in them until the spring, when they could build houses. The conductors also reminded the Indians that the government would support them for one year, starting on the date they arrived on their new reserve. Their annuities would find their way west, too, along with profits from the sale of their land back in Ohio, once the expenses of their emigration were deducted.[60]

By the time the conductors arrived back in Ohio, the sale of the Indian reserves was already under way. The government moved the local land office from Piqua to Wapakoneta. Surveyors drew a six-mile-by-six-mile square block around Wapakoneta and Hog Creek and named it Duchouquet Township after the French fur trapper whom Gardiner had gotten drunk before the treaty negotiations in what seemed like a lifetime ago. Sections of the Hog Creek Reserve were opened for sale in November 1832, even though eighty Shawnee were still living there, while Wapakoneta was subdivided and sold in January 1833. Many farmers moved into the cabins of the Shawnee, and even into the council house where Black Hoof once governed his tribe. If a settler found an apple orchard on his land, he counted this treasure as one more blessing left behind by the Indians. Oquanoxa's village on the Auglaize would soon become the town of Charloe, while the Ottawa reserve at Old Tawa Town on Blanchard's Fork would be known as Ottawa.[61]

Hundreds of miles away, no one recorded what the Shawnee, Seneca, and Ottawa thought of all they had suffered to make this possible. But if they had, it might have been close to what George Bluejacket, son of the great Shawnee chief Bluejacket, had written down in Wapakoneta right before his people went west:

> Our tribe is no more a great people. Our old Chiefs most all gone. Our warriors sit down most like E-qui-wa (women). We take what our White Father gives us. Now we must go to the new land. Soon more times we will have to move again. Soon there will be no more Shawanoes. Our hearts (are) full of sorry (sorrow) for all the tribes. But we will listen to the voice of our Mish-e-me-ne-toc (Good Spirit) in the great Me-to-quegh-ke (Forest) and he tells his A-pe-te-the (Children) when they all gone from this Mel-che-a-sis-ke (Poor land or poor earth) he will lead them to their Wa-ch-a-sis-ke (Good land) where all place is for Indian, where pale-face never come. Then poor Indian (once) more again may (be) happy.[62]

NINE

The Passing of the Ottawa

In the summer of 1832, when Colonel James Gardiner was making final preparations to remove the Shawnee and Seneca from Wapakoneta and Lewistown and the Ottawa from the Auglaize River valley, Lewis Cass wrote to George Porter, his successor as the governor of the Michigan Territory, directing him to negotiate a treaty with the Ottawa of the Maumee River valley to give up their remaining reserves and head with their relatives across the Mississippi. He told Porter that the Ottawa were living on two reserves—a thirty-four-square-mile tract on the eastern bank of the Maumee granted to them at the Foot of the Rapids in 1817, and a four-mile square tract at Maumee Bay granted at Detroit in 1807—and wanted to join the other Indians who were leaving Ohio for Kansas. For the moment, Cass had forgotten that the Ottawa were also living farther up the Maumee at Roche de Boeuf, Wolf Rapids, and at a nearby river island.[1]

Cass added an important piece of advice for Porter: do not let the Ottawa, he explained, go west to pick out a new homeland on their own. Nothing could be gained by this delaying tactic, since the American government, not the Ottawa, would decide where the tribe would live. Cass knew that other officials who had tried to discuss removal with the Ottawa, including their former sub-agent Benjamin Stickney and current subagent James Jackson, always faced the same dilemma. The Ottawa would say they were ready to sell their land and would then ask to go west across the Mississippi to choose the best place for their new home; but they would always change their minds about going, leading everyone to suspect that they would never leave the Maumee River valley.[2]

American traders who lived among the Ottawa would have confirmed this. No matter what the tribe told their agents or the War Department, the Ottawa would never willingly abandon their beautiful valley. John Anderson, who ran a trading post on the site of old Fort Miamis, just below the Foot of the Rapids, said many Ottawa told him that if their land were taken away they would simply wander up and down the Maumee forever. Several bands of the Ottawa had first come into the valley in the 1720s when, like so many other tribes, they needed to escape the crowded conditions around the French fort at Detroit. There were so many Indians living there, anxious to exchange furs for guns, ammunition, cloth, needles, iron pots and pans, and blankets, and to receive food throughout the difficult winter months, that the Ottawa could no longer find enough animals to hunt and trade. The Maumee River valley, with a deep bay at its mouth and white-water rapids upstream, would provide the tribe with fish and birds for food. The rolling, wooded countryside along its banks was full of otter, deer, fox, mink, and bear, whose skins and pelts could be traded for manufactured goods. Every spring the rich bottomland flooded and was perfect for growing corn, beans, and pumpkins.[3]

The Ottawa's greatest chief, Pontiac, may well have been born in the Maumee River valley, probably in 1720. After his confederation against the British failed and he lifted the siege of Detroit in October 1763, he retreated to Missionary Island in the Maumee, where Presbyterians were now growing corn and potatoes to supply their Indian school. Just one year later, his family and closest supporters followed him into the valley, where they established four villages: one at the mouth of the bay, another at Presque Isle near the rapids of the river, and two others at Roche de Boeuf and Wolf Rapids. More Ottawa came from Detroit in the next twenty years and settled farther south along the Auglaize River at

Oquanoxa's village and Blanchard's Fork. After he finally made peace with the British in a meeting at Oswego, New York, in 1766, Pontiac told them that he had brought his people back to the Maumee for the plentiful wildlife and to keep them safe from liquor, which flowed freely in Detroit. While Pontiac died three years later, shot in the back by an Indian in the Illinois Country, his most devoted followers remained safe and protected in the riches of the Maumee River valley.[4]

British traders soon came among the Ottawa and established posts from just below the Foot of the Rapids and upriver to the mouth of the Auglaize. The Ottawa, Algonquin for "trader," often served as middle men for the other tribes—trading furs in Detroit, now a British fort since the French and Indian War, and bringing back manufactured goods for distribution along the Maumee. When the American Revolution broke out just a decade later, the Ottawa joined the British against the colonists and fought throughout the Ohio River valley from Pittsburgh to Vincennes. Their villages along the Maumee remained safe throughout the long conflict. Actual fighting came no farther north than the Sandusky Plains, where Colonel Crawford was taken prisoner and executed in June 1782. But the Ottawa were not so lucky after their country was handed over to the Americans in the Treaty of Paris, which ended the revolution in 1783. Now they were at the center of the fight to preserve the Ohio River as the border between the tribes and the United States. Pontiac's descendants, led by their war chief Egushawa, who lived in the tribe's village at Maumee Bay, were instrumental in defeating the armies of Josiah Harmar and Arthur St. Clair, sent west to defeat the Indian confederation formed to halt the advance of the Americans across the Ohio.[5]

In the year leading up to the Battle of Fallen Timbers, Egushawa helped organize the fight against Anthony Wayne. Acting as "chief of staff" for the confederated tribes, he sent scouting parties to track Wayne's movements, and kept the lines of communication open between the many Ohio tribes and so coordinated their actions. When Wayne, after nearly two years of training his men outside of Pittsburgh and Cincinnati, finally took his army north from Fort Washington in the early fall of

1793, Egushawa sent the Ottawa chief Negig, or the Little Otter, south from the Maumee River valley to harass his supply lines. Negig and his warriors attacked Wayne's army near Fort Jefferson on October 16, killing upwards of thirty soldiers and taking ten more prisoner. One week later Negig delivered the scalps of the murdered soldiers to Egushawa at a council at the Foot of the Rapids. The Ottawa's continuing harassment of Wayne's supply lines forced him to halt his advance into Indian country, and retreat to the huge fort he built at Greeneville. Here he waited until the following summer when he continued his advance north into the Maumee River valley, heading for the newly erected British post at Fort Miamis.[6]

The Ottawa, whose villages had been spared from the fighting during Pontiac's War and the American Revolution, now bore the brunt of Wayne's destruction. He defeated the confederated tribes and their British allies on August 20, 1794, near the site of Presque Isle, the Ottawa village on the Maumee rapids just two miles south of Fort Miamis, forever known thereafter as Fallen Timbers. He then proceeded to burn to the ground every Ottawa town and all the surrounding fields nearly ripe for harvest, from the Foot of the Rapids back to the mouth of the Auglaize where he had built Fort Defiance. General Wayne torched every British trading post, too. One year later, at Fort Greeneville, the Ottawa chiefs from the Maumee River valley, along with the chiefs of other confederated tribes, finally made peace with Wayne and the United States. With his people starving, Egushawa was the first of six Ottawa chiefs from Ohio to make his mark on the Treaty of Greeneville. Despite the humiliation of treating with General Wayne, or the "Black Snake" who never slept as the Indians called him, the Ottawa saw much of their land in the Maumee River valley restored to them, with the exception of the Twelve-Mile Reserve, which was centered at Fort Miamis and included Presque Isle; a four-mile square reserve at the mouth of Swan Creek, which became Fort Industry (now Toledo); and a one-mile-square reserve farther upriver, across from present-day Waterville.[7]

With peace restored and the British ousted from the valley, American traders, many of French descent, settled along the Maumee. They set up stores over the ashes of the British posts destroyed by Wayne. The Ottawa chiefs rebuilt their villages throughout the valley. A few American settlers came into the valley, too, and carved out farms on land granted to them by the tribe. For nearly a dozen years, everyone lived peacefully side by side. In 1807, the Ottawa signed the Treaty of Detroit, in which they agreed to live on three small reserves along the Maumee River. But things changed dramatically five years later, when the War of 1812 broke out. Detroit fell quickly to the British and their Indian allies. Most of the younger Ottawa chiefs in the Maumee River valley joined Tecumseh. One such leader was Pontiac's son, Otussa, who played a key role in the defeat of the Americans along the River Raisin in January 1813. Soon traders along the Maumee were warning everyone to flee for their lives before the Ottawa warriors descended on them.

As predicted, the Ottawa were soon on the attack, setting fire to American trading posts and storehouses along the Maumee. Most of the settlers escaped in the nick of time; but a few, including a man who returned to harvest his corn on a river island, were killed. One of the worst incidents occurred farther east, at a place called Cold Creek along Sandusky Bay. Ottawa warriors from the Maumee River valley led an attack on several American farms along the creek. Many women and children were taken prisoner and forced to march back toward Canada, where they were to be ransomed. A pregnant mother, unable to keep up, was tomahawked and her child torn from her womb; and three other children, who also fell behind, were murdered. These were the attacks that led Matthew Elliot, superintendent of Indian affairs at Fort Malden, to reprimand the Ottawa for their cruelty.[8]

When the war was finally over, the Ottawa found that all was forgiven once again. First at Greeneville in 1814, and then at Springwells in 1815, they were welcomed back into their beautiful valley. The chiefs who had joined Tecumseh in the War of 1812 now worked for a lasting peace with the Americans. They retained the tract at Maumee Bay, granted to them in 1807, and ten years later they acquired more land for their tribe by signing the Treaty at the Foot of the Rapids, which gave the Ottawa a large reserve at McCarty's village. In exchange for the loss of Presque Isle, which lay within the Twelve-Mile Reserve secured by General Wayne for the United States in the Greeneville treaty, they won reserves at Roche de Boeuf and Wolf Rapids along the Maumee farther south. They also secured the use of two smaller tracts around Oquanoxa's village on the Auglaize, and Old Tawa Town on Blanchard's Fork.

During this time, traders returned to the Maumee and set up stores near small towns throughout the valley. The Ottawa brought furs and maple syrup to these posts and traded them for manufactured goods. While more and more farmers were settling along the Maumee, the Ottawa hoped that somehow they could still survive. Surely the traders would always welcome their furs and syrup, and that the missionary family at Ebenezer, near Tontogony Creek, would look out for them and even try to help them overcome the plague of drinking. No matter what rumors Lewis Cass might hear about the Ottawa wanting to move, and, more important, no matter what treaties they might sign with his commissioners, they would never leave the Maumee River valley.[9]

While Cass understood the tribe's reluctance to move, he had received many reports that the Ottawa were a troubled people. They were suffering from the usual ills that came from contact with the whites. One report had come to the War Department a year earlier from Reverend Isaac McCoy, a Baptist minister who was a strong supporter of removal as the only way to save the Indians. Congress had appointed McCoy to survey lands across the Mississippi River as possible sites for future Indian reserves. Several Ottawa chiefs, along with chiefs of the Pottawatomi, Chickasaw, Choctaw, and Creek, traveled west with him. They gave McCoy a petition asking the government to remove their people from Ohio and send them across the Mississippi. In the document, the Ottawa chiefs explained that their children were starving and that wildlife were disappearing from their beautiful valley. There were no animals to hunt and so no skins to trade. Even worse, the chiefs complained, "wicked white men" came among their people selling liquor, which the Ottawa could not resist. Surely there must be a "better country" where the tribe could live? They asked the president to find them this country and pay the tribe's way there. If this was done, then the chiefs promised that "our nation shall concede to go."[10]

Jackson's War Department would soon learn from Governor Porter about the declining health of the Ottawa. Oscar White, a physician from Maumee, had been hired by the government to inoculate the tribe against smallpox. Doctor White traveled throughout McCarty's village, the tribe's large tract on the eastern bank of the Maumee River, vaccinating as many Ottawa as he could find. He then wrote a letter to Porter telling him of the diseases that afflicted the Ottawa. White described the tribe as a very sickly people who suffered from rheumatism, ulcers, whooping cough, syphilis, and the measles. Since he used the common practice of injecting live smallpox cultures into the Ottawa when vaccinating them, he added that a few had contracted the dreaded disease as a result of the very measure he had taken to save them. He did not have to list drunkenness as a problem among the tribe since every Indian agent, trader, and missionary who worked with them had reported the horrific toll that whiskey was taking on Ottawa men and women alike.[11]

While people like Dr. White wrote sympathetically about the Ottawa, Lewis Cass also heard from local citizens who were less understanding. They considered the tribe a sad reminder of the past that was fast disappearing. When he was still governor of the Michigan Territory, Cass had received a petition from the leading citizens of Port Lawrence, one of the new towns that had been plotted out by businessmen around old Fort Industry on the Maumee, just opposite the Ottawa's largest reserve at McCarty's village. These men believed in the commercial potential of both sides of the Lower Maumee Valley. The river was perfect for handling the growing steamboat traffic coming across the lake from Buffalo, Cleveland, Sandusky, and Detroit. By 1836, 330 steamboats, with names like *Enterprise, General Wayne*, and *Andrew Jackson*, were plying the western waters of Lake Erie and heading upriver as far as Perrysburg and Maumee. Just one year later, their numbers had more than doubled to 736. The ships brought settlers and manufactured goods west and carried raw materials and farm goods back east.[12]

The Maumee was equally important for the future of canals, the next great advance in America's transportation revolution. The successful completion of the Erie Canal in 1825, which had connected the Hudson River valley, and thus New York City and the Atlantic to the Great Lakes, inspired politicians and entrepreneurs in Ohio to do the same. Indian agents who knew the Maumee well, like Benjamin Stickney and John Johnston, were early advocates of making the river valley a vital part of a statewide canal system. Neither man, however, calculated the cost of such a canal to the Ottawa. As Stickney explained in 1817, the Maumee River would provide the best route for a future canal connecting Lake Erie to the Ohio and so provide "an uninterrupted navigation from the bay of St. Lawrence to the Gulf of Mexico." By the time the citizens of Port Lawrence had sent their petition to Lewis Cass in 1831, the state of Ohio had completed the Ohio and Erie Canal, which connected Cleveland on Lake Erie to Portsmouth on the Ohio. John Johnston and other members of the state's canal commission were investigating whether the mouth of the Maumee would be the best terminus for a western route through the state. Port Lawrence and the adjacent towns of Vistula and Manhattan were competing against each other to win the terminus, and so become the gateway to any canal heading through western Ohio.[13]

According to Port Lawrence's leading citizens, the Maumee River valley would boom once the Ottawa were removed. The tribe's large reserve at McCarty's village sat on prime real estate along the eastern bank of the river from Maumee Bay down to the new Presque Isle, now the docks of East Toledo. If this land were sold to people who knew how to develop its commercial potential, then the Maumee River valley would prosper like the rest of the state. Docks and warehouses could be built where Ottawa villages now stood. Steamboats loaded with workers willing to build more canals would land there. Settlers would come ready to drain the Black Swamp and cultivate the rich soil hidden under the tangled forests. Warehoused crops could be transferred across Lake Erie to the rest of the world. Once the river's western bank was part of a canal system linking northwest Ohio to Fort Wayne, Dayton, and Cincinnati, then little villages like Port Lawrence and Vistula, at the mouth of the Maumee; Perrysburg and Maumee, at the Foot of the Rapids; Waterville, at Roche de Boeuf; Providence, at Wolf Rapids; and Defiance, at the mouth of the Auglaize, would prosper as major trade centers. The canal would draw more settlers down the Maumee who would open up some of the richest farm-land in the country. Once trade and transportation were established, manufacturing would not be far behind.

But none of this would happen if the Ottawa stayed in the valley. As the petitioners from Port Lawrence explained to Lewis Cass, the tribe was blocking progress. If they were removed from the area, then northwest Ohio would become one of the nation's greatest economic success stories to date. The petitioners reminded Cass that the Indian Removal Act had just been passed. The law should be applied to the Ottawa, who must be rounded up and sent west across the Mississippi. If this were not possible, they asked that the Ottawa be placed on a smaller reserve somewhere "beyond the line" of white settlement. Their message was clear. The Ottawa, so lost in the past and with no purpose in the present, must be sent out of the Maumee River valley to make way for its glittering future.[14]

Knowing well the contested history of the Maumee River valley, Porter headed there in late September 1832. He realized that many settlers at the mouth of the river, along with the War Department, wanted the Ottawa out. While he was convinced the Ottawa were willing to sell their land, he was certain they would never go west. He thought most of the tribe would head to Canada and live there with relatives. As many as 350 Ottawa had already left the Maumee River valley and moved to Manitoulin Island in Lake Huron (in Chippewa, Manitoulin means "Spirit Island").

The Ottawa were closely related to the Chippewa and the Pottawatomi. Members of the three tribes believed they had originally descended from three brothers. The Ottawa, Chippewa, and Pottawatomi had been settling on Manitoulin Island since the end of the War of 1812. The three tribes would cede the island to the British government in 1836, which in turn would grant it back to the Indians as a refuge for any tribe that would like to move there.[15]

The council between Porter and the Ottawa chiefs opened in Maumee on September 21, 1832. The governor asked the Ottawa if they really wanted to sell their land in the Maumee River valley, promising to support them no matter their decision. The chiefs sat silently, certain he was lying, and finally answered they needed another day to think about what he had said. The next day, they chose a half-breed Ottawa named John King to speak for them, but Porter refused to listen, saying he would only speak to the chiefs through his chosen interpreter. The two sides argued back and forth, with the Ottawa asking for a few months, and then a few days, to make their decision.

Finally, on September 23, the chiefs said they would sell their land to the United States, but only if their demands were met. They asked for $40,000 for their reserves but then raised the price to $50,000, saying they would use the extra money to pay off their debts. Next the chiefs demanded that a tribal cemetery be granted to Peter Manor, better known as Yellow Hair, the adopted son of chief Tontogony. This was necessary so that Manor "might preserve for them the home of their fathers." Finally, they requested that a five-acre tract at Wolf Rapids and a nearby island in the Maumee be set aside as permanent reserves for the tribe. When Porter responded that $50,000 was too much, the chiefs said the council was over and they would leave on the next day.[16]

While settlers in the Maumee Valley often described the Ottawa as a degraded people who cared only for whiskey, Porter found them to be determined negotiators who could not be easily swayed. Before they departed on the morning of September 24, they handed him a list of more tracts of land they wanted assigned to traders who had lived among them, and to their own chiefs. The Navarre brothers—Peter, Jacques, Robert, Antoine, Francis, and Alexis—were each to receive a section of land at Presque Isle on the eastern side of the Maumee, south of the bay. Several Ottawa chiefs and their family members were to receive whole or partial sections nearby. Robert Forsyth, an American trader from Maumee, was to receive 320 acres at Halfway Creek on the turnpike road out to Lower Sandusky and another 320 acres of his choice on Ottawa land. Without a formal treaty, Porter could not authorize any of these grants on behalf of the Ottawa, but he promised to send their requests to the War Department.

Porter believed the Ottawa were still angry at Colonel Gardiner for the tactics he employed during treaty negotiations in 1831, and that that was why they were so determined in the negotiations. They complained that he had lied to their chiefs from Roche de Boeuf and Wolf Rapids. Gardiner had promised them money for every acre sold and for every improvement on their land, but they had received none. With the memory of this wrongdoing "so fresh" in their minds, and with many of the citizens of Maumee siding with the Ottawa against Gardiner, Porter decided further treaty negotiations should be delayed until late fall at the earliest. The chiefs refused to set a date for a council, demanding instead they be allowed to travel to Kansas to see the land for which they were supposed to be exchanging their beautiful valley.[17]

In the face of such bitter opposition to any treaty, Governor Porter decided to wait until February 1833 to reopen negotiations with the Ottawa. Even with the delay, it was clear right from the start that the tribe meant to stay put along the Maumee. Porter found this out from the chiefs from Roche de Boeuf and Wolf Rapids, who had signed the removal treaty with Colonel Gardiner in 1831. They told Porter they would not leave the temporary reserves set up for them when the three years were up because Gardiner had taken advantage of their chiefs during the treaty negotiations. They would long tell the tale of how he had gotten Chief Thunderbolt, who resisted his efforts to rob them of their land, drunk and then held his hand to a pen and forced him to sign the treaty.[18] Gardiner had lied to all of them, they said, promising the tribe seventy cents for every surrendered acre. According to their calculations, even after all their debts to various traders were deducted from the total, the government still owed the tribe at least $18,000. Because the Ottawa from Roche de Boeuf and Wolf Rapids had never received any of this money, they now refused to go west to their new reserve along the Kansas River.[19]

The Ottawa were determined to make their case to the government. They handed Porter a list filled with complaints about Colonel Gardiner and the treaty they had signed with him. They said again that he had promised them $40,000 for their land. They would be willing to settle for $18,000, but only if the government paid their outstanding debts as part of the deal. "We ask this as our just due," the chiefs explained, "and hope it will be granted." The petition was signed by eighteen chiefs and had the support of local traders who had been at the negotiations with Gardiner, and who confirmed what the Ottawa said about the 1831 treaty. Porter promised to send the chiefs to Washington to request upward of $30,000 from the War Department.[20]

But he remained resolute in negotiating a new treaty that would remove the Ottawa from the Lower Maumee valley. He made his strongest case by describing the country across the Mississippi River as more beautiful than Ohio. The tract set aside for the Ottawa in the 1831 treaty was considered by government surveyors to be the best in Kansas, even better than the reserves of the Shawnee, Delaware, Pottawatomi, or Sac and Fox. The land was rolling countryside with good soil that was well watered by many streams from the Kansas and Osage rivers. The Ottawa reserve had groves of black walnut, hickory, oak, elm, and cotton-wood, trees that were missing from most reserves across the Mississippi, and also included a sandstone quarry and plenty of salt just across its border.[21]

After Porter finished speaking, all eyes turned to Ottokkee, the head chief of the Ottawa, who sat with his eyes fixed on the ground. Minutes passed before be stood up. He was a tall man, at least six feet, and stout, too, weighing about 200 pounds. Folding his arms and looking directly at Governor Porter, he was clearly torn over whether his people should cede their land and head west, or fight to remain in the Maumee River valley. Ottokkee acknowledged that the "pale-face chief" had spoken like a "bird" about the land across the Mississippi. Many of his young men were now excited to go west to Kansas, but the old men wished to stay near the graves of their fathers and keep the council fires burning. How could they leave the land given to them by the Great Spirit? Ottokkee noted that Porter spoke of the beauty of the West, but neither he nor his children were moving; instead, they would remain in the shade of the trees and among the flow-ers of Ohio. If he loved the "beautiful land toward the sun-down" so much, why not go there himself?

Although he challenged Governor Porter, there were many things that Ottokkee left unsaid. His people were hungry, their game was disappearing, and their addiction to whiskey was driv-ing many of them to ruin. Even worse, they were nearly penniless.

Soon they would have to follow the Ottawa from Oquanoxa's village and Blanchard's Fork west, if only to receive a share of the tribe's annuities. For these reasons, and not any argument about which country was more beautiful, Ottokkee decided to surrender most of the Ottawa's remaining land in the Maumee River valley to the United States. To Porter, he said:

> Go to the wigwam of the great father [President Andrew Jackson], and tell him that his red children will give the 'beautiful land' to their pale-face brothers, and they will sleep where their fathers' sleep, and their last council fire shall go out on the banks of their beautiful Me-aw-mee. Go tell this to the great father.[22]

On February 18, 1833, Governor Porter, Ottokkee, and twenty-one other Ottawa chiefs signed a treaty that was less than satisfactory for all sides. In fact, this treaty was more like the one at the Foot of the Rapids than like the other removal treaties, primarily because the Ottawa gave up their two remaining reserves in exchange for smaller local tracts of land granted to their major chiefs. Ottokkee was given 320 acres on the eastern side of the Maumee River, which contained an important Ottawa burial ground at Presque Isle. Chief Wauseon, Ottokkee's younger brother, received 160 acres, which included the cabin of their father Tushquaguan, better known as McCarty. Chief Cheno was granted 80 acres of land near a small creek, while Chief Wausaonquet received 160 acres on Pike Creek fronting Maumee Bay. Two other chiefs, Auschcush and Ketuckkee, were each given 160 acres on the north side of the Ottawa River. A woman named Petau won 80 acres where her cabin and farm stood. Even though the Ottawa had given up about 29,000 acres, they clearly intended to stay in the Maumee River valley for as long as possible, staking out holdings on good farmland and at strategic points along the river that would allow them to continue trading with the Americans.[23]

The Ottawa also made sure that traders who had lived among them were amply rewarded. They asked that an 800-acre tract of land be granted to the Navarre brothers—namely Peter, Jacques, Robert, Francis, and Alexis, their "valuable friends" who were married to Ottawa women. Another Frenchman named Leon

Guoin, who, like the Navarres, had lived among the Ottawa for many years, helping them especially during hard times, would get 80 acres. The tribe also remembered Albert Ranjard, who had paid them $300 for 80 acres in the Maumee River valley right before the War of 1812. At the outbreak of the war, Ranjard fled to Fort Stephenson, where he died shortly thereafter. The tribe insisted the treaty include that his descendants were to be awarded a deed to the land he had purchased.[24]

Several American traders were each given two quarter land sections for their "many acts of kindness" toward the Ottawa. John Hunt, who had a trading post in Maumee, received 160 acres on the turnpike between the Foot of the Rapids and the Western Reserve, and another 160 acres on the Maumee. Robert Forsyth, the Maumee trader for whom the Ottawa had requested land in their first list of demands, received identical tracts adjacent to the land granted to Hunt. While Hunt and Forsyth were grateful for the land they received, they demanded to be paid for the outstanding debts owed to them by the Ottawa. Of the $29,440 promised to the Ottawa for the sale of their land, the entire amount would be doled out to Hunt, Forsyth, and six other traders and the companies they represented. Hunt would receive $9,929; Forsyth, $10,890; and John Hollister and his company, $7,365.

Attached to the treaty were three schedules listing the specific people that Hunt, Forsyth, and Hollister would in turn pay from these lump sums. Four other traders would receive another $1,256. If the tribe was to receive extra money from the sale of their land, or in essence receive some portion of the 30 to 37.5 cents per acre assigned to each tribe according to the government's calculations, this was not stated in the treaty. Nor did the treaty explain that these new grants of land could only be sold back to the United States and not to private individuals. The Ottawa were only certain of the fact that for the time being they were out of debt and still retained 1,120 acres, or one and three-quarter sections, along the Maumee.[25]

Unlike the removal treaties with the Seneca, Shawnee, and other Ottawa in Ohio, this treaty failed to designate any reserve out west that the Ottawa of the Lower Maumee River valley would receive in exchange for the two reserves they had just surrendered. Without the certainty of a future home across the Mississippi, they told Governor Porter that they would not go west. One year later, when the time limit was up for occupation of the three reserves at Roche de Boeuf, Wolf Rapids, and the nearby island, the Ottawa of the Upper Maumee Valley also refused to leave for Kansas. Despite this resistance, Lewis Cass remained as determined as ever to send the remaining Ottawa out of Ohio. However, Governor Porter would not be the official who would negotiate the removal of the tribe. Porter had died of cholera in Detroit in July 1834. Secretary Cass would instead send US Army lieutenant I. P. Simonton into the Maumee River valley to convince the Ottawa now was the time to leave.

Arriving in northwest Ohio in September 1834, Simonton invited several Ottawa chiefs to travel with him out past Independence, Missouri, and take a look at the land along the Kansas River. After exploring the western country, the chiefs were even more reluctant to move and returned home. Many of them said they would head to Canada, where the British were still supplying them with yearly gifts. Others said the tribe should just wander on its own, finding a new home for themselves on the way west or even farther south. Still more would simply stay where they were, hoping to remain in their beautiful valley. They may even have hoped to escape removal altogether by delaying any further discussion until after Andrew Jackson left office in 1837. If they could survive past the end of his second term, maybe they could remain along the Maumee River forever.[26]

If this was their hope, then the Ottawa were disappointed when Martin Van Buren, Jackson's handpicked successor, was sworn into office in March 1837. He had no intention of stopping the removal of the tribes. Just one month after Van Buren's inauguration, his War Department ordered Henry Schoolcraft, Michigan superintendent of Indian affairs, to meet with the Ottawa and convince them to leave. Schoolcraft was able to accomplish what none had previously been able to do; but only because the Ottawa were now homeless. They had recently sold the tracts granted to them in the 1833 treaty with Governor Porter to the Maumee Land and Railroad Company. Without any land, the tribe now wandered along the Maumee, scratching out an existence on what patches of ground they could find. This would become even more difficult now that Port Lawrence and Vistula had joined together as the new city of Toledo, and Ohio had granted the state's western canal terminus to Manhattan at the mouth of the Maumee River. Making matters worse, the British in Canada had just announced that they would no longer be handing out yearly presents to tribes visiting from the United States. Without these extra gifts, and with no land left to sell or farm in the increasingly crowded Maumee River valley, the Ottawa had no choice but to head west to Kansas as soon as possible.[27]

In June 1837 Carey Harris, a Tennessee newspaperman appointed as the new commissioner of Indian affairs for his loyalty to President Jackson, asked John McElvain, the Indian agent who had overseen the removal of the Seneca from Sandusky, to act as the superintendent of Ottawa emigration. He was to round up the tribe and escort them to the Osage River Agency in eastern Kansas, where many of their "friends" from Ohio were already living. This would be the sixth "trail of tears" out of Ohio. McElvain had resigned as the state's Indian agent two years before. But Harris asked him to return to government service until the Ottawa were removed. The commissioner had already purchased most of the goods the tribe would need for the trip, including blankets and tents.

McElvain was more than happy to accept the position, believing for years that the tribe, surrounded by encroaching farmers and whiskey traders, would disappear if they stayed much longer in Ohio. By early July, he had organized a council with the Ottawa chiefs at the town of Maumee. They assured him they wanted to leave for Kansas and would help him get their people ready for the long trip west. Based on the annuities paid to the tribe in the previous year, McElvain estimated there were probably four hundred Ottawa living along the Maumee River valley from Wolf Rapids down to the bay. But he admitted he would not know the exact number until the morning of their departure.

He planned to pick a day in August when he would bring the Ottawa to the docks in Maumee at the Foot of the Rapids where they would board lake steamers for Cleveland. From there they would travel on the Ohio and Erie Canal to Portsmouth, on the

Ohio River, where McElvain would hire a steamboat to take them down the Ohio, up the Mississippi, and finally west along the Missouri toward the town of Westport. From there, they would go by wagon train to the Osage River Agency. It would be up to the officials at the agency to determine if the Ottawa from the Maumee River valley would live on the reserve granted to the Ottawa from Roche de Boeuf and Wolf Rapids or on the reserve granted to the Ottawa from Oquanoxa's village and Blanchard's Fork. After the disastrous overland journey of the Seneca in 1831, under the supervision of his old rival Henry Brish, Colonel McElvain was certain no one would question the wisdom of sending the Indians west by water.[28]

But he was not prepared for the resistance of Maumee townsfolk, especially the Indian traders, to the departure of the Ottawa. At first he assumed they supported the tribe's removal since they had presented numerous gifts to the chiefs—and as McElvain surmised, to get them to leave. But many of these same traders were torn about the departure, some realizing they would have to find a new livelihood when the Ottawa left, while others were worried that the tribe would leave before paying their debts. More wanted the Ottawa to stay so they could keep selling them liquor. McElvain did his best not to offend the "good citizens" of the town; but he lost his patience with fur traders, who threatened to detain the Ottawa unless every penny they owed was paid, and he had the same contempt for the whiskey traders.

What kind of people, McElvain asked in a broadside distributed in Maumee on August 17, would threaten the "fallen Ottawas?" They were homeless and spent their days roaming the Maumee Valley with no place to call their own. Their only chance for survival lay across the Mississippi River.[29] McElvain ordered any trader who held outstanding debts against the tribe to come directly to him for payment. If debts owed to them were part of a past treaty, they would be paid out in a lump sum relatively quickly; for new debts accumulated since the last treaty in 1833, then McElvain would make arrangements for the Ottawa to pay them off in installments over two or three years. But no matter what, anyone who had previously sold the whiskey to the Indians must "do so no-more."[30]

There were a few people along the Maumee River who were working sincerely to keep the Ottawa in the valley. At the Maumee Indian Mission overlooking the river at Tontogony Creek, Reverend Isaac Van Tassel was doing everything in his power to stop the removal of the tribe. His mission had continued to grow since opening in 1822. Besides the main building and school, there was a stove house, a blacksmith shop, and a stable for the mission's two horses. During its first decade, the school averaged thirty "scholars" each year who were mainly Ottawa, along with a few children of local settlers. The older Indian boys took care of the fifty acre-mission farm. They also helped to raise cattle, sheep, and hogs for the school.[31]

Though the number of students averaged about twenty, and he had only converted a few Ottawa to the faith, Van Tassel was certain he was making progress. If nothing else, the Ottawa respected the missionaries and considered them their protectors. This was proven true when many of them came to see Van Tassel after they signed the removal treaty with Colonel Gardiner in 1831. They told him that they never intended to sell their land, but had been pressured into it. Their chiefs were even forced to participate in treaty negotiations on the Sabbath. Though they eventually signed away their land on the Auglaize River and at Roche de Boeuf and Wolf Rapids for a new reserve in Kansas, they said they would "never leave this country."

Reverend Van Tassel came up with a solution. He asked the Presbyterian Synod in Pittsburgh to buy land near the Maumee Indian Mission, where Ottawas desiring to remain in Ohio could stay. As he explained to the synod members:

> If they can find no place to stay, they will spend the rest of their days in walking up and down the Maumee, mourning over the wretched state of their people. Some have said that they would place themselves under our protection, and stay by us as long as we remain.

This new reserve would ensure the survival of the Ottawa and the mission. Van Tassel wanted to continue the school, but he did not see how this would be possible if the Ottawa, who made up the majority of students, were removed from Ohio. The reverend also asked the synod to help him remove the whiskey traders from the Maumee River valley.[32]

A few miles farther upriver, the Howard family also wanted the Ottawa to stay. After coming to Ohio from New York in 1822, they had set up two trading posts: one near Wolf Rapids, and the other one down a trail to the west at a village named for the Pottawatomi chief Winameg. The Howards made a good living trading furs with the Ottawa and saw no reason to leave. They counted about a 1,000 settlers in the Upper Maumee River valley. The few hundred Indians who lived among them posed no threat and were generally peaceful, only getting a little rowdy when they were drinking, and even then they were more a danger to themselves than to the Americans. The Howards had always refused to sell them whiskey, but sadly so many others did.

Dresden Howard, the boy who had been schooled alongside Indian children at Reverend Van Tassel's mission, and who together had raced down the snow-covered banks of the Maumee on their homemade sleds, was now a young man. He often listened with wonder to the Ottawa chiefs, most especially Ottokkee, who came to meetings under the Council Elm near Wolf Rapids. In May 1835, when Howard was just seventeen, Peter Manor asked him to serve as interpreter at a council between Ottokkee and the Ottawa's subagent James Jackson. He long remembered how the chief asked the colonel why their "Great Father," the president of the United States, stood by and did nothing when Americans came onto Ottawa land, stealing their corn, killing their animals, and abusing their women. Jackson said he would report all of this to the president, and young Howard relayed this promise to the chiefs.

Two years later, Dresden Howard acted as interpreter for Ottawa and Pottawatomi chiefs during their meetings with officials about their pending removal. These took place under the ancient Council Oak at Winameg. Howard knew that many Ottawa, along with some of the Pottawatomi who lived with them, had already escaped down woodland trails that led from Winameg into the Michigan Territory, where superintendents and conductors, sent to take them across the Mississippi, would never find them. While ninety-five-year-old chief Winameg said he would never leave Ohio, Ottokkee and the other Ottawa chiefs felt they had no choice but to promptly head for Kansas. Young Howard even volunteered to join members of Ottokkee's band who planned to go west on their own by wagon train in the fall of 1838. After he had gotten everyone safely across the Mississippi, he would take to the woods, traveling along the northern Great Lakes into the Wisconsin Territory, where he would make a living for himself as a fur trader.[33]

While missionaries, like the Van Tassels, and traders, like the Howards, did not want the Ottawa to leave, John McElvain could not understand why anyone would want them to stay. He saw the Ottawa as a dying people. They were hungry, landless, and often drunk, and would not last through one more winter in the Maumee River valley. The only way to save them was to move the tribe across the Mississippi River to a country of their own, where, far from the reach of land speculators and whiskey traders, they could learn to support themselves on farms and ranches. With this in mind, on Thursday, August 31, 1837, two weeks to the day after he had delivered his broadside to the people of Maumee, John McElvain ushered, by his count, 174 Ottawa onto a lake steamer at the Maumee docks. Chief Ottokkee was not one of them.

McElvain's muster roll revealed just how young the Ottawa were in this second group to leave Ohio. Eighty percent were under 25 years of age, of whom 30 percent were under 10, almost equally divided between 25 boys and 27 girls. Half of the rest were adolescents and young adults ranging in age from 11 to 24, the men outnumbering women by a 2 to 1 ratio. Only six people—one man and five women—were over 50. Thirty-eight ranged in age from 25 to 50 (17 men compared to 21 women). Of the thirty-six heads of households, seven were single, and the remaining twenty-nine had families numbering from two to eleven, seven being the average.[34]

The editor of the *Maumee Express* seemed more amused than troubled by the spectacle of the Ottawa heading through his town toward the river. He had already dismissed them as a remnant of a once-great people in the pages of his newspaper. They were something out of a distant past that the many people settling along the Maumee had heard about but never seen. Their story now bore an antique quality not nearly as exciting as the local commercial news, or the tales of Seminole warriors still fighting the government, which filled the pages of his weekly journal. He made no mention of the many children among the Ottawa and instead wrote of the drunken chiefs who stumbled toward the docks, completely unmoved by the tears of the women they were leaving behind. Yet, he admitted that there was a melancholy in the air as the babies cried and the dogs wailed to be taken west with their masters, and as the low sound of Indian flutes could be heard through the confusion.[35]

A thirteen-year-old girl named Mary Blackwood Copeland, who watched the Ottawa leave, was far more sympathetic. Perhaps because she was a child herself, she took pity on the boys and girls leaving for the Far West. She, in fact, would never forget the sight of these people, many of them very young, shuffling down along the docks with their heads hanging low. The only sound she heard was "one continuous pitiful wail" that the Ottawa made as they boarded the boat that would take them across Maumee Bay to Cleveland. Years later, when she was married to Dresden Howard, who had returned to the Maumee River in 1842, after his father died, she still remembered the "sad, sad day" when the Ottawa left their beautiful valley, knowing they would never see it again, and not knowing for certain where they were going.[36]

As McElvain had planned, the Indians headed first to Cleveland and then down the Ohio and Erie Canal to the Ohio River. By September 15, they had made it to Portsmouth, where they boarded a steamboat that arrived in St. Louis on September 22. There William Clark gave them the rest of the goods that the commissioner of Indian affairs had purchased for them, including axes and rifles. They continued up the Mississippi and made the turn west along the Missouri to Westport. From there they traveled overland to the Osage River Agency in eastern Kansas, where 170 of them arrived on October 11, 1837. They decided to stay with the Shawnee through the winter before moving to the reserve where Ottawa from the Auglaize River valley were already living. In his final report to the War Department, McElvain claimed he lost only four of his charges. A young man named Pantee, with no family of his own, had left the tribe in Cleveland. Two infants died on the long trek west, one as the Ottawa passed Waverly, Ohio, on the canal ride to Portsmouth, and the other just fifteen miles from their final destination in Kansas; and a woman, whose name McElvain did not record, died in St. Louis.[37]

If he kept a Journal of Occurrences, as he was required to do, the document has not survived. But a twenty-four-page letter from McElvain did arrive safely at the Office of Indian Affairs. In the letter, he recited everything that he had been through since being appointed superintendent of Ottawa emigration. The letter told a tale of hardship, trauma, and the toll that removal took, not so much on the Indians as on their conductor. On the long nightmarish trek west, he put up with childish chiefs, unscrupulous traders, and so many wagons. "At best," he explained, "the removal of the Indians is a most vexatious responsible and troublesome business." He concluded with a warning. No man could understand how terrible Indian removal truly was until he had made the trip west himself.[38]

About 150 Ottawa, including their head chief Ottokkee, still remained behind. Some of them fled to Canada, where they starved or froze to death during the brutal winter of 1838. If there were to be another removal of the tribe to Kansas, John McElvain would not lead it. His last letters to the War Department were filled with complaints that he had never been paid for relocating the Ottawa. At the rate of five dollars a day for 127 days of work, he figured the government owed him exactly $635. Many people in the Maumee River valley were relieved that McElvain would not be taking more Ottawa west. They disliked him and instead admired Capt. W. E. Cruger, the young army officer who had served as disbursing agent on the trip. Many said that if Cruger had been the superintendent of Ottawa emigration, the entire tribe would have willingly left with him. This was because Cruger, unlike McElvain, was a decent and upstanding fellow.

As long as someone of Cruger's caliber oversaw the next round of removal, settlers throughout the Maumee River valley were convinced that the remaining Ottawa would happily go. The honorable man chosen for the task was Robert Forsyth, the trader from Maumee who had received money and land in the 1833

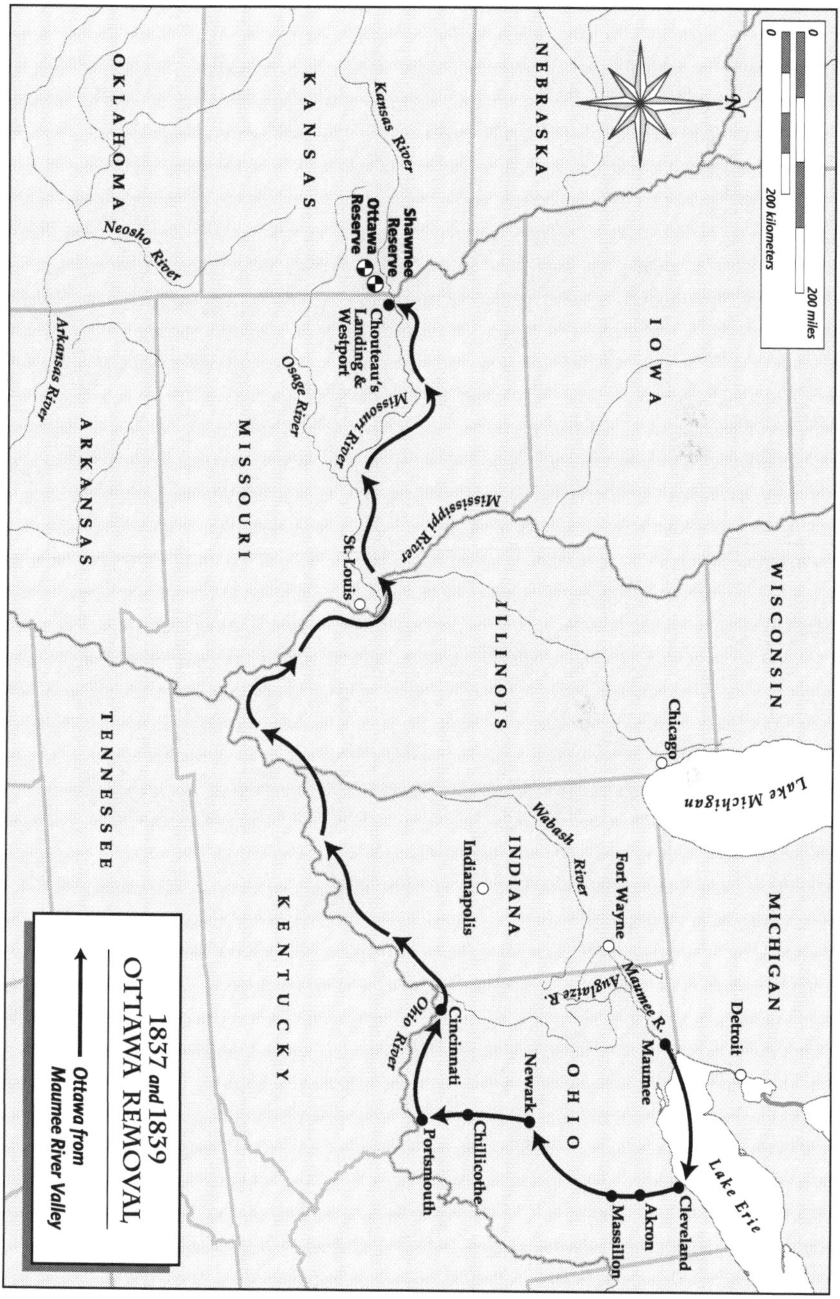

Map 6. The Ottawa Removal, 1837 and 1839.

treaty with the Ottawa. He had also purchased some of the first lots in Port Lawrence and was a newly appointed judge of the Michigan Territory. In 1839 Thomas Hartley Crawford, the latest commissioner of Indian affairs, just appointed by President Martin Van Buren, named Forsyth as the next superintendent of Ottawa removal. Crawford had replaced Harris, who was dismissed for holding stock in a company that speculated in the sale of Creek land following the tribe's removal to the West.[39]

Judge Forsyth was determined to be a better superintendent than McElvain had been. He was committed to ensuring that every Ottawa who left the Maumee River valley would arrive safely in Kansas a few weeks later. He was certain he could accomplish this because he had the support of their head chief Ottokkee. Forsyth kept an accurate muster roll of the 108 Ottawa who would be heading across the Mississippi. Like the group that McElvain had taken west two years before, these people were very young. Sixty percent of them were children and young adults under twemty-five years of age. Of the thirty-eight adults who accompanied them, only five were over fifty.[40] Just as important, Judge Forsyth had also been appointed disbursing agent and thus was in charge of the funds. McElvain had spent $5,400 just on the trip from Portsmouth to St. Louis. Forsyth was determined to make the whole trip from the Maumee to Kansas for less than that. He estimated that it would cost exactly $3,901.70 with $1,860 for transportation, $680 for subsistence, and $1,361.70 for "contingencies."[41]

But even with all of his careful planning, things went wrong right from the beginning. He planned to move in the spring of 1839, but he could not convince the Ottawa to leave then. Fur prices were unusually high, and the Ottawa wanted to take full advantage of that. They continued their last winter hunt in Ohio well into the spring. When everything was finally set for the tribe's removal in July, Forsyth noticed that forty to fifty Ottawa were nowhere to be found. While he had promised to do a better job looking after the Ottawa than McElvain, clearly not everyone in the tribe trusted him. At least thirty had gone to hide among the Navarres. Forsyth followed them to the family's land near Maumee Bay, where he discovered that most of them were women and children. He ordered them back to the rendezvous point across the river, but they refused to go, even when he warned them that the government was prepared to force them off their land next year. He could only stand and watch as the Navarres loaded the women and children into canoes and headed farther east, where they would never be found.[42]

Forsyth headed back to the docks in Maumee, where 108 Ottawa were waiting for him. He did not want to take any chances that they would escape in the night, so he escorted them onto the *Commodore Perry* on the evening of July 24, 1839. He also took along Dr. James Colby, a physician, since he was determined to have even fewer deaths than McElvain had experienced. He was glad that his assistant superintendent and two assistant conductors all spoke some Ottawa. Also accompanying him was William McKnabb, a well-known interpreter in the Maumee River valley.

Early on the morning of July 25, the *Commodore Perry* pulled away from the dock to the cheers of hundreds of onlookers and the silent sorrow of the Ottawa. Even for a man as disciplined as Judge Forsyth, watching the Ottawa as they took a last look at the country they would never see again was almost unbearable. The calm waters of Lake Erie on this summer day made the trip from Maumee to Sandusky a pleasant one. By nightfall, when the lights of Cleveland came into view, much of the homesickness everyone felt had eased. Forsyth found a warehouse with a wide overhang under which the Ottawa could rest safely for the night.[43]

On the next morning, Judge Forsyth gave the Indians their rations, and they cooked them behind the building where they had spent the night. They then boarded two canal boats for the five-day trip down the Ohio and Erie Canal from Cleveland to Akron, Massillon, Newark, Chillicothe, and finally Portsmouth. Forsyth noted that the Indians were amazed at the country through which they were passing. There was something new for the Ottawa to see at every turn: towns that were centers of trade and manufacturing, and the countryside filled with neatly ordered farms and dairies. Soon, the Maumee River valley would resemble this, once the canal was completed in the western part of the state. Along the way, people came out to meet the Ottawa. Most had never seen Indians before and treated them kindly.

The Ottawa accepted the daily routine of leaving the boats at night to camp on shore, cooking the day's rations in the evening and right after dawn, and then boarding the boats by the early morning. A few Ottawa could not resist the temptation of going into towns at night to buy whiskey. But the conductors kept a watchful eye on them, making sure all were onboard each morning, and even saving a few from falling overboard.

The Ottawa's greatest problem was getting used to eating daily rations of beef and flour, some preferring to purchase fruit from local farmers in the canal towns. Many Ottawa were soon troubled with upset stomachs and diarrhea, and Dr. Colby, whom children often fled at his approach, was sent to dole out remedies and explain that eating only fruit made their condition worse. Judge Forsyth was grateful that Ottokkee helped Dr. Colby coax the Ottawa, especially the children, to swallow the medicine. Forsyth commended the leadership of Ottokkee, Wauseon, and the other chiefs in his daily journal, saying they made all the difference in lifting the spirits of everyone on the long trip west. Slowly, most of the sick improved, especially since families and friends watched over them through the night. Both Forsyth and Colby were happy that everyone seemed to recover, except for one woman and an eight-year-old girl.[44]

At seven o'clock on the morning of August 1, the Ottawa finally reached Portsmouth, on the Ohio River. Forsyth hoped that a steamboat headed for Cincinnati, or even St. Louis, would come by, but none arrived. The Ottawa pitched their tents on shore, cooked their rations, and took care of the sick. The river was low at this time of the year, and many steamboats were upriver waiting for the water to rise. Finally, on the afternoon of August 3, a mail packet called the *Bedford* came by and took everyone on board. The Ottawa were so happy to be moving again that they lined up on the side of the *Bedford* and gave a "parting yell" to the people of Portsmouth. At ten o'clock on the next morning, the Queen City of Cincinnati came into view. Everyone was amazed to see steamboats lined up for a mile along the shore. When the *Bedford* docked, Judge Forsyth went off to find a steamboat large enough to take the Ottawa all the way to St. Louis, and with enough stoves for the Ottawa to cook their meals. While Forsyth searched for a boat, the Ottawa made their way into the city, where they enjoyed the many museums. Onlookers came with them, and the museum owners let the Indians in for free, since they brought in many customers. Crowds followed the Ottawa back to the river and tried to climb onboard the *Monsoon*, the steamboat that Forsyth had secured for the journey west. The captain had to pull out into the river to keep the Ottawa safe and the curious away.[45]

It took six days, from August 5 to August 11, for the Ottawa to make their way from Cincinnati to the Mississippi River. At times the trip was pleasant, with the boat cutting the waters of the "noble Ohio" at a clip of twelve miles an hour; but at other times, the ship battled sandbars. Once the Ottawa and their conductors had to get off the boat and walk alongside it on shore to lighten the load. Even with this precaution, the steamboat still stalled in a sandbar and could not be dislodged until the water level rose. Once everyone was back on board, Forsyth was impressed with all the Ottawa, not just the chiefs, for their endurance and good humor.

The weather was terrible, with the sun beating down and not one breath of wind moving. Even the Indians, who never seemed to mind the heat or cold, had to take shelter "under the decks, from the burning rays of the sun." Mosquitos swarmed the boat, biting the faces of the Ottawa so badly that they looked like they had smallpox; yet they uttered not one word of complaint, staying calm in the heat by sleeping, lounging, or playing cards in the shade.[46]

On August 12, the *Monsoon* entered the Mississippi River and turned north, and took only one day to get to St. Louis, where the Ottawa disembarked and set up camp. Forsyth went off to find a boat to take everyone up the Missouri to Chouteau's Landing. The Ottawa were happy to receive the rifles promised to them, but said they would not be able to use them until they started farms in their new reserve. They were glad to buy fruit again, even though many became sick. Dr. Colby was certain that the well water in St. Louis was making the children ill. A few men could not resist the lure of the big city and went off for a "frolic." Before the Ottawa could leave St. Louis on August 16, Forsyth had to return to town and look for them. He found them locked up for disorderly conduct. He paid the $9.25 fine and got them back onboard for the final leg of the trip west.[47]

Forsyth and the Ottawa found the journey upriver on the Missouri as disturbing as other groups that had come west from Ohio, since the country seemed empty and desolate. Rock formations more than a hundred feet high came right up from the river's edge. Cedars growing at the top seemed barely able to cling to the thin soil. The oppressive heat made breathing difficult, and mosquitos plagued the Ottawa by day, with relief coming only at night as they camped along the Missouri. Here they cooked their meals and finally got some rest in the cool evening air. In these miserable conditions, the little girl who had been sick since leaving Ohio was failing. When Dr. Colby told her parents and friends that he could not save her, they wept so loudly that everyone on board heard them. The child finally died on the morning of August 21. The ship's captain made her a coffin. Her parents begged Judge Forsyth to keep her body on board until they reached the reserve, where they would bury her; but he said no, because the smell would be unbearable in the terrible heat. She would have to be buried at Chouteau's Landing, the next stop that they would reach in a few hours.[48]

Upon reaching Chouteau's Landing—named for Auguste Chouteau, who years earlier had helped to negotiate treaties at Portage des Sioux—Forsyth rode to Westport, just seven miles away, to hire wagon teams to transport the Ottawa to their reserve. Meanwhile, the Ottawa encamped on the Missouri shore and were greatly relieved to be in the cooler air. They buried the little girl who had just died; and on August 26, after five days at Chouteau's Landing, they finally set off in a long wagon train toward their new home. Forsyth was amazed that "hardly a man, woman, or child" would ride. They were happy to be walking at last. There was something awe inspiring and even frightening in this new country. The Ottawa were "astonished" at the sight of the endless horizon opening before them. As Forsyth put it, "these grand prairies were beyond their comprehension." The landscape was so different from their beautiful valley in Ohio with its river marked by silver rapids and lined with elms. Here the land was flat with few trees and little water. Some became disheartened because they had been promised a country rich in wildlife. Except for a few birds, they saw none. This meant they would not be able to survive as hunters until they established their farms. They felt better by the evening when they finally found a grove of trees near a stream where they could make camp for the night.[49]

On the morning of August 28, the Ottawa sent one of their young men ahead to inform families and friends of their impending arrival, which was in fact only a day away. Around noon something wonderful happened. The Ottawa saw riders on the distant horizon far ahead of them. They were racing toward the wagon train, coming closer and closer, and finally leaping from their horses. They were young Ottawa men who had come west in 1837. They took hold of the people at the head of the caravan and then ran through the wagon train looking for their mothers and fathers. Even Judge Forsyth had to admit that he was deeply moved by this loving reunion.

The Ottawa camped for their last night on the road in a large grove of trees. Early on the morning of August 29, they set out on the final leg of their trip. Several men went to the head of the wagon train, walking as fast as possible to get to the reserve. They got so far in front of the caravan that they had to stop and give everyone a chance to catch up with them. The Ottawa wanted to meet the rest of their tribe as one people. After traveling just four or five miles, they saw many Indians approaching; and as Forsyth described the scene, "Our arrival on the land caused quite a sensation." The Ottawa who had come west two years earlier flocked around their relatives and friends from the Maumee River valley. They took them to a place where they could camp until they had the time to go out across the tribe's reserve and pick the best sites for their homes and farms. Judge Forsyth and his assistants stayed with the Ottawa for five more days before wishing them well and heading home to Ohio.[50]

Forsyth was elated that he had overseen the Ottawa's removal from the Maumee Valley, down the seventh "trail of tears," with the loss of only one child. He was more convinced than ever that the removal of the tribe from Ohio had been the right thing to do, and agreed in the end with McElvain that the Ottawa were a dying people who would have disappeared from the face of the earth if they had not found a refuge in the West. The life they had led along the Maumee and Auglaize could not compare to the one they would lead along the Kansas and Osage, where they would give up hunting to become successful farmers, and set down the rifle and take up the plow, ax, and hoe. They would build sturdy log homes, grow acres of corn, and raise livestock. All memories of their days as "half famished, ragged, and emaciated" vagabonds would disappear in the happy world they now inhabited. Forsyth even volunteered to collect the remaining Ottawa who were wandering in the Maumee River valley and bring them west.[51]

The Van Buren administration, however, was no longer interested in removing any more Ottawa from Ohio. If some of them remained along the Maumee or Auglaize rivers, no one would come looking for them. Reports of "stragglers," who drifted poor and alone, would come into the Office of Indian Affairs for the next forty years. The Howard family took care of many of them near their old trading posts. They let them hunt on their land and helped them when they were hungry or sick. When old chief Winameg, who had refused to go west to Kansas, finally died, the Howards buried him on their land and watched over his grave for generations. They protected another Indian named Tee-Na-Beek, believed to be the last Ottawa in the Maumee River valley.

Dresden Howard had grown up with Tee-Na-Beek, who became gravely ill in 1850. His wife and three small children came to Howard begging him for help. Howard immediately called for a doctor, but his childhood friend, only thirty-five years old, was past saving. When Tee-Na-Beek finally died, Howard wrapped him in his best blanket and buried him with his weapons next to his own family's cemetery plot near Wolf Rapids. His grave can be seen to this day, just off Main Street in downtown Grand Rapids, Ohio. Howard's wife, Mary Copeland, loaded the canoe of Tee-Na-Beek's wife and children with food and supplies for their long trip north to Canada, where they would live with relatives. Unable to forget the Ottawa, the Howards named towns, such as Ottokkee and Wauseon, in honor of the many chiefs who had tried to remain in Ohio. They named their first-born son Osceola after the Seminole warrior who carried on the fight for his people even as the Ottawa were sent west.[52]

Other wandering Ottawa became legendary among the growing number of settlers who sympathized with their plight. There was Francis Buono, who founded the town of Bono just east of Toledo, and his wife, Mary Angeline Caderat. They raised six children, and both lived into the twentieth century, Francis dying in 1901, and Mary in 1906. Farther south in the Auglaize River valley, Chief Peter Charloe, who had signed the 1831 removal treaty with Colonel Gardiner, never went to Kansas and gave his name to the town that grew up around his people's abandoned reserve. A woman of Ottawa, Chippewa, and French descent named Victoria Cadaract, who supported her family by making baskets, was long considered the last Indian to survive in Ottawa County. Born in northwestern Ohio in 1828, she remembered hearing her grandfather's tales about the many battles that the Indians fought along the Maumee, especially the attacks on Fort Meigs. He had joined Tecumseh in the War of 1812 and for many years thereafter proudly dressed in a bright red British uniform. "He swung a British sword at his side and strutted about," she recalled, "much to the merriment of the braves about him." She died in 1915 and was buried in the Allen Township Cemetery.[53]

The Van Tassels tried to remain as long as possible in the Maumee River valley, and operated the mission school for several years after the Ottawa left. When it finally closed, they stayed on and ran the farm for a while longer. Finally, they left the mission, abandoning the buildings and fields, and headed for a new life in the nearby town of Bowling Green. Lucia Van Tassel knew that most people who heard the story of the Maumee Indian Mission would dismiss it as a failure. They would argue that the missionaries had been unable to take the Ottawa out of a dying past, and place them squarely on the road to the future. She, however, never thought of it that way. For a brief time she and her fellow missionaries had helped the Ottawa to stay longer in their beautiful valley, and for this the tribe was always grateful. If you helped the Indians, Mrs. Van Tassel liked to tell her neighbors, they would always greet you with the same words, "Wawanee, wawanee," or "Thank you, thank you." In a world where proud Ohioans, moving so swiftly on the leading edge of their nation's history, regularly counted up one success after another, she could say that numbers did not matter. The fact that she brought "30 souls" among the Ottawa to Christ did.[54]

Isaac Van Tassel left the Maumee River valley knowing he had done his best to save the Ottawa from the rush of time. His request to set aside a reserve for those wishing to remain in Ohio was at first met with the approval of the Presbyterian Synod. But then so many conditions were placed on the Ottawa who hoped to live there that none could accept the offer. The synod demanded that the tribe build homes for themselves, clear fields for farming, and abandon their traditional ways. They must start religious instruction in the Christian faith and send their children to the white man's school. Above all else, they must stop drinking right away. Van Tassel knew that these changes could not be made overnight, but would take time. He was also concerned that local farmers were urging traders to boost the production and sale of whiskey to the Ottawa so they would never be acceptable to the Presbyterians. His plan for a reserve came to nothing. What would become of the "poor Indians" once they were dismissed from their valley, the reverend could not foresee. But he believed a day of reckoning was coming, not for the tribes but for the United States. As Van Tassel explained, "when I reflect that God is just, I tremble in view of those awful judgments that await our beloved country."[55]

TEN

The Wyandot Farewell

With the Ottawa on their way out of the valley of the Maumee, there was only one tribe still left in Ohio: the Wyandot. About seven hundred members of the nation once known as the Huron were living on the Grand Reserve at Upper Sandusky and the smaller tract just to the north called Big Spring. More than any other tribe in Ohio, they had done everything asked of them by the American government. They had become successful farmers and now cultivated some of the best land in the state. Travelers to their country noticed the fine log houses with sash windows and stone chimneys, the acres of corn growing alongside apple orchards, and the herds of cattle and horses on the Wyandot reserves.[1]

But this success stirred a great impatience in many of the American settlers who surrounded them. Any interest they might have had in "civilizing" the tribes ended once the Indian Removal Act was signed into law. Now their only concern was for the Wyandot to pack up and follow the Delaware, Seneca, Shawnee, and Ottawa west across the Mississippi River. Then all the farms and fields sitting on the richest soil in northwest Ohio would be theirs. The Wyandot who wanted to stay, slightly more than half of the tribe, could take some comfort that miracles did happen.

They knew from the Bible that long ago Joshua had won a battle against the Amorites when the sun stood still. Even if no miracle of this magnitude occurred, they might still delay the Americans, who were so determined to take every acre in Ohio for themselves.

Leaving Ohio would not be easy for a people who had made it their home for nearly a century. The country along the Sandusky, a Wyandot word meaning "water within pools of water," had been a refuge for the tribe fleeing from the ravages of war. The Wyandot remembered that they once lived in towns far to the north along the Georgian Bay in Canada. But in 1648, the Iroquois attacked their villages, destroying most of them and forcing the Wyandot to abandon the rest. The Iroquois were determined to claim the western country as hunting grounds for themselves alone, thereby dominating the fur trade. Some Wyandot fled farther north toward Hudson Bay, others went east to Quebec, and a third group, the ancestors of the Ohio Wyandot, headed south of Lake Erie. But wherever they went, first to the Blue Ridge Mountains and later west to Green Bay, the Iroquois were never far behind. Finally, they found safety outside the walls of the new French fort at Detroit. But when other tribes crowded about the post, making hunting more difficult and fur trading less profitable, they followed French Jesuits to a new home along the Sandusky. Every Protestant minister who came among the Wyandot in Ohio saw the old people still wearing crucifixes and holding rosaries, and took note of the number who returned to Detroit each spring to celebrate Easter.

The other Indians who found refuge in Ohio, but who were now all gone, respected the Wyandot for their courage and wisdom. They joined the Wyandot against the British during the French and Indian War and against the Americans during their revolution. Together they continued the fight against the United States all the way to Fallen Timbers, giving up finally at Greeneville. When the Ohio tribes split over Tecumseh and the Prophet a decade later, with many warriors following the Shawnee brothers, most of the Wyandot remained loyal to the Americans. Later, after peace was restored at Springwells, the Wyandot regained their position as the leader of the Indians in Ohio for the next twenty years. Even after the other tribes moved west in the

1830s, they still wanted the Wyandot to come live with them. The Shawnee and the Delaware were especially anxious for their "grandfathers" to give up the fight against the American settlers, who inched closer to their reserves every day. They even offered to sell some of their land along the Kansas River to the Wyandot.[2]

Nearly half of the Wyandot living in Ohio wanted to follow their brother tribes across the Mississippi River. Their leader was Chief Warpole, who a decade before had opposed the efforts of Reverend Finley to convert the tribe to the white man's religion. Even though he had joined the Methodist Church, he and his supporters still had many complaints about Ohio. Their main concern was the fact that American settlements were encroaching closer to the Wyandot reserves each year. Between 1825 and 1835, five new towns—Marseilles, Tymochtee, McCutcheonville, Little Sandusky, and Wyandot—had been established nearby. Nine townships around the tribe's Grand Reserve had been surveyed and opened for settlement. People were already buying plots of ground from the land office in Bucyrus and were even establishing farms in Crane Township, home of the Grand Reserve. The Overland Stagecoach route that connected Buffalo to Cincinnati ran straight through Upper Sandusky and made regular stops there. The Mad River Valley Railroad was laid out all the way to Tiffin, and would soon run a line east and west directly across the Grand Reserve, having obtained permission to do so from President Andrew Jackson himself. More and more whites came onto the reserve each day, renting land from the Wyandot or sharecropping for them. Some even hired themselves out as laborers on Wyandot farms.[3]

The close proximity of so many whites brought whiskey to the reserves, and whiskey in turn brought violence. What seemed a necessity for settlers on the frontier was a curse for the Indians. Even the Methodist missionaries who had lived on the Grand Reserve for decades had not been able to stem the tide of traders coming into the Indian country to sell liquor. Drinking led to fighting and even murder. Many offenders spent time in the tribal jail, built high on a bluff overlooking the Sandusky River, awaiting trial and punishment. Members of the tribe who wanted to go west were generally sympathetic to the young men who got drunk and accidentally killed someone in a rage. They usually favored banishing the offender from the Grand Reserve, but the Wyandot who wanted to stay in Ohio were less forgiving. They often demanded death for a murderer and carried out the sentence by firing squad. However, the tribe's leaders banded together whenever their young men were thrown into jail in an American settlement. Whether they supported or opposed removal, the chiefs went together to bail out their sons and defend them against whatever charges they faced.[4]

Despite these problems, the Wyandot who hoped to remain in Ohio argued that the tribe had accomplished great things since moving to their reserves at Upper Sandusky and Big Spring. Most of these Wyandot were Methodists who had converted to the faith when James Finley, and before that John Stewart, lived among them. Even after Stewart died and Finley moved on to other assignments, the mission school remained open. All the government observers sent to report on the progress of the Wyandot "scholars" were impressed with the determination of the children to master reading, writing, and arithmetic. A few of the students went on to become ministers, traders, and even lawyers. The mission church was still active, with many Wyandot deeply devoted to their faith. James Wheeler, their current minister, had promised to follow his congregation west if the Wyandot ever decided to head for Kansas. While their greatest preacher, Between the Logs, had died of consumption, new ministers, like Squire Grey Eyes and Matthew Peacock, had risen from the Wyandot to take his place.[5]

The Wyandot who wanted to stay in Ohio were equally proud of how prosperous the tribe had become, especially since the Grand Reserve was divided among individual landowners in 1827. Most families had cleared at least 5 to 10 acres, and nearly every head of a household had multiple properties. Some individuals owned several farms with 75 to 100 improved acres each. Robert Robertail, son of Chief Squire Grey Eyes, had two of the biggest farms on the Grand Reserve: one was 56 acres and had three cabins and a stable, and the other was 65 acres with a hewed log house that was surrounded by pastureland. George Wright had one of the largest individual homesteads in Salem Township, a 125

The Wyandot Mission
Church, Upper Sandusky,
in 1847. (*Historical
Collections of Ohio* by
Henry Howe)

1/2-acre farm that had a log home, a springhouse, a deep well, a meadow for pasture, and twenty apple trees. All Wyandot farmers, along with numerous settlers who rented property on the tribe's reserves, hauled their corn and wheat to a place called Indian Mill for grinding. The government had built the mill on the Sandusky River in section sixteen of Crane Township in accordance with a provision in the Treaty at the Foot of the Rapids.[6]

While the old tribal villages had disappeared, Upper Sandusky, or Mononcue, as the Wyandot called the town, on the western bank of the Sandusky River became the cultural center of the Grand Reserve. The Wyandot built a new council house, one of the finest public buildings in the region, at the center of the town. It was one-and-a-half stories high, with a wide porch and dormers on the second floor that let in the light. Here the tribe gathered to debate the great issues of the day, most notably whether they should remain in Ohio or leave for the Far West. Here they also agreed on a new method for choosing a head chief. When Tarhe's successor, Deonquod, died, they decided the tribe's leader would no longer be chosen from only two royal clans—the Wolf and the Porcupine—but could instead be selected from any of the seven surviving clans. The chief's position would also be changed from a lifetime appointment to a one-year term. On January 1, the tribe would vote for a new head chief and six other chiefs who would act as his council of advisors during the upcoming year. Just as important, there was the Walker's store near the council house; the family used a portion of the tribe's yearly annuities to purchase items in New York City, and then sold them to the Indians for a very small profit, an arrangement that ensured high-quality, reasonably priced goods. The Walkers also established the Overland Inn on the stagecoach route that ran through Upper Sandusky where guests could buy food, drink, and a bed for the night.[7]

Colonel James Gardiner had cared about none of this when he headed to the Grand Reserve in the early fall of 1831 to negotiate a treaty that would remove the Wyandot west of the Mississippi River. For him, the Wyandot were simply the last tribe on the list slated for removal from Ohio. They also happened to be sitting on some of the best farmland in the state. He knew that a treaty with the Wyandot would be "highly important" to both Ohio and the United States, and even calculated how much money the government would make by selling the Grand Reserve at Upper Sandusky. At the rate of 70 cents per acre, the Wyandot's land, which he estimated to be 162,000 acres, would yield about $113,000. Even after calculating the cost of "all contingencies," this would still "leave a large balance in favour of the United States."

Gardiner had no doubt that he was the man to win the treaty that would make these high profits possible. With the exception of the Ottawa of the Lower Maumee River valley, he had successfully negotiated removal treaties with all the other Ohio tribes. He had worked out these treaties like clockwork at regular three-week intervals throughout the summer of 1831. The Mixed Band of Shawnee and Seneca from Lewistown had signed theirs on July 20, the Shawnee of Wapakoneta and Hog Creek on August 8, and the Ottawa of the Auglaize and Upper Maumee on August 30. As he headed for Upper Sandusky in late September 1831, he was certain that he would have a deal with the Wyandot well before he had to escort the Shawnee, Ottawa, and Seneca to their new homes in Kansas and Oklahoma.[8]

But Gardiner quickly discovered that the Wyandot were not as easy to handle as the other tribes. He called them a wise, intelligent, and "crafty" people who could best him on every point. Before they would even begin a serious discussion about removal, they demanded that a delegation of their leading citizens be sent west to see if this new land was worth anything.[9] Since he badly wanted a treaty that would complete his work among the Ohio tribes, Gardiner had no choice but to acquiesce to the demands of the Wyandot. The tribe chose five men, among them William Walker Jr., to lead the expedition across the Mississippi. While Walker openly opposed removal, he promised to fairly evaluate the western country and report his findings to the tribe.

As Gardiner prepared to head west with the delegation, he did not understand how much the Wyandot respected Walker. He was the son of William Walker Sr., who had been taken as a boy on the Virginia frontier, and his Wyandot wife, Catherine Rankin. The younger Walker was a devout Methodist and proud supporter of the mission school, where he had worked as a teacher and where his children were educated. He had continued his studies in literature and language as an adult. He was known for his intelligent conversation, his poetry, and his fluency in English, French, and Wyandot. He often served as an interpreter and secretary for government officials during their negotiations with the Ohio tribes. Walker was also a successful businessman who managed the tribe's store in Mononcue and who helped his sister Nancy and her husband, William Garrett, run the Overland Inn. He built one of the finest frame homes in northwest Ohio, served as US postmaster for Upper Sandusky, and was a founding member of a Masonic lodge on the Grand Reserve.[10]

William Walker and the rest of the Wyandot delegation headed for Kansas with Colonel Gardiner in the fall of 1831. They planned to be in the Far West for about six weeks and would return to Ohio around Christmastime. The exploring party made its way to the juncture of the Kansas and Missouri rivers and then headed farther to the northwest along the Platte. The Wyandot were impressed with the soil, which in most places was deep and black, but they were worried about the steep, treeless ravines. The trees that did grow there were only good for firewood. The Wyandot were also disappointed when they could find no sugar maples. They finally did find a few of them, thirty to be exact, but they were spread out across ten acres. The wildlife also seemed sparse. They saw many deer, raccoons, and bears, but knowing what good hunters they were, the Wyandot said these animals would soon disappear if the tribe emigrated west. Yet, what most troubled the Wyandot were the Missourians, who spoke openly that the Indians were a "nuisance" and a "curse to the state." The worst were the poor whites, who had come up from the South to settle, whom Walker described as "an abandoned, dissolute and wicked class of people." They would undoubtedly have only one thing to trade with the Wyandot and that would be whiskey.

Walker noted, too, that many people in Missouri were slave-holders, the "greatest and most merciless oppressors" of Indians "among all the American population." He considered whites who owned slaves the moving force behind the removal of the tribes. If the Wyandot left for Kansas, the slaveholders, having filled up the country from Georgia to Arkansas with their cotton plantations, would be waiting for them. The tribe would be caught in the cross fire between white planters and slaves, who would escape to the tribe's new reserve, just as they escaped to Negro Town north of Upper Sandusky. Who would keep the peace? Surely not the soldiers at Fort Leavenworth, Walker answered. They couldn't even keep whiskey out of the hands of traders. How could they protect the Wyandot from clashing with poor whites, wealthy slaveholders, and runaway slaves? Twenty years before it actually happened, William Walker clearly envisioned his people trapped in "Bleeding Kansas."[11]

Another terrible irony in Kansas that Walker and his fellow Wyandot could clearly see, but which advocates of Indian removal could not understand, was that those who favored the removal of the eastern tribes to the western plains argued that this would give the Indians a chance to become civilized, meaning the Indians would give up the ways of the warrior and hunter, and settle down as farmers and ranchers. Walker and his companions knew they were more civilized than the poor whites they passed in Missouri and far more cultured than the pioneers who were trying to scratch out a life for themselves in the woods around the Grand Reserve.

Because they were so advanced, and in fact were already substantial landowners, the Wyandot had nothing in common with the nomadic tribes who lived between Kansas and the Rocky Mountains. Walker even referred to these Indians as "savages." On the return trip to Ohio, when the Wyandot delegation stopped in St. Louis to visit William Clark, Walker observed Flathead Indians who had come all the way from the Rockies to learn more about the white man's religion. He wrote to a friend back east about these wild people who flattened the backs of their heads and who hoped to become Christians. His letter was published in a Methodist newspaper, which encouraged the movement of missionaries and settlers to the Oregon Territory.[12]

As the Wyandot made their way from St. Louis to Upper Sandusky, Colonel Gardiner was unaware of Walker's opinions and was still certain he could negotiate a removal treaty with the tribe in four to five weeks. When he learned that Walker meant to oppose him in future councils, Gardiner exploded in a rage and poured out his frustration in angry letters to the War Department, claiming that the delegation had only good things to say about the western country when they met with Clark. The Indians had so enjoyed hunting bears in western Missouri that Gardiner had never been able to move them very far up the Kansas River. They never saw the country where they would probably be moving and so he could not report fairly on it. He was so angry at William Walker that he had another member of the exploring party and Henry Brish, who had met the group in St. Louis when he was taking the Seneca to their new reserve, swear out depositions attesting that the Wyandot loved the western country. He went on to complain that Walker was against removal because he was a half blood, actually more white than Indian, and thus never had any intention of leaving Ohio. He railed against the whites who had intermarried with the Wyandot and who were trying hard to keep the tribe in the state. They did this only so they could continue collecting annuities from the government along with the rest of the tribe. Gardiner was now convinced that if he only negotiated with full bloods, whom he called the "Pagan" or "savage" party, since many of them were not Christians, he could convince them to give up their land in Ohio and move west.[13]

Like many Americans who supported the removal of the eastern tribes, Gardiner could not comprehend that the Wyandot had more in common with the settlers who surrounded them than with the Indian tribes of the Far West. They had been fierce warriors and able hunters during the long years of fighting with the French and the English, but those days had ended for most of the tribe after Greeneville and for the rest of the tribe after

Springwells. In just twenty years, since the close of the War of 1812, they had become some of the wealthiest people in Ohio. Their homes, farms, and orchards were a source of wonder for every passing traveler to behold. During the entire time they lived in Ohio, whether as "wild" Indians or "settled" farmers, they had always accepted whites into their tribe. More than any other Indians that lived in Ohio, the Wyandot protected whites, mainly women and children, who had been captured on the frontier. They often saved captives of other Indians and adopted them as full members of their tribe. When peace came to Ohio after the War of 1812, the Wyandot frequently intermarried with pioneer families who lived near them as well as with the now-grown children of Methodist missionaries. Some of the most respected families on the Grand Reserve could boast Indian and white ancestors.[14]

Along with the Walkers, the Armstrong family was another good example of mixed bloods among the Wyandot. The founder of the clan was Robert Armstrong, who had been captured by Delaware Indians on the Ohio frontier when he was only four. He was ransomed by the Wyandot and lived among them for the rest of his life, eventually marrying Sarah Zane, a granddaughter of Tarhe the Crane. His son, John Armstrong, had been educated at the mission school and was now a practicing attorney in Bucyrus. His other son, Silas, owned one of the best farms on the Grand Reserve and had accompanied his friend William Walker Jr. west to Kansas.[15] Like Walker, Armstrong saw no reason why the Wyandot, who had done everything the Americans had asked of them and who were now respectable citizens of Ohio, whether recognized as such or not, should have to leave. Only a misguided romanticism which demanded that Indians of the present must be like Indians of the past could drive the Wyandot across the Mississippi River.

But Colonel Gardiner saw no contradiction in the government's position. He had been sent among the Wyandot, civilized or not, to convince them to sell their land. If he could not get the Grand Reserve out of the clutches of the half-breed "Christian" party, then he would negotiate with the full bloods who lived at Big Spring and take their reserve away from them. Between the Logs had won this small tract, slightly less than a full township just north of the Grand Reserve, during the treaty negotiations at St. Mary's in 1818. The place got its name from the "big spring" that formed the headwaters of the Blanchard River. On January 19, 1832, just three weeks after returning with the exploring party from the western country, Gardiner signed a treaty with the Wyandot of Big Spring at McCutcheonville, named for its founder, Joseph McCutcheon, who was a justice of the peace and active participant in the negotiations.

A careful look at the opening lines of the treaty gives a clear picture of the arguments that Gardiner must have used to convince the Wyandot to sell their land. This little band, surrounded by whites whose numbers were ever increasing, would never be happy in Ohio. In order to preserve the morals of their people from the corrupting influence of the whites, they were willing to sell the 16,000 acres of the Big Spring Reserve to the United States, which was willing to purchase it. The government would immediately survey the land into sections and open them for settlement. The Wyandot would receive $1.25 in US silver coins for every acre sold. One half section, or 320 acres, would be set aside for the old Chief Roenunas, who would be allowed to live out the remainder of his days there. The Wyandot would also be paid for any improvements on their land, with McCutcheon acting as surveyor along with another person chosen by the Wyandot.

Gardiner, who had been so careful to follow Cass's original instructions, wrote no provision in the treaty for a specific grant of land in the West that the Wyandot would receive in exchange for Big Spring. Instead, the treaty stated that they could head to Canada or the Huron River in the Michigan Territory, where their relatives lived, or they could obtain land from another Indian tribe. Gardiner later told the War Department that the Wyandot of Upper Sandusky were so furious at their brethren from Big Spring for signing the treaty that they threatened to drive them away or even kill them. They only relented, he claimed, when they realized that profits from the sale of Big Spring could supplement the tribe's annuities. They then welcomed the Big Spring Wyandot to live with them on the Grand Reserve.[16]

In reality, William Walker Jr., on behalf of his tribe, had written immediately to Elbert Herring, commissioner of Indian

Affairs, asking him why a treaty had been written with the Wyandot at Big Spring, and who gave Joseph McCutcheon the authority to participate in the negotiations? Instead of a direct answer to either question, Herring reminded Walker that the removal of the Indians was the policy of the government, explaining it was mutually beneficial to the tribes and "our people," meaning the Americans. As head of the Office of Indian Affairs, he was grateful to Joseph McCutcheon or any individual who helped negotiate a removal treaty. After all, this was being done for the good of everyone. Herring then concluded his letter with a sarcastic jab. If Walker or anyone else would like to help with removal, their services would be greatly appreciated.[17]

The Wyandot who wished to remain in Ohio could take some comfort that they had at least learned two valuable lessons in their dealings with Gardiner. First, they realized that they could use the negotiating process to delay removal and perhaps even prevent it. Second, they could sell part of their land to the government if they ever needed ready cash. The Wyandot employed the delaying tactic two years later, when the next round of commissioners arrived in Upper Sandusky demanding the surrender of the Grand Reserve. Settlers in northwest Ohio, eyeing the valuable property of the Wyandot and dreaming of their own prosperous farms there, petitioned the state government in Columbus to remove the tribe. On January 18, 1834, almost two years to the day since an angry James Gardiner won the cession of Big Spring from the Wyandot, the state legislature passed a resolution asking the federal government to reopen negotiations with the tribe for their removal. Jackson's administration welcomed Ohio's request as proof of the wisdom of its Indian policy. Exactly five months later, Congress appropriated money to pay for the negotiations, and Lewis Cass appointed Robert Lucas, the first Democratic governor of Ohio and a staunch Jackson man, as the next commissioner to try and negotiate the removal of the Wyandot.[18]

Secretary of War Lewis Cass was as clear in his instructions to Governor Lucas as he had been to Colonel Gardiner. Since the Wyandot were among the last tribes remaining in the East, they must be "speedily removed." Lucas was to tell them how they were surrounded by "dense settlements" of Americans bent on destroying them. Cass promised to send a map indicating where all the other tribes had agreed to live. Only the Wyandot, Menominee, and the New York Indians had not yet chosen new reserves across the Mississippi River. Cass was so anxious for the removal process to be over that he promised the Wyandot that they could have any piece of territory still available equaling 148,000 acres, his estimate of the size of the Grand Reserve, and up to 74,000 acres more. The Wyandot chiefs could also decide whether they wanted to remove their people themselves, or be conducted west by government agents. But no matter what the chiefs decided, the government would support the Wyandot financially for one year once they reached their new home in the Far West.[19]

Confident that with terms like these he would have more success with the Wyandot than Gardiner had had, Governor Lucas notified John McElvain, who was the Indian agent for the state of Ohio, to gather the tribe for a council in Upper Sandusky in the late summer of 1834. McElvain warned Lucas that negotiations might not go well, since another exploring party had just returned from the West. Much as William Walker had described the country nearly three years previously, the two chiefs just back from Kansas drew a stark picture of the place as worthless country. One of these men was Summundewat, a full-blooded chief deeply respected by his tribe, who put to rest Gardiner's argument that only half-breeds who intermarried with whites would want to stay in Ohio. The two chiefs had spoken about their trip to the entire tribe in a meeting that lasted from sunup to sundown, admitting that while there were a few good streams and quarries in Kansas, overall the land could not compare with Ohio.

When his council with the tribe opened on September 23, Governor Lucas attempted to counter this dark picture of the Far West. He laid out the map Cass had sent him showing where the Wyandot might settle. This "wide and extended" country was perfect for grazing large herds of horses and cattle, and Lucas added that Congress was presently debating a bill which would allow the Indians to set up their own territorial government in the Far West. He concluded with an argument he was certain no Wyandot could refute. Look around the council house, he said, at the handful of people who are left from this once mighty tribe. He then pointed to the west and told the Wyandot to go there and plant the last remnant of their nation in its soil, because only then would the tribe flourish once again. The governor made one more promise. Any chiefs who had received grants of land in previous treaties could stay behind and become citizens of Ohio.[20]

Henry Jacques, the tribe's current head chief, answered that the Wyandot would need several weeks to consider everything they had heard. A disappointed Governor Lucas returned to Columbus, hoping to continue the negotiations in late October. He noticed the tribe seemed evenly split on the matter of removal. As he explained to Lewis Cass, "some are anxious to join their brethren in the West, while others are loath to abandon the land of their fathers." But as of now, they were in no hurry to decide one way or the other. Lucas would travel back to Upper Sandusky in late October, and maybe then, after they had received their annuity payments, the tribe would be more amenable to removal.[21]

But when he arrived back at the Wyandot council house on October 23, Lucas learned that the tribe had no intention of moving west. They had chosen Summundewat to explain their position. The young chief said that his people had discussed the matter for three full days. They had taken a vote on removal, and the result was "negative." How had they come to this conclusion when Governor Lucas had described so powerfully that they were a nation on the brink of extinction? Summundewat said they remembered something a young man had told them after they signed the Treaty at the Foot of the Rapids in 1817. At the time, the young man worked in the Indian service at Detroit, and told the Wyandot "never to part with their reservation." They saw no reason to ignore his advice, even though he was now the secretary of war and had changed his mind on the question of removal.[22]

In the Wyandot's opinion, they had made an irrefutable argument to Governor Lucas. Lewis Cass, who had sent Lucas to buy the Grand Reserve, was the same man who had once told them never to sell their land. No matter what Lucas argued from this point forward, the Wyandot would not listen, at least not at the present time. The desperate governor launched a series of questions at them. Are you more prosperous now than you were five years ago? Aren't you more in debt than you were then? Don't you want to live on land you have chosen and under laws you have written? Summundewat answered that a vote of the entire nation had been taken and could not now be overturned.[23]

For their part, the Wyandot had survived two official attempts to remove them from Ohio. They had also learned the value of delay in extending negotiations to the point at which the government retreated, probably only for the moment and certainly to return at a later date. Before that happened, the Wyandot who wanted to stay in Ohio, still slightly more than half of them, hoped to strengthen the tribe's position by making improvements on the Grand Reserve, specifically to the mission school, to the Indian Mill on the Sandusky River, and to the many roads that connected farms around Upper Sandusky. The tribe's annuities, however, were not enough to fund these projects. When William Walker Jr. became head chief in January 1836, he decided to raise these much-needed funds by implementing the second lesson Colonel Gardiner had taught them at McCutcheonville. He would sell part of the Wyandot's remaining land to the government to procure enough money to make the necessary improvements. Along with John Barnett and Matthew Peacock, he headed for the War Department in Washington, where he offered to sell two tracts of Wyandot land in exchange for money paid directly to the chiefs.

Cass, serving in his final days as Jackson's secretary of war, appointed John Bryan to negotiate the treaty with the Wyandot. Bryan had served as Governor Lucas's secretary during the failed negotiations just two years earlier. On April 23, 1836, William Walker Jr., John Barnett, and Matthew Peacock signed a treaty that would bring much-needed revenue to their tribe. The Wyandot chiefs agreed to sell a five-mile-wide strip on the eastern edge of the Grand Reserve to the United States. They also gave up the one-mile-square tract in the Cranberry Swamp on Broken Sword Creek won in the Treaty of St. Mary's in 1818. The strip at the eastern edge of the Grand Reserve would be opened for immediate settlement. Officials appointed to oversee the survey and sale of the tract would be chosen by the president, the Senate, and the Wyandot chiefs. Records of the land sale would be carefully maintained. If the chiefs were dissatisfied with how the sale was proceeding, they could stop it and report their concerns to the War Department. In turn, the War Department would notify the president who would set a new date for the sale.[24]

The details of the treaty showed just how much the younger Walker distrusted the American government. He made sure the agreement clearly stated that up to $20,000 of the profits from the land sale would go directly to the chiefs, who would use the money specifically for the mission school, the Indian Mill, and the roads on the Grand Reserve. Walker further added a provision that would resolve a long-standing conflict between the Wyandot and the government. In the treaty signed at the Foot of the Rapids, seven Wyandot chiefs had each been promised two sections of land in the tribe's new reserves; yet these tracts had never been assigned. Just a year earlier, in February 1835, Warpole, Mononcue, John Hicks, George Punch, and Matthews, along with the descendants of Between the Logs and Deonquod, had sent a petition to the War Department asking for their land and the right to sell one of the sections for money for their "old age." William Walker Jr. won a guarantee from the government that the five surviving chiefs and the designated heirs of the two deceased chiefs would each receive 640 acres in the surrendered territory. This would secure several hundred dollars for each man and would also give Walker the satisfaction of making the government live up to its promises.[25]

But Walker's treaty did not stop the determination of people in Ohio to take the Grand Reserve away from the Wyandot. When the original architects of Indian removal left office, local politicians came forward to take their place. In 1836, Cass stepped down as secretary of war in order to become the ambassador to France. In the same year, Andrew Jackson chose not to run for a third term and planned instead to retire to the Hermitage, his plantation in Tennessee, while Governor Lucas was defeated in his bid for reelection by his Whig opponent, Joseph Vance. In the absence of so many former leaders, Congressman William H. Hunter of Sandusky took up the challenge to rid his state of this "once great people." Elected as a Democrat to the House of Representatives in November 1836, he dedicated himself to winning the final purchase of the Grand Reserve from the Wyandot.

Joseph McCutcheon, who had helped James Gardiner negotiate the sale of Big Spring, and Henry Brish, the Indian agent who had taken the Seneca west to the part of Indian Territory that is now Oklahoma, were equally determined to push the Wyandot out of Ohio. They believed they could accomplish this by buying tribal land from chiefs who supported removal. In 1837, instead of treating with John Barrett, the tribe's current head chief and his ruling council, which included William Walker Jr., they negotiated with Warpole, a known advocate of removal, and several chiefs who agreed with him. When the Wyandot ruling council learned of the transaction, they disavowed the sale and placed Warpole and his top supporter, Standing Stone, under arrest in the tribe's jail on the Grand Reserve, on the grounds that they had violated the law, recently passed by the tribe, which mandated that no individual Wyandot could sell land to the Americans.

This new law was in keeping with the government's long-standing policy that Indians could only sell their land as a tribe to the United States and not to individuals. A date for a tribal council was set to determine the fate of Warpole and Standing Stone. But before this could take place, McCutcheon and Brish had a judge issue a writ of habeas corpus, which released the imprisoned chiefs. Both sides petitioned Joel Roberts Poinsett, the new secretary of war under President Martin Van Buren, for his support. The War Department directed the local district attorney to decide the matter, and he ruled that the Wyandot were fully under the laws of the state of Ohio and had no right to pass their own statutes. Individual Wyandots were free to sell land to anyone as they saw fit.

A triumphant Warpole now forwarded petitions, signed by Wyandot men and women who wanted to move west, to the government, and planned to go to Washington, to explain to President Van Buren what had transpired. A horrified William Walker Jr., acting on behalf of the Wyandot's head chief and the other members of the ruling council, wrote to the people of Ohio in an article published in the *Ohio State Journal* (Columbus) on September 16, 1837. Calling himself "One of the Nation," he explained how the Indian tribes had always sold their land to the United States, not to individuals, and that this policy was being violated on the Grand Reserve in a desperate effort to force his people off their land. He now asked the people of Ohio a direct question: Did they want the Wyandot to remain in their state? He concluded his powerful essay with the confident belief that their answer would be yes.[26]

With the tribe deadlocked, the many Wyandot who were opposed to removal believed the political tide would soon turn in their favor. Andrew Jackson's Democratic Party finally appeared on the brink of losing the White House and the Congress; and if the Wyandot could survive every attempt to remove them until this happened, then they could stay in Ohio forever. The next attempt came from William Hunter, who remained determined to rid Ohio of the Wyandot. Even after he lost his bid for reelection to Congress in November 1838, he met with the tribe in a five-day council in the following May, urging them to move west. He took another exploring party across the Mississippi and later claimed he won an agreement from the Shawnee and Delaware to sell 55,000 acres in Kansas to the tribe. Luckily for the Wyandot who wanted to stay in Ohio, the Office of Indian Affairs ignored Hunter's unofficial efforts to remove them.[27]

But the tribe faced a more serious threat when the lame-duck Democratic Congress appropriated $3,000 on March 3, 1841, to pay for more negotiations with the tribe. The Wyandot held out hope that their old friend William Henry Harrison, who would be inaugurated as the new Whig President on the following day, would remember how Tarhe and his warriors had fought at his side against Tecumseh and the British in the last days of the War of 1812. Harrison would surely overturn the policy of Jackson and his party and let the tribe stay on the Grand Reserve. Sadly for the Wyandot who had such faith in him, the new president had no intention of changing the nation's Indian policy. Instead, he had already told John Johnston, whom he had known since they were both boys on the Ohio frontier, that he would hire him to negotiate treaties with the Wyandot, undoubtedly for the purpose of removing them. Johnston had come to Washington after the election seeking such a position. On March 26 Harrison's secretary of war, John Bell, appointed Johnston as the commissioner who would negotiate the final treaty with the Wyandot. Johnston headed back to Upper Sandusky, determined to remove the tribe from the state.[28]

Johnston was convinced that the Wyandot must go west for their own sake. If they did not leave Ohio soon, they would be overrun by American settlers and would literally disappear as a people. He knew the tribe was evenly divided over the prospect of removal, and believed he could tip the balance in favor of removal, because he understood the Wyandot better than the previous commissioners. As an old Indian agent, he also believed he could argue better than any chief and outlast them when they tried to delay the inevitable. Even if the negotiations took a year or more, he would win the removal treaty that younger men in the opposing party had failed to achieve. As he would later explain to the War Department, "I never yet failed in any undertaking with them— patience, perseverance and fair dealing will accomplish anything with them but cannot be hurried." In the end, the removal treaty became a matter of personal honor for Johnston—the last survivor of Wayne's army in the Miami River valley, as he proudly described himself—to be the person who removed the last Indian from Ohio.[29]

Thomas Hartley Crawford, now serving as commissioner of Indian Affairs under John Tyler, who became president in 1841 after the unexpected death of William Henry Harrison, was even more dedicated to Indian removal than his predecessors. He had made a name for himself as a congressman from eastern Pennsylvania who voted for Jackson's Indian Removal Bill over the objections of his own constituents. Instead of slowing down removal, he wanted the process expedited, always claiming he was doing this to protect and civilize the Indians. He gave Johnston detailed instructions on how to remove the Wyandot from Ohio. First, Johnston was to do everything in his power to obtain the 109,144 acres that he calculated the Wyandot still owned. As Crawford simply put it, "The object is the cession of all their lands in Ohio." Second, he told Johnston what the government was willing to offer in return for this land. The tribe's annuities would be raised from $6,900 to $12,000. The Wyandot could deduct $2,000 from this amount to operate a school for their children. They would receive another $2,000 annually for the next ten years to buy farm equipment. Furthermore, all debts up to $10,000 would be paid off.

The tribe would not be rushed west, but would have two years to move. Once they were across the Mississippi, the government would support them for one year and ensure that no white settlers encroached on their land. They would also receive a sawmill, a gristmill, and a blacksmith's shop with a blacksmith, whose salary would be paid by the government. Finally, and perhaps most important, Crawford told Johnston that he was not to allow any more Wyandot to go west in exploring parties; enough Wyandot had already traveled across the Mississippi, and sending another group would be a waste of time. Johnston was only to relent if the matter became a sine qua non for a final treaty. He could also offer an extra half section of 320 acres to every adult with a family to sweeten the deal.[30]

With these instructions in hand, Colonel Johnston arrived in Upper Sandusky in May 1841. He found the Wyandot greatly changed from the days when he was their Indian agent more than a dozen years before. He was most surprised to see that they were not so much surrounded by whites as intermarried with them. These many "half breeds" and "quadroons," as Johnston described them, had a great influence over the tribe. Instead of fearing the whites who daily drew closer to Upper Sandusky, they actually encouraged them to move onto the Grand Reserve as tenant farmers and day laborers. The tribe also now had a fellow Wyandot, John Armstrong, as their attorney. He came to the negotiations armed with facts and figures to confirm how valuable his tribe's land truly was.[31]

Armstrong shared the same facts and figures with the commissioner of Indian Affairs. He wrote to Crawford in June 1841, reminding him that the Grand Reserve was in the "heart of a flourishing country." The land had many natural advantages, such as its "superior" soil and abundant streams, and also man-made assets, such as buildings and roads. At a public auction, the Grand Reserve would go for at least $5.00 an acre; and even if the government only got $4.00 per acre, the United States would still collect over $430,000. After estimating that the tribe's removal costs, including annuities, travel expenses, debt payment, subsistence for one year, and surveying and land sale costs, would amount to $125,000, not $300,000, as Johnston had estimated, Armstrong concluded that the government would still clear a hefty profit. If the government invested this money, it would provide the Wyandot with a permanent annuity of $20,000.[32]

Johnston wrote Commissioner Hartley, too, promising he could get a treaty, even in the face of so many Wyandot half-breeds and their attorney. He would accomplish this by convincing the tribe that they were a disappearing people, and by reminding them that forty years ago, before Tippecanoe and the War of 1812, there were at least 2,500 Wyandot, but that no more than 700 or 800 were left, just a third of the tribe that Johnston had known as a young man. Maybe the half-breeds and their leaders, such as the current head chief, John Hicks, were "educated, well-informed and intelligent," but the "pure" Indians, who made up at least half of the tribe, were "abandoned, degraded, drunk, vagrant" men and women; these people were suffering from the "withering effect" of the nation's Indian policy, and would benefit from a "speedy removal" to the West.

Having identified the deep division within the tribe, Colonel Johnston proposed a deal that he thought a majority of Wyandot would accept. He asked that their annuity be raised to $15,000. He agreed with John Armstrong that the government could afford a higher annuity even if the Grand Reserve sold for only $4.00 an acre. A tidy profit would still be left over for the US Treasury. The government would be able to make even more money on the sale of the Wyandot tract along the Huron River in the Michigan Territory. Johnston was certain that the band would emigrate with their relatives in Ohio and asked Commissioner Crawford for permission to treat with them.[33]

Johnston and Crawford argued back and forth throughout the summer of 1841 over what else the government should offer the Wyandot to convince them to leave. Crawford commissioned Johnston to negotiate a removal treaty with the Wyandot band living in Michigan, but he refused to increase their annuities any higher than $12,000, as he was not sure the Grand Reserve would fetch a high price. Land around Bucyrus, including the Big Spring Reserve, was only selling for $2.78 an acre. Crawford told

Johnston to remind the Wyandot that they would receive the same amount of land in the West that they held in the East. The government would auction the Grand Reserve within one year after the tribe left for Kansas. Once all the removal costs were deducted from the total, the remaining funds would be invested to provide an annual 5 percent return for the Wyandot. But because he sympathized with the Wyandot, and did not want to "rob" them, Crawford offered to sell them more land in the West at $1.25 an acre. Johnston responded that demanding payment for extra land in Kansas would be "unanimously rejected by my Indians."[34]

The old agent was correct. The Wyandot rejected any discussion of making them pay for more land and held firm to their demand for a $20,000 annuity. After meeting with the Wyandot in councils for several months, Johnston went home to his farm in Piqua, hoping to resume negotiations sometime after Christmas. He was frustrated that the Wyandot, both the advanced half-breeds and the degraded full bloods, as he designated them, did not seem to understand what was happening around them. While Johnston worried that the Mad River Railroad would soon cross the western boundary of the Grand Reserve, the half-breeds looked forward to this, because the value of their land would increase. In a similar way, the full bloods failed to comprehend how much the encroaching whites were changing the land around the Grand Reserve. Trees were coming down, farmsteads were going up, and everywhere the wild fur-bearing animals were disappearing. Instead, they had just gone off on their annual hunt in September as if nothing had changed in northwest Ohio in the last thirty years.[35]

But Colonel Johnston was wrong if he believed that the Wyandot were unaware of the changes. They had been involved in a great debate among themselves about these changes and what they meant for the future of their tribe since coming to live on the Grand Reserve twenty-five years earlier. They may have delayed negotiations on their possible removal by raising the stakes over the size of their annuities, but they continued to discuss whether they should remain in Ohio or leave for Kansas. In November 1841, they finally decided to authorize their chiefs to enter into treaty negotiations with the United States to sell their land in

Ohio and then head west across the Mississippi River. They were currently in discussions with the Shawnee and Delaware to buy land from one or both of the tribes. They were also now willing to accept an increase of their annuities to only $17,500.

The Wyandot chiefs informed Johnston of all this after the New Year in 1842, and chided him a bit for his impatience by reminding him how a democracy works. While they knew he was clearly in favor of removal, they explained that in a democracy, whether that of the United States or the Wyandot nation, the majority rules:

> We hold it as a rule that when a question of importance is submitted to the nation for its decision, the minority however respectable its numbers and intelligence, must acquiesce in the decision, be what it may, and must cooperate with the majority in sustaining that decision.[36]

The Wyandot, however, did not tell Colonel Johnston what had caused the shift in favor of removal. The change had come after the murder of their beloved chief Summundewat. He had been a man at home in two worlds, both among the full-bloods, who usually supported removal, and among the Christians, who with rare exceptions, like Warpole, opposed it. Summundewat was a tall man, at least six feet, who always wore a traditional feather headdress. He had an excellent memory and could recall the history and legends of his tribe with ease. But he was also a devout Methodist, a gifted preacher, and a trustee of the Mission Church. In the fall of 1841, he had gone west to Williams County on his tribe's winter hunt. He invited Nancy Coon and her husband, Tall Fighter, a Seneca Indian who was the brother of his wife Mary, to come with him. On their way back to the Grand Reserve, they stopped near Turkey Foot Creek in Henry County. When two white men came upon their camp, Summundewat offered them food and invited them to rest.

During the night, the men murdered the chief and his brother-in-law with an ax as they slept. Nancy escaped into the woods, but they caught up with her and murdered her, too. They fled with the furs that Summundewat had collected, along with his horses and dogs. On the following day, the Wyandot came looking for their

chief and his companions, and found them buried under logs and
fallen leaves. The two criminals were later captured and jailed, but
local officials let them escape. The murder of Summundewat and
the escape of his murderers shook the Wyandot to their very core.
Suddenly, all the warnings from government officials about the
dangers of white people creeping closer to their reserve made
sense. Many who had opposed removal were now prepared to vote
for it.[37]

At the same time, Colonel Johnston had an experience that
made him determined to negotiate a treaty with the Wyandot. In
the early winter of 1842, he was riding on a bridge over a swift-
moving stream when his horse stumbled and fell over the edge.
Johnston went under the water with the horse. Try as he might, he
could not pull his right foot free from the stirrup. Finally, with
only seconds to spare, he got loose and rose to the surface. He and
his horse swam back to shore and rode fourteen miles in the bitter cold to his home. His leg was severely injured, and it took several weeks for him to recover.[38] But his brush with death seemed
to embolden him. As much as it pained the "old public servant,"
he decided to ignore the last set of instructions from
Commissioner Crawford. He knew the Wyandot would never
accept Crawford's complicated formula for their annuities. They
had to have a set amount paid to them annually. If the government did not relent on this point, then, there would be no chance
for a treaty.

He strongly believed that failure to win a treaty would be a
tragedy for the Wyandot. He now saw the tribe as victims of "vile"
whites, the "most abandoned of their race," who had invaded their
land as "renters," "croppers," and "squatters." Johnston counted at
least 400 of these degraded people on the Grand Reserve. They
had turned Upper Sandusky into an "asylum for every species of
lawless violence," the kind of violence that had taken the life of
Summundewat. Johnston was horrified when he learned of the
murder of the chief and his companions. He tracked down one of
the escaped killers to the county jail in Perrysburg, Ohio, where he
was being held for counterfeiting, but no official in Tyler's administration would help Johnston prosecute him for the murders.
This further convinced Johnston that the Wyandot would only be

safe if they sold their remaining land in Ohio and headed west, where they could retain their tribal identity, unsullied by the presence of poor whites. The more advanced Wyandot could begin again in their new home, while the less advanced would have time to settle down, give up their old ways, and learn to become civilized at last. Then, too, the Grand Reserve could be opened for settlement by decent, hardworking Americans.[39]

In early March, Johnston made his own offer to the Wyandot. The tribe would cede all land in Ohio and Michigan for an equal amount of territory across the Mississippi River. They could choose their new home from land unclaimed by other eastern tribes. Johnston also proposed that several acres of the Grand Reserve, containing the Methodist church and tribal cemeteries, be permanently set aside. The Wyandot would forever own this land which could never be sold. Acknowledging the importance of the mission school, Johnston promised that the government would give $500 a year for a new school in the western country. Lastly, acknowledging the hard work that the Wyandot had invested in their land at Upper Sandusky, he vowed that the president would appoint honest people to assess the tribe's improvements and pay a fair price, and that they would receive this money as soon as they arrived across the Mississippi. The tribe's annuities would also be raised to $17,500.[40]

The Wyandot chiefs met in council with Johnston throughout the first week of March. They also met in councils with their own people. Finally, on March 17, 1842, they gathered the men together in the council house to vote on the question of removal. Those who were in favor moved to one side of the room, while those who opposed it went to the other. For the first time in voting, the balance tipped in favor of leaving Ohio by a slight majority. No one rejoiced but instead nearly every man cried. The Wyandot who had opposed removal accepted the decision and wept with those who had supported it. The chiefs then worked out the final details of the treaty with Johnston. Most of the provisions that Johnston had proposed in the last round of negotiations, along with some additional promises on the part of the government, were included. The Wyandot would be able to harvest their crops planted in the upcoming year, and could use the improvements on their land until the spring of 1844. The chiefs would also receive an extra $10,000 to help their people during the removal process. They would receive $5,000 when the first group of Wyandot left the Grand Reserve, and the rest when the entire nation assembled west of the Mississippi.[41]

As they had done since they signed the Treaty at the Foot of the Rapids, the Wyandot used the negotiations to guarantee property to certain members of the tribe by birth or adoption. Twenty-four individuals would receive 640 acres each in the West by fee simple. They could pass this land on to their descendants, but could only sell it to someone else with the approval of the president. The descendants of Cherokee Boy, who had been granted 640 acres in the Treaty of St. Mary's, were allowed to sell 480 acres of the original tract if the president approved. The Walker family would receive $3,000 for damages caused by the British to the farm of William Walker Sr. in the Michigan Territory during the War of 1812. His sons—William and Joel—would each receive $250 for acting as interpreters during treaty negotiations. Even Warpole would receive money owed to him, and would be paid $150 for traveling to Washington, in 1839 to inform President Van Buren that the Wyandot wanted to move west. After every account had been settled, Francis Hicks, the current head chief, signed his name under the signature of John Johnston, while his six counselors—James Washington, Squeendehtee, Henry Jacques, Tauroone, George Armstrong, and Squire Grey Eyes—made their marks below his name on the treaty that officially removed their people from Ohio.[42]

In a strange coincidence, renowned British author Charles Dickens was on a tour of the United States and arrived in Upper Sandusky one day after the Wyandot had voted to go west. He was on his way by stagecoach from Cincinnati to Sandusky, where he would board a lake steamer for Buffalo on his return trip to England. Dickens was impressed with the beautiful Ohio countryside, but unimpressed with most of the Americans he met along the way. He found accommodations at the Overland Inn, where he stayed for the night, less than desirable. When he tried to order a brandy for a friend who was traveling with him, he was told no one could sell liquor on an Indian reserve. "The legislature had banned the sale of spirits to the Indians by tavern keepers," Dickens later explained in his work *American Notes* (1842), adding snidely that the "precaution is quite inefficacious for the Indians never fail to procure liquor of a worse kind at a dearer price from travelling peddlars."

But Dickens's opinion of Americans changed for the better when he met Colonel Johnston, whom he described as a "mild old gentleman." Johnston explained that he had concluded a treaty with the Wyandot who lived in this village to move "just a little way beyond St. Louis." He described exactly how the vote was taken, with the "ayes" moving to one side of the council house and the "nays" to the other. Johnston said he had been through this process many times before with other tribes, and that the experience was always a sad one. The Indians were deeply attached to the land of their fathers, and leaving their homeland would be difficult; but they had voted to go west, and so they would. Dickens could not understand how the Wyandot who wanted to remain in Ohio could accept this decision so "cheerfully." When he boarded the Overland Stage and headed out of Upper Sandusky, he looked with pity at the poor Indians riding on their shaggy ponies. They seemed a "restless and wandering people," just like the gypsies he knew in England. Dickens left never knowing that the orderly farms that he admired everywhere in Upper Sandusky belonged to these wild people and would soon be for sale.[43]

Dickens also did not understand that the Wyandot were one people and meant to stay that way, whether in Ohio or Kansas, and that they had added a provision to their removal treaty to make certain they remained together. The treaty promised that every Wyandot who migrated west would be guaranteed the benefits of tribal citizenship and government annuities. If anyone refused to relocate to Kansas, or left once the tribe arrived there, they would no longer be a Wyandot or enjoy the tribe's annuities.[44] Since neither the state of Ohio nor the United States had offered citizenship, and the protection that citizenship gave under the law, the Wyandot would only have a legal standing if they remained a tribe. Any Wyandot who stayed behind in Ohio would be a person without a country. A handful of Wyandot told the chiefs they would never leave, preferring to spend the remainder of their lives wandering the river valleys between Upper Sandusky and Columbus; but most readied themselves for Kansas.

As the Wyandot planned for their future in the West, John Johnston notified Commissioner Crawford that he had won a treaty with the tribe. He apologized for ignoring explicit instructions from the secretary of war, but he did what he had to do to secure an agreement. He was proud that he had overcome the resistance of whites living on the Grand Reserve who wanted the tribe to stay in Upper Sandusky. He had also proved wrong state politicians who believed the tribe could never be removed from Ohio. Johnston was relieved when the Office of Indian Affairs congratulated him for his hard work. The Senate quickly approved the treaty, making only one minor change that raised the amount paid for Wyandot debts from $10,000 to $23,860. Since the Wyandot from Michigan had been unable to attend the negotiations in Upper Sandusky, due to high water and flooding in the late winter of 1842, the Senate amended the treaty to include the purchase of their land along the Huron River. A relieved Colonel Johnston headed on a 267-mile journey across the state attempting to determine exactly how much the Wyandot owed to various people. He discovered that the hardworking Ohioans, the kind of people who would soon buy the Grand Reserve once it was surveyed and opened for settlement, were not always honest. As he complained to Crawford, trying to find out exactly what the Wyandot owed and to whom was a "most perplexing affair." The final list of individuals to whom the Wyandot owed money ran eleven pages long. The people on the list claimed the tribe owed them over $30,000, but Johnston concluded the actual amount was closer to $24,000.[45]

After estimating the tribe's debt, Johnston had no further dealings with the Wyandot. Unlike the other tribes who had left Ohio, the Wyandot took total control of the removal process. Their chiefs planned to use the $10,000 they had received in the treaty to pay for the journey west. While the government would oversee the sale of their improvements—that is, houses, fields, and orchards—there would be no superintendent, disbursing agent, or conductor and assistant conductors on this trip. Instead, the chiefs, led by Henry Jacques and his six counselors, would organize their people, prepare wagons for the journey to Cincinnati, and pay for steamboat passage to Missouri. From there they would hire more wagons to take the tribe to Kansas. The Wyandot would sell much of their personal property, including furniture, livestock, and farm equipment. But they would not leave their horses behind or sell them at the docks in Dayton like the Seneca did in 1831. Instead Matthew Walker, a brother of William Walker Jr., would select several responsible young men who would help him take the tribe's horses and ponies from Upper Sandusky to Cincinnati and then overland to Kansas.[46]

For the chiefs, whether they had been for removal or against it, there was no turning back. They decided to take at least one year to prepare their people to move west. They hoped to leave in June 1843, but when they were delayed because they had so much personal property to sell, they pushed back the target date to July 12. One of their first moves was to hire another blacksmith and set up an extra shop for him to outfit their wagons and horses. They next welcomed 55 members of their tribe from the Huron River valley in Michigan and another 30 Wyandot who came south from Canada to join the migration to Kansas. The chiefs prepared a muster roll in order to have an exact count of the families heading west. On the final roll, prepared in July 1843, they listed a total of 664 people, including 609 individuals from Ohio, along with the Wyandot from Michigan and Canada. There were 144 heads of households, who matched almost exactly the list of property owners at Upper Sandusky that government surveyors would prepare in 1844 before opening the Grand Reserve for sale and settlement.[47]

The roll also revealed that the Wyandot who would travel west were very young. Only 20 people were over 50, while 150 were children under 10. There were many notable figures from the nation's long battle over removal on the list. One of them was Warpole, now close to 70, who would finally go west with his people to Kansas. Jonathan Pointer, the black man who had been Tarhe the Crane's servant and a supporter of the Methodist missionaries in Upper Sandusky, was also ready to leave. But there were many others who had figured prominently in the tribe's long history in Ohio who were not on the muster roll. One of them was Catherine Rankin Walker. Now 72, she decided to stay on the Grand Reserve, where she died in 1844. She was buried near the grave of her husband, who had died twenty years earlier, in the Old Indian Cemetery, not far from the Wyandot council house.

But Mononcue, an early convert to Christianity who had long opposed removal, would be heading with his own family to Kansas, as would the woman once married to Tarhe the Crane and Between the Logs. Now a widow for the third time with the new name of Sally Frost, she would head west alone; and so would another prominent widow, Mary Summundewat, and her two young children. All the leading "half-breed" families, as James Gardiner and John Johnston referred to them, like the Walkers, Armstrongs, and Zanes, descendants of the Wyandot and their white captives, were on the muster roll. Whites who had intermarried with the Wyandot once peace came to the frontier also readied their families for the trip to Kansas. George Garrett, who had married into the Walker clan, sold his interest in the Overland Inn, while Lucy Bigelow, the daughter of Methodist missionaries and who was married to John Armstong, loaded her children onto the prize buggy her husband had built for her and waited to start on the long trek west.[48]

The preparations for removal among the Wyandot, whether they were young or old, full-bloods or half-bloods, supporters or opponents of removal, were so calm that Purdy McElvain, the son of John McElvain and the tribe's last subagent, could only comment on the wonder of it all in his letters to the Office of Indian Affairs. Remarkably, just as Charles Dickens had first noted, they were ready to go "cheerfully."[49] But despite their outward calm, the Wyandot were troubled by several things as they prepared for their journey. Much of the new equipment they wanted to take with them, including wagons and heavy iron plows, would not be ready until after the tribe left Upper Sandusky. They would have to be stored at McElvain's agency until the following spring, when Joel Walker would bring them west. The Wyandot also worried that at least fifty people, members from eight to ten families, were too sick to make the long trip. Hopefully they would be strong enough to head west with Joel Walker's wagon train next spring.

The chiefs were also troubled by the many whites who came onto to Cherokee Boy's land to chop down trees. This section had been specifically designated for sale by his heirs. McElvain finally had to step in and threaten to prosecute anyone who stole lumber from them.[50] Another worry came over obtaining the payment for the tribe's many improvements. The men hired to evaluate them estimated they were worth more than $122,000. The Wyandot would not receive this money until they were settled in Kansas. An even more significant problem was that the tribe still had no definite place to live once they crossed the Mississippi River.

The Shawnee had promised to sell them a part of their reserve south of the Kansas River, but in the spring of 1843, just as the Wyandot were making final preparations to depart, they decided against the sale. The Wyandot chiefs were furious, remembering that a century earlier their tribe had "spread the deerskin" and invited the wandering Shawnee to settle in Ohio. They hoped that the Delaware would still be willing to sell them land when they arrived in Kansas. In order to scout out the best place, the chiefs sent an exploring party ahead of them in May 1843, consisting of Silas Armstrong, George Clarke, and their families, as well as Jane Tillies, a young woman who had been raised by the Armstrongs. They instructed Armstrong to set up a store for the Wyandot as soon as he arrived in Westport, Missouri, to ensure goods were immediately available when they arrived. The exploring party reported back that the best place to settle was at the juncture of the Kansas and Missouri rivers.[51]

In the days immediately preceding the Wyandot's departure, the chiefs often gathered with their people in the council house—which would soon serve as the first Wyandot County courthouse—making last minute preparations for the trip. People also attended the mission church to pray and hold services. In one of their last acts before leaving Ohio, the Wyandot moved the remains of Chief Summundewat and the black preacher John Stewart to the cemetery next to the mission. They placed stone markers over their graves. Then the Wyandot and many of their white neighbors crowded into the church to hear Reverend James Wheeler preach for the last time before he left with the tribe for Kansas. Then they listened to Squire Grey Eyes, who gave the final sermon. He would be heading west with his family, including his daughter, Margaret. As a little girl, she was taken by her father to the mission school when it first opened, but now she was a married woman who had given birth to seven children, two of whom lay buried in the mission church's cemetery.

Finally, on Wednesday morning, July 12, 1843, the Wyandot were ready to leave Ohio. The long wagon train pulled out of Upper Sandusky and headed for Cincinnati down the eighth and final "trail of tears" from Ohio. Matthew Walker and the young men he had hired rode the tribe's horses and ponies at the rear of the caravan. They would follow their people to Cincinnati before heading west through Indiana and Illinois and joining the main body of the tribe in Missouri. The chiefs calculated that it would take about a week to get to Cincinnati. They headed down the old Indian trail, which now ran through the frontier village of Marseille, that long ago connected Upper Sandusky to the Shawnee town of Wapatomica. By the end of the first day, they were at Grassy Point, just south of Kenton in Hardin County, and on the next they were in Bellefontaine, once the home of the Shawnee chief Bluejacket. From there they headed through Urbana, Springfield, Clifton, and Xenia, until after traveling for six days they camped just four miles north of Cincinnati. The chiefs took another day to arrange travel by steamboat for their people. On July 20, just eight days after leaving Upper Sandusky, the Wyandot boarded the *Republic* and the *Nodaway* and headed down the Ohio for Kansas.[52]

All along the way, from Upper Sandusky to Cincinnati, people had come out to see the Wyandot and their long caravan of wagons and horses. Many had never laid eyes on an Indian before. They thought of them as wild children of the forest and could not understand why these people looked so much like themselves. At Bellefontaine, a reporter from the local *Logan Gazette* saw them pass by on the afternoon of July 13. He admired their "stout hearts" as they walked and rode by calmly in the dust and heat. A wave of guilt passed over the writer as he watched the proud "Red Man" at last driven off his land by the "rapacious cupidity of the White Man." He could only offer up a simple prayer for their protection on the long way west. "May the Good Spirit guide and protect them."

A reporter for the *Xenia* (Ohio) *Torch-Light* saw them on Sunday, July 16, as they passed through his town on their way to Cincinnati. The Wyandot had hoped to stop and rest on the Sabbath; but whiskey traders had come into their camp the night before, and a few Wyandot who could not resist the temptation had gotten drunk. Fearing the peace of their wagon train would be disrupted if they stayed here any longer, the chiefs led their people farther south down the road through Xenia toward Cincinnati. The reporter for the *Torch-Light* was amazed at the caravan passing before him. By his count there were 625

Margaret Grey Eyes Solomon, c. 1880. Her family was among the last Wyandot to leave Ohio. (*Ohio Historical Society*)

Wyandot from Ohio and another 125 from Michigan and Canada. He was impressed with how well dressed the Indians were, like white people, he noted, and how many wagons and horses they had. He counted 80 wagons owned by the tribe and 55 more they had hired to make the trip to the Ohio River. The wagons were loaded with provisions and cooking utensils. There were at least three hundred horses and ponies. He was amazed, too, at the parade of fine buggies that went by. Like the reporter in Bellefontaine, he seemed unable to comprehend that the Wyandot were not wild savages, but wealthy farmers. In his mind, Indians still lived primarily by hunting deep in the forest. How tragic, he wrote, that they must leave their hunting grounds, douse their council fires, and abandon their wigwams. Everyone who saw them should utter a silent prayer to the "Great Spirit," asking that they would safely reach their new home in the West.[53]

In Cincinnati, where they remained for two days, newspapers reported that the trip was taking its toll on the Wyandot. A woman who had become sick in the extreme heat had died and was buried just outside the city. Chief John Hicks, a "fine-looking fellow," had gotten so drunk that he fell into the Ohio River. Although the paper reported the chief had drowned, he was instead rescued and would arrive safely in Kansas. A more sympathetic observer, Jacob Burnet, caught sight of the Wyandot as they boarded two steamboats for the West. As a justice on the Ohio Supreme Court, he had restored the land taken from the Seneca Nimble Jemmy. Later, as an Ohio senator, he had voted against the Indian Removal Bill, but now he could only stand by as the "final catastrophe" for this "noble race" unfolded before him. Along with many of the people of Cincinnati, he saw the Wyandot board the boats that would take them out of Ohio forever. Burnet was heartsick as he watched the tribe bravely face this "hopeless banishment." He noticed that the Wyandot, on the *Republic* and the *Nodaway*, seemed to linger for a moment and look back to the north as if saying one last farewell to their beloved homeland. He imagined they were saying good-bye to the graves of their children and the tombs of their ancestors. How terrible for the tribe to leave the place of their birth and the country of their fathers only to head into an unknown future.[54]

The Wyandot said two farewells to Ohio, one quite formal, and one more heartfelt. After the tribe arrived in Urbana, their head chief, Henry Jacques, headed for Columbus to meet with Governor Wilson Shannon. He went, in part, to ask that a young Wyandot man in the state penitentiary be released in order to go west with his tribe. But he also went to offer an official good-bye to the people of Ohio on behalf of the Wyandot. He reminded everyone that his tribe had been at peace with the Americans since 1795, when they signed the treaty with General Wayne at Fort Greeneville. From then on, even though the Wyandot had been surrounded by white people, there was never any conflict between them. If settlers in the Far West asked them what the people in Ohio were like, Jacques said he would tell them that they were kind, faithful, and honest. If anyone from Ohio visited the new Wyandot country across the Mississippi, the chief promised that they would be welcomed. Echoing the words of Jesus, he said if they were hungry, they would be fed. If they were thirsty, they would receive drink. If they were naked, they would be clothed. If they were sick, they would be healed. "The chain of peace and friendship" between the Wyandot and the citizens of Ohio would never be broken.[55]

The tribe gave a more personal farewell at North Bend, just down the river from Cincinnati, as they passed the tomb of

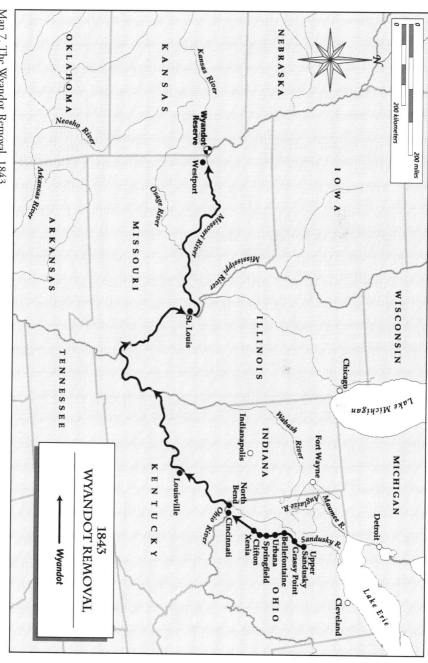

Map 7. The Wyandot Removal, 1843.

William Henry Harrison. He had died a few days after his administration appointed John Johnston to remove the Wyandot from Ohio. The tribe did not hold their removal against Harrison, but rather loved him as their "White Chief." Many of the men had served with Old Tippecanoe during the War of 1812, right up to the Battle of the Thames River. Harrison's tomb on his family's farm sat high on a bluff overlooking the Ohio. As the Wyandot approached this hallowed ground, Henry Jacques asked the steamboat captain to have the "big gun" loaded. Then he and the men who served with General Harrison climbed up to the highest deck of the ship and faced his resting place. As they passed, the cannon boomed, and the Wyandot men took off their hats and waved them in the air toward Harrison's grave. Henry Jacques stepped forward and shouted, "Farewell, Ohio, and her brave."[56]

All went smoothly until the Wyandot arrived in Louisville, where the chiefs made the first payment for their people's fare west. They planned to make the next one at St. Louis, and the last installment at Lexington, Missouri, near their final destination. But as soon as they handed their money to the captain of the *Nodaway*, he let them know that he did not like traveling with Indians. There had been no problems since leaving Cincinnati, except for trouble with the prisoner that Henry Jacques had gotten out of the state penitentiary. He was an angry young man who shouted insults at the other passengers. The chiefs silenced him by keeping him chained up throughout the rest of the trip; but this was not enough for the captain. For some reason that he never explained, he decided to take up all the carpets from his boat and store them away until he had deposited the Wyandot in Missouri.

On July 28, when the *Nodaway* was close to its final destination of Westport, the captain ordered the tribe off his ship. Local residents told him there was only one house nearby, and that he should let the Wyandot stay on board for the night. But he refused, saying that he had to get to St. Joseph by nightfall. Without tents or any kind of covering, the Wyandot had to huddle together throughout the night. When they woke up on the following morning, they saw the *Nodaway* still docked nearby on the Missouri River. The captain had spent the night ordering his crew to take the carpets out of storage and lay them down throughout his boat now that the Indians were gone. Many Wyandot would take some comfort a year later when they learned that the *Nodaway* was wrecked beyond repair.[57]

Just two days later, the rest of the Wyandot arrived on the *Republic*. Their horses were still in Illinois and would not join them for several weeks. The chiefs hired wagons to transport their people and goods to the site picked out by the advance party sent ahead in May. The US Army had planned to build a major fort on this strip of land, measuring three sections, at the juncture of the Kansas and Missouri rivers. But when Colonel Henry Leavenworth saw the spot chosen for the post, he refused to build it there, saying the land was too low. Since a fort should be on high ground, he picked a location farther up the Missouri River for Fort Leavenworth. The Wyandot went to work building temporary homes on the abandoned site. In October, they moved west to thirty-six sections that adjoined this original tract. They officially purchased all thirty-nine sections from the Delaware in December. The Wyandot agreed to pay the Delaware $46,080 for the 24,960 acres in installments. They would pay $6,080 in 1844, and then $4,000 annually for the next ten years. The two tribes also agreed that the president would have to approve this transaction, which must then be duly recorded by the War Department.[58]

On their new reserve, the Wyandot did their best to restore their tribal life. Their capital, Wyandotte, would eventually become part of Kansas City, Kansas. Overnight they built log cabins, turned over the soil and planted corn, beans, and potatoes, and laid out roads to link their farms together. At their new store in Westport, just as in Upper Sandusky, the Wyandot could buy whatever goods they needed at reasonable prices. But they were even more interested in using their tribe's resources to build a church and a school. When whiskey traders descended on the Wyandot, as the first exploring party to the West had feared, the tribe responded by founding a temperance society and building another school. Even with these successes, the toll that removal had taken on the Wyandot was heavy. Within the first year of arriving in Kansas, more than 60 people died, and their numbers were down to 565 just a short while later. Yet many Wyandot remembered this time in Kansas as their tribe's "halcyon days."[59]

But others never quite got over the heartbreak of leaving Ohio. William Walker Jr. was one of them. He tried to describe what it was like for his people to move out onto the grassy plains, where the horizon was endless. Like Moses in the land of Midian, he explained, we were "strangers in a strange land." Years later, after so many Wyandot, including Warpole, Sally Frost, Squire Grey Eyes, and Walker's two wives and all of his children, lay buried in graves under the boomtown of Kansas City, he wrote of his sadness. "Now I stand like a blasted oak in a desert," he said, "its top shivered by a bolt hurled from the armory of Jove." Despite the success that came to many of his people, and the honors that he received, he never fully recovered from the trauma of moving west. His people were convinced that when he died in 1874 it was from a broken heart.

While he left behind another poem about his tribe's new settlement in Kansas, he could easily have been remembering Ohio and all the tribes that had come from there down so many "trails of tears" to the Far West:

Sweet vale of Wyandotte, how calm could I rest
In thy bosom of shade with friends I love best;
When the storms which we felt in this cold world shall cease,
Our hearts like thy waters shall mingle in peace.[60]

Epilogue

A Last Goodbye

In Ohio today the effect of the removal of the tribes is readily apparent, for their names are everywhere, but they themselves are nowhere. Perhaps this is why the question "*Could* it have been otherwise?" still haunts us. Maybe the better question to ask is, "*Should* it have been otherwise?"

Looking back to the years immediately following the end of the War of 1812, many said yes. The British at Ghent tried and failed to win a permanent homeland for the tribes. But even by trying, they showed they believed that the sad tale of the removal of the tribes was not inevitable. By demanding the inclusion of Article IX in the final treaty, they meant to put an end to the conflict that had bloodied the North American continent for centuries. The implication was clear. If everyone lived in peace with everyone else, then surely a compromise on how to share the remaining land and so live side by side with one another could be reached.

The chiefs who signed the many treaties to remove their tribes to smaller pieces of ground within their old homeland certainly agreed. On their reserves, particularly those of the Seneca, Shawnee, and Wyandot, they would make the transition to a new economy, while at the same time retaining their own identity as tribes. The missionaries who came west to Ohio to help the tribes make the transition proved by the simple actions of their daily lives that removal to the Far West was not necessary, and in fact was immoral. When the final drive to remove the Indians across the Mississippi River came in 1830, many Ohioans, including the state's two senators and most of its representatives, tried to prevent it. Perhaps the sixty-two ladies of Steubenville best expressed the belief that it should have been otherwise when they petitioned the Congress to halt the removal of the tribes:

> We solemnly and honestly appeal, to save this remnant of a much injured people from annihilation, to shield our country from the curses denounced on the cruel and ungrateful, and to shelter the American character from lasting dishonor.[1]

But even if we regret the removal today, we must honestly admit that there were many people who believed it should not be otherwise. First and foremost in this group was the Prophet, who spent much of his life fighting assimilation with the whites. He was joined by Colonel Lewis, who believed that Tecumseh's dream for a permanent Indian homeland still had a chance to be realized across the Mississippi River. Even tribes that appeared on the surface to be fully assimilated, like the Seneca of Sandusky, were anxious to head west, thus keeping themselves from being swallowed up by the Americans.[2] Territorial governors, like Lewis Cass and William Clark, along with Indian agents, like John Johnston, saw the damaging effects of the collision of the tribes and the whites—especially the tragedy of alcoholism—and joined in the chorus of those who thought the Indians should be moved west for their own good and survival. Politicians, beginning with President James Monroe and his secretary of war, John C. Calhoun, and culminating with President Andrew Jackson, agreed. Anxious settlers who watched as land ran out in the northwest corner of Ohio, and some of the politicians who represented them, like Governor Robert Lucas, demanded that the last of the tribes must go.

Whether they left willingly or unwillingly, Ohio's tribes did not find the permanent refuge they were promised in the West. Instead, the Americans who had pushed them into an unwanted country coveted the place within a decade of the parting of the Wyandot, the last Indians to leave Ohio. William Walker's warning of the trouble that the tribes would face across the Mississippi River came true with a vengeance. Kansas turned "bloody" within a dozen years of the arrival of the Wyandot, as the region was swept up in the fight over slavery. Even before the Kansas-Nebraska Act had officially opened the country to settlement, and ultimately to the strife that led to the Civil War, wagon trains were already making their way through the reserves of the "Emigrant Tribes," as the eastern Indians were now called.

In 1843, the year that the Wyandot left the Grand Reserve, another "Great Migration," like the one that brought people to Ohio nearly thirty years before, occurred west of the Mississippi. Thousands of Americans made their way to the Pacific Northwest along the Oregon Trail, which ran through the northeastern corner of Kansas. After gold was discovered at Sutter's Mill in California in 1848, prospectors headed down the Santa Fe Trail, which also ran directly through Kansas. Even worse, countless squatters, town boosters, and railroad men overran the new Indian reserves as the next step on their march westward.

Less than five years after Gold Rush fever first swept through the United States, the Congress in Washington, under great pressure from railroad companies especially, authorized President Franklin Pierce to negotiate treaties with the emigrant tribes to allow Americans to settle on their reserves. At first the government did not plan to remove the Indians completely from Kansas. Instead, just as had occurred after the War of 1812, the tribes would be urged to surrender most of their land in exchange for smaller pieces of ground in Kansas, now called "diminishing reserves," a slight increase in annuities, and the assignment of "trust lands" that the government would manage and sell to provide future income for the Indians. George Manypenny, appointed commissioner of Indian Affairs in 1853, was charged with writing the treaties. During his four years in office, he negotiated the surrender of nearly eighteen million acres of land from the Delaware, Shawnee, and ten other tribes in the territory. He also wrote a treaty in 1855 with the Wyandot, who accepted American citizenship and individual plats of land in exchange for most of their remaining reserve in Kansas. After all the treaties were negotiated, the holdings of the tribes had been reduced to only 1,342,000 acres.[3]

Although the Manypenny Treaties, as they are known, opened the way for the implementation of the Kansas-Nebraska Act, the commissioner of Indian Affairs was not happy with the result. He was troubled by the attitudes of both his fellow citizens and the Indians during the negotiations. Without so much as a glance backward, the Americans took most of the reserves that had been promised to the eastern tribes just twenty years before. The Indians, torn apart by rivalries within their own tribes, divided themselves over the issue of slavery, and, misled by land speculators and railroad officials, signed away their land without a fight. In the end, Manypenny judged the entire process a "crime" for which the "whole country suffered a penalty." By taking most of Kansas away from the Indians and opening the territory to American settlers, including Free Soilers from the North and "Border Ruffians" from the South, he said the "seed was sown which bore fruit and resulted in our civil war."[4]

After Commissioner Manypenny left office in 1857, the press of railroad companies for every bit of remaining Indian land grew even more relentless. Rival companies competed for tracts for their chosen routes, along with land on either side of their railroads, to sell to farmers. Squatters continued to settle on the surviving Indian reserves, and no civil authority, whether local or national, was able to stop them. In 1860 the Delaware, following the example of the Wyandot, gave up most of what was left of their land in Kansas. They sold 224,000 acres in exchange for 80-acre allotments given to every member of the tribe. In 1862 the Ottawa made a similar deal, which granted individual plots of land and American citizenship to tribal members, plus 20,000 acres of land for a university. The Kansas, along with bands of the Sac and Fox, both from Missouri and Mississippi, also sold hundreds of thousands of acres to railroad companies.

In March 1863, Congress authorized President Abraham Lincoln, who had led the fight to open the western plains for settlement, to obtain the remaining land still held by Indians in Kansas. Lincoln's only worry was where to put the remnants of eastern tribes that might want to retain their tribal identity after selling off their reserves. He decided they would have to go onto the reserves of the Shawnee and Seneca from Ohio, who had settled in the part of Indian Territory that is now northeastern Oklahoma. Once the South had been defeated in the Civil War, the government decided that Indians from Kansas could also be granted land taken from the Cherokee and the other southern tribes in Oklahoma, ostensibly as punishment for their support for the Confederacy.

Between 1863 and 1873, most of the tribes that still held land in Kansas, including all the Indians who had come west from Ohio, sold their remaining lands to the United States. Tribes splintered as many individuals accepted allotments and American citizenship in Kansas, while others crowded onto tiny reserves plotted out for them in Oklahoma. Only the Kickapoo, Chippewa, Munsee, Prairie Pottawatomi, and Sac and Fox of Missouri retained small tribal holdings in Kansas.

In 1887, just fourteen years after the Miami, the last tribe to leave Kansas, concluded a treaty with the government, the tribes lost most of their remaining land in Oklahoma with the passage of the Dawes Severalty Act. In exchange for giving up their tribal land, heads of households received 160 acres, single adults and orphans eighteen and older received 80 acres, and children under eighteen received 40 acres, all still measured out in accordance with the Land Ordinance of 1785.[5]

As the tribes struggled to make a life for themselves, both in Kansas and Oklahoma, from the 1840s to the 1870s, Ohioans were swept up in waves of nostalgia over the passing of the Indians from their state. Many looked back with regret at all that the tribes had suffered during the process. Local newspapers ran stories and poems about pioneer life in general, and the departed Indians in particular, both of which had passed from view so quickly. One of the most popular poems, often copied in local and county histories written in the late nineteenth century, was entitled "The Wyandot Farewell." The poem appeared originally in an 1845 edition of Upper Sandusky's *Democratic Pioneer*, a newspaper that was the first business to set up shop in the abandoned council house of the Wyandot. The anonymous poem had actually been written by James Rankin Jr., the younger brother of Catherine Walker, who two years before had moved with his people from Ohio to Kansas. In his poem, Rankin tried to capture something of what the Wyandot had felt as they faced the prospect of heading west. He also conveyed a keen sense of the passage of time that had affected them so dramatically.

Adieu to the graves where my fathers now rest!
For I must be going afar to the West.
I've sold my possessions; my heart's filled with woe.
To think I must lose them. Alas! I must go . . .

Sandusky, Tymochtee, and Brokensword streams,
Nevermore shall I see you except in my dreams.
Adieu to the marshes where the cranberries grow
O'er the great Mississippi, Alas! I must go . . .[6]

While Ohioans were touched by Rankin's anonymous poem, they were troubled by the final sermon given in the Wyandot mission church. They printed the words that Squire Grey Eyes had spoken just before he headed west in their local histories. The chief had seen no need for regret as he made ready to follow his tribe to their new home across the Mississippi River. He believed that everything happening to his people occurred merely in time, that there was a better world in eternity. Before he left for Kansas in the summer of 1843, he reminded his fellow Ohioans that every piece of ground for which they had fought so long and so relentlessly would someday pass away:

> It is but a little time for us till we leave our earthly home for a Better Country—that of a heavenly home; for here we are no continuing city, but we seek one that is to come, whose builder and maker is God.[7]

Things had happened so quickly for the Wyandot and the other Ohio tribes. Only thirty years separated the death of Tecumseh from the departure of the last Indian for Kansas. In less than a lifetime, the tribes had seen the boundary between themselves and the Americans give way and surround them as the borders of their township reserves. Here they were expected almost overnight to become successful farmers. While most of them accomplished that task in less than a decade, it was still not quick enough. Many Americans, but not all of them, had to have every acre of every section of every township in Ohio right away and so the Indians must go west. But once the tribes headed to Kansas and Oklahoma, they were swept up in another thirty-year cycle that saw their new reserves sold out from under them. In the rush toward the future, no one bothered anymore to debate how far the Indians had come down the road toward the white man's civilization. There was no time for that, as the once limitless supply of land on this huge continent finally ran out.

Just as the first story of the removal of Ohio's tribes was forgotten against the mythic struggle of Andrew Jackson and the Cherokee, so the second tale of the loss of tribal lands in Kansas disappeared completely from the wider American narratives of the opening of the Great Plains, the Civil War, the battle to end slavery, and the final defeat of the Plains Indians.

To this day, the only tribes that most Americans know, including the Cherokee of Georgia, are the ones who put up the last fight against the United States, like the Sioux, the Cheyenne, and the Apache, and who entered the American consciousness through westerns in literature and films and on television. Historians H. Craig Miller and William E. Unrau, authors of one of the best studies of the removal of the tribes from Kansas, were troubled about how the second removal could have happened so quickly, why no one rose up to stop it, and how the story can be totally forgotten today. In the conclusion to *The End of Indian Kansas* (1977), they, too, asked the question posed by this epilogue. "Could it have been different? Must it have happened this way?" Acknowledging that "one of the lessons of history is that nothing is inevitable," they could only conclude that "human nature being what it is," the rights of minority cultures are often trampled by the majority.[8]

Still amid the rapid fire of Indian reserves giving way to Bloody Kansas, the Civil War, and then to a patchwork of towns, farms, and railroads, all filled with descendants of the nation's first pioneers heading west, Confederates and freedmen coming up from the ruined South, and recent immigrants arriving from the fading empires of Europe, Miller and Unrau ask why someone in some place and at some time could not have found a better solution to whatever challenges existed, other than removal. Even though an answer was never found, they concluded that this does not "prevent the modern student from joining those who, at the time, hoped that leadership somewhere would rise above the level of common expectation to bring about one of those surprising reversals that fill human history with hope."[9]

There have been many attempts in the last century to rectify some of the misery caused by the removal of the tribes, first from the East and then from the West. In 1924, Congress awarded American citizenship to every Indian living in the United States who still did not have it. A decade later, the administration of President Franklin D. Roosevelt took an even more dramatic step with the passing of the Indian Reorganization Act, which allowed tribes to reform once again and purchase communal land for tribal use. In 1946, during Harry Truman's presidency, the Indian Claims Commission was established, which gave tribes the right to petition the government for money owed for past land sales and for broken treaties. But while these laws helped lead to a rebirth of tribal identity, including the return of millions of dollars to descendants of Indians who suffered mightily, especially in the early nineteenth century, a deep wound in the consciousness of the tribes and the nation still exists. No amount of government programs on tribal reserves, whether part of the New Frontier or the Great Society, nor any amount of money collected through federally regulated gaming in tribal casinos, seems able to heal these memories and so make things right at last.

In his beautiful book *Violence over the Land* (2008), which is both a history of Indians in the early American West and a personal memoir of his people, the Shoshone, historian Ned Blackhawk argues that remembering Indian history takes place against "a larger struggle, a contest for reconciliation." Much like a troubled family that has been "bereft by tragedy," the United States has been unable or unwilling to "confront its past." Blackhawk concludes that the many strands describing what the tribes suffered, which up until now "have not been equally shared or appropriately recognized," must be woven into the fabric of the "epic of America."[10]

Yet what makes American history so challenging to write is not merely the fact that the stories of so many people have been forgotten. Even when all the threads of the past, drawn out against the passage of time, are woven together, tragedy remains. The suffering of a group of people, like the Delaware, Seneca, Shawnee, Ottawa, and Wyandot, often gives rise to the triumph of another, like the millions of farmers, townspeople, factory workers, immigrants, and city dwellers who filled up the land in Ohio left behind by the tribes. Until we have figured out a way for all Americans to live side by side, fulfilling personal dreams for a better future but never at the expense of someone else's life, we will be left wondering with Squire Grey Eyes, whose remains lie buried in the Indian Cemetery in Kansas City, if the consequences of the immense tragedies we bring into the lives of one another will ever be resolved in time or eternity.[11]

Notes

PROLOGUE: MANY TRAILS OF TEARS

1. The "trail where tears were shed" is a translation of the Choctaw phrase for their removal.
2. Robert Remini, *Andrew Jackson and His Indian Wars* (New York: Viking, 2001), 180.
3. Ibid., vii, 181.
4. Jon Meacham, *American Lion: Andrew Jackson in the White House* (New York: Random House, 2008), 93–97.

CHAPTER ONE: TURNING BACK THE CLOCK AT GHENT

1. Fred L. Engelman, *The Peace of Christmas Eve* (New York: Harcourt, Brace & World, 1962), 122–127, 134; Brian Jenkins, *Henry Goulburn, 1784–1856: A Political Biography* (Montreal and Kingston: McGill-Queens University Press, 1996), 81.
2. "James Monroe to Thomas Jefferson, June 7, 1813," *The Writings of James Monroe*, edited by Stanislaus Murray Hamilton (New York and London: G. P. Putnam's Sons, 1901), 267–268; Engelman, *The Peace of Christmas Eve*, 3–4.
3. Engelman, *The Peace of Christmas Eve*, 92–94.
4. "Albert Gallatin to James Monroe, June 13, 1814," as quoted in Engelman, *The Peace of Christmas Eve*, 111.
5. John Quincy Adams, "April 11," *Diary of John Quincy Adams, 1794–1845*, edited by Alan Nevins (New York: Frederick Ungar, 1951), 117; Marie B. Hecht, *John Quincy Adams: A Personal History of an Independent Man* (New York: Macmillan, 1972), 208–209, 217.
6. Paul C. Nagel, *John Quincy Adams: A Public Life, A Private Life* (New York: Alfred A. Knopf, 1999), 218.
7. Ibid., 219.
8. Adams, "July 8," *Diary of John Quincy Adams*, 120; "Jonathan Russell to Henry Clay, July 2, 1814," *The Papers of Henry Clay*, Volume I, *The Rising Statesman 1797–1814*, James F. Hopkins, Editor (Lexington: University of Kentucky Press, 1959), 940–941.
9. James Monroe, "Instructions to the American Commissioners, January 28, 1814," *Papers of Henry Clay, Volume I*, 857–862.
10. Christopher Hibbert, *Wellington: A Personal History* (Reading, Massachusetts: Addison–Wesley, 1997), 160–166; Elizabeth Longford, *Wellington: The Years of the Sword* (New York: Harper & Row, 1969), 370–375.

11. "William Crawford to Henry Clay, June 10, 1814," *Papers of Henry Clay, Volume I*, 933.

12. Harry Ammon, *James Monroe: The Quest for National Identity* (New York: McGraw Hill, 1971), 4–35.

13. James Monroe, "Instructions to the American Plenipotentiaries, February 14 and June 27, 1814," *The Writings of James Monroe*, 370–373.

14. Adams, *Diary of John Quincy Adams*, 122; Henry Clay, "Journal of Ghent Negotiations, August 7–10," *Papers of Henry Clay*, Volume I, 952–953.

15. The original letter of Adams to Monroe, dated September 5, 1814, is in the National Archives. The quote is taken from Jenkins, *Henry Goulburn*, 81.

16. Ibid., 77–78.

17. Adams, "August 8," *Diary of John Quincy Adams*, 122–123.

18. Adams, "August 8," *Diary of John Quincy Adams*, 122–123; Henry Clay, "Journal of Ghent Negotiations, August 7–10," *Papers of Henry Clay*, Volume I, 954.

19. Samuel Flagg Bemis, *John Quincy Adams and the Foundations of American Foreign Policy* (New York: Alfred A. Knopf, 1949), 204.

20. Benjamin Drake, *Life of Tecumseh and His Brother the Prophet with a Historical Sketch of the Shawnee Indians* (Cincinnati: E. Morgan and Co., 1841), 160–163.

21. J.F.H. Claiborne, *Life and Times of General Sam. Dale, the Mississippi Partisan* (New York: Harper & Brothers, 1860), 50–51, 59–61; "Tecumseh Visits Malden and Invites British Help," Carl Klinck, Editor. *Tecumseh: Fact and Fiction in Early Records* (Englewood Cliffs: Prentice–Hall, 1967), 79–80.

22. "William Henry Harrison to Secretary of War William Eustis, August 6, 1810, August 6, 1811, and August 7, 1811," *Governor's Message and Letters: Messages and Letters of William Henry Harrison*, Volume II, edited by Logan Esarey (Indianapolis: Indiana Historical Society, 1922), 456–459, 542–546, and 548–551.

23. "William Eustis to William Henry Harrison, September 18, 1811," *Territorial Papers of the United States, 8 Volumes*, edited by Clarence E. Carter (Washington, D.C.: Government Printing Office, 1939), 8:133–34.

24. J. Wesley Whickar, Editor, "Shabonee's Account of Tippecanoe," *Indiana Magazine of History* 17 (December 1921): 354–357; Benson J. Lossing, *Pictorial Field-Book of the War of 1812* (Portsmouth: New Hampshire Publishing Company, 1976), 204–206.

25. "Excerpt from Tecumseh's Speech at Tuckabatchee," Mike Bunn and Clay Williams, *Battle for the Southern Frontier: The Creek War and the War of 1812* (Charleston: History Press, 2008), 163–164.

26. Joel W. Martin, *Sacred Revolt: The Muscogees' Struggle for a New World* (Boston: Beacon Press, 1991), 124–125.

27. R. David Edmunds, *The Shawnee Prophet* (Lincoln and London: University of Nebraska Press, 1983), 117, 119; Drake, *Life of Tecumseh*, 156.

28. Lossing, *Pictorial Field–Book of the War of 1812*, 362.

29. Reginald Horsman, *The War of 1812* (New York: Alfred A. Knopf, 1969), 17–18; Reginald Horsman, *The Causes of the War of 1812* (New York: A. S. Barnes, 1961), 229–232.

30. Colonel David G. Fitz-Enz, *The Final Invasion, Plattsburgh, The War of 1812's Most Decisive Battle* (New York: Cooper Square Press, 2001), 156.

31. John Sugden, *Tecumseh: A Life* (New York: Henry Holt, 1997), 90.

32. Robert S. Allen, *His Majesty's Indian Allies: British Indian Policy in the Defence of Canada 1774–1815* (Toronto: Dundurn Press, 1993), 57–86, 88–110; Alan Taylor, *The Civil War of 1812: American Citizens, British Subjects, Irish Rebels, & Indian Allies* (New York: Alfred A. Knopf, 2010), 35–72.

33. Allen, *His Majesty's Indian Allies*, 109–113.

34. R. David Edmunds, *Tecumseh and the Quest for Indian Leadership* (Boston: Little, Brown, 1984), 165–167.

35. James Laxler, *Tecumseh & Brock: The War of 1812* (Toronto: Anansi Press, 2012), 109–162; Jenkins, *Henry Goulburn*, 76–78.

36. Drake, *Life of Tecumseh*, 165–167; "Brock to Hull, August 15, 1812," *Historical Register of the United States*, Part II (1812–1813), in *Tecumseh: Fact and Fiction*, 159; Jenkins, *Henry Goulburn*, 76–78; Edmunds, *Tecumseh and the Quest for Indian Leadership*, 171–172.

37. Engelman, *The Peace of Christmas Eve*, 71.

38. James Monroe, "Letter to Thomas Jefferson, June 7, 1813," *The Writings of James Monroe*, 259–267.

39. William Stanley Hatch, *A Chapter in the History of the War of 1812 in the Northwest* (Cincinnati: Miami Printing & Publishing Company, 1872), 129; Drake, *Life of Tecumseh*, 166; "Captain Zachary Taylor to Governor Harrison, September 13, 1812," *Presidential Papers Microfilm*; Emilius O. Randall, Editor, "Ohio in the War of 1812: Excerpts from Early Ohio Newspapers," *Ohio Archaeological and Historical Society Proceedings* 28 (July 1919): 321; Lossing, *Pictorial Field-book of the War of 1812*, 745–748.

40. Lossing, *Pictorial Field-book of the War of 1812*, 4–6.

41. Gilbert Auchinleck, *A History of the War between Great Britain and the United States of America during the Years 1812, 1813, & 1814* (Toronto: Arms and Armour Press, 1972), 39.

42. William McAffee, *History of the Late War in the Western Country* (Bowling Green, Ohio: Historical Publications Company, 1910), 9–19.

43. Laxer, *Brock & Tecumseh*, 163–178; Gilbert, *God Gave Us This Country*, 293–294.

44. Sugden, *Tecumseh*, 368–380; Drake, *Life of Tecumseh*, 193.

45. Adams, "August 9," *Diary of John Quincy Adams*, 123–125; Henry Clay, "Journal of Ghent Negotiations, August 7–10," *Papers of Henry Clay*, Volume I, 955–956.

46. Jenkins, *Henry Goulburn*, 78.

47. Jenkins, *Henry Goulburn*, 125–129; Henry Clay, "Journal of Ghent Negotiations, August 7–10," *Papers of Henry Clay*, Volume I, 968–970; for the exact location of the Treaty of Greeneville line, see "Treaty with the Wyandot, August 3, 1795," *Indian Affairs: Laws and Treaties*, Volume II, compiled and edited by Charles J. Kappler (Washington, D.C.: Government Printing Office, 1904), 39–45.

48. John Quincy Adams, "July 18," *Diary of John Quincy Adams*, 121; Engelman, *The Peace of Christmas Eve*, 155; "The American to the British

Commissioners, September 9, 1814," *American State Papers, Foreign Relations*, III, 715–717.

49. See "The Menace of War and Peace" (map insert), in Bemis, *John Quincy Adams and the Foundation of American Foreign Policy*, between pages 210 and 211 for how Adams expected the map of North America to be redrawn by the British.

50. April 15, 1814.

51. Engelman, *The Peace of Christmas Eve*, 139 and 153.

52. "Earl Bathurt to George Prevost, June 3, 1814," as quoted in Fitz-Enz, *The Final Invasion*, 50–52.

53. Adams, *Diary of John Quincy Adams*, 129; Robert Remini, *Henry Clay: Statesman for the Union* (New York: William Morrow, 1991), 22–23, 119.

54. Engelman, *The Peace of Christmas Eve*, 196; "Treaty of Greeneville, July 22, 1814," *Indian Affairs: Laws and Treaties*, Volume II, 105–106; "William Crawford to Henry Clay, September 26, 1814," *Papers of Henry Clay*, 978.

55. Joel W. Martin, *Sacred Revolt: The Muscogees' Struggle for a New World* (Boston: Beacon Press, 1991), 124–125; Jay Lamar, "Preface," *Tohopeka: Rethinking the Creek War and the War of 1812*, Kathryn E. Holland Braun, Editor (Tuscaloosa: University of Alabama Press, 2012), 10–16; Mike Bunn and Clay Williams, *Battle for the Southern Frontier: The Creek War and the War of 1812* (Charleston: History Press, 2008), 31–46.

56. Bunn and Williams, *Battle for the Southern Frontier*, 73–115.

57. Engelman, *The Peace of Christmas Eve*, 168–174; Lossing, *Pictorial Field-Book of the War of 1812*, 932–936.

58. Fitz-Enz, *The Final Invasion*, 101–170; Lossing, *Pictorial Field–Book of the War of 1812*, 947–964.

59. "Henry Clay to James Monroe, October 26, 1814," *Papers of Henry Clay*, Volume I, 996–997; Longford, *Wellington*, 347, 351, 363–365.

60. Engelman, *The Peace of Christmas Eve*, 235–236, 248–251.

61. Adams, "November 27," *Diary of John Quincy Adams*, 144; Ammon, *James Monroe*, 333–338, 343.

62. "Treaty of Ghent, December 24, 1814," *American State Papers, Foreign Relations*, III, 745–753.

63. Ibid., 745–753.

64. Engelman, *The Peace of Christmas Eve*, 282–285; Lossing, *Pictorial Field-Book of the War of 1812*, 1035; "Henry Clay to William H. Crawford, September 20, 1814," *Papers of Henry Clay*, Volume I, 978.

65. Jackson's men completed the three foot high barricade that ran nearly a mile along the Rodriguez Canal at sundown on December 23, 1814; see Lossing, *Pictorial Field-Book of the War of 1812*, 1034.

CHAPTER TWO: STARTING OVER AT SPRINGWELLS

1. Irving Brant, *James Madison: Commander in Chief*, Volume VI (Indianapolis: Bobbs-Merrill, 1956), 363–364.

2. Ammon, *James Monroe*, 346.

3. W.P. Cresson, *James Monroe* (Chapel Hill: University of North Carolina Press, 1946), 276.

4. "Andrew Jackson to Robert Hays, January 26, 1815," *Correspondence of Andrew Jackson*, Volume II, edited by John Spencer Bassett (Washington, D.C.: Carnegie Institution of Washington, 1926–35), 156.

5. "James Monroe to Judge Hugh L. White, January 26, 1815," *Writings of James Monroe*, Volume 7, 93–103; Cresson, *James Monroe*, 274; John Elting, *Amateurs to Arms: A Military History of the War of 1812* (Chapel Hill: Algonquin Books, 1991), 321.

6. Walter Borneman, *1812: The War that Forged a Nation* (New York: Harper Collins, 2004), 294–297.

7. George Morgan, *The Life of James Monroe* (Boston: Small, Maynard and Company, 1921), 346–347.

8. James Madison, "To the Senate of the United States, February 15, 1815," *American State Papers, Foreign Relations*, Volume III, 730.

9. Donald Hickey, *The War of 1812: A Forgotten Conflict* (Urbana and Chicago: University of Illinois Press, 1989), 297–298.

10. James Madison, "Message at the Commencement of the Fourteenth Congress, First Session," *American State Papers, Foreign Relations*, Volume IV, 1–4.

11. "The American Plenipotentiaries to the Secretary of State, December 25, 1814," *American State Papers: Foreign Affairs*, Volume III, 732–733; "Albert Gallatin to James Monroe, December 15, 1814," *American State Papers, Foreign Relations*, Volume IV, 810.

12. "James Monroe to William Clark, Ninian Edwards, and Auguste Choteau, March 11, 1815," *American State Papers; Indian Affairs: Laws and Treaties*, II, 6.

13. Jerome O. Steffen, *William Clark, Jeffersonian on the Frontier* (Norman: University of Oklahoma Press, 1977), 55–58.

14. "William Clark to the Honorable Secretary of War, May 22, 1815," *American State Papers, Indian Affairs*, Volume II, 7.

15. Timothy Flint, *Recollections of the Last Ten Years* (New York: A.A. Knopf, 1932), 160.

16. "James Monroe to William Clark, March 25, 1815," *American State Papers, Indian Affairs*, Volume II, 6.

17. Shirley Christian, *Before Lewis and Clark: The Story of the Chouteaus, the French Dynasty That Ruled America's Frontier* (New York: Farrar, Straus and Giroux, 2004), 198–201.

18. Flint, *Recollections of the Last Ten Years*, 142; "Alexander Dallas to the Governors of Tennessee. Kentucky, Georgia, Indiana Territory, and Mississippi Territory, June 14, 1815," *American State Papers, Indian Affairs*, Volume II, 8.

19. "William Clark to the Honorable Secretary of War, July 11, 1815," *American State Papers, Indian Affairs*, Volume II, 8–9.

20. Copies of the individual treaties signed at Portage des Sioux can be found in the *American State Papers, Indian Affairs*, Volume II, 3–5.

21. "William Clark, Ninian Edwards, and Auguste Chouteau to William Crawford, October 18, 1815," *American State Papers, Indian Affairs*, Volume II, 9–11.

22. Christian, *Before Lewis and Clark*, 200–201; Christian draws her information from a document entitled "Auguste Chouteau on Boundaries of Various Indian Nations," in the National Archives in Washington, D.C.

23. See Chapter One, "Turning Back the Clock at Ghent," for a description of the Treaty of Greeneville, 1814 and related sources.

24. "A. J. Dallas to William Henry Harrison, Duncan McArthur, and John Graham, June 9, 1815," *American State Papers, Indian Affairs*, Volume II, 13–14; Gillum Ferguson, *Illinois in the War of 1812* (Champaign and Urbana: University of Illinois Press, 2012), 164, 185–196.

25. Henry Howe, *Historical Collections of Ohio: Containing a Collection of the Most Interesting Facts, Traditions, Biographical Sketches, Anecdotes, Etc. Relating to the General and Local History with Descriptions of Its Counties, Principal Towns and Villages* (Columbus: Henry Howe and Son, 1891), 573.

26. John Vogel, *The Indians of Ohio and Wyandot County* (New York: Vantage Press, 1975), 1–4; Emil Schlup, "Tarhe–The Crane," *Ohio Archaeological and Historical Quarterly* 14 (April 1905) 2: 132–138.

27. "Entry for August 15, 1815," in "Journal of the Commissioners Appointed to Treat with the Northwest Indians at Detroit," *American State Papers, Indian Affairs*, Volume II, 13.

28. T.A. Buser, "Tarhe: Grand Sachem," and Tarhe the Crane, "Address of Tarhe, Grand Sachem of the Wyandot Nation to the Assemblage at the Treaty of Greenville July 22, 1795," posted on the official website of the Wyandot Nation of Kansas (www.wyandot.org).

29. Schlup, "Tarhe – The Crane," 132–138; "Sally Frost b. Caty Sage," Thelma Marsh: Wyandot Indian Genealogical Cards, 1724–1932 (MS193mf) (Center for Archival Collections) (Bowling Green State University); William L. Curry, "The Wyandot Chief Leather Lips: His Trial and Execution," *Ohio Archaeological and Historical Quarterly* 12 (January 1903) 1: 30–36. Curry's article is a reprint of an essay published in the *Hesperian* in 1838 describing Benjamin Sells's eyewitness account of the execution of Leather Lips.

30. E. L. Taylor, "Harrison-Tarhe Peace Conference," *Ohio Archaeological and Historical Quarterly* 14 (April 1905) 2: 121–131. James Gardiner, the reporter who recorded the meeting between Harrison and Tarhe on June 2, 1813, in his newspaper *The Freeman's Chronicle* (June 25, 1813), will be the agent who has the primary responsibility for removing the Ohio tribes under Jackson's administration. Taylor's article is a reprint of Gardiner's original newspaper account.

31. Springwells, first named Bellefontaine by the French for its clear springs, had been occupied for centuries before Harrison held his council there in 1815. Indian mounds were once built in the area near the Detroit River. Pontiac also held one of his most important councils here in May 1763 when it was the site of a Pottawatomi village. Many French families and traders made their homes at Springwells. Today it is part of the city of Detroit. See Clarence Monroe Burton, William Stocking, and Gordon K. Miller, eds., *The City of Detroit, Michigan, 1701–1922*, Volume 2 (Detroit and Chicago: S. J. Clarke, 1922), 886, 1583; "Major Edward Barrak to William Henry Harrison, August 27, 1815," *American State Papers, Indian Affairs*, Volume II, 15.

32. "Speech of the Crane, August 31, 1815," in "Journal of the Commissioners Appointed to Treat with the Northwest Indians at Detroit," ibid., 19–20.

33. Drake, *Life of Tecumseh*, 209.

34. "Speech of the Crane, August 31, 1815," in "Journal of the Commissioners Appointed to Treat with the Northwest Indians at Detroit," 19–20.

35. "Speech of William Henry Harrison, August 31, September 1, 2, and 4, 1815," ibid., 20–23.
36. "Speech of the Shawnee Prophet, September 4, 1815," ibid., 23.
37. "Speech of William Henry Harrison, September 5, 1815," ibid., 24–25.
38. "Treaty of Springwells, September 8, 1815 (Ratified December 26, 1815)," *Indian Affairs: Laws and Treaties*, II, 117–119.
39. James Madison, "Message at the Commencement of the Fourteenth Congress, First Session, December 5, 1815," *Annals of Congress*, 14th Congress, 1st Session (Senate), 13.
40. "Speech of a Chief of the Pattawatamies, September 8, 1815," in "Journal of the Commissioners Appointed to Treat with the Northwest Indians at Detroit," 25.

Chapter Three: Boundaries Long Gone

1. As mentioned in Chapter One, for the exact location of the Treaty of Greeneville line, see "Treaty with the Wyandot, August 3, 1795," *Indian Affairs: Laws and Treaties*, II, 39–45.
2. "William Henry Harrison to Alexander J. Dallas, June 26, 1815," quoted in Cleaves, *Old Tippecanoe*, 231.
3. Tecumseh's quote is taken from Edmunds, *Tecumseh and the Quest for Indian Leadership*, 134.
4. Charles B. Galbreath, *History of Ohio*, Volume I (Chicago and New York: American Historical Society, 1928), 258.
5. Sleeper-Smith, Susan, "Cultures of Exchange in a North Atlantic Frontier," *Rethinking the Fur Trade: Cultures of Exchange in an Atlantic World*, edited by Susan Sleeper-Smith (Lincoln and London: University of Nebraska Press, 2006), xvii–xx.
6. For the Treaty of Fort Industry, see "Treaty with the Wyandot, July 4, 1805," *Indian Affairs: Laws and Treaties*, II, 77–78.
7. See "Trade and Intercourse Act, March 30, 1802," and "President Jefferson on Indian Trading Houses, January 18, 1803," in Francis Paul Prucha, editor, *Documents of United States Indian Policy* (3rd Edition) (Lincoln: University of Nebraska Press, 2000), 17–22.
8. "Peltry & Other Produce to Sundries for the Following Articles," Miscellaneous Accounts of the Sandusky Factory (Box 1) (National Archives).
9. This north-south line would become the Michigan Meridian used in surveying the Michigan lands. See William Edward Peters, *Ohio Lands and Their Subdivision* (Athens, Ohio: Messenger Printery Company, 1918), 34.
10. "Treaty with the Ottawa, November 17, 1807" (Treaty of Detroit), *Indian Affairs: Laws and Treaties*, II, 92–95.
11. Charles Elihu Slocum, *History of the Maumee River Basin from the Earliest Accounts to Its Organization into Counties* (Defiance, Ohio: Published by the author, 1905), 254.
12. The same tribes (along with the Shawnee and Delaware) had already given up their claims to the Connecticut Western Reserve by the Treaty of Fort Industry in 1805 and would allow a road to be built from the Western Reserve to the Maumee Rapids (and so connect eastern Ohio to the Michigan Territory)

by the Treaty of Brownstown in 1808; see the "Treaty with the Wyandot, July 4, 1805" (Treaty of Fort Industry), "Treaty with the Ottawa, November 17, 1807" (Treaty of Detroit), and "Treaty with the Chippewa, November 25, 1808" (Treaty of Brownstown), *Indian Affairs: Laws and Treaties*, II, 77–78, 92–95, 99–100. The explanation of why the Presque Isle reserve was never surveyed can be found in Article 2 of the treaty that removed the Ottawa from the Auglaize and Upper Maumee river valleys in 1831. See "Treaty with the Ottawa, August 30, 1831, ibid., 335.

13. Information on the Black Swamp past and present can be found at the website of the Black Swamp Conservancy (www.blackswamp.org).

14. Patrick M. Tucker, *Ottawa Culture and Ethnohistory in the Maumee Valley, 1812–1838* (Master's Thesis) (Toledo, Ohio: University of Toledo, no date given), 10–17.

15. "Treaty with the Chippewa, November 25, 1808" (Treaty of Brownstown), *Indian Affairs: Laws and Treaties*, II, 99–100.

16. "Tarhe and Wyandot Chiefs to Governor Huntington, May 8, 1810," John Johnston Papers (Ohio Historical Society) (MSS 553).

17. For a description of the destruction of Delaware villages in the War of 1812, see the "Thomas Rotch Letters (Letterbook) 1816–1819" (original in the Massillon Public Library; digital images posted at Ohio Memory Website at www.ohiomemory.org). Rotch submitted a list of Delaware property destroyed in the War of 1812 to the Congress for redress.

18. Excerpted from Morris Birkbeck, "Notes on a Journey in America, London, 1818," 25–28, 31–33 in Martin Ridge, editor, *America's Frontier Story: A Documentary History of the Westward Expansion* (New York: Holt, Rinehart and Winston, 1969), 274–279.

19. Francis P. Weisenburger, *The Passing of the Frontier* (Volume II in *The History of the State of Ohio*, edited by Carl Wittke) (Columbus: Ohio Archaeological and Historical Society, 1941), 3–4; Benjamin Drake and Edward Deering Mansfield, *Cincinnati in 1826* (Cincinnati: Morgan, Lodge, and Fisher, 1827), 19.

20. "Agreement with the Seneca, September 15, 1797," *Indian Affairs: Laws and Treaties*, II, 1027–1030.

21. Henry Schoolcraft, *History of the Indian Tribes of the United States of America* (Philadelphia: J. P. Lippincott, 1857), 377–378.

22. Frank B. Woodward, *Lewis Cass: The Last Jeffersonian* (New Brunswick, New Jersey: Rutgers University Press, 1950), 123–124.

23. See "Henry Knox to George Washington, June 15, 1789," *American State Papers, Indian Affairs*, I, 12–14, for insights into their Indian policy; Anthony F. C. Wallace, *Jefferson and the Indians: The Tragic Fate of the First Americans* (Cambridge: Belknap Press, 1999), 165–170; "Thomas Jefferson to William Henry Harrison, February 27, 1803," as quoted by Joseph A. Parsons in "Civilizing the Indians of the Old Northwest, 1800–1810," *Indiana Magazine of History* 56 (September 1960): 195; Thomas Jefferson, "Fifth Annual Message to Congress, December 3, 1805," *The State of the Union Messages of the Presidents*, 3 volumes, edited by Fred Israel (New York: Chelsea House–Robert Hector Publishers, 1966), 1:82.

24. Schoolcraft, *History of the Indian Tribes of the United States of America*, 383–384; 396, 404–405; "Civilization Fund Act, March 3, 1819," *Documents of United States Indian Policy*, 33.

25. Daniel Preston, Editor, *The Papers of James Monroe: A Documentary History of the Presidential Tours of James Monroe, 1817, 1818, 1819* (Westport, Connecticut: Greenwood Press, 2003), 428–438; Willard Carl Klunder, *Lewis Cass and the Politics of Moderation* (Kent, Ohio: Kent State University Press, 1996), 26.

26. "George Graham, Acting Secretary of War, to Lewis Cass and Duncan McArthur, May 19, 1817," *American State Papers: Indian Affairs*, II, 137; "Talk Addressed to the Wyandot, Seneca, and Delaware Nations, November 18, 1817, ibid., 140; "Treaty with the Cherokee, July 8, 1817," *Indian Affairs: Laws and Treaties*, II, 140–144.

27. Freeman Cleaves, *Old Tippecanoe: William Henry Harrison and His Times* (New York: Charles Scribner's Sons, 1939), 236.

28. John Johnston, "Recollections of Sixty Years," in Leonard U. Hill, *John Johnston and the Indians in the Land of the Three Miamis* (Columbus, Ohio: Stoneman Press, 1957), 178–179.

29. R. Douglas Hurt in *The Ohio Frontier: Crucible of the Old Northwest, 1720 to 1830* (Bloomington: Indiana University Press, 1997), 364, quotes the *Cincinnati Liberty Hall* (1817) to show some Ohioans understood the treaty's significance: "The Treaty with the Wyandot altered the land base of the Ohio Indians for all time."

30. Slocum, *History of the Maumee River Basin from the Earliest Accounts to Its Organization into Counties*, 375; Slocum takes the story from the manuscript memoir of John E. Hunt, an American trader in the Maumee River valley.

31. Leggett, Conaway, and Company, *The History of Wyandot County, Ohio, Containing a History of the County: Its Townships, Towns, Churches, Schools, etc.* (Chicago: Leggett, Conaway, and Company, 1884), 268.

32. The Treaty at the Foot of the Rapids was signed on September 29, 1817, and proclaimed by the U.S. Senate on January 4, 1819; *Indian Affairs: Laws and Treaties*, II, 145–155.

33. Johnston, "Recollections of Sixty Years," 176; "Cherokee Boy," Wyandot Indian Genealogical Cards.

34. Charles Sumner Van Tassel, *Story of the Maumee Valley, Toledo, and the Sandusky Region*, Volume I (Chicago: S.J. Clarke, 1929), 47.

35. Woodward, *Lewis Cass: The Last Jeffersonian*, 99.

36. Woodward, *Lewis Cass*, 119; for the full text of Monroe's 1st message to Congress, see James Monroe, "First Annual Message, December 2, 1817," *The Writings of James Monroe*, Volume VI (New York: AMS Press, 1969), 33–43.

37. "Message of President Monroe on Indian Removal, January 27, 1825," *Documents of United States Indian Policy*, 39–42.

38. Charles Elliott, *Indian Missionary Reminiscences, principally of the Wyandot Nation. In which is exhibited the efficacy of the gospel in elevating ignorant and savage men* (New York: Lane & Scott, 1850), 172.

39. Many historians follow John Johnston who places Tarhe's death in 1818, immediately after the signing of the Treaty at the Foot of the Rapids. See Johnston, "Recollections of Sixty Years," 174. However, there is solid evidence

pointing to the death of Tarhe before 1818. See Carl G. Klopfenstein, "The Removal of the Ohio Tribes," in Randall L. Buchman, editor, *The Historic Indian in Ohio: A Conference to Commemorate The Bicentennial of The American Revolution* (Columbus: Published for The Ohio American Bicentennial Advisory Commission by the Ohio Historical Society, 1976), 28–29. Also see the schedule of individuals attached to the Treaty at the Foot of the Rapids which lists the "widow of the Crane" as one of the recipients. Thelma Marsh placed his death in November 1816 in "Tarhe" in her Wyandot Indian Genealogical Cards.

40. Schlup, "Tarhe—The Crane," 133–135.

41. Johnston, "Recollections of Sixty Years," 175–176.

42. Ibid., 178, 187.

Chapter Four: A Race Against Time

1. "Amendments Proposed to the Treaty with the Wyandots, Senecas, Delawares, Shawanees, Pattawatomies, Ottowas, and Chippewas, December 29, 1817," *American State Papers, Indian Affairs*, II, 148–149.

2. Ibid., 149–150.

3. "Treaty with the Wyandot, Etc., September 17, 1818" (Treaty of St. Mary's), *Indian Affairs: Laws and Treaties*, II, 162.

4. Ibid., 163.

5. "Treaty with the Wyandot, September 20, 1818," ibid., 164.

6. Henry Howe, *Historical Collections of Ohio,* Volume II (Columbus: Henry Howe and Son, 1891), 902.

7. Bob Blaisdell, editor, *Great Speeches by Native Americans* (New York: Dover Thrift Edition, 2000), 62–63.

8. "Treaty with the Miami, October 6, 1818," *Indian Affairs: Laws and Treaties,* II, 171–174; "Treaty with the Pottawatomi, October 2, 1818," ibid., 168; "Treaty with the Wea, October 2, 1818," ibid, 169; "Treaty with the Delaware, October 3, 1818," October 6, 1818," in ibid., 170–171.

9. Jerry E. Clark, *The Shawnee* (Lexington: University Press of Kentucky, 1993), 38–47.

10. Johnston, "Recollections of Sixty Years," 92–93; Johnston gives estimates for all but the Ottawa based on the annuities recorded for 1816.

11. Grant Foreman, *The Last Trek of the Indians* (Chicago: University of Chicago Press, 1946), 80–81.

12. "Lewis Cass and Duncan McArthur to John C. Calhoun, September 18, 1818," *American State Papers, Indian Affairs*, Volume II, 177; "Duncan McArthur to John C. Calhoun, September 18, 1818," T494 (Documents Relating to the Negotiations of Ratified and Unratified Treaties) (Roll 1) (National Archives Microfilm); Treaty with the Delaware, October 3, 1818," October 6, 1818," *Indian Affairs: Laws and Treaties*, II, 170–171.

13. Henry Harvey quotes the entire letter from Dearborn to the Shawnee in Harvey, *History of the Shawnee Indians*, 129–131; also see Hill, *John Johnston and the Indians*, 100.

14. Harvey, *History of the Shawnee Indians*, 35.

15. Ibid., 30–31.

16. Johnston, "Recollections of Sixty Years," 187.

17. Harvey, *History of the Shawnee Indians*, 51–54, 79–80, 143.

18. Ibid., 118–119.

19. Calloway, *The Shawnee and the War for America* (New York: Penguin Library, 2007), 119–122.

20. Calloway, *The Shawnee and the War for America*, 122–123; Harvey, *History of the Shawnee Indians*, 137–140, 169.

21. Slocum, *History of the Maumee River Basin*, 392–395; Johnston, "Recollections of Sixty Years," 189.

22. Harvey, *History of the Shawnee Indians*, 142.

23. Ibid., 145.

24. Johnston, "Recollections of Sixty Years," 187.

25. "William Henry Harrison to William Eustis, August 1810," *Governors Messages and Letters*, Volume I, 487.

26. James Howard, *Shawnee: The Ceremonialism of a Native American Tribe and Its Cultural Background* (Athens: Ohio University Press, 1981), 224–226.

27. Harvey, *History of the Shawnee Indians*, 144.

28. Slocum, *History of the Maumee Basin*, 396–398.

29. Presbyterian Church in the U.S.A. General Assembly, *Minutes of the General Assembly of the Presbyterian Church in the United States of America from A.D. 1821 to A.D. 1835 Inclusive* (Philadelphia: Presbyterian Board of Publications, 1894), 110.

30. Helen Waugh, "A Chronicle of Devoted Lives: The Story of the Growth and Development of the First Presbyterian Church, Bowling Green, Ohio, 1855–1955," *Commemorative Pamphlet from the 100th Anniversary of First Presbyterian Church, Bowling Green, Ohio 1955* (Bowling Green, Ohio: First Presbyterian Church, 1955), 4–6, 10 (Appendix); Ralph Phelps, *Historic Maumee Valley* (Toledo: Toledo Blade Company, 1957), 50–51.

31. Howe, *Historical Collections of Ohio*, Volume I, 662.

32. Phelps, *Historic Maumee Valley*, 51.

33. Reverend John O. Choules and Reverend Thomas Smith, *The Origin and History of Missions; A Record of the Voyages, Travels, Labors, and Successes of the Various Missionaries, Who Have Been Sent Forth by Protestant Societies and Churches to Evangelize the Heathen*, Volume II (New York: Robert Carter, 1848), 395; see "John Seib to Governor Cass, October 1, 1823," M1 (Roll 17) (National Archives Microfilm), for a description of the Maumee Indian Mission. Judge John Seib had come west to evaluate the impact of education on the Indians.

34. Howe, *Historical Collections of Ohio*, Volume I, 662, 665–666.

35. Ibid., 663–664.

36. Choules and Smith, *Origin and History of Missions*, 395.

37. Howe, *Historical Collections of Ohio*, Volume I, 664; Choules and Smith, *Origins and History of Missions*, 395.

38. Slocum, *History of the Maumee River Basin*, 396–400.

39. "Benjamin F. Stickney to Lewis Cass, December 16, 1821; January 4, 1822; March 24, 1824; and March 31, 1824," *Correspondence of the Maumee (Ottawa) Sub-Agency: Selected Letters (1820–1836)*, compiled by Jon. A. Sturm (Toledo, Ohio: Toledo Lucas County Public Library, 1989), 3–12.

40. "Benjamin F. Stickney to Lewis Cass, March 31, 1824," ibid., 12–14.

41. Thelma R. Marsh, *Moccasin Trails to the Cross: A History of the Mission to the Wyandott Indians on the Sandusky Plains* (Sandusky, Ohio: Published by the John Stewart United Methodist Church, 1974), 48.

42. Johnston, "Recollections of Sixty Years," 186–187.

43. The first work ever published on John Stewart was *The Missionary Pioneer, or a Brief Memoir of the Life, Labors, and Death of John Stewart (Man of Colour), Founder, under God, of the Mission Among the Wyandotts at Upper Sandusky, Ohio*, Published by Joseph Mitchell and Printed by John C. Totten (Bowery, 1827). It was later reprinted by the Joint Centenary Committee of the Methodist Episcopal Church (New York, 1918). Mitchell was the first assistant to Stewart. He also gave credit for writing the book to Moses Henkle, another assistant, and to letters donated to him by the Walker Family. His work contains the essential story of Stewart that is repeated by every other historian.

44. Marsh, *Moccasin Trails to the Cross*, 71.

45. Ibid, 70–74.

46. Marsh, *Moccasin Trails to the Cross*, 70–72; James B. Finley, *Life among the Indians, or Personal Reminiscences and Historical Incidents Illustrative of Indian Life and Character* (Cincinnati: Cranston and Curts, 1853), 233–282.

47. Finley, *Life among the Indians*, 67–87.

48. James B. Finley, *History of the Wyandott Mission, at Upper Sandusky, Ohio Under the Direction of the Methodist Episcopal Church* (Cincinnati: J. F. Wright and L. Swormstedt, 1840), 257–258; the Christian Wyandot disliked their tribe's subagent John Shaw for many reasons including the fact that he ignored the Sabbath; see "John C. Calhoun to John Shaw, August 17, 1824," Lewis Cass Collection (Microfilm Roll 41) (Bentley Historical Library).

49. Finley, *Life among the Indians*, 258.

50. "John Johnston to Bishop McKendree, August 23, 1823," Finley, *History of the Wyandott Mission*, 193.

51. William Bullock, "Sketch of a Journey through the Western States" (London, 1827), xviii, as quoted in Weisenburger, *The Passing of the Frontier*, 34–35.

Chapter Five: On the Edge of Eternity

1. James B. Finley, *Life Among the Indians*, 309.

2. Finley, *History of the Wyandott Mission*, 118–119.

3. Finley, *Life Among the Indians*, 292–294.

4. James B. Finley, *Autobiography of Rev. James B. Finley; or, Pioneer Life in the West*. Edited by W. P. Strickland, D.D. (Cincinnati: Jennings and Graham, 1853), 449.

5. Finley, *History of the Wyandott Mission*, 347.

6. Finley, *Autobiography*, 449.

7. Ibid., 445.

8. Finley, *History of the Wyandott Mission*, 392–395.

9. Ibid., 375–376.

10. Finley, *Life Among the Indians*, 326–327; Marsh, *Moccasin Trails to the Cross*, 108–109.

11. Finley, *Life Among the Indians*, 327–331.

12. William Elsey Connelley, *Wyandot Folk-Lore* (Topeka: Crane & Company, 1900), 46–49; Georges E. Sioui, *Huron Wyandot Heritage: The Heritage of the Circle* (Vancouver and Toronto: UBC Press, 1999), 16–19.

13. Anthony F. C. Wallace, *The Death and Rebirth of the Seneca.* (New York: Alfred A. Knopf, 1970), 7–8, 297–298.

14. Henry Howe, *Historical Collections*, 575.

15. Elizabeth Tooker, *The Iroquois Ceremonial of Midwinter* (Syracuse: Syracuse University Press, 1970), 118–123.

16. Finley, *Life Among the Indians*, 331; "James Finley to Lewis Cass, March 15, 1825," Lewis Cass Collection (Microfilm Roll 42) (Bentley Historical Library).

17. Finley, *Autobiography*, 463–467.

18. Edmunds, *The Shawnee Prophet*, 142–143.

19. Ibid., 157.

20. Antal, *A Wampum Denied*, 387.

21. Ibid., 150–151.

22. Ibid., 152–157.

23. The growing legend of Tecumseh emphasized his mercy toward others, his leadership, and his oratory. For examples, see Glenn Tucker, *Tecumseh: Vision of Glory* (Indianapolis: Bobbs-Merrill, 1956), 322–325, and Drake, *Life of Tecumseh*, 225–228.

24. Edmunds, *The Shawnee Prophet*, 157–164; Sugden, *Tecumseh: A Life*, 386.

25. *Sketches of the Life and Public Service of Gen. Lewis Cass* (Washington, D.C.: Printed at the Congressional Globe Office, 1848), 2; Klunder, *Lewis Cass and the Politics of Moderation*, 4–5, 9–14.

26. Cass's changing attitudes can be traced in the many articles he wrote for the *North American Review.* See Lewis Cass, "Indians of North America," *North American Review* (January 1826): 53–119; "Policy and Practice of the United States and Great Britain in Their Treatment of Indians," ibid. (April 1827): 365–442; and "Removal of the Indians," ibid. (January 1830): 62–121.

27. Answers to Cass's many questionnaires helped him write two important studies of Indian history and culture. See Lewis Cass, *Inquiries Respecting the History, Traditions, Languages, Manners, Customs, Religion, &c. of the Indians Living Within the United States* (Detroit: Sheldon & Reed, 1823) and "Structure of the Indian Languages," *North American Review* (April 1828): 357–403; see note 21 in chapter three for a complete reference to Schoolcraft's book.

28. Edmunds, *The Shawnee Prophet*, 170–172; Gregory Evans Dowd wrongly dismisses the Prophet as an "accomodationist" for helping the Americans remove the Shawnee, claiming that Tenkswatawa, who had once defended the Northern Indians against American expansion, now "collaborated with them." This analysis ignores the fact that the Prophet, like Colonel Lewis, saw removal as a last chance to fulfill Tecumseh's dream of a separate nation for the tribes; see Dowd, *A Spirited Resistance: The North American Indian Struggle for Unity, 1745–1815* (Baltimore and London: Johns Hopkins University Press, 1992), 194.

29. Harvey, *History of the Shawnee Indians*, 84; Sugden, *Tecumseh: A Life*, 52–33; Colin Calloway, *The Shawnees and the War for America*, 158.

30. Johnston, "Recollections of Sixty Years," 186; C. A. Weslager, *The Delaware Indian Westward Migration* (Wallingford, Pennsylvania: Middle Atlantic Press, 1978), 67–69.

31. Ibid., 71–77; "Treaty with the Delaware, September 24, 1829," Kappler, *Indian Affairs: Laws and Treaties*, II, 304.

32. James B. Finley, *Life Among the Indians*, 512–513.

33. Charles Russell Logan, *The Promised Land: The Cherokees, Arkansas, and Removal, 1794–1839* (Little Rock: Arkansas Historic Preservation Program, 1997), 5–11.

34. "Preamble" of the "Treaty with the Cherokee, July 8, 1817," *Indian Affairs: Laws and Treaties*, II, 140–141.

35. Ibid., 141–144.

36. John H. Finger, *The Eastern Band of Cherokees, 1819–1900* (Knoxville: University of Tennessee Press, 1984), 10; "Treaty with the Cherokee, February 17, 1819, *Indian Affairs: Laws and Treaties*, II, 177–181.

37. Kathleen DuVal, *The Native Ground: Indians and Colonists in the Heart of the Continent* (Philadelphia: University of Pennsylvania Press, 2006), 196–244; Logan, *The Promised Land*, 11–14; Anthony F. C. Wallace, *The Long, Bitter Trail: Andrew Jackson and the Indians* (New York: Hill and Wang, 1993), 9–11.

38. "Treaty with the Osage, September 25, 1818," *Indian Affairs: Laws and Treaties*, II, 167–168; "Treaty with the Osage, June 2, 1825," ibid., 217–221.

39. One of the best sources on Colonel Lewis and his relationship with the Cherokee chief Takatoka can be found in M1 (Records of the Michigan Superintendency of Indian Affairs, 1814–1851) (Roll 28) (National Archives Microfilm). Information coming into the Office of Indian Affairs about the Ohio tribes, including the actions of Colonel Lewis, was forwarded to Lewis Cass. For example, see "Thomas McKenney to Lewis Cass, March 9, 1825" in this location; see also Logan, *The Promised Land*, 14–16.

40. "William Clark to John C. Calhoun, September 5, 1823," as quoted in Grant Foreman, *Indians and Pioneers* (Norman: University of Oklahoma Press, 1936), 189. The original letter is in the John Graham Collection in the Missouri Historical Society.

41. "In Council with General Clark, January 6, 1825," M1 (Roll 28) (National Archives Microfilm); references to Colonel Lewis's plans and the death of Takatoka can be found in the letters of the Secretary of War John C. Calhoun, specifically "John C. Calhoun to Delegates of the Shawnee Residing in Missouri, March 2, 1825" and "John C. Calhoun to Cherokees from Arkansas, March 2, 1825," M1 (Roll 28) (National Archives Microfilm).

CHAPTER SIX: THE FUTURE UNRAVELS

1. Edmunds, *The Shawnee Prophet*, 170–171.

2. "Civilization Fund Act, March 3, 1819," *Documents of United States Indian Policy*, 33.

3. "Andrew Jackson to James Monroe, March 4, 1817, John S. Bassett, Editor, *Correspondence of Andrew Jackson* (Washington, D.C.: Carnegie Institute, 1926–35), 2: 277–82; Theda Purdue and Michael Green, *The Cherokee Nation and the Trail of Tears* (New York: Penguin, 2007), 42–68.

4. Reginald Horsman, *The Origins of Indian Removal 1815–1824* (Lansing: Published by the Michigan State University Press for the Historical Society of Michigan, 1963), 4–7.

5. "Treaty with the Cherokee, July 8, 1817," *Indian Affairs: Laws and Treaties*, II, 140–144; "Treaty with the Creek, October 18, 1828," ibid., 191–195.

6. "Establishment of Government Trading Houses, April 18, 1796), *Documents of United States Indian Policy*, 16–17; "Trade and Intercourse Act, March 30, 1802," ibid., 17–21; "President Jefferson on Indian Trading Houses, January 18, 1803," ibid., 21–22.

7. "Secretary of War Crawford on Trade and Intercourse, March 13, 1816," *Documents of United States Indian Policy*, 26–28.

8. "Secretary Calhoun on the Indian Trade, December 5, 1818," *Documents of United States Indian Policy*, 31–33; "Names and Pay of All Persons Employed in the Indian Department, April 12, 1822, *American State Papers, Indian Affairs*, Volume II, 364–365. Clark stepped down from the position temporarily but reassumed it from 1824 until his death in 1838.

9. Douglas Hurt, *The Indian Frontier*, 138.

10. Calhoun's report was delivered to Monroe in January 1825; it is quoted almost in total in Schoolcraft, *History of the Indians of the United States of America*, 409–414.

11. James Monroe, "Address to the Senate, January 27, 1825," *A Compilation of the Messages of the Presidents*, edited by James D. Richardson (Reprint) (Whitefish, Montana: Kessinger Publishing, 2004), 374; Monroe's speech is quoted extensively in Gloria Jarhoda, *The Trail of Tears: The Story of American Indian Removal* (New York: Holt, Rinehart and Winston, 1975), 31.

12. "Delegates of the Shawnee from Ohio, John Lewis to John C. Calhoun, February 28, 1825," M1 (Roll 28) (National Archives Microfilm).

13. "John C. Calhoun to John Lewis, March 2, 1825," "John C. Calhoun to Delegates from the Shawnee Residing in Missouri, March 2, 1825," and "John C. Calhoun to the Cherokees from Arkansas, March 2, 1825," ibid.

14. Douglas Hurt, *The Indian Frontier*, 138.

15. Charles D. Lowery, *James Barbour: A Jeffersonian Republican* (Tuscaloosa: University of Alabama Press, 1984), 153–163.

16. Horseman, *The Origins of Indian Removal*, 17.

17. "Treaty with the Osage, June 2, 1825," *Indian Affairs: Laws and Treaties*, II, 217–221; "Treaty with the Kansas, June 3, 1825," ibid., 222–225.

18. Edmunds, *The Shawnee Prophet*, 170–171.

19. "William Clark to G. B. Porter, January 1, 1829," M1 (Roll 28) (National Archives Microfilm); Clark kept excellent records of the Shawnee who left Ohio in 1827, including a detailed list of the improvements they left behind. See his "Enumeration of All the Shawnee Living in Ohio, April 9, 1830" and "An Enumeration of All the Mixed Bloods, Shawanese & Seneca of Lewistown Who Yet Remain East of the Mississippi, April 9, 1830," M1 (Roll 28) (National Archives Microfilm).

20. Edmunds, *The Shawnee Prophet*, 171–172.

21. William Clark, "In Council with Indians Agency South of Kansas River, April 10, 1830," M1 (Roll 28) (National Archives Microfilm).

22. Edmunds, *The Shawnee Prophet*, 171–173.

23. Thomas L. McKenney and James Hall, *History of the Indian Tribes of North America*, Volume I (Philadelphia: E. C. Biddle, 1836–1844), plate facing page 81. The many paintings that McKenney commissioned to line the walls of the War Department remain among the most valuable sources of American Indian history in the early nineteenth century.

24. "Treaty with the Creeks, February 12, 1825," *Indian Affairs: Laws and Treaties*, II, 214–217.

25. "Treaty with the Creeks, January 24, 1826," ibid., 264–268.

26. Lowery, *James Barbour*, 158–159.

27. Ibid., 163–165.

28. Ibid., 166–167.

29. Johnston, "Recollections of Sixty Years," 155, 188; Howard, *Shawnee*, 29–30.

30. Howard, *Shawnee*, 155.

31. Richard Butler's journal for October and November 1785 can be found in Neville B. Craig, editor, *The Olden Time*, Volume II, October 1847, Number 10 (Cincinnati: Reprinted by Robert Clarke & Co., 1876), 433–464; the journal reflects Butler's character and makes an interesting reference to young James Monroe who was traveling with Butler in the West; Judge Jacob Burnet, *Notes on the Early Settlement of the Northwestern Territory* (Cincinnati: Derby, Bradley & Co., 1847), 123–125, gives one of the best accounts of St. Clair's defeat that Howe excerpts in his own *Historical Collections*.

32. There is some confusion about the date of the attack on Polly Butler as seen in Harvey, *History of the Shawnee*, 169–180. The event is described as occurring in both 1819 and 1823 on pages 169 and 180 respectively. But the event most probably occurred in 1825 after the Prophet, who is clearly identified as the instigator (ibid., 170), had returned to Wapakoneta. The fact that the Harvey family left Wapakoneta in the fall of 1825 (ibid., 181) points to the later date as well. Also see Slocum, *History of the Maumee River Basin*, 393–395. See also "John Johnston to Lewis Cass, September 28, 1825," Lewis Cass Collection (Microfilm Roll 43) (Bentley Historical Collection).

33. Hill, *John Johnston and the Indians in the Land of the Three Miamis*, 110.

34. Edmunds, *The Shawnee Prophet*, 173–174; "John Johnston to Lewis Cass, September 9, 1826," M1 (Roll 19) (National Archives Microfilm).

35. William Clark calculated the most accurate numbers during his council with Cornstalk in April 1830; see William Clark, "An Enumeration of Shawnee Who Have Migrated West, April 8, 1830," "Enumeration of All the Shawnee Living in Ohio, April 9, 1830" and "An Enumeration of All the Mixed Bloods, Shawanese & Seneca of Lewistown Who Yet Remain East of the Mississippi, April 9, 1830," M1 (Roll 28); "John Johnston to Lewis Cass, October 7, 1826," M1 (Roll 19) (National Archives Microfilm).

36. See Foreman, *The Last Trek of the Indians*, 53–55, for the quote from the *Vincennes Western Sun* (December 13, 1826).

37. "Pierre Menard to William Clark, February 22, 1827," M234 (Letters Received by the Office of Indian Affairs) (Roll 748) (National Archives Microfilm).

38. "William Clark to John Barbour, March 8, 1827," ibid.

39. "Major Richard Graham to William Clark, April 4, 1827," and "Pierre Menard to William Clark, September 30, 1825," ibid.

40. "Treaty with the Shawnee, November 7, 1825," *Indian Affairs: Laws and Treaties*, II, 261–264.

41. Eastern Kansas was part of the Tallgrass Prairie ecosystem which at that time covered 170 million acres in the center of North America. Today only 4% of the region remains. The Tallgrass Prairie National Reserve in the Flint Hills of Kansas (www.nps.gov/tapr) gives a sense of what the Shawnee and other Ohio tribes first experienced when they arrived in their reserves across the Mississippi River.

42. "William Clark to James Barbour, March 8, 1827," M234 (Roll 748) (National Archives Microfilm).

43. R. David Edmunds, *The Shawnee Prophet*, 174–183.

44. Ibid., 181–183.

45. William Clark, "Memorial of a Talk by the Shawnee, April 2, 1827," M234 (Roll 498) (National Archives Microfilm). The Prophet's grave is at 3813 Ruby Avenue, a private residence in Kansas City, Kansas. It is on the National Register of Historic Places. The grave was unmarked until 1897 when the editor of the *Kansas City Sun* asked Shawnee head chief Charles Bluejacket, who had been present at the Prophet's death, to identify it. The grave was marked for sometime by an iron post that Bluejacket placed there, but it eventually disappeared. A historical marker was placed in front of the residence in 1978. The Prophet's village and his grave are somewhere in the ravine along the creek that borders the property. The application for the marker can be viewed under "White Feather Spring" at the National Register of Historic Places on the National Park Service website (www.nps.gov).

46. James H. O'Donnell III, *Ohio's First Peoples* (Athens: Ohio University Press, 2004), 121; Baughman, *History of Seneca County*, 199.

47. The first petition from the Seneca was forwarded by John McElvain to Thomas McKenney on December 18, 1828; see Klopfenstein, "The Removal of the Indians from Ohio," 31, 37; "The Removal Act of May 28, 1830," Appendix A in Ronald N. Satz, *American Indian Policy in the Jackson Era* (Lincoln: University of Nebraska Press, 1975), 296–298.

CHAPTER SEVEN: THE EXODUS OF THE SENECA

1. Wallace, *The Death and Rebirth of the Seneca*, 149–179; see the official Web site of the Seneca Nation of Indians (www.sni.org) for a description of the tribe's name, "O-non-dowa-gah," meaning the "Great Hill People." Nineteenth century authors often transcribed the tribe's name as "Nundawaoro."

2. A. J. Baughman, editor, *History of Seneca County: A Narrative Account of Its Historical Progress, Its People, and Its Principal Interests*, Volume I (Chicago and New York: Lewis Publishing Company, 1911), 15, 20; Howe, *Historical Collections of Ohio*, 573.

3. Wallace, *The Death and Rebirth of the Seneca*, 179–183; "Agreement with the Seneca, September 15, 1797," *Indian Affairs: Laws and Treaties*, II, 1027–1030.

4. Baughman, *History of Seneca County*, 20.

5. William Bullock, "Sketch of a Journey through the Western States" (London, 1827), xviii, as quoted in Weisenburger, *The Passing of the Frontier*, 34–35.

6. "An Indian Talk, Washington City, March 5, 1831," *New Hampshire Patriot and State Gazette*, May 16, 1831; the local paper in Concord, New, Hampshire, reprinted the speech that was originally published in the *Washington Globe* with the note: "The following talk of some Indians of the Seneca tribe was published, a few days ago, in the *Washington Globe*. We recommend it to the special attention of those who honestly believe that it is more necessary to raise money, by every possible device, for sending *missionaries* to administer to the supposed spiritual necessities of the 'Poor Indians,' than to supply the temporal wants of the needy nearer home."

7. Baughman, *History of Seneca County*, 23–24. There are many references to Seneca John in early state and county histories of Ohio. These same works give conflicting information on the identity of the suspected witch and her relationship to Seneca John. Most imply she was a medicine woman who was either burnt at the stake or tomahawked. At least one record says that Seneca John's wife was the suspect because she was a Christian and so was hated by the Seneca. One pioneer remembered that she had been shot and killed trying to escape from her accusers. See *The Firelands Pioneer, June 1864* (published by Firelands Historical Society).

8. W. W. Williams, *History of the Fire Lands, Comprising Huron and Erie Counties, Ohio* (Cleveland: Leader Printing Company, 1879), 38.

9. William Lang, *History of Seneca County from the Close of the Revolutionary War to July, 1888* (Springfield, Ohio: Transcript Printing Company, 1880), 127.

10. Henry Howe's description of Seneca John's death in his *Historical Collections* is the best version and most historians of Ohio's counties draw extensively from it. For information on Seneca John, he interviewed Sardis Birchard, the uncle of Rutherford B. Hayes, who ran a store that Seneca John frequented; see Howe, *Historical Collections of Ohio*, 574–574.

11. Horace S. Knapp, *History of the Maumee Valley: Commencing with Its Occupation by the French in 1680* (Toledo: Blade Mammoth Printing and Publishing House, 1872), 282–283; Henry Brish, Sardis Birchard, and Judge David Higgins of the Court of Common Pleas are listed as sources for the account of the trial of Coonstick before the Ohio Supreme Court as mentioned in Basil Meek, "Seneca John, Indian Chief, His Tragic Death, Erection of Monument in his Memory," *Ohio Archaeological and Historical Quarterly* XXX (1922): 128–141; incomplete Sandusky County records that survive show Justice Porter Hitchcock frequently presiding over the Ohio Supreme Court in Lower Sandusky in 1828 when Seneca John was killed. Justices Jacob Burnet and Charles Robert Sherman, the father of William Tecumseh Sherman, also heard cases in Lower Sandusky. See "Sandusky County/Clerk of Courts Supreme Court Journal, 1823–1851" (Microfilm Roll 55) (Center for Archival Collections) (Bowling Green State University).

12. "In Council, Seneca Village, September 22, 1830, to Andrew Jackson, Our Great Father, President of the United States," *Correspondence on the Subject of the Emigration of the Indians Between 30th November, 1831 and 27th December,*

1833 with Abstracts of Expenditures by disbursing Agents, in the removal and Subsistence of Indians, Etc., Furnished in Answer to a Resolution of the Senate of 27th December, 1833, by the Commissary General of Subsistence, Volume 2, Part 1 (Washington, DC: Printed by Duff Green, 1836), 169; the Seneca's Indian agent John McElvain forwarded this version of the petition in 1830 as a follow-up to the one he sent in 1829. McElvain assured the Seneca that he had forwarded the original petition and was awaiting a response. The tribe grew so anxious that they turned to their subagent Henry Brish for help.

13. Andrew Jackson, "Third Annual Message, December 6, 1831," James Richardson, editor, *A Compilation of the Messages of the President*, Volume 3 (New York: Bureau of National Literature, 1897), 1107–1121.

14. Andrew Jackson, "First Annual Message, December 8, 1829," ibid., 1005–1026; Andrew Jackson, "First Inaugural Address, March 4, 1829," ibid., 999–1001.

15. "Extinguishment of Indian Title to Lands in Georgia, Communicated to the House of Representatives, April 5, 1824," *American State Papers, Indian Affairs*, Volume II, 490–491; Wallace, *The Long Bitter Trail*, 37–38.

16. A record of Jackson's views on land ownership can be found in a "Secret Journal of Negotiations of the Chickasaw Treaty of 1818" accessible at the Avalon Project of the Yale Law School (www.avalon.law.yale.edu). Written by Robert Butler, the secretary of Andrew Jackson, and Isaac Shelby, the two officials who negotiated the treaty, the diary was controversial in its day for implying the commissioners bribed the chiefs to sell their land. The diary was repressed by both the Tennessee Legislature and the U.S. Senate on the grounds that the information might lead to the death of the chiefs who signed the treaty. The document became an issue in the 1828 election when Jackson's opponents argued that the treaty negotiations gave Jackson's land company the right to profits from the sale of salt on a small reserve on the surrendered land. See "Charles Todd to Henry Clay, October 10, 1828," and the related footnote in *The Papers of Henry Clay*, Volume 7," edited by Robert Seager II (Lexington: University Press of Kentucky, 1982), 488–489. Jackson's negotiations are covered in detail in Arrell Morgan Gibson, *The Chickasaws* (Norman: University of Oklahoma Press, 1971), 99–103. But the controversy over Jackson's actions has obscured the equally important content in the document which shows the arguments that Jackson made to the tribes about land ownership. It clearly states the position which Jackson had made previously to President Monroe that the Americans, and not the Indians, owned all the land in the eastern United States.

17. Andrew Jackson, "First Annual Message, December 8, 1829," *A Compilation of the Messages of the President*, Volume 3, 1005–1026; Andrew Jackson, "First Inaugural Address, March 4, 1829," ibid., 999–1001.

18. Kathleen DuVal, *The Native Ground*, 227–248; "Treaty with the Western Cherokee, May 6, 1828," *Indian Affairs: Laws and Treaties*, II, 288–292.

19. "Lewis Cass to Thomas McKenney, March 11, 1830," M234 (Roll 427) (National Archives Microfilm); Herman J. Viola, "Thomas McKenney (1824–30)," Robert M. Kvasnicka and Herman J. Viola, editors, *The Commissioners of Indian Affairs, 1824–1977* (Lincoln and London: University of Nebraska Press, 1979), 1–8.

20. "William Clark to James Barbour, March 8, 1827," M234 (Roll 748) (National Archives Microfilm).

21. Andrew Jackson, "Second Annual Message, December 6, 1830," James Richardson, editor, *A Compilation of the Messages of the President*, Volume 3, 1063–1092; see Robert Remini, *The Life of Andrew Jackson* (New York: Harper Perennial, 2010), 68–85, for a description of the brutality of the Creek War.

22. Jackson first addressed the problem of Indian reserves as states within states in his First Annual Message on December 8, 1829.

23. Andrew Jackson, "Fourth Annual Message, December 4, 1832," *A Compilation of the Messages of the President*, Volume 3, 1154–1169; "Fifth Annual Message, December 3, 1833," ibid., 1238–1254; "Sixth Annual Message, December 1, 1834," ibid., 1316–1342; "Seventh Annual Message, December 7, 1835," ibid., 1366–1396; and "Eighth Annual Message, December 5, 1836," ibid., 1455–1469.

24. "An Act to Provide for an Exchange of Lands with the Indians Residing in Any of the States or Territories and for Their Removal West of the Mississippi River, May 28, 1830," *Statutes of the United States*, 21st Congress, 1st Session, *A Century of Lawmaking for a New Nation, U. S. Congressional Documents and Debates, 1774–1875* (www.memory.loc.gov).

25. Senator Theodore Frelinghuysen on the Indian Removal Act of 1830, 21st Congress, 1st Session, *Register of Debates of the Senate of the United States of America* (April 9, 1830): 236–239; Senator Peleg Sprague on the Indian Removal Act of 1830, 21st Congress, 1st Session, ibid. (April 9, 1830): 252–254; for a discussion of Jackson's abuse of power with regard to Indian removal, see Alfred A. Cave, "Abuse of Power: Andrew Jackson and the Indian Removal Act of 1830," *Historian*, Volume Five, Issue 6 (December 2003): 1330–1353.

26. William A. Taylor, *Ohio in Congress from 1803 to 1901* (Columbus: The XX Century Publishing Co., 1900), 48 (Ruggles), 56–57 (Burnet); for more information on Judge Burnet, see his memoir *Notes on the Early Settlement of the Northwestern Territory* (New York: Appleton & Co., 1847) and D. K. Este, *Discourse on the Life and Public Services of the Late Jacob Burnet*; Senate Roll–Call Vote on the Indian Removal Act of 1830, 21st Congress, 1st Session, *Journal of the Senate of the United States of America, 1789–1873* (April 26, 1830): 269; also see the *Register of the Debates of the Senate* (April 24, 1830), 381, for the vote of Ohio's two Senators Burnett and Ruggles. See a reference to *Nimble Jemmy v. McNutt* in the case of *Chaffee v. Garret* in Charles Hammond, editor, *Cases Decided in the Supreme Court of Ohio in Bank*, Volume VI (Cincinnati: Robert Clarke & Co., 1872), 472.

27. Representative Jabez Huntington on the Indian Removal Act of 1830, 21st Congress, 1st Session, *Register of Debates of the House of Representatives of the United States of America* (May 14, 1830): 6–7, 12; Representative William Storrs on the Indian Removal Act of 1830, 21st Congress, 1st Session, ibid. (May 15, 1830): 994–1014; Representative William Ellsworth on the Indian Removal Act of 1830, 21st Congress, 1st Session, ibid. (May 17, 1830): 1026–1030; Representative George Evans on the Indian Removal Act of 1830, 21st Congress, 1st Session, ibid. (May 18, 1830): 994–1014; Representative

Isaac Bates on the Indian Removal Act of 1830, 21st Congress, 1st Session, ibid. (May 19, 1830): 1049–1054; Representative John Test on the Indian Removal Act of 1830, 21st Congress, 1st Session, ibid. (May 19, 1830): 1103–1108.

28. Representative Richard Wilde on the Indian Removal Act of 1830, 21st Congress, 1st Session, *Register of Debates of the House of Representatives of the United States of America* (May 14, 1830): 1092.

29. Congress, House of Representatives, Roll-Call Vote on the Hemphill Amendment, Register of Debates, 21st Congress, 1st Session, *Register of Debates* (May 18, 1830), 1132–1133.

30. Congress, House of Representatives, Roll-Call Vote on the Indian Removal Act of 1830, 21st Congress, 1st Session, *Journal of the House of Representatives of the United States of America, 1789–1873* (May 26, 1830): 732; *Ohio in Congress* contains descriptions of the Ohio representatives serving in the 21st Congress, 1st Session.

31. Weisenburger, *The Passing of the Frontier*, 35–36.

32. "Memorial from the Ladies of Steubenville Against the Forcible Removal Without the Limits of the United States, February 15, 1830," 21st Congress, 1st Session. House of Representatives [Rep. No. 209].

33. "In Council, Seneca Village, September 22, 1830, to Andrew Jackson, Our Great Father, President of the United States," *Correspondence on the Emigration of Indians*, Volume II, Part 1, 169; "Memorial of the Citizens of Seneca County, January 31, 1831," M234 (Roll 601) (National Archives Microfilm).

34. Buchman, "Gardiner, James B. (1789–1837)," Daniel F. Littlefield, Jr. and James W. Parins, editors, *Encyclopedia of American Indian Removal*, Volume I (Santa Barbara: Greenwood, 2011), 83.

35. "Treaty with the Seneca, February 28, 1831," *Indian Affairs: Laws and Treaties*, II, 325–327.

36. "John Eaton to James Gardiner, March 29, 1831," *Correspondence on the Emigration of Indians*, Volume II, Part 1, 270–273. Thomas L. McKenney, "Report of the Commissioner of Indian Affairs, November 17, 1829," and Elbert Herring, "Report of the Commissioner of Indian Affairs, November 19, 1831," *The American Indians in the United States: A Documentary History*, Volume I, edited by Wilcomb Washburn (New York: Random House, 1973), 14, 19; the Delaware were given $2,000 upon signing the treaty while the remaining $1,000 would be paid out in horses and other supplies when they left Ohio; see the "Treaty with the Delawares, August 3, 1829," *Indian Affairs: Laws and Treaties*, II, 303–304, which required the Delaware to join their kinsmen in the West by January 1, 1830; Grant Foreman, *The Last Trek of the Indians* (Chicago: University of Chicago Press, 1946), 65–66; the 1825 U.S. Census is quoted in Weisenburger, *The Passing of the Frontier*, 35.

37. Gardiner made two requests for a book on Indian treaties. See "James B. Gardiner to Colonel Samuel S. Hamilton, August 17, 1831," *Correspondence Concerning the Emigration of Indians*, Volume II, Part 1, 56, and "James B. Gardiner to Colonel Samuel S. Hamilton, September 16, 1831," ibid., 592–593.

38. "John McElvain to Thomas McKenney, September 14, 1830," *Correspondence Concerning the Emigration of Indians*, Volume II, Part 1, 86–87.

39. In "Samuel S. Hamilton to John McElvain, May 31, 1831," *Correspondence on the Emigration of Indians*, Volume II, Part 1, 298, the Commissioner of Indian Affairs states, "It is to be regretted that there is any misunderstanding between you." See also "Samuel S. Hamilton to John McElvain, July 18, 1831," ibid., 507–508; for the government's response to McElvain's request to fire Brish, see "Samuel S. Hamilton to John McElvain, May 21, 1831," ibid., Volume II, Part 2, 293–294.

40. "Henry Brish to Lewis Cass, September 20, 1831," *Correspondence Concerning the Emigration of Indians*, Volume II, Part 1, 596.

41. Henry Brish, "Agent Sale, September 8, 1831," ibid., 597; the "List of Sales" for sale of the Seneca's private property covers 24 pages in Volume IV of *Correspondence on the Emigration of Indians*.

42. "John McElvain to John Eaton, June 12, 1831," *Correspondence Concerning the Emigration of Indians*, Volume II, Part 1, Volume 2, Part 1, 471–472; "John McElvain to Lewis Cass, November 15, 1831," ibid., 684–685; "John McElvain to John Eaton, September 7, 1831," ibid., 588–589.

43. "John McElvain to Lewis Cass, December 8, 1831," *Correspondence Concerning the Emigration of Indians*, Volume II, Part 1, 652–655.

44. "John McElvain to Lewis Cass, November 15, 1831," *Correspondence Concerning the Emigration of Indians*, Volume II, Part 1, 684–685; "John McElvain to Lewis Cass, December 8, 1831," ibid., 652–655.

45. "Henry Brish to Samuel S. Hamilton, November 28, 1831," *Correspondence Concerning the Emigration of Indians*, Volume II, Part 1, 691–692.

46. "John McElvain to Lewis Cass, November 15, 1831," *Correspondence Concerning the Emigration of Indians*, Volume II, Part 1, 684–685.

47. Foreman, *The Last Trek of the Indians*, 68–71, 73.

48. "William Clark to William B. Lewis, Second Auditor of the Treasury, November 18," *Correspondence on the Emigration of Indians*, Volume IV, 112–114; "Henry Brish to Samuel S. Hamilton, November 28, 1831," ibid., Volume II, Part 1, 691–692; "William Clark to Elbert Herring, December 20, 1831," ibid., Volume III, 722–723.

49. "Letter from Seneca Who Have Stopped at Muncie Town, Delaware County, December 10, 1831," *Correspondence on the Emigration of Indians*, Volume IV, 9–10; "Henry Brish to William Clark, July 16, 1832," ibid., Volume V.

50. Klopfenstein, "The Removal of the Indians from Ohio," 34.

51. "Treaty with the Seneca and Shawnee, December 29, 1832," *Indian Affairs: Laws and Treaties*, II, 383–385; Muriel H. Wright, *A Guide to the Indian Tribes of Oklahoma* (Norman: University of Oklahoma Press, 1986), 149–152.

52. Foreman, *The Last Trek of the Indians*, 341; Baughman, *History of Seneca County*, 50–51.

Chapter Eight: The Shawnee Exile

1. Harvey, *History of the Shawnee Indians*, 81–85; Jerry Clark, *The Shawnee*, 5–27; Calloway, *The Shawnee and the War for America*, 85–108; Howard,

Shawnee, 1–23; George Bluejacket, "An Indian's Own Story," transcribed and edited by John Allen Rayner, *Kansas Historical Society* (Indian History Coll. 590 Box 6 Subgroup XXII Series E): 1–2. This document can be accessed at the Kansas Memory site of the Kansas Historical Society (www.kansasmemory.org).

2. Harvey, *History of the Shawnee Indians*, 184.

3. Ibid., 190–199.

4. Ibid., 184.

5. "Henry Dearborn to the Chiefs of the Delawares and Shawnee Nations of Indians, 1802," quoted in its entirety in Harvey, *History of the Shawnee Indians*, 129–131.

6. "John Johnston to Lewis Cass, September 28, 1825," *Correspondence on the Subject of the Emigration of Indians*, Volume I, 25.

7. Harvey, *History of the Shawnee Indians*, 186–189.

8. "John Eaton to James B. Gardiner, March 29, 1831," *Correspondence on the Subject of the Emigration of Indians*, Volume II, Part I, 270–273.

9. Ibid.

10. Ibid.

11. James McPherson of Carlisle, Pennsylvania, was taken prisoner while fighting against the British and Indians during the American Revolution. He was placed with the British Indian Department and was released as a result of the Treaty of Greeneville in 1795. He remained among the Indians who called him "Squa-la-ka-ke" or "Red Face;" see John G. Hover et. al., *Memoirs of the Miami Valley*, Volume I (Chicago: Robert O. Law, 1919), 175.

12. "Treaty with the Seneca and Shawnee, July 20, 1831," *Indian Affairs: Laws and Treaties*, II, 327–330.

13. "Treaty with the Shawnee, August 8, 1831," ibid., 331–334.

14. "Treaty with the Ottawa, August 30, 1831," ibid., 335–339.

15. Harvey, *History of the Shawnee Indians*, 200–201, 208–213, 224; "John Johnston to Lewis Cass, August 24, 1831," M234 (Roll 601) (National Archives Microfilm). Harvey mentions the noted orator Wayweleapy and Spybuck accompanying John Perry. He is mistaken, however, when he says Black Hoof also went with them to Washington since the chief had died earlier in 1831.

16. Weisenburger, *The Passing of the Frontier*, 36–37; Randall Buchman, "Gardiner, James B. (1789–1837)," *Encyclopedia of American Indian Removal*, Volume I, 83.

17. Lewis Cass, "Indians of North America," *North American Review* (January 1826): 53–119; Lewis Cass, "Policy and Practice of the United States and Great Britain in Their Treatment of Indians," ibid., (April 1827): 365–442; Lewis Cass, "Removal of the Indians," ibid., 62–121; "Lewis Cass to Thomas McKenney, March 11, 1830," M234 (Roll 427) (National Archives Microfilm).

18. See Jackson's use of the word "emigration" in his "First Annual Message, December 8, 1829;" "Lewis Cass to Andrew Jackson, February 6, 1831," *Correspondence on the Subject of the Emigration of Indians*, Volume II, 767–782; Klunder, *Lewis Cass and the Politics of Moderation*, 67–68.

19. Frederick Webb Hodge, Editor, *Handbook of American Indians North of Mexico*, Part Two (Washington, D.C.: Government Printing Office, 1910),

107; R. David Edmunds, "Samuel S. Hamilton (1830–31)," *The Commissioners of Indian Affairs*, 9–12; Ronald N. Satz, "Elbert G. Herring (1831–36), ibid., 13–16.

20. D. L. Birchfield, General Editor, *The Encyclopedia of the North American Indian*, Volume X (Tarrytown: Marshall Cavendish Corporation, 1997), 1302; Klunder, *Lewis Cass and the Politics of Moderation*, 71–72.

21. Lewis Cass, "Regulations Concerning the Removal of the Indians, May 15, 1832," *Correspondence on the Subject of the Emigration of Indians*, Volume I, 343–349.

22. Ibid.

23. "Lewis Cass to James Gardiner, May 17, 1832," *Correspondence on the Subject of the Emigration of Indians*, Volume I, 338–339.

24. "James B. Gardiner to Lewis Cass, June 2, 1832 and June 20, 1832," ibid., 686–692.

25. Ibid.

26. Numerous letters on this topic were written between Gardiner and both Cass and Gibson in the summer of 1832. For examples, see "James B. Gardiner to Lewis Cass, June 23, 1833," *Correspondence on the Subject of the Emigration of Indians*, Volume I, 693–700, and "James B. Gardiner to George Gibson, June 3, 1832," ibid., 692–693. For Jackson's approval of a land route, see "J. H. Hook, Acting Commissary General, to James B. Gardiner, September 1, 1832," ibid., 153.

27. "James B. Gardiner to Lewis Cass, June 23, 1833," *Correspondence on the Subject of the Emigration of the Indians*, Volume I, 693–700.

28. "James B. Gardiner to Lewis Cass, May 17, 1832," ibid., 338–339.

29. "James Gardiner to George Gibson, September 17, 1832," ibid., 702–703.

30. "Colonel J. F. Lane to George Gibson, August 18, 1832," *Correspondence on the Subject of the Emigration of the Indians*, Volume I, 726–727; records in the War Department related to the removal of the Shawnee, Seneca, and Ottawa list the Disbursing Agent only as "J. F. Lane;" he was undoubtedly Colonel John F. Lane (1810–1836) who graduated from West Point in 1828. He served in several posts following his work as the Disbursing Agent for the removal of the Ohio tribes. In 1836, he was made a Captain of the 2nd Dragoons and given command of the Creek Brigade in the Second Seminole War. He is credited with inventing the pontoon boat. He contracted brain fever while fighting near Tampa Bay which led him to commit suicide. See George W. Cullum, *Biographical Register of the Graduates of the United States Military Academy*, Vol. I, 1802–1840 (New York: D. Van Nostrand, 1868), 328.

31. Harvey, *History of the Shawnee Indians*, 227–228.

32. "Daniel Dunihue to Alexander Dunihue, October 11, 1832," in the "Dunihue Correspondence of 1832," *Indiana Magazine of History* 35 (December 1939): 422; Dunihue made the comment about his uncle when the caravan ran out of money in Indianapolis and Gardiner said that he would kill and eat every public horse rather than stop the removal.

33. "Daniel Dunihue to Alexander Dunihue, September 11, 1832," "Dunihue Correspondence," 419; "James B. Gardiner to George Gibson, September 17, 1833," *Correspondence on the Subject of the Emigration of Indians*, Volume I, 702–703.

34. Howe, *Howe's Historical Collections*, I, 299; Daniel Dunihue's Diary, July 1–December 11, 1832, Sunday, September 2, 1832, Dunihue Collection, Conner Prairie Museum Archive (www.connerprairie.org). Daniel Dunihue was required to keep a "Journal of Occurrences," but he also kept this personal diary with many details missing from the formal government account.

35. Harvey, *History of the Shawnee Indians*, 233.

36. Howe, *Historical Collections of Ohio*, I, 299; Foreman, *The Last Trek of the Indians*, 83. Foreman cites a story in the *St. Louis Beacon* as the source for the 105-year-old white woman among the Shawnee.

37. Daniel Dunihue's Diary provides the best evidence of the daily schedule.

38. Hill, *John Johnston and the Indians*, 116–117; Harvey, *History of the Shawnee Indians*, 230–232.

39. "Journal of Judge Shelby, October 6 and October 12, 1832," Randall Buchman, Editor, *A Sorrowful Journey* (Defiance, Ohio: Defiance College Press, 2007), 25, 28. A typed copy of Judge Shelby's journal is also housed in the Center for Archival Collections at Bowling Green State University.

40. "James B. Gardiner to George Gibson, October 3, 1832," *Correspondence on the Subject of the Emigration of the Indians*, Volume I, 703.

41. "Judge Shelby's Journal, October 6, 1832," 24; Dunihue Diary, Wednesday, October 3.

42. "Daniel Dunihue to Alexander Dunihue, September 11, 1832," "Dunihue Correspondence in 1832," 418.

43. "Colonel J. F. Lane to George Gibson, October 3, 1832," *Correspondence on the Subject of the Emigration of Indians*, Volume I, 732–733; "Daniel Dunihue to Alexander Dunihue, October 23, 1832," "Dunihue Correspondence," 423.

44. "James B. Gardiner to Daniel Dunihue, July 26, 1832," "Dunihue Correspondence," 414.

45. "James B. Gardiner to George Gibson, October 8, 1832," *Correspondence on the Subject of the Emigration of Indians*, Volume I, 705; "Colonel J. F. Lane to George Gibson, November 5, 1832," ibid., 736–737; for more detailed information on Abert's military career, see Cullum, *Biographical Register of the Graduates of the United States Military Academy*, Vol. I, 1802–1840, 121–122.

46. Peter T. Harstad, "Disease and Sickness on the Wisconsin Frontier: Cholera," *Wisconsin Magazine of History*, Volume 43, Number 3 (Spring 1960): 203–220; Charles E. Rosenberg, *The Cholera Years: The United States in 1832, 1849, and 1866* (Chicago and London: University of Chicago Press, 1987), 13–17, 36–39.

47. "James B. Gardiner to Lewis Cass, October 21, 1832," Buchman, Editor, *A Sorrowful Journey*, 31–32; "Daniel Dunihue to Alexander Dunihue, October 23, 1832," "Dunihue Correspondence," 423.

48. "Daniel Dunihue to Alexander Dunihue, October 23, 1832," "Dunihue Correspondence," 423; Daniel Dunihue Diary, Monday, October 29; "Judge Shelby's Diary, October 22, 1832," 32–33.

49. "James B. Gardiner to Lewis Cass, October 21, 1832," Buchman, Editor, *A Sorrowful Journey*, 31–32.

50. Daniel Dunihue Diary, Sunday, October 28; "Report of Lt. Col. J. J. Abert, Special Commissioner of the Emigration, to Lewis Cass, November 5, 1833," *Correspondence on the Subject of the Emigration of Indians*, Volume III, 4–8.

51. Colonel Gardiner's final report on the removal of the Shawnee is quoted nearly in total in Foreman, *The Last Trek of the Indians*, 77–78, and completely in Buchman, Editor, *A Sorrowful Journey*, 66–71; see also Gardiner's detailed lists of expenses paid from Ohio to the Shawnee reserves which concludes *Correspondence on the Subject of the Emigration of Indians*, Volume I, 1125–1152. Sources on what became of Gardiner after this point are sparse. There is one reference to him a few years later as the "Printer to the State" of Ohio as seen in the *Journal of the Senate of the State of Ohio* (Columbus: 1834).

52. Foreman, *The Last Trek of the Indians*, 84; the *Missouri Intelligencer* source is from November 12, 1832.

53. "Judge Shelby's Journal, October 26 to November 19, 1832," Buchman, Editor, *A Sorrowful Journey*, 37–48.

54. "Judge Shelby's Journal, November 20 to November 29, 1832," ibid., 48–55.

55. "Judge Shelby's Journal, November 30, 1832," ibid., 55.

56. "Report of Lt. Col. J. J. Abert to Lewis Cass, January 5, 1833," *Correspondence on the Subject of the Emigration of Indians*, Volume IV, 4–10; Foreman, *The Last Trek of the Indians*, 84–85.

57. Dunihue Diary, Monday, October 29, Saturday October 3, and Sunday October 4.

58. Dunihue Diary, Friday, November 9, Saturday, November 17, and Tuesday December 11, 1832.

59. Foreman, *The Last Trek of the Indians*, 82–83; "Remarks of Daniel Dunihue, Enrolling Agent, December 18, 1832," *Correspondence on the Subject of the Emigration of Indians*, Volume III, 77; Henry. L. Ellsworth and John F. Schermerhorn, two members of the three–man committee appointed to evaluate the western land, negotiated the "Treaty with the Shawnee and Seneca, December 29, 1832," *Indian Affairs: Laws and Treaties*, II, 383–385.

60. "Report of Lt. Col. J. J. Abert, Special Commissioner of the Emigration, to Lewis Cass, November 5, 1833," *Correspondence on the Subject of the Emigration of Indians*, Volume III, 4–8; "Statement of Richard W. Cummins (Resident Agent) and G. W. Pool, December 2, 1832," ibid., 9.

61. Robert C. Brown, *History of Hancock County, Ohio* (Chicago: Warner, Beers, & Co., 1886), 197; Knapp, *History of the Maumee Valley*, 403. Charloe was named for the Ottawa Chief Peter Charloe who refused to leave with the rest of his tribe in 1832. The town was platted out in June 1839 by Benjamin Hollister who had been the Conductor for the Ottawa Removal. See Ann Sherry, *The Melrose Area* (Defiance, Ohio: Hubbard Company, 1969), 70, and *Antwerp Bee-Argue, "A Village by a Stream:" A Pictorial History, in Memory of the Last Indian Chief in Northwestern Ohio* (Antwerp, Ohio: Antwerp Bee-Argue, 1962) 5–6, 16–17.

62. George Bluejacket, "An Indian's Own Story," 4.

CHAPTER NINE: THE PASSING OF THE OTTAWA

1. An excellent source on the Ottawa holdings in the Maumee River valley prior to their removal can be found in Robert Baumann, *The Ottawas of Ohio: 1704–1840*, Volume VI (Toledo: University of Toledo, 1984). Baumann worked for a Cleveland law firm from 1947 to 1955 researching the Ottawa holdings as part of a claim against the U.S. government for which the Ottawa won more than $263,000.

2. Cass wrote two letters about this to Porter. In the first, he told him to find a reputable person to do the negotiating, and in the second letter, he told Porter to go himself. See "Secretary Lewis Cass to Governor, George Porter, July 4, 1832 and September 11, 1832," National Archives, Office of Indian Affairs, Letters Sent, Volume 8, 517, and Volume 9, 233.

3. Nevin Otto Winter, *A History of Northwest Ohio: A Narrative Account of Its Historical Progress and Development from the First European Exploration of the Maumee and Sandusky Valleys and the Adjacent Shores of Lake Erie, Down to the Present Time*, Volume I (Chicago and New York: Lewis Publishing Company, 1917), 199.

4. David M. Stother and Patrick M. Tucker, *The Fry Site: Archaeological and Ethnohistorical Perspectives in the Maumee River Ottawa in Northwest Ohio* (Morrisville, North Carolina: Lulu Press, 2006), 22–25.

5. Ibid., 26.

6. Stother and Tucker, *The Fry Site*, 31; "Anthony Wayne to Henry Knox, October 23, 1793," Wayne Papers (Historical Society of Pennsylvania), Volume 30.

7. Stother and Tucker, *The Fry Site*, 31; for the Treaty of Greeneville, see "Treaty with the Wyandot, August 3, 1795," *Indian Affairs: Laws and Treaties*, II, 39–45.

8. Stother and Tucker, *The Fry Site*, 42–27.

9. An excellent source on the early days of trading in the Lower Maumee River valley can be found in Richard J. Wright, Editor, *The John Hunt Memoirs: Early Years of the Maumee Basin, 1812–1835* (Maumee, Ohio: Maumee Valley Historical Society, 1978).

10. George A. Schultz, *An Indian Canaan: Isaac McCoy and the Vision of an Indian State* (Norman: University of Oklahoma Press, 1971), 101–116; "Reverend Isaac McCoy to Samuel Lykins, March 4, 1831," M234 (Roll 428) (National Archives Microfilm).

11. "Dr. Oscar White to Governor George Porter, September 30, 1832," M234 (Roll 421) (National Archives Microfilm).

12. "Inhabitants of Port Lawrence, Ohio to Lewis Cass, August 2, 1830," M234 (Roll 421) (National Archives Microfilm); Winter, *A History of Northwest Ohio*, 247–248.

13. Winter, *History of Northwest Ohio*, 250; Hill, *John Johnston and the Indians*, 140–141.

14. Winter, *History of Northwest Ohio*, 251–252; "Inhabitants of Port Lawrence, Ohio to Lewis Cass, August 2, 1830," M234 (Roll 421) (National Archives Microfilm).

15. "George Porter to Lewis Cass, July 13, 1832," M234 (Roll 421) (National Archives Microfilm); Robert F. Baumann, "The Migration of the Ottawa Indians from the Maumee Valley to Walpole Island," *Northwest Ohio Quarterly*, Volume XXI (Summer 1949), 3:10–25.

16. "George Porter to Lewis Cass, September 29, 1832," M234 (Roll 421) (National Archives Microfilm).

17. "George Porter to Lewis Cass, September 29, 1832" with the attached "Memorandum of Reserves," M234 (Roll 421) (National Archives Microfilm).

18. The story of Thunderbolt can be found in Joseph B. King's memoir, "The Ottawa Indians in Kansas and Oklahoma," in Lewis H. Barlow, Charles Dawes, and Tom Doyle, *The Ottawa Indian Tribe of Oklahoma: Past, Present, Future: A Comprehensive Planning Document* (No Publisher Listed, 1981), 15.

19. "Treaty with the Ottawa, August 30, 1831," *Indian Affairs: Laws and Treaties*, II, 334–339; "Memorial of the Ottawa Indians of the Maumee River, Maumee to Governor George B. Porter, Michigan Territory, February 15, 1833," M234 (Roll 421) (National Archives Microfilm).

20. "George Porter to Elbert Herring, Commissioner of Indian Affairs, February 18, 1833," M234 (Roll 421) (National Archives Microfilm).

21. Clinton Carter Hutchinson, *A Colony for an Indian Reserve* (Lawrence, Kansas: State Journal Steam Press Print, 1863), 4–5. This document can be accessed at the Kansas Territorial Online 1854–1861 Website (www.kansasterritoralonline.org).

22. Lewis Cass Aldrich, "Otto-wau-kee Speaks for His People," *The Ohio Frontier: An Anthology of Early Writings*, edited by Emily Foster (Lexington: University Press of Kentucky, 2000), 170–171. Aldrich attended the negotiations to remove the Ottawa from the Maumee River valley when he was a boy. He included the speech of Ottokee in his 1888 work *History of Henry and Fulton Counties, Ohio* (Syracuse: D. Mason and Co., 1888); see Dresden Howard's description of Ottokkee in "Fulton County" in Howe, *Historical Collections of Ohio*, I, 664.

23. "Treaty with the Ottawa, February 18, 1833," *Indian Affairs: Laws and Treaties*, II, 392–393.

24. Ibid., 393.

25. Ibid., 393–394. There is no record of to whom the money was owed. Kappler states on page 394 that the schedules are not on file in Washington. The treaty only gives the total amount each man received to pay to others: Hunt would pay $2,675; Forsyth would pay $4,410; and Hollister and Company would pay $1,395.

26. Foreman, *The Last Trek of the Indians*, 89–92; Klopfenstein, "The Removal of the Ohio Tribes," 35; Slocum, *The History of the Maumee River Basin*, 414–418.

27. Winter, *History of Northwest Ohio*, 340; Robert F. Bauman, "Kansas, Canada, or Starvation," *Michigan History* 36 (1952): 287–299.

28. Ronald N. Satz, "Carey Allen Harris (1836–38)," *The Commissioners of Indian Affairs*," 17–22; War Department, "Advertisement for Sealed Proposals in the *New York Times* and *Evening Post*, July 26, 1836," M234 (Roll 427) (National Archives Microfilm); the same proposals for bids for rations and wag-

ons for Ottawa removal were also published in the August 12, 1837, and August 19, 1837, editions of the *Maumee Express*; "John McElvain to Carey Harris, June 6, June 21, July 8, July 11, and September 3, 1837," *Maumee Express*; "Statement of Letters Written by John McElvain for Month of July 1837," ibid.; "Statement of Letters Received by John McElvain in the Month of August, 1837," ibid.; "John McElvain to William Clark, August 13, 1837," ibid.

29. Winter, *History of Northwest Ohio*, 340; John McElvain, "Notice, August 17, 1830," M234 (Roll 427) (National Archives Microfilm).

30. "John McElvain to William Clark, August 13, 1837," *Maumee Express*; McElvain's broadside was also printed in the *Maumee Express*, a local weekly newspaper, on August 19 and August 26, 1837.

31. Waugh, "A Chronicle of Devoted Lives," 4–5; John Seib, "A List of Scholars belonging to the Missionary School on the Miami, with their ages, degree of blood & state of advancement in their education, October 1, 1823" M1 (Roll 17) (National Archives Microfilm).

32. "Reverend Isaac Van Tassel, Ebenezer Mission, Maumee, Ohio to the Presbyterian Synod of Pittsburgh, Pennsylvania, 1831," *Missionary Herald at Home and Abroad*, Volume 27: 387–388.

33. Howe, *Historical Collections of Ohio*, 665–667; "James Jackson to Elbert Herring, May 31, 1835," M234 (Roll 421) (National Archives Microfilm); Frank H. Reighard, *A Standard History of Fulton County: An Authentic Narrative of the Past, with an Extended Survey of Modern Developments*, Volume I (Chicago and New York: Lewis Publishing Company, 1920), 61–63; Robert F. Baumann, Editor, "The Removal of the Indians from the Maumee River Valley: A Selection from the Dresden W. H. Howard Papers," *Northwest Ohio Quarterly* 30 (Winter 1957–1958) 1: 10–25. Some Pottawatomi lived with the Ottawa in villages in northwest Ohio. The government considered the Pottawatomi a tribe of Indiana or the Michigan Territory. Between 1818 (the date of the signing of the Treaty of St. Mary's) and 1837, various bands of the Pottawatomi signed 20 treaties with the U.S. government (usually negotiated by Lewis Cass, as governor of the Michigan Territory, or the current governor of Indiana) which first removed them to smaller reserves in the eastern United States and finally surrendered their remaining territory in exchange for land in Kansas. In 1846, the government united the Pottawatomi, Chippewa, and Ottawa who had signed these treaties into one group called the Pottawatomi Nation. From then on, negotiators dealt with them as one tribe. An excellent book on the removal of the Pottawatomi form northern Indiana is Daniel McDonald, *Removal of the Pottawattomie Indians from Northern Indiana; Embracing also a brief statement of the Indian policy of the government, and other historical matter relating to the Indian question* (Volume 2) (Plymouth, Indiana: D. McDonald and Company, 1898).

34. "Muster Roll of a Company of Ottoway Indians in the Year 1837," Barlow, Dawes, and Doyle, *The Ottawa Indian Tribe of Oklahoma*, 18.

35. *Maumee Express*, September 2, 1837.

36. Mary Copeland Dresden was born in Seneca County, New York, in 1824 and died in Winameg, Ohio, in 1915; for her memories of the removal of the Ottawa, see Reighard, *A Standard History of Fulton County*, 61.

37. Foreman, *The Last Trek of the Indians*, 89–91; Klopfenstein, "The Removal of the Ohio Tribes," 35; "Muster Roll of a Company of Ottoway Indians in the Year 1837," Barlow, Dawes, and Doyle, *The Ottawa Indian Tribe of Oklahoma*, 18.

38. "John McElvain to the Office of Indian Affairs, March 21, 1838," M234 (Roll 427) (National Archive Microfilm).

39. "Report of Auditor's Office, June 21, 1842," M234 (Roll 427) (National Archive Microfilm); "Citizens of Maumee City to Captain W. E. Cruger, September 2, 1837," ibid.; "John Garland to Judge R. Forsyth, September 24, 1838," ibid.; Ronald N. Satz, "Thomas Hartley Crawford (1838–45)," *The Commissioners of Indian Affairs*, 23–27.

40. "Muster Roll of a Company of Ottawa Indians about to Emigrate west of the Mississippi River under the direction of R. A. Forsyth Superintendent and Disbursing Agent, August 30, 1839," M234 (Roll 427) (National Archive Microfilm); a copy entitled "Muster Roll of a Company of Ottoway Indians in the Year 1839," can also be found in Barlow, Dawes, and Doyle, *The Ottawa Indian Tribe of Oklahoma*, 19.

41. "Estimate of Funds required in the Removal and Subsistence of the Emigrating Ottawa Indians, for the Quarter ending in September 1839 with the Application in detail, intended to be made of them by R. A. Forsyth Distributing Agent," M234 (Roll 427) (National Archive Microfilm); "Estimate of Funds required in the Removal and Subsistence of the Emigrating Ottawa Indians, for the Quarter ending 31st December 1837 with the Application in detail, intended to be made of them by W. E. Cruger Distributing Agent," ibid.

42. "R. A. Forsyth to T. Hartley Crawford, May 30 and July 26, 1839," M234 (Roll 427) (National Archive Microfilm).

43. R. A. Forsyth, "Robert Forsyth's Journal of Occurrences in the Ottawa Emigration, between 24th July and 29th August 1839," July 24 and 25, 1839, ibid.

44. Forsyth, "Journal of Occurrences," July 26, 27, 28, 29, 30, and 31, 1839, ibid.

45. Forsyth, "Journal of Occurrences," August 1, 2, 3, and 4, 1839; Foreman, *The Last Trek of the Indians*, 92.

46. Forsyth, "Journal of Occurrences," August 5, 6, 7, 8, 9, 10, and 11, 1839, M234 (Roll 427) (National Archives Microfilm); the *Louisville Advertiser* commented on the arrival of the Ottawa in his city, stating that Ottokkee and the younger chief Petonoquette were "very good men, well informed, and not much inclined to barbarity." The story was printed in the September 21, 1839, edition of the *Maumee Express*.

47. Forsyth, "Journal of Occurrences," August 12, 13, 14, 15, and 16, 1839, M234 (Roll 427) (National Archives Microfilm).

48. Ibid., August 17, 18, 19, 20, and 21, 1839.

49. Ibid., August 22, 23, 24, 25, 26, and 27, 1839.

50. Ibid., August 28 and 29, 1839.

51. Forsyth, "Journal of Occurrences," Concluding Remarks, M234 (Roll 427) (National Archive Microfilm); "R. A. Forsyth to T. Hartley Crawford, July 7, 1843," ibid.

52. "Arnold Maham to the Secretary of the Interior, November 5, 1868," M234 (Roll 461) (National Archives Microfilm); Reighard, *A Standard History of Fulton County*, 60; Barlow, Dawes, and Doyle, *The Ottawa Indian Tribe of Oklahoma*, 14–15.

53. Sherry, *The Melrose Area*, 70; Robert C. Levee, *Memories of Genoa, Ohio 1868–1968* (Genoa: Published by the author, 1968), 1, 11–17.

54. Phelps, *Historic Maumee Valley*, 51–52.

55. "Reverend Isaac Van Tassel, Ebenezer Mission, Maumee, Ohio to the Presbyterian Synod of Pittsburgh, Pennsylvania, 1831," *Missionary Herald at Home and Abroad*, Volume 27: 387–388.

CHAPTER TEN: THE WYANDOT FAREWELL

1. George Knepper, *Ohio and Its People* (Kent, Ohio: Kent State University Press, 2003), 112–113. Knepper quotes a British traveler named Thomas Wharton who visited the Wyandot reserves and noted the "most delightful" countryside filled with prosperous farms and a people "far advanced in civilization."

2. Sioui, *Huron Wyandot Heritage*, 90–92; Vogel, *The Indians of Ohio and Wyandot County*, 1–4; Eric R. Seeman, *The Huron-Wendat Feast of the Dead: Indian-European Encounters in Early North America (Witness to History)* (Baltimore: Johns Hopkins University Press, 2011), 6–22; Reverend Joseph Badger, "A Sketch of the Wyandot Tribe of Indians," in A. J. Baughman, Editor, *Past and Present of Wyandot County, Ohio: A Record of Settlement, Organization, Progress and Achievement*, Volume I (Chicago: S. J. Clarke, 1913), 38–40; see also the best scholarly work on the Wyandot written by the contemporary Wendat scholar George Sioui, *Huron Wendat: The Heritage of the Circle*, translated by Jane Brierley (Vancouver: University of British Columbia Press, 2000).

3. Vogel, *Indians of Ohio and Wyandot County*, 61–62; "John McElvain to Elbert Herring, October 2, 1833," *Correspondence on the Subject of the Emigration of Indians*, Volume 3, 581–584; "Warpole," Wyandot Indian Genealogical Cards.

4. Leggett, Conaway, and Company, *History of Wyandot County*, 225.

5. "School Report to Governor Cass from John L Lieb, October 1, 1825;" Thelma Marsh, *Daughter of Grey Eyes: The Story of Mother Solomon* (Upper Sandusky, Ohio: Published by the author, 1989), 56.

6. Lonny L. Honsberger, *A Book of Diagrams and Index of Indian Landholders on Wyandot Reservation, Wyandot County, Ohio at the Time of Cession* (Upper Sandusky, Ohio: Published by the author, 1989), 4–7.

7. Finley, *History of the Wyandot Mission*, 392–394; Leggett, Conaway, and Company, *History of Wyandot County*, 296.

8. "James Gardiner to John Eaton, September 26, 1831," M234 (Roll 421) (National Archives Microfilm).

9. Ibid.

10. "Obituary for Governor William Walker, March 5, 1799–February 18, 1874," *Wyandotte Herald*, February 19, 1874; William Walker's house can still be seen at 132 North Fourth Street in Upper Sandusky. It is on the National Register of Historic Places.

11. William Walker, "Report to the Chiefs of the Wyandot Nation, December 15, 1831," *Correspondence on the Subject of the Emigration of Indians*, Volume 4, 166–168.

12. "William Walker to G. P. Disosway, January 19, 1833," Kansas Historical Society Website (www.kansasmemory.org).

13. "James B. Gardiner to Lewis Cass, January 5 and 28, 1832," *Correspondence on the Subject of the Emigration of Indians*, Volume 4, 10–11, 153–156; "Deposition of Henry Brish, January 23, 1832," ibid., 161–163; "James B. Gardiner to George Gist, January 16, 1832," ibid., 163–164. John McElvain also frequently complained to the government that whites, who infiltrated the tribes for its annuities, behaved like a "privileged class." See "John McElvain to Elbert Herring, May 20, 1833," M234 (Roll 601) (National Archives Microfilm).

14. Vogel, *Indians of Ohio and Wyandot County*, 288–289; Baughman, *Past and Present of Wyandot County, Ohio*, 63–64.

15. Paul Armstrong Youngman, *Heritage of the Wyandots and "The Armstrong Story,"* Kansas City, Kansas Public Schools Website (www.kckps.org).

16. "Treaty with the Wyandot, January 19, 1832" (usually referred to as the Treaty of McCutcheonville since it was signed in McCutcheonville, Ohio), *Indian Affairs: Laws and Treaties*, II, 339–341.

17. "Elbert Herring to William Walker, December 7, 1832," *Correspondence on the Matter of the Emigration of Indian*s, Volume II, Part 2, 960–961.

18. Dwight L. Smith, Editor, "Documents: An Unsuccessful Negotiation for Removal of the Wyandot Indians from Ohio, 1834, *Ohio Archaeological and Historical Quarterly* 58 (July 1949), 310.

19. "Lewis Cass to Robert Lucas, July 11, 1834," ibid., 310–313.

20. "Journal of Proceedings, August 1834 to September 27th," ibid., 319–322

21. "Robert Lucas to Lewis Cass, August 19, 1834," ibid., 314–315.

22. "Journal of Continuing Proceedings," ibid., 325–327.

23. Ibid., 328–329.

24. "Treaty with the Wyandot, April 23, 1836," *Indian Affairs: Laws and Treaties*, II, 460.

25. *Indian Affairs: Laws and Treaties*, II, 461; "John McElvain to Elbert Herring, February 10, 1835" (with the attached petition from the seven chiefs), M234 (Roll 601) (National Archives); Van Buren appointed David Evan Owen, a popular local Democratic politician, as the receiver of public monies for the region. His records show that he paid $22,212 to Wyandot chiefs from his appointment in June 1838 to his dismissal following the Whig victory in 1840; see Lang, *History of Seneca County*, 304–305.

26. Records detailing the fight among the Wyandot over land sales to individual Americans can be found in the Correspondence of the Bureau of Indian Affairs: Ohio Agency (MMS 244, Roll 2) (Center for Archival Collections, Bowling Green State University) including "A Law Against Ceding Lands to the United States, June 28, 1837," Walker's anonymous piece entitled "The Wyandot Indians," *Ohio State Journal*, September 16, 1837, and the petition of Warpole and his supporters, "To Our Great Father the President of the United States, October 23, 1838."

27. Taylor, *Ohio in Congress*, 175; Hunter flooded the Office of Indian Affairs with one letter after another about his plans and activities. See "William Hunter to T. Hartley Crawford, May 7, 1839," Correspondence of the Bureau of Indian Affairs: Ohio Agency (MMS 244, Roll 2) (Center for Archival Collections, Bowling Green State University), as an example. Hunter died under mysterious circumstances in 1842 and was buried in the Cholera Cemetery in Sandusky just in case he had succumbed to the disease.

28. Hill, *John Johnston and the Indians*, 120.

29. "John Bell to John Johnston, March 26, 1841," Hill, *John Johnston and the Indians*, 120.

30. "T. Hartley Crawford to John Johnston, March 26, 1841," ibid., 121–122.

31. "John Johnston to T. Hartley Crawford, May 11, 1841," ibid., 122.

32. "John Armstrong to T. Hartley Crawford, June 21, 1841," ibid., 123–125.

33. "John Johnston to T. Hartley Crawford, June 19, 1841," ibid., 125–126.

34. "T. Hartley Crawford to John Johnston, July 7, 1841," ibid., 126; "John Johnston to T. Hartley Crawford, August 6, 1841," ibid., 126–127.

35. "John Johnston to T. Hartley Crawford, November 11, 1841," ibid., 128.

36. "Wyandot Chiefs to John Johnston, January 4, 1842," ibid., 129.

37. Howe, *Historical Collections of Ohio*, 898; most sources place Summundewat's death in the fall of 1841 including the official website of the Wyandotte Nation of Kansas as seen in Jeremy Turner's essay on "Catherine Coon Johnson." Thelma Marsh lists the date as September 1840 in "Summundewat" in her Wyandot Genealogical Cards. Reverend N. B. C. Love in "The Old Mission Church," *The Ladies' Repository: A Monthly Periodical, Devoted to Literature, Arts, and Religion*, Volume 3, Issue 2 (February 1869), 127–129, claims Summundewat died in 1843.

38. "John Johnston to T. Hartley Crawford, February 9, 1842," Hill, *John Johnston and the Indians*, 130.

39. "John Johnston to T. Hartley Crawford, March 14, 1842," ibid., 130–131; Johnston's efforts to bring the murderer to justice can be found in Roll 45 of the Lewis Cass Collection at the Bentley Historical Library.

40. "John Johnston to T. Hartley Crawford, February 9, 1842," Hill, *John Johnston and the Indians*, 131–132.

41. "Treaty with the Wyandot, March 17, 1843," *Indian Affairs: Laws and Treaties* II, 534–536.

42. Ibid., 537.

43. Charles Dickens, *American Notes for General Circulation*, Volume II, Third Edition (London: Chapman and Hall, 1842), 166–170.

44. "Treaty with the Wyandot, March 17, 1843," Article 11, *Indian Affairs: Laws and Treaties* II, 535.

45. "John Johnston to T. Hartley Crawford, April 15, 1842," Hill, *John Johnston and the Indians*, 133; the 11 page chart forwarded to the Office of Indian Affairs showed the estimated debt as $30,279.76 and the actual debt as $24,014.43; see "Purdy McElvain to Thomas Hartley Crawford, December 20, 1842," Correspondence of the Bureau of Indian Affairs: Ohio Agency (MMS 244, Roll 2) (Center for Archival Collections, Bowling Green State University).

46. "Purdy McElvain to the Office of Indian Affairs, March 3, 1843," M234 (Roll 952) (National Archives Microfilm); Marsh, *Moccasin Trails to the Cross*, 117–125.

47. "Muster Roll of the Wyandott Indians Who Departed Upper Sandusky, Ohio," Marsh, *Daughter of Grey Eyes*, 59–60.

48. Marsh, *Daughter of Grey Eyes*, 59–60; James H. Anderson, Editor, *Life and Letters of Judge Thomas J. Anderson and Wife* (Columbus: Press of F. J. Heer, 1904), 42–43. See also "Warpole," "Jonathan Pointer," "Catherine Walker," "William Walker, Sr.," and "Sally Frost," in Wyandot Indian Genealogical Cards.

49. "Purdy McElvain to T. Hartley Crawford, March 3, 1843," M234 (Roll 952) (National Archives Microfilm).

50. "Purdy McElvain to T. Hartley Crawford, July 12, 1843," ibid.

51. Perl W. Morgan, Editor, *History of Wyandotte County, Kansas and Its People*, Volume I (Chicago: Lewis Publishing Company, 1915), 69–70.

52. "Journal of Reverend James Wheeler, Monday July 10, 1843 – Thursday July 20," Wyandotte Nation of Kansas Website (www.wyandot.org); Foreman, *The Last Trek of the Indians*, 97; Leggett, Conaway, and Company, *History of Wyandot County*, 299; Marsh, *Moccasin Trails to the Cross*, 121–122; Frank N. Wilcox, *Ohio Indian Trails* (Kent: Kent State University Press, 1970), 110–112. The route of the Wyandot from Upper Sandusky to Cincinnati closely paralleled Ohio Route 67 and Ohio Route 68.

53. Several other newspapers reported on the passage of the Wyandot on their departure from Ohio in 1843 including the Bellefontaine *Logan Gazette*, July 13, 1843, the Springfield *Republic*, July 21, 1843, the *Xenia Torch-Light*, July 20, 1843, and the *Cincinnati Daily Chronicle*, July 17, 1843. There appears to be some confusion on the exact dates that the papers reported the passage of the Wyandot through their towns. Foreman noted this in *The Last Trek of the Indians* (page 96) and, taking the dates without question, concluded the Wyandot took a circuitous route backtracking from Xenia before heading to Cincinnati. But this seems unlikely with a wagon train and at least 300 horses.

54. Knepper, *Ohio and Its People*, 113.

55. "Speech of Jacques to Governor Shannon," Leggett, Conaway, and Company, *History of Wyandot County*, 299–300. The source for the speech, which is printed in its entirety, is the *Ohio State Journal*.

56. The story of the farewell to Harrison first appeared in the *St. Louis Republican*, July 25, 1843. See Foreman, *The Last Trek of the Indians*, 97.

57. William C. Cutler, *History of the State of Kansas* (Chicago: A.T. Andreas, 1883), Wyandotte County, Part 2, Wyandot Nation, Part 1.

58. "D. D. Mitchell to T. Hartley Crawford, August 14, 1843," M234 (Roll 952) (National Archives Microfilm); James Wheeler, "Letter Written July 28, 1843 from a Missouri Riverboat," Wyandot Nation of Kansas Website (www.wyandot.org); "Agreement with the Delawares and Wyandot, 1843," *Indian Affairs: Laws and Treaties*, II, 1048.

59. Morgan, *History of Wyandotte County, Kansas*, 68–73; Lucy B. Armstrong, "Letter to the Editor," *Wyandotte Gazette*, December 19, 1870.

60. Morgan, *History of Wyandotte County, Kansas*, 71; for descriptions of Wyandot cemeteries in Kansas City, Kansas, see the Federal Writers' Project, *Kansas: A Guide to the Sunflower State* (New York: Viking Press, 1939), 215–217.

EPILOGUE: A LAST GOODBYE

1. "Memorial from the Ladies of Steubenville Against the Forcible Removal Without the Limits of the United States, February 15, 1830," 21st Congress, 1st Session. House of Representatives [Rep. No. 209].

2. John Johnston observed that the Seneca "labour more steadily, have better houses and farms, and appear more like white people in their dress and manners, than any other Indians in Ohio," in "Recollections of Sixty Years," 188.

3. The Wyandot retained a few acres including tribal cemeteries and a Methodist Church and school in Kansas City, Kansas; see the "Treaty with the Wyandot, January 31, 1855," *Indian Affairs: Laws and Treaties*, II, 677–681; Foreman, *The Last Trek of the Indians*, 229–234; H. Craig Miner and William E. Unrau, *The End of Indian Kansas: A Study of Cultural Revolution, 1854–1871* (Lawrence; Regents Press of Kansas, 1978), 1–11; descendants of the Wyandot remaining in Kansas bought land in Kansas City from money awarded to them from a lawsuit against the U.S. government in 1956 for underpayment of the true value of the Grand Reserve which is today the site of the tribe's Seventh Street Casino.

4. George W. Manypenny, *Our Indian Wards* (Cincinnati: Robert Clarke & Co., 1880), 133.

5. William Frank Zornow, *Kansas: A History of the Jayhawk State* (Norman: University of Oklahoma Press, 1977), 96–105; the Dawes Severalty Act can be found on the website of the National Archives at www.ourdocuments.gov.

6. "The Wyandot's Farewell Song," *Upper Sandusky Democratic Pioneer* (October 24, 1845) as quoted in Schenk, *The History of Wyandot County, Ohio*, 301; the author is identified in Hill, *John Johnston and the Indians*, 136; see also "Descendents of James Rankin" (www.kcps.org).

7. Marsh, *Moccasin Trails to the Cross*, 121.

8. Miner and Unrau, *The End of Indian Kansas*, 139.

9. Ibid., 140.

10. Ned Blackhawk, *Violence over the Land: Indians and Empires in the Early American West* (Cambridge and London: Harvard University Press, 2006), 293.

11. Federal Writers' Project, *Kansas*, 215.

Bibliography

PRIMARY SOURCES

Adams, John Quincy. *Diary of John Quincy Adams, 1794–1845.* Edited by Alan Nevins. New York: Frederick Ungar, 1951.

American State Papers, Foreign Relations.

American State Papers, Indian Affairs.

Anderson, James H., Editor. *Life and Letters of Judge Thomas J. Anderson and Wife.* Columbus: F. J. Heer, 1904.

Annals of Congress.

Anthony Wayne Papers (Historical Society of Pennsylvania), Volume 30.

Armstrong, Lucy B. "Letter to the Editor," *Wyandotte Gazette*, December 19, 1870.

Bassett, John S., Editor. *Correspondence of Andrew Jackson.* Washington, D.C.: Carnegie Institute, 1926–35.

Bellefontaine *Logan Gazette*, July 13, 1843.

Black Swamp Conservancy Website (www.blackswamp.org).

Blaisdell, Bob, Editor. *Great Speeches by Native Americans.* New York: Dover Thrift Edition, 2000.

Bluejacket, George. "An Indian's Own Story." Transcribed and edited by John Allen Rayner, Kansas Historical Society, Indian History Coll. 590 Box 6 Subgroup XXII Series E.

Buchman, Randall, Editor. *A Sorrowful Journey.* Defiance, Ohio: Defiance College Press, 2007.

Burnet, Judge Jacob. *Notes on the Early Settlement of the Northwestern Territory.* Cincinnati: Derby, Bradley & Co., 1847.

Carter, Clarence, Editor. *Territorial Papers of the United States*, 8 Volumes. Washington, D.C.: Government Printing Office, 1939.

Cass, Lewis. "Indians of North America," *North American Review* (January 1826): 53–119.

————. *Inquiries Respecting the History, Traditions, Languages, Manners, Customs, Religion, &c. of the Indians Living Within the United States.* Detroit: Sheldon & Reed, 1823.

————. "Policy and Practice of the United States and Great Britain in Their Treatment of Indians," *North American Review* (April 1827): 365–442.

————. "Removal of the Indians," *North American Review* (January 1830): 62–121.

————. "Structure of the Indian Languages," *North American Review* (April 1828): 357–403.

Center for Archival Collections, Bowling Green State University
  Bureau of Indian Affairs. Ohio Agency, Correspondence, 1824–1881.
  John Shelby, Journal, 1832.
  Kenneth Smith. Ohio Native Genealogical Cards, 1724–1932.
  Sandusky County Records, Supreme Court Journal, 1823–1851.
  Seneca County Records, Supreme Court Index to Journals, 1826–1884, and
  Journals, 1825–1843.
  Thelma G. Marsh. Wyandot Indian Genealogical Cards, 1795–1910.
*A Century of Lawmaking for a New Nation, U. S. Congressional Documents and
  Debates, 1774–1875.*
Choules, Reverend John O. and Smith, Reverend Thomas. *The Origin and
  History of Missions; A Record of the Voyages, Travels, Labors, and Successes of the
  Various Missionaries, Who Have Been Sent Forth by Protestant Societies and
  Churches to Evangelize the Heathen,* Volume II. New York: Robert Carter,
  1848.
Cincinnati *Daily Chronicle,* July 17, 1843.
Claiborne, J. F. H. *Life and Times of General Sam. Dale, the Mississippi Partisan.*
  New York: Harper & Brothers, 1860.
Clay, Henry. *The Papers of Henry Clay,* Volume I, *The Rising Statesman 1797-
  1814.* Edited by James F. Hopkins. Lexington: University of Kentucky Press,
  1959.
Conner Prairie Museum Interactive History Website (www.conner prairie.org).
*Correspondence on the Subject of the Emigration of Indians Between 30th November,
  1831 and 27th December, 1833 with Abstracts of Expenditures by disbursing
  Agents, in the removal and Subsistence of Indians, Etc., Furnished in Answer to a
  Resolution of the Senate of 27th December, 1833, by the Commissary General of
  Subsistence,* 8 Volumes. Washington, D.C.: Printed by Duff Green, 1836.
Craig, Neville B., Editor. *The Olden Time,* Volume II, October 1847, Number
  10. Cincinnati: Reprinted by Robert Clarke & Co., 1876.
Cruikshank, Ernest A., Editor. *Documents Relating to the Invasion of Canada
  and the Surrender of Detroit, 1812.* New York: Arno Press, 1971.
Cullum, George W. *Biographical Register of the Graduates of the United States
  Military Academy,* Vol. I, 1802–1840. New York: D. Van Nostrand, 1868.
Daniel Dunihue's Diary July 1-December 11, 1832, Sunday September 2,
  1832, Dunihue Collection, Conner Prairie Museum Archive.
Dickens, Charles. *American Notes for General Circulation,* Volume II, Third
  Edition. London: Chapman and Hall, 1842.
Drake, Benjamin. *Life of Tecumseh and His Brother the Prophet with a Historical
  Sketch of the Shawnee Indians.* Cincinnati: E. Morgan and Co., 1841.
Drake, Benjamin and Mansfield, Edward Deering. *Cincinnati in 1826.*
  Cincinnati: Morgan, Lodge, and Fisher, 1827.
"Dunihue Correspondence of 1832," *Indiana Magazine of History* 35
  (December 1939): 408–426.
Elliott, Charles. *Indian Missionary Reminiscences, principally of the Wyandot
  Nation. In which is exhibited the efficacy of the gospel in elevating ignorant and
  savage men.* New York: Lane & Scott, 1850.

Este, D. K. *Discourse on the Life and Public Services of the Late Jacob Burnet.* Cincinnati: Steam Press of the Cincinnati Gazette Co., 1853.

Finley, James B. *Autobiography of Rev. James B. Finley; or, Pioneer Life in the West.* Edited by W. P. Strickland, D.D. Cincinnati: Jennings and Graham, 1853.

_____. *History of the Wyandott Mission, at Upper Sandusky, Ohio Under the Direction of the Methodist Episcopal Church.* Cincinnati: J. F. Wright and L. Swormstedt, 1840.

_____. *Life Among the Indians.* Edited by D. W. Clark. Cincinnati: Cranston & Curts, 1854.

Flint, Timothy. *Recollections of the Last Ten Years.* New York: A.A. Knopf, 1932.

Foster, Emily, ed. *The Ohio Frontier: An Anthology of Early Writings,* edited by Emily Foster. Lexington: University Press of Kentucky, 2000.

Hammond, Charles, Editor. *Cases Decided in the Supreme Court of Ohio in Bank,* Volumes I to VI. Cincinnati: Robert Clarke & Co., 1872.

Harrison, William Henry. *Governor's Message and Letters: Messages and Letters of William Henry Harrison,* 2 Volumes. Edited by Logan Esarey. Indianapolis: Indiana Historical Society, 1922.

Hutchinson, Clinton Carter. *A Colony for an Indian Reserve.* Lawrence, Kansas: State Journal Steam Press Print, 1863.

"An Indian Talk, Washington City, March 5, 1831," *New Hampshire Patriot and State Gazette,* May 16, 1831.

Israel, Fred, Editor. *The State of the Union Messages of the Presidents,* 3 Volumes. New York: Chelsea House-Robert Hector Publishers, 1966.

Jackson, Andrew. *Correspondence of Andrew Jackson,* Volume II. Edited by John Spencer Bassett. Washington, D.C.: Carnegie Institution of Washington, 1926–35.

"Journal of Reverend James Wheeler, Monday July 10, 1843 – Thursday July 20."

Journal of the Senate of the United States of America, 1789-1873.

Kansas Historical Society Kansas Memory Website (www.kansas memory.org).

Kansas Territorial Online 1854–1861 Website (www.kansasterritorialonline.org).

Kappler, Charles J., Editor. *Indian Affairs: Laws and Treaties,* Volume II. Washington, D.C.: Government Printing Office, 1904.

Klinck, Carl, Editor. *Tecumseh: Fact and Fiction in Early Records.* Englewood Cliffs: Prentice-Hall, 1967.

Letters Sent to the Commissary General of Subsistence (National Archives)

Lewis Cass Collection, 1814–1847. Bentley Historical Library, University of Michigan.

Library of Congress American Memory Website (www.memory.loc.gov).

Manhattan Advertiser, 1837–1841

Maumee Express, 1837–1840

McKenney, Thomas L. and Hall, James. *History of the Indian Tribes of North America,* Volume I. Philadelphia: E. C. Biddle, 1836–1844.

Miscellaneous Accounts of the Sandusky Factory (Box 1) (National Archives).

Mitchell, Joseph. *The Missionary Pioneer, or a Brief Memoir of the Life, Labors, and Death of John Stewart (Man of Colour), Founder, under God, of the Mission Among the Wyandotts at Upper Sandusky.* Bowery: Printed by John C. Totten, 1827.

Monroe, James. *The Writings of James Monroe.* Edited by Stanislaus Murray Hamilton. New York and London: G. P. Putnam's Sons, 1901.

_____. *The Writings of James Monroe*, Volume VI. New York: AMS Press, 1969.

"Obituary for Governor William Walker, March 5, 1799–February 18, 1874," *Wyandotte Herald*, February 19, 1874.

Presbyterian Church in the U.S.A. General Assembly. *Minutes of the General Assembly of the Presbyterian Church in the United States of America from A.D. 1821 to A.D. 1835 Inclusive.* Philadelphia: Presbyterian Board of Publications, 1894.

Presidential Papers Microfilm (William Henry Harrison).

Preston, Daniel, Editor. *The Papers of James Monroe: A Documentary History of the Presidential Tours of James Monroe, 1817, 1818, 1819.* Westport, Connecticut: Greenwood Press, 2003.

Prucha, Francis Paul, Editor. *Documents of United States Indian Policy* (3rd Edition). Lincoln: University of Nebraska Press, 2000.

Randall, Emilius O., Editor. "Ohio in the War of 1812: Excerpts from Early Ohio Newspapers," *Ohio Archaeological and Historical Society Proceedings* 28 (July 1919).

Records of the Office of Indian Affairs (Record Group 95) (National Archives Microfilm).

M1, Records of the Michigan Superintendency of Indian Affairs, 1814–1851.

M234, Letters Received by the Office of Indian Affairs, 1818–1860.

M348, Report Books of the Office of Indian Affairs.

M574, Special Files of the Office of Indian Affairs.

T494, Documents Relating to the Negotiations of Ratified and Unratified Treaties.

Register of Debates of the House of Representatives of the United States of America.

Register of Debates of the Senate of the United States of America.

"Reverend Isaac Van Tassel, Ebenezer Mission, Maumee, Ohio to the Presbyterian Synod of Pittsburgh, Pennsylvania, 1831," *Missionary Herald at Home and Abroad* (Volume 27): 387–388.

Richardson, James D., Editor. *A Compilation of the Messages of the Presidents.* (Reprint) Whitefish, Montana: Kessinger Publishing, 2004.

_____. *A Compilation of the Messages of the Presidents*, Volume III. New York: Bureau of National Literature, Inc., 1897.

Ridge, Martin, Editor. *America's Frontier Story: A Documentary History of the Westward Expansion.* New York: Holt, Rinehart, and Winston, 1969.

Schoolcraft, Henry. *History of the Indian Tribes of the United States of America.* Philadelphia: J. P. Lippincott, 1857.

Seager II, Robert, Editor. *The Papers of Henry Clay*, Volume 7. Lexington: University Press of Kentucky, 1982.

"Secret Journal of Negotiations of the Chickasaw Treaty of 1818" (www.avalon.law.yale.edu).

Sketches of the Life and Public Service of Gen. Lewis Cass. Washington, D.C.: Printed at the Congressional Globe Office, 1848.

Smith, Dwight L., Editor. "Documents: An Unsuccessful Negotiation for Removal of the Wyandot Indians from Ohio, 1834," *Ohio Archaeological and Historical Quarterly* 58 (July 1949): 305–331.

Springfield *Republic*, July 21, 1843.

Stickney, Benjamin F. *Correspondence of the Maumee (Ottawa) Sub-Agency: Selected Letters (1820-1836).* Compiled by Jon. A. Sturm. Toledo, Ohio: Toledo Lucas County Public Library, 1989.

Tallgrass Prairie National Reserve (Kansas) (www.nps.gov/tapr).

"Tarhe and Wyandot Chiefs to Governor Huntington, May 8, 1810," John Johnston Papers, Ohio Historical Society, MSS 553.

Thomas Rotch Letters (Letterbox) 1816–1819, Ohio Historical Society.

Toledo Blade, 1837–1843.

Toledo Herald, 1843.

Washburn, Wilcomb, Editor. *The American Indians in the United States: A Documentary History*, Volume I. New York: Random House, 1973.

Whickar, J. Wesley, Editor. "Shabonee's Account of Tippecanoe," *Indiana Magazine of History* 17 (December 1921).

"William Walker to G. P. Disosway, January 19, 1833," Kansas Historical Society (www.kshs.org).

Wright, Richard J., ed. *The John Hunt Memoirs: Early Years of the Maumee Basin, 1812-1835.* Maumee, Ohio: Maumee Valley Historical Society, 1978.

Xenia Torch-Light, July 20, 1843.

SECONDARY SOURCES

Abel, Annie H. "The History of the Events Resulting in Indian Consolidation West of the Mississippi River," *Annual Report for the Year 1906*, 2 Volumes. Washington, D.C.: American Historical Association, 1908.

Allen, Robert S. *His Majesty's Indian Allies: British Indian Policy in the Defence of Canada 1774–1815.* Toronto: Dundurn Press, 1993.

Ammon, Harry. *James Monroe: The Quest for National Identity.* New York: McGraw-Hill, 1971.

Anderson, Indiana. Official Web site (www.cityofanderson.com).

Antal, Sandy. *A Wampum Denied: Procter's War of 1812.* Ottawa: Carleton University Press, 1998.

Antwerp *Bee-Argue*. "A Village by a Stream:" A Pictorial History, in Memory of the Last Indian Chief in Northwestern Ohio. Antwerp, Ohio, 1962.

Auchinleck, Gilbert. *A History of the War between Great Britain and the United States of America during the Years 1812, 1813, & 1814.* Toronto: Arms and Armour Press, 1972.

Barlow, Lewis H., Dawes, Charles, and Doyle, Tom. *The Ottawa Indian Tribe of Oklahoma: Past, Present, Future: A Comprehensive Planning Document.* No Publisher Listed, 1981.

Bartlett, C. J. *Castlereagh*. New York: Charles Scribner's Sons, 1966.

Baughman, A. J., Editor. *History of Seneca County: A Narrative Account of Its Historical Progress, Its People, and Its Principal Interests*, Volume I. Chicago and New York: Lewis Publishing Company, 1911.

_____, Editor. *Past and Present of Wyandot County, Ohio: A Record of Settlement, Organization, Progress and Achievement*, 2 Volumes. Chicago: S. J. Clarke Company, 1913.

Bauman, Robert F. "Kansas, Canada, or Starvation," *Michigan History* 36 (1952): 287–299.

_____. *The Ottawas of Ohio: 1704–1840*, 6 Volumes. Toledo: University of Toledo, 1984.

Bemis, Samuel Flagg. *John Quincy Adams and the Foundations of American Foreign Policy.* New York: Alfred A. Knopf, 1949.

Birchfield, D. L., General Editor. *The Encyclopedia of the North American Indian*, Volume X. Tarrytown: Marshall Cavendish Corporation, 1997.

Blackhawk, Ned. *Violence over the Land: Indians and Empires in the Early American West*. Cambridge and London: Harvard University Press, 2006.

Borneman, Walter. *1812: The War that Forged a Nation*. New York: Harper Collins, 2004.

Brands, H.W. *Andrew Jackson: His Life and Times*. New York: Doubleday, 2005.

Brant, Irving. *James Madison: Commander in Chief*, Volume VI. Indianapolis: Bobbs-Merrill, 1956.

Braun, Kathryn E. Holland, Editor. *Tohopeka: Rethinking the Creek War and the War of 1812*. Tuscaloosa: University of Alabama Press, 2012.

Brown, Robert C. *History of Hancock County, Ohio*. Chicago: Warner, Beers, & Co., 1886.

Buchman, Randall L., Editor. *The Historic Indian in Ohio: A Conference to Commemorate The Bicentennial of The American Revolution*. Columbus: Published for the Ohio American Bicentennial Advisory Commission by the Ohio Historical Society, 1976.

Bunn, Mike and Williams, Clay. *Battle for the Southern Frontier: The Creek War and the War of 1812*. Charleston: History Press, 2008.

Buser, T. A. "Tarhe: Grand Sachem," and Tarhe the Crane, "Address of Tarhe, Grand Sachem of the Wyandot Nation to the Assemblage at the Treaty of Greeneville July 22, 1795," posted on the official website of the Wyandotte Nation (www.wyandotte-nation.org).

Calloway, Colin G. *Crown and Calumet: British-Indian Relations, 1783–1815*. Norman and London: University of Oklahoma Press, 1987.

_____. *One Vast Winter Count: The Native American West before Lewis and Clark*. Lincoln and London: University of Nebraska Press, 2007.

_____. *The Shawnees and the War for America*. New York: Penguin Library, 2007.

Cave, Alfred. "Abuse of Power: Andrew Jackson and the Indian Removal Act," *Historian*, Volume 65 (December 2003): 1330–1353.

Christian, Shirley. *Before Lewis and Clark: The Story of the Chouteaus, the French Dynasty That Ruled America's Frontier*. New York: Farrar, Straus and Giroux, 2004.

Clark, Jerry E. *The Shawnee*. Lexington: University Press of Kentucky, 1993.

Cleaves, Freeman. *Old Tippecanoe: William Henry Harrison and His Times*. New York: Charles Scribner's Sons, 1939.

Connelley, William Elsey. *Wyandot Folk-Lore*. Topeka: Crane & Company, 1900.

Cresson, W.P. *James Monroe*. Chapel Hill: University of North Carolina Press, 1946.

Curry, William L. "The Wyandot Chief Leather Lips: His Trial and Execution," *Ohio Archaeological and Historical Quarterly* 12 (January 1903): 30–36.

Cutler, William C. *History of the State of Kansas*. Chicago: A.T. Andreas, 1883.

"Descendents of James Rankin" (www.kcps.org).

Dowd, Gregory Evans. *A Spirited Resistance: The North American Indian Struggle for Unity, 1745–1815*. Baltimore and London: Johns Hopkins University Press, 1992.

Drinnon, Richard. *Facing West: The Metaphysics of Indian-Hating and Empire-Building*. Minneapolis: University of Minnesota, 1980.

DuVal, Kathleen. *The Native Ground: Indians and Colonists in the Heart of the Continent*. Philadelphia: University of Pennsylvania Press, 2006.

Edmunds, R. David. *Tecumseh and the Quest for Indian Leadership*. New York: HarperCollins, 1984.

_____. *The Shawnee Prophet*. Lincoln and London: University of Nebraska Press, 1983.

Elting, John. *Amateurs to Arms: A Military History of the War of 1812*. Chapel Hill: Algonquin Books, 1991.

Engelman, Fred L. *The Peace of Christmas Eve*. New York: Harcourt, Brace & World, 1962.

Federal Writers' Project. *Kansas: A Guide to the Sunflower State*. New York: Viking Press, 1939.

Ferguson, Gillum. *Illinois in the War of 1812*. Champaign-Urbana: University of Illinois Press, 2012.

Finger, John H. *The Eastern Band of Cherokees, 1819–1900*. Knoxville: University of Tennessee Press, 1984

Fitz-Enz, Colonel David G. *The Final Invasion, Plattsburgh, The War of 1812's Most Decisive Battle*. New York: Cooper Square Press, 2001.

Foreman, Grant, *Indians and Pioneers*. Norman: University of Oklahoma Press, 1936.

_____. *The Last Trek of the Indians*. Chicago: University of Chicago Press, 1946.

Galbreath, Charles B. *History of Ohio*, Volume I. Chicago and New York: American Historical Society, 1928.

Gibson, Arrell Morgan. *The Chickasaws*. Norman: University of Oklahoma Press, 1971.

Gilbert, Bil. *God Gave Us This Country: Tekamthi and the First American Civil War*. New York: Atheneum, 1989.

Harstad, Peter T., "Disease and Sickness on the Wisconsin Frontier: Cholera," *Wisconsin Magazine of History*, Volume 43, Number 3 (Spring 1960): 203-220.

Hatch, William Stanley. *A Chapter in the History of the War of 1812 in the Northwest*. Cincinnati: Miami Printing & Publishing Company, 1872.

Hecht, Marie B. *John Quincy Adams: A Personal History of an Independent Man*. New York: Macmillan, 1972.

Hibbert, Christopher. *Wellington: A Personal History*. Reading, Massachusetts: Addison-Wesley, 1997.

Hickey, Donald. *The War of 1812: A Forgotten Conflict*. Urbana and Chicago: University of Illinois Press, 1989.

Hill, Leonard U. *John Johnston and the Indians in the Land of the Three Miamis*. Columbus, Ohio: Stoneman Press, 1957.

Hodge, Frederick Webb, Editor. *Handbook of American Indians North of Mexico*, Part Two. Washington, D.C.: Government Printing Office, 1910.

Honsberger, Lonny L. *A Book of Diagrams and Index of Indian Landholders on Wyandot Reservation, Wyandot County, Ohio at the Time of Cession*. Upper Sandusky, Ohio: Published by the author, 1989.

Horsman, Reginald. *The Causes of the War of 1812*. New York: A. S. Barnes, 1961.

_____. *The Origins of Indian Removal 1815–1824*. Lansing: Published by the Michigan State University Press for the Historical Society of Michigan, 1963.

_____. *The War of 1812*. New York: Alfred A. Knopf, 1969.

Hover , John G. et. al. *Memoirs of the Miami Valley*, Volume I. Chicago: Robert O. Law, 1919.

Howard, James. *Shawnee: The Ceremonialism of a Native American Tribe and Its Background*. Athens: Ohio University Press, 1981.

Howe, Henry, *Historical Collections of Ohio: Containing a Collection of the Most Interesting Facts, Traditions, Biographical Sketches, Anecdotes, Etc. Relating to the General and Local History with Descriptions of Its Counties, Principal Towns and Villages*. Columbus: Henry Howe and Son, 1891.

Hurt, R. Douglas. *The Ohio Frontier: Crucible of the Old Northwest, 1720 to 1830*. Bloomington: Indiana University Press, 1997.

Jarhoda, Gloria. *The Trail of Tears: The Story of American Indian Removal*. New York: Holt, Rinehart and Winston, 1975.

James, Marquis. *Andrew Jackson: Portrait of a President*. New York: Grosset & Dunlap, 1937.

Jenkins, Brian. *Henry Goulburn, 1784–1856: A Political Biography*. Montreal and Kingston: McGill-Queens University Press, 1996.

Klunder, Willard Carl. *Lewis Cass and the Politics of Moderation*. Kent, Ohio: Kent State University Press, 1996.

Knapp, Horace S. *History of the Maumee Valley: Commencing with Its Occupation by the French in 1680*. Toledo: Blade Mammoth Printing and Publishing House, 1872.

Knepper, George. *Ohio and Its People*. Kent, Ohio: Kent State University Press, 2003.

Lang, William. *History of Seneca County from the Close of the Revolutionary War to July, 1888*. Springfield, Ohio: Transcript Printing Company, 1880.

Laxler, James. *Tecumseh and Brock: The War of 1812*. Toronto: Anansi Press, 2012.

Leggett, Conaway, and Company. *The History of Wyandot County, Ohio, Containing a History of the County: Its Townships, Towns, Churches, Schools, etc.* Chicago: Leggett, Conaway, and Company, 1884.

Levee, Robert C. *Memories of Genoa, Ohio 1868–1968.* Genoa: Published by the author, 1968.

Littlefield, Daniel F., Jr. and Parins, James W., Editors. *Encyclopedia of American Indian Removal,* Volumes I and II. Santa Barbara: Greenwood, 2011.

Logan, Charles Russell. *The Promised Land: The Cherokees, Arkansas, and Removal, 1794–1839.* Little Rock: Arkansas Historic Preservation Program, 1997.

Longford, Elizabeth. *Wellington: The Years of the Sword.* New York: Harper & Row, 1969.

Lossing, Benson J. *Pictorial Field-Book of the War of 1812.* Portsmouth: New Hampshire Publishing Company, 1976.

Love, Reverend N. B. C. "The Old Mission Church," *The Ladies' Repository: A Monthly Periodical, Devoted to Literature, Arts, and Religion,* Volume 3, Issue 2 (February 1869), 127–129.

Lowery, Charles D. *James Barbour: A Jeffersonian Republican.* Tuscaloosa: University of Alabama Press, 1984.

Lutz, Regan A. *West of Eden: The Historiography of the Trail of Tears* (Ph.D. dissertation). Toledo: University of Toledo, 1995.

Manypenny, George W. *Our Indian Wards.* Cincinnati: Robert Clarke & Co., 1880.

Marsh, Thelma R. *Daughter of Grey Eyes: The Story of Mother Solomon.* Upper Sandusky, Ohio: Published by the author, 1989.

_____. *Moccasin Trails to the Cross: A History of the Mission to the Wyandott Indians on the Sandusky Plains.* Sandusky, Ohio: Published by the John Stewart United Methodist Church, 1974.

Martin, Joel W. *Sacred Revolt: The Muscogees' Struggle for a New World.* Boston: Beacon Press, 1991.

McAffee, William. *History of the Late War in the Western Country.* Bowling Green, Ohio: Historical Publications Company, 1910.

McDonald, Daniel. *Removal of the Pottawattomie Indians from Northern Indiana; Embracing also a brief statement of the Indian policy of the government, and other historical matter relating to the Indian question,* Volume 2. Plymouth, Indiana: D. McDonald and Company, 1898.

McLoughlin, William G. *After the Trail of Tears: The Cherokees' Struggle for Sovereignty.* Chapel Hill and London: University of North Carolina Press, 1993.

Meacham, Jon. *American Lion: Andrew Jackson in the White House.* New York: Random House, 2008.

Meek, Basil. "Seneca John, Indian Chief, His Tragic Death, Erection of Monument in His Memory," *Ohio Archaeological and Historical Quarterly* XXX (1922): 128–141.

Miner, H. Craig and Unrau, William E. *The End of Indian Kansas: A Study of Cultural Revolution, 1854–1871.* Lawrence: Regents Press of Kansas, 1978.

Morgan, George. *The Life of James Monroe.* Boston: Small, Maynard and Company, 1921.

Morgan, Perl W., Editor. *History of Wyandotte County, Kansas and Its People,* Volume I. Chicago: Lewis Publishing Company, 1915.

Nagel, Paul C. *John Quincy Adams: A Public Life, A Private Life.* New York: Alfred A. Knopf, 1999.

Nelson, Paul. *Anthony Wayne: Soldier of the Early Republic.* Bloomington: Indiana University Press, 1985.

O'Donnell III, James H. *Ohio's First Peoples.* Athens: Ohio University Press, 2004.

Ohio Historical Society Ohio Memory Website (www.ohiomemory.org).

Owsley, Frank. *Struggle for the Gulf Borderlands: The Creek War and the Battle for New Orleans, 1812–1815.* Gainesville: University Press of Florida, 1981.

Parsons, Joseph A. "Civilizing the Indians of the Old Northwest, 1800–1810," *Indiana Magazine of History* 56 (September 1960): 195–216.

Parsons, Lynn. "A Perpetual Harrow upon My Feelings: John Quincy Adams and the American Indian," *New England Quarterly* 46 (September 1973): 344–355.

Parton, James. *The Life of Andrew Jackson,* 3 Volumes. New York: Mason Brothers, 1860.

Pessen, Edward. *Jacksonian America: Society, Personality, and Politics.* Homewood, Illinois: Dorsey Press, 1969.

Peters, Edward. *Ohio Lands and Their Subdivision.* Athens, Ohio: Messenger Printery Company, 1918.

Phelps, Ralph. *Historic Maumee Valley.* Toledo: Toledo Blade Company, 1957.

Purdue, Theda and Green, Michael. *The Cherokee Nation and the Trail of Tears.* New York: Penguin, 2007.

Reighard, Frank H. *A Standard History of Fulton County: An Authentic Narrative of the Past, with an Extended Survey of Modern Developments,* Volume I. Chicago and New York: Lewis Publishing Company, 1920.

Remini, Robert. *Andrew Jackson and His Indian Wars.* New York: Viking, 2001.

_____. *Henry Clay: Statesman for the Union.* New York: William Morrow, 1991.

_____. *The Life of Andrew Jackson.* New York: Harper Perennial, 2010.

Richter, Daniel K. *Before the Revolution: America's Ancient Pasts.* Cambridge and London: Belknap Press of Harvard University Press, 2011.

_____. *The Ordeal of the Longhouse: The Peoples of the Iroquois League in the Era of European Colonization.* Chapel Hill and London: Published for the Institute of Early American History and Culture by the University of North Carolina Press, 1992.

Rogin, Michael Paul. *Fathers & Children: Andrew Jackson and the Subjugation of the American Indian.* New York: Alfred A. Knopf, 1975.

Roosevelt, Theodore. *The Winning of the West, Part IV, The Indian Wars, Franklin, Kentucky, Ohio, and Tennessee.* New York and London: G.P. Putnam's Sons, 1906.

Rosenberg, Charles R. *The Cholera Years: The United States in 1832, 1849, and 1866.* Chicago and London: University of Chicago Press, 1987.

Satz, Ronald N. *American Indian Policy in the Jacksonian Era*. Lincoln: University of Nebraska Press, 1975.

Schlesinger, Arthur. *The Age of Jackson*. Boston: Little, Brown, 1953.

Schlup, Emil. "Tarhe–The Crane," *Ohio Archaeological and Historical Quarterly* 14 (April 1905): 132–38.

Schultz, George A. *An Indian Canaan: Isaac McCoy and the Vision of an Indian State*. Norman: University of Oklahoma Press, 1971.

Seeman, Eric R. *The Huron-Wendat Feast of the Dead: Indian-European Encounters in Early North America (Witness to History)*. Baltimore: Johns Hopkins University Press, 2011.

Seneca Nation of Indians. Official Web site (www.sni.org).

Sheehan, Bernard. *Savagism & Civility: Indians and Englishmen in Colonial Virginia*. Cambridge: Cambridge University Press, 1990.

_____. *Seeds of Extinction: Jeffersonian Philanthropy and the American Indian*. New York: W.W. Norton, 1974.

Sherry, Ann. *The Melrose Area*. Defiance, Ohio: Hubbard Company, 1969.

Silver, Timothy. *A New Face on the Countryside: Indians, Slaves, and Colonists in South Atlantic Forests, 1500–1800*. Cambridge: Cambridge University Press, 1990.

Sioui, George. *Huron Wendat: The Heritage of the Circle*. Translated by Jane Brierley. Vancouver: University of British Columbia Press, 2000.

Sleeper-Smith, Susan, Editor. *Contested Knowledge: Museums and Indigenous Perspectives*. Lincoln and London: University of Nebraska Press, 2009.

_____. *Rethinking the Fur Trade: Cultures of Exchange in an Atlantic World*. Lincoln and London: University of Nebraska Press, 2009.

Slocum, Charles Elihu. *History of the Maumee River Basin from the Earliest Accounts to Its Organization into Counties*. Defiance, Ohio: Published by the author, 1905.

Steffen, Jerome O. *William Clark, Jeffersonian on the Frontier*. Norman: University of Oklahoma Press, 1977.

Stother, David M. and Tucker, Patrick M. *The Fry Site: Archaeological and Ethnohistorical Perspectives in the Maumee River Ottawa in Northwest Ohio*. Morrisville, North Carolina: Lulu Press, 2006.

Sugden, John. *Tecumseh: A Life*. New York: Henry Holt, 1999.

Sumner, William Graham. *Andrew Jackson as a Public Man: What He Was, What Chances He Had, and What He Did With Them*. Boston and New York: Houghton Mifflin, 1882.

Taylor, Alan. *The Civil War of 1812: American Citizens, British Subjects, Irish Rebels, & Indian Allies*. New York: Alfred A. Knopf, 2010.

_____. *The Divided Ground: Indians, Settlers, and the Northern Borderland of the American Revolution*. New York: Alfred A. Knopf, 2006.

Taylor, E. L. "Harrison-Tarhe Peace Conference," *Ohio Archaeological and Historical Quarterly* 14 (April 1905): 121–131.

Taylor, William A. *Ohio in Congress from 1803 to 1901*. Columbus: XX Century Publishing Co., 1900.

Tooker, Elizabeth. *The Iroquois Ceremonial of Midwinter*. Syracuse: Syracuse University Press, 1970.

Tucker, Glenn. *Tecumseh: Vision of Glory*. Indianapolis: Bobbs-Merrill, 1956.

Tucker, Patrick M. *Ottawa Culture and Ethnohistory in the Maumee Valley, 1812–1838* (Master's Thesis). Toledo, Ohio: University of Toledo, No date given.

Turner, Wesley B. *British Generals in the War of 1812: High Command in the Canadas*. Montreal and Kingston: McGill-Queen's University Press, 1999.

Van Tassel, Charles Sumner. *Story of the Maumee Valley, Toledo, and the Sandusky Region*, Volume I. Chicago: S.J. Clarke, 1929.

Vogel, John. *The Indians of Ohio and Wyandot County*. New York: Vantage Press, 1975.

Wallace, Anthony F. C. *The Death and Rebirth of the Seneca*. New York: Alfred A. Knopf, 1970.

_____. *Jefferson and the Indians: The Tragic Fate of the First Americans*. Cambridge: Belknap Press, 1999.

_____. *The Long, Bitter Trail: Andrew Jackson and the Indians*. New York: Hill and Wang, 1993.

Walsh, Martin W. "The 'Heathen Party': Methodist Observation of the Ohio Wyandot." *American Indian Quarterly*, Volume 16, No. 2 (Spring 1992): 189–211.

Waugh, Helen. "A Chronicle of Devoted Lives: The Story of the Growth and Development of the First Presbyterian Church, Bowling Green, Ohio, 1855–1955," *Commemorative Pamphlet from the 100th Anniversary of First Presbyterian Church, Bowling Green, Ohio 1955*. Bowling Green, Ohio: First Presbyterian Church, 1955.

Weisenburger, Francis P. *The Passing of the Frontier*. Volume II in *The History of the State of Ohio*. Edited by Carl Wittke. Columbus: Ohio Archaeological and Historical Society, 1941.

Weslager, C. A. *The Delaware Indian Westward Migration*. Wallingford, Pennsylvania: Middle Atlantic Press, 1978.

Wilcox, Frank N. *Ohio Indian Trails*. Kent, Ohio: Kent State University Press, 1970.

Wilentz, Sean. *Andrew Jackson*. New York: Times Books, 2005.

Williams, W. W. *History of the Fire Lands, Comprising Huron and Erie Counties, Ohio*. Cleveland: Leader Printing Company, 1879.

Willig, Timothy D. *Restoring the Chain of Friendship: British Policy and the Indians of the Great Lakes, 1783-1815*. Lincoln: University of Nebraska Press, 2008.

Winter, Nevin Otto. *A History of Northwest Ohio: A Narrative Account of Its Historical Progress and Development from the First European Exploration of the Maumee and Sandusky Valleys and the Adjacent Shores of Lake Erie, Down to the Present Time*, Volume I. Chicago and New York: Lewis Publishing Company, 1917.

Woodward, Frank B. *Lewis Cass: The Last Jeffersonian*. New Brunswick, New Jersey: Rutgers University Press, 1950.

Wright, Muriel H. *A Guide to the Indian Tribes of Oklahoma*. Norman: University of Oklahoma Press, 1986.

Wright, Richard. *The Middle Ground: Indians, Empires, and Republics in the Great Lakes Region, 1650–1815.* Cambridge: Cambridge University Press, 1991.

Wyandotte Nation of Kansas Website (www.wyandot.org).

Youngman, Paul Armstrong. *Heritage of the Wyandots and "The Armstrong Story."* Kansas City, published by the author.

Zornow, William Frank. *Kansas: A History of the Jayhawk State.* Norman: University of Oklahoma Press, 1977.

Acknowledgments

I am especially grateful to the members of the Ohio Academy of History who accepted my paper "Many Trails of Tears: The Removal of the Ohio Tribes" for presentation at their annual conference in April 2009. Their enthusiasm for the topic inspired me to continue my research which ultimately led to this book. Like every historian who has worked on the story of the removal of the Indians, I was inspired by Grant Foreman's *The Last Trek of the Indians* which remains the most comprehensive study of the subject to date. His work guided me to the National Archives and the Library of Congress which house valuable records on the history of the removal of the Ohio tribes. I am thankful to the staff of both institutions for their support for myself and the many scholars who come their way each year. I am also especially thankful to Bruce H. Franklin of Westholme Pubishing for accepting my book and overseeing its publication with kind attention.

On a more personal note, I would like to thank my sister Roberta Stockwell, an artist and professional cartographer, for the maps that accompany this work. She was able to create beautiful images which accurately reflect the movement of the tribes onto reserves in Ohio and later in Kansas and Oklahoma. She is also a wonderful editor and proofreader in her own right. I am grateful for her many suggestions and corrections. Finally, I must thank my sister Kathleen Stockwell for her support during the research and writing of this work. Even though she was struggling with a terminal illness, she often came with me to libraries as I searched for more facts in this complex tale. She even helped me copy articles and books, and gave me advice until the end on how to stay focused. I will always remember that she took her last trip with our family, including my little spaniel Jamie, and Adam, her Westie, to visit the Wyandot Mission Church in Upper Sandusky the summer before she died. It was a moving experience that helped me understand how fleeting our time on earth is and how well the Ohio tribes must have understood this when they traveled west down so many "Trails of Tears."

Index

Made in the USA
Lexington, KY
17 December 2019